# Springer Series on Social Work

## Albert R. Roberts, D.S.W., Series Editor
*Graduate School of Social Work, Rutgers, The State University of New Jersey*

1984 **Battered Women and Their Families:** Intervention Strategies and Treatment Programs, *Albert R. Roberts, D.S.W.*

1984 **Social Policy and the Rural Setting:** *Julia M. Watkins, Ph.D., and Dennis A. Watkins, Ph.D.* (out of print)

1984 **Clinical Social Work in Health Settings:** A Guide to Professional Practice with Exemplars, *Thomas Owen Carlton, D.S.W.*

1984 **Social Work in the Emergency Room** *Carole W. Soskis, M.S.W., J.D.* (out of print)

1984 **Disability, Work, and Social Policy:** Models for Social Welfare *Aliki Coudroglou, D.S.W., and Dennis L. Poole, Ph.D.* (out of print)

1984 **Foundations of Social Work Practice** *Joseph Anderson, D.S.W.* (out of print)

1985 **Task-Centered Practice with Families and Groups** *Anne E. Fortune, Ph.D.* (out of print)

1986 **Widow-to-Widow** *Phyllis R. Silverman, Ph.D.* (out of print)

1986 **Elder Abuse and Neglect:** Causes, Diagnosis, and Intervention Strategies, *Mary Joy Quinn, R.N., M.A., and Susan K. Tomita, M.S.W.*

1986 **Law and Social Work Practice** *Raymond Albert, M.S.W., J.D.*

1987 **Information and Referral Networks:** Doorways to Human Services, *Risha W. Levinson, D.S.W.*

1988 **Social Work in the Workplace:** Practice and Principles, *Gary M. Gould, Ph.D., and Michael Lane Smith, Ph.D.*

1988 **The Human Bond:** Support Groups and Mutual Aid, *Harry Wasserman, D.S.W., and Holly E. Danforth, M.S.W.*

1988 **Social Work:** The Membership Perspective *Hans S. Falck, Ph.D.*

1990 **Social Work Practice in Maternal and Child Health** *Terri Combs-Ome, Ph.D.*

1990 **Program Evaluation in the Human Services** *Michael J. Smith, D.S.W.*

1990 **Journeys to Recovery** *Milson Trachtenberg, A.C.S.W., C.A.C.*

1990 **Evaluating Your Practice:** A Guide to Self-Assessment, *Catherine Alter, Ph.D., and Wayne Evens, M.S.W.*

1990 **Violence Hits Home:** Comprehensive Treatment Approaches to Domestic Violence, *Sandra M. Stith, Ph.D., Mary Beth Williams, L.C.S.W., and Karen Rosen, M.S.*

1991 **Breast Cancer in the Life Course:** Women's Experiences, *Julianne S. Oktay, Ph.D., and Carolyn Ambler Walter, Ph.D.*

1991 **Victimization and Survivor Services:** A Guide to Victim Assistance, *Arlene Bowers Andrews, Ph.D.*

1992 **The Family Functioning Scale:** A Guide to Research and Practice, *Ludwig L. Geismar, Ph.D., and Michael Camasso, Ph.D.*

1994 **Dilemmas in Human Services Management:** Illustrative Case Studies, *Raymond Sanchez Mayers, Ph.D., Federico Souflee, Jr., Ph.D., and Dick J. Schoech, Ph.D.*

1994 **Managing Work and Family Life,** *Viola M. Lechner, D.S.W., and Michael A. Creedon, D.S.W.*

1996 **Total Quality Management in Human Service Organizations,** *John J. Gunther, D.S.W., and Frank Hawkins, D.S.W.*

1997 **Multicultural Perspectives in Working with Families,** *Elaine P. Congress, D.S.W.*

1997 **Research Methods for Clinical Social Workers:** Empirical Practice, *John S. Wodarski, Ph.D.*

1997 **Elder Abuse and Neglect:** Causes, Diagnosis, and Intervention Strategies, 2nd Edition *Mary Joy Quinn, R.N., M.A., and Susan Tomita, M.S.W., Ph.D.*

**Mary Joy Quinn, RN, MA,** is the director of Probate Court Services for the California Superior Court, City and County of San Francisco. She is a public health nurse and since 1973 has focused exclusively on frail elders. She formerly directed a geropsychiatric day treatment center and has published numerous articles and book chapters on elder mistreatment.

**Susan K. Tomita, MSW, PhD,** is an associate director of social work at Harborview Medical Center, Seattle, Washington. She is also the manager of the Medicine-Surgery Social Work Unit and social worker in the Senior Care Program. Her current research acivities are in the area of cultural variables and their relationship to elder mistreatment.

# Elder Abuse and Neglect

## SECOND EDITION

## Causes, Diagnosis, and Intervention Strategies

**MARY JOY QUINN**
**SUSAN K. TOMITA**

 Springer Publishing Company

Springer Publishing Company, Inc.
536 Broadway
New York, NY 10012-3955

*Cover design by: Margaret Dunin*
*Acquisitions Editor: Bill Tucker*
*Production Editor: Susan Gamer*

97 98 99 00 01 / 5 4 3 2 1

---

**Library of Congress Cataloging-in-Publication Data**

Quinn, Mary Joy.
    Elder abuse and neglect : causes, diagnosis, and intervention
strategies / Mary Joy Quinn, Susan K. Tomita.—2nd ed.
        p.     cm.—(Springer series on social work)
    Includes bibliographical references and index.
    ISBN 0-8261-5121-3 (HB)
    ISBN 0-8261-5122-1 (PB)
    1. Abused aged—United States.   2. Social work with the aged—
United States.   3. Abused aged—Services for—United States.
I. Tomita, Susan K.   II. Title.   III. Series.
HV6626.3.Q56   1997
362′6—dc21                                                    97-2104
                                                                  CIP

---

Printed in the United States of America

*In memory of*

*Frank A. Quinn*
*E. Joy Stine and Walter T. Stine*
*Susumu Tomita*

*and to*
*Hiroko Miura Tomita*
*Clifford J. Barda*
*Jason Rabbitt-Tomita*

*Whose love sustains us and*
*whose caring continues to teach us to care for others*

# Contents

# Foreword to the First Edition

## Congressman Claude Pepper

Elder abuse. The phrase still sends shock waves among the majority of Americans. Most find it hard to believe how widespread and frequent this problem is. Most would prefer not to acknowledge that elder abuse, which flies in the face of traditional American ideals, exists.

Eight years ago the Select Committee on Aging began an investigation into the problem of elder abuse. A series of field hearings and considerable research revealed the sad truth—elder abuse was far from an isolated and localized problem involving a few frail elderly and their pathological offspring. The problem was a full-scale, national epidemic which existed with a frequency few dared imagine. In fact, abuse of the elderly by loved ones and caregivers existed with a frequency and rate only slightly less than child abuse. Subsequent work in this area has shown that the problem has increased dramatically through the years. Our latest figures show that 1.1 million, or one out of every 25, elderly persons are victims of abuse each year.

I think Ms. Quinn and Ms. Tomita are to be congratulated for their very comprehensive work on elder abuse. A recurring observation in the Committee's 1985 survey of state adult protective service workers was the dearth of information on elder abuse—particularly how to spot victims and provide appropriate intervention. I feel *Elder Abuse and Neglect: Causes, Diagnosis, and Intervention Strategies* will prove useful to anyone concerned with elder abuse—social worker, scholar, legislator, caregiver, or ordinary citizen.

We have a long way to go if we are to eliminate elder abuse in this nation. In the meantime, proper detection and intervention can ease the pain. I welcome the appearance of this important and timely book.

CLAUDE PEPPER
*Chairman, Subcommittee*
*on Health and Long-Term Care*
*U.S. House Select Committee on Aging*

# Foreword to the Second Edition

## Lisa Nerenberg

When *Elder Abuse and Neglect: Causes, Diagnoses, and Intervention Strategies* was first published in 1986, elder abuse prevention was still in its infancy. Very little was known about the etiology of abuse, the risk factors, or the defining features of victims, abusers, and the circumstances surrounding abuse. Few service programs existed to treat effects of abuse, and practitioners in the field who encountered abuse had little guidance in devising intervention strategies. The book was seminal in translating the knowledge available at the time into practice approaches and techniques that could be used by practitioners from a wide range of disciplines. It further presented related models developed in other fields, including domestic violence and caregiving, to broaden the reader's perspective and understanding of this complex problem. The book's impact has been far-reaching. It contains the information, concepts, and ideas reflected in virtually all training manuals, outreach brochures, and articles on elder abuse that have emerged since its initial publication. Through this revised volume, the authors review and interpret new findings and developments, alerting us to their relevance and application.

Elder abuse prevention has evolved substantially in the 10 years since the book was first released. This can be credited to a great extent to the leadership provided by the federal government. A year after publication of the First Edition, amendments to the Older Americans Act mandated states to develop procedures for receiving and investigating abuse reports and to conduct public education and outreach activities aimed at identifying cases. In 1990, Congress approved its first appropriation of just under $3 million for these activities. A subsequent amendment enacted in 1992 created a new elder rights title, Title VII, which combined all of the sections of the Older

Americans Act that focus on protecting the rights of older persons into a separate title. Title VII includes provisions for the long term care ombudsman, legal assistance, and services to prevent elder abuse. The appropriation slowly grew to almost $5 million.

The federal government futher advanced the field of elder abuse through its support of research, demonstration, and training projects. Through Title IV of the Older Americans Act, the Administration on Aging (AoA) providing funding for research and the piloting and evaluation of a variety of model projects which explored alternative approaches to service delivery. The most recent project is aimed at developing services for older battered women. The AoA has also provided funding for a national resource center and is currently collaborating with the Administration on Children and Famlies in sponsoring a 3-year study to measure the incidence of elder abuse, neglect, and exploitation. Elder abuse was also a prominent issue at the 1995 White House Conference on Aging, which brought together 2,000 service providers, advocates, and seniors.

Regrettably, the federal government seems to be relinguishing its leadership role in elder abuse prevention. As this book goes into publication, the future of federal initiatives is in jeopardy. Congress has proposed significant cuts in program funding and the elimination of Title VII as a separate title. It has further targeted Title IV for significant reductions and has challenged states to pick up the lead in abuse prevention activities.

The research and demonstration projects funded by the federal government and other institutions have revolutionized abuse prevention. As Quinn and Tomita point out, the research has emerged in waves, each wave helping us achieve a clearer understanding of the scope and nature of the problem. When the book was first released, the "typical" victim of abuse was an older woman who was mistreated by well-meaning but overburdened adult children. In light of this image, it is not surprising that the first wave of policy and practice mirrored approaches developed to address child abuse which reflect society's commitment to protecting those who are less able to act in their own self-interest. It also led to an emphasis on interventions aimed at reducing caregivers' burdens and stress. While the authors acknowledge that caregiver stress and the broader issue of dependency are still significant factors, they maintain that the dynamics between dependent individuals and their caregivers are much more complex than had previously been imagined. They single out, for example, how aggressive behavior among some impaired older adults may contribute to, trigger, or reinforce abusive conduct.

Another breakthrough in the field was the discovery that rather than one single profile of abuse, there are in fact several discrete profiles. When one distinguishes physical abuse from financial exploitation and neglect, very different patterns emerge. The characteristics of victims, perpetrators, and risk factors correspond to the specific types of abuse. These studies also point out that abusers' characteristics (as opposed to victims') are more significant in predicting abuse and that perpetrator dysfunction is a particularly significant predictor of abuse. Studies which have been conducted since the book's initial publication have further suggested that the prevalance of spousal abuse among the elderly actually exceeds that of abuse by adult offspring, leading to speculation about the relationship between elder abuse and other forms of domestic violence.

These new discoveries into the causes and risk factors associated with abuse have signaled the need for new approaches to treatment and preventive interventions. When elder abuse was thought to be mainly a result of caregiver stress, helping the caregiver was the preferred treatment option. Common interventions involved bringing in supportive services such as homemaker assistance, home-delivered meals, and personal care. Although these services still figure prominently in elder abuse care plans, the new research has suggested the need for alternative approaches. For example, the discovery that perpetrators are often financially and emotionally dependent on their victims (in cases of physical abuse) suggests the need for interventions which reduce this dependency, including vocational counseling and job placement. The strong association between abuse, mental illness, and substance abuse suggest the need for drug treatment and mental health services for the abusers as well.

Recognition that abuse is frequently perpetrated between spouses is reflected in the authors' emphasis on domestic violence approaches. The infusion of ideas and insights from the field of domestic violence promises to have far-reaching impact. Strategies and interventions which are common to domestic violence practice reflect a far greater understanding of help-seeking behavior, the power of peer support, and the influence of societal values and norms in perpetrating abuse than those employed in the field of elder abuse. Domestic violence approaches to ensuring victims' safety through the use of shelters, restraining orders, and prosecution also hold promise for preventing elder abuse.

New insights into dependency and caregiving have prompted the authors to revisit common approaches to addressing caregiver stress. While the early literature on abuse assumed that stress caused or triggered abuse, it failed to explain why some heavily burdened caregivers were abusive while others are not. The authors offer an explanation by introducing neutralization theory, which was developed to describe delinquent behavior by adolescents. When applied to elder abuse, it assumes that in some caregiving systems, abusive behavior is minimized, rationalized, and slowly reinforced. The authors present a variety of abuse interventions within this framework.

Criminal prosecution of abusers has become increasingly common in recent years, with law enforcement personnel assuming a more prominent role in abuse prevention activities. Because service providers are increasingly called upon to participate in the criminal justice system, Tomita and Quinn have presented a comprehensive and practical discussion of the legal process.

The authors trace other significant developments in the past 10 years which include rapid proliferation of multidisciplinary teams in assessing complex abuse cases. Some teams have specialized in handling certain types of abuse while others have expanded their membership to include disciplines which were not previously considered to be part of the elder abuse or aging service network, including clergy, bankers, and certain paraprofessionals.

An extremely important development in the field is that the banner of elder abuse prevention has been taken up by prominent national advocacy organizations such as the American Association of Retired Persons (AARP), the Older Woman's League (OWL), and the National Organization of Women (NOW). AARP sponsored the first national forum on older battered women in 1992, bringing together researchers and advocates from the fields of aging and domestic violence. In 1994, OWL published a report and organized a congressional hearing on the issue. NOW assembled a committee to look at older women as part of its broader initiative in domestic violence. These initiatives have breathed new life and energy into the field, and have fused a bond between service providers and senior advocates.

The establishment and growth of the National Committee for the Prevention of Elder Abuse has also fueled the development of research and practice in the field. Through its *Journal of Elder Abuse and Neglect,* the Committee provides a mechanism for presenting and exchanging knowledge and ideas. In recent years, the Committee launched a program of local affiliates aimed at catalyzing the growth of state and local programs and coalitions.

This revised version of *Elder Abuse and Neglect: Causes, Diagnoses and Intervention Strategies* broadens our understanding of the complex dynamics in elder abuse cases. The authors present new information, including recent findings about self-neglect, sexual abuse, and abuse in nursing homes, and translate this new information into practical, pragmatic applications. They also present for our consideration, new models to augment, complement, or reinforce those which have predominated in the field, pointing out their significance and instructing us in how they can be applied. Finally, the book provides practical, "hands-on" advice and suggestions in how to conduct investigations and interventions and how to demystify the diverse and complex systems which make up the service delivery network. The First Edition created a structure or conceptual skeleton; the Second Edition now extends the scope of the field. In so doing, this revision will continue to guide the field for many more years to come.

LISA NERENBERG, MSW, MPH
*Coordinator, Consortium for Elder Abuse Prevention*
*UCSF/Mount Zion Center on Aging*
*San Francisco, California*

# Preface

This book was written for anyone who works with elders and is concerned about their well-being. It is intended to serve both as an introduction to the subject of elder abuse and neglect and as a guide to effective intervention. It is our hope that the book will contribute to the information, sustenance, and energy that are needed to work with these challenging situations.

The case examples cited throughout the book are real. For the most part, they have been drawn from the authors' clinical experience, although a few cases came from newspaper accounts and from examples shared with the authors by other practitioners.

So many people gave generously of their time, experience, support, and wisdom in the preparation of this book that it is not possible to name them all. We wish to thank those known and anonymous who have contributed their ideas, insights, and knowledge.

In the preparation of this second edition, Mary Grace Luke and Bill Tucker, Springer's acquisitions editors, very patiently supported the development of the manuscript, always respecting our need for more time, given unforeseen circumstances. They may not know it, but a few kind words during trying periods kept us going. Patricia Brownell, at the Fordham University School of Social Work, generously provided valuable feedback on an earlier version of the manuscript. The skillful guidance of Louise Farkas, Springer's Editorial/Production Manager, contributed significantly to the successful completion of this project. The meticulous editing by Production Editor Susan Gamer brought clarity to the book. Our appreciation goes to Publisher Ursula Springer for her abiding interest in the field of gerontology.

The generous sharing of recent studies conducted by researchers Rosalie Wolf and Karl Pillemer, Jill Korbin and Georgia Anetzberger, and Toshi Tatara and the staff of the National Center on Elder Abuse made writing portions of this book effortless. Candice Heisler, Assistant District Attorney of the San Francisco District Attorney's Office, contributed to the refinement of Chapter 9. Lisa Nerenberg, Coordinator of the San Francisco Consortium on Elder Abuse Prevention, carefully reviewed the manuscript and kindly provided the foreword for the second edition.

Ms. Quinn would like to thank Judge Isabella Horton Grant and Commissioner Carol Yaggy for their unfailing support, their deep appreciation for the human condition, and the administration of justice leavened by humor and compassion. Ms. Quinn is especially grateful to her colleagues Maria Amader, John Black, Angela Buscovich, John Cushner, Shauna Gillespie-Ford, Joyce Henson, Cynthia Jones, Tim Kneis, Elina Leino, Susan Lee, Jeanine Lim, Pamela Meyers, Caridad Morata, Christine Nahnsen, John Norton, Stella Pantazis, Ron Ross, Manuel Valenzuela, and Ella Yip for their assistance during the preparation of the manuscript and for their dedication to the people who come before the Probate Court.

Dr. Tomita ignored her family and friends during this project. Thank you to Wendy Lustbader and Barry Grosskopf, Karen and Larry Matsuda, Irene Fujitomi and Mike Nishiyama, Harriette de Mers Rower, Alan and Joyce Tomita, Neal Tomita and Cheryl Lippman for allowing her to be a social isolate and absent friend or sister, for taking care of some of her responsibilities and her son's needs on her behalf, and for remaining kind without expecting any reciprocity on her part. David Redick was always available when she had a computer problem. Dr. Tomita's parents, the late Susumu Tomita, and Hiroko Tomita, taught her the values that were put to use during this project. They exemplify parental devotion and unselfishness. Last, Dr. Tomita is extremely fortunate to have Cliff Barda and Jason Rabbitt-Tomita, who ran around and refused to throw anything away ("But dear—but Mom—every item is a memory"), distracted her when it was needed, and humored her during this project.

MARY JOY QUINN
SUSAN K. TOMITA

# The Phenomenon of Elder Mistreatment

Part One examines the developing phenomenon of elder mistreatment, including the nature and types of mistreatment, findings from several phases of research, and various hypotheses as to why older adults are being abused and neglected in our society.

Chapter 1 explores the hidden nature of elder mistreatment. Other forms of domestic abuse, such as child abuse and neglect and spousal abuse, have been recognized for over 30 years, but it is within only approximately 15 years that the mistreatment of elderly family members has come to the attention of the public and professional groups.

Chapter 2 provides a case history that highlights common aspects of elder mistreatment: a combination of physical and financial abuse and medical neglect. Findings from the several phases of research are described. The first phase consisted mainly of exploratory studies that confirmed the existence of elder mistreatment. In the second phase, the focus of interest shifted to characteristics of abusers, with abuser dependency, not elder dependency, surfacing as a significant contributor to elder mistreatment. The prevalence of elder mistreatment is also estimated in this phase. Pioneering studies on elder mistreatment in nursing facilities, within the relationship between caregiver and impaired elder, and among several ethnic groups are dominant activities in the last few years.

Chapter 3 describes the various types of elder mistreatment. Physical abuse, sexual abuse, physical neglect, self-neglect, failure to thrive, obsessive-compulsive hoarder's syndrome, psychological abuse and neglect, financial abuse, and violation of rights are described and are accompanied by case examples. Most people, even those who work with other forms of domestic violence, have difficulty visualizing exactly how elder mistreatment is manifested. In some instances, it closely resembles child or spousal abuse. However, there are some unique aspects to elder mistreatment, such as financial abuse. Children and women typically do not own real estate or do not have other assets. Elders usually do, and this can make them a target for mistreatment.

Chapter 4 focuses on the hypothesized causes of elder mistreatment, including societal attitudes such as ageism and sexism, which create a climate for the maltreatment of older people. Recent studies that revisit the concepts of caregiver stress and elder dependency as factors associated with elder mistreatment are discussed. As yet no specific theories have been proved or disproved by methodical research, but these various hypotheses offer a framework which practitioners will be able to utilize.

# CHAPTER 1

# Aging and Elder Mistreatment

Home is the place where,
    When you have to go there
They have to take you in.
("The Death of the Hired Man," Robert Frost)

A decade ago, preliminary steps had been taken to address the problems of domestic elder mistreatment. But the subject had not yet received the same attention as other forms of domestic violence, namely child abuse and neglect, child sexual assault, woman battering, and rape. When the subject of abuse or neglect of the elderly was mentioned, the general public usually thought of abuse in nursing homes, crime in the streets, or fraudulent insurance schemes. Now, a decade later, domestic elder mistreatment is widely acknowledged both by the public and by professionals who deal with the elderly. Many steps have been taken to combat the problems, such as passage of legislation in every state, education of practitioners, formation of multidisciplinary teams, and the development of innovative techniques for intervention, including criminal prosecution of some alleged abusers. Conferences devoted exclusively to elder mistreatment are beginning to appear, and there are more efforts to link all types of domestic violence to find common characteristics and solutions. Even with all these efforts, however, elder mistreatment remains hidden to a large extent and for many reasons.

## A HIDDEN PROBLEM

Why have elder abuse and neglect remained hidden and unacknowledged? Some reasons are rooted deeply in the traditional nature of the family; others can be traced to the dynamics at work between domestic abusers and their victims. Still other reasons flow from the ambivalent feelings society holds about growing old. On the practitioner's part, there has been a lack of information, a lack of procedures, and a lack of intervention protocols. Practitioners have also been handicapped by the absence of support services for victims, such as counseling and shelters, and by the lack of treatment for abusers of the elderly. In addition, agencies have had difficulty creating and funding procedures and policies that address elder mistreatment effectively.

Those who work in the field of family violence know that it is one of the toughest societal problems and that, even after 20 to 35 years of awareness, there is still a great deal of work to be done to bring child abuse and spouse abuse fully into the consciousness of this country. Until recently, both types of abuse were sanctioned as proper behavior. Children and wives were viewed as chattel, the rightful property of the male head of the household, and it was his duty to discipline them if they "went astray." There was very little interference from the state; harsh treatment was rarely viewed with concern, but rather was seen as a righteous effort to discipline a disobedient child or a wayward spouse.

Violence in the family and the neglect of helpless family members are emotionally charged issues. The home is traditionally the place where people feel the most secure. To think that one would not be safe there is nearly incomprehensible. The private home has been traditionally looked upon as a sanctuary from any governmental interference. Indeed, this country was founded on that principle (among others) and many of those who left their homelands to come here did so to escape governmental interference in their private lives. Secrecy and isolation are a common dimension in all forms of intimate abuse especially in a perpetrator-victim relationship in the family system (American Association of Retired Persons, 1992). Straus (1979a) notes that the norms of American society make behavior inside the home a private affair, and that even after violence occurs, the rule of family privacy is so strong that it works to prevent victims from seeking help. Many continue to feel that violence in the family is best resolved within the family. This view is termed the "traditional position" in the Final Report of the

Attorney General's Task Force on Family Violence (1984), which notes that until this century, wife battering and child abuse were viewed as private matters exempt from public scrutiny or jurisdiction. The Task Force also notes that this traditional view is still widely held by the public as well as by some law enforcement officers, prosecutors, and judges.

## Why Elder Abuse Victims Don't Tell

Many older people are concerned about their family's privacy and the privacy of their relationships, and that is why they do not report the abuse and neglect they are suffering, or why they do not accept services aimed at stopping the mistreatment or why they refuse to take any action that might appear to be aimed against the alleged abuser. They fear public exposure, and the embarrassment and humiliation they are sure such exposure will bring. They worry that they will not be believed, because the alleged abuser acts differently in public. When the alleged abuser is an adult child, the victim may feel shame at having raised a child who would hurt him or her in any way. Victims do not want anyone to know that their lives have come to such a pass. When the alleged abuser is a demented spouse and the victim is the caregiver, the victim may not want others to know for fear they will think he or she cannot properly take care of a spouse. The couple may have promised each other years ago that they would always care for one another if illness struck, and the victim may fear that they will be separated.

Linked to these feelings of shame and embarrassment is anxiety about what will happen if an "outsider" finds out about the abuse. The older person may realistically fear that if the abuse is reported the perpetrator will retaliate with still more mistreatment. Alleged abusers may threaten to inflict more severe abuse, destroy property or pets, or even kill their victims, other loved ones, or themselves (Breckman & Adelman, 1988). There is also often concern that the abuser, who is usually a family member or a caregiver the older person has come to rely upon, will be put in jail and that as part of that process, the older person will have to testify in court against the abuser. This means still more public exposure and possible rupturing of intimate relationships. Victims of elder abuse and neglect also worry that reporting means incarceration for the perpetrator, who may be the only caregiver or even the only relationship the elder has. This in turn raises the specter of placement in a nursing home, a fate most people view with horror:

Almost all older people view the move to a home for the aged or to a nursing home with fear and hostility. . . . All old people—without exception—believe that the move to an institution is the prelude to death. . . . [The old person] sees the move to an institution as a decisive change in living arrangements, the last change he will experience before he dies. . . . Finally, no matter what the extenuating circumstances, the older person who has children interprets the move to an institution as rejection by his children. (Shanas, 1962)

Other family ties may also prevent the older person from reporting abuse. The victim may resist out of parental love, or out of a sense that a parent should protect, nurture, and financially support an adult child no matter what the child has done. Some victims deny or minimize the abuse out of family loyalty or for fear that they will alienate whatever family they have:

One man who lived in a nursing home was aware that his son had taken $90,000 from his bank account. He told the state ombudsman that he did not want his son prosecuted and he did not want to take any steps to recover the money. "The money isn't important," he said. " My son is. After all, some family is better than none. He's all I got." The son rarely visited his father in the nursing home.

Victims of child abuse fear losing parental affection, and battered women fear losing the affection of their batterers; both fear the disruption of the status quo (Walker, 1984). Elderly victims of mistreatment are no different; they too fear rejection and disruption of their lives, even though they may be badly abused.

Some elders minimize or deny the mistreatment they are suffering out of pride in survival. They reason that they have survived two world wars, several recessions, a major depression and various personal misfortunes. They reason that the mistreatment is not that bad and surely will not last forever. Other older people feel they deserve the abuse and accept it fatalistically. There may be a religious justification or a belief that suffering in the present will bring rewards in the future. An older person may feel that God means for him or her to suffer and that the suffering has a purpose that will be revealed in due time.

Sometimes a female victim of elder abuse will not report the abuse or prosecute the abuser because she has never been very assertive or effective in getting what she wants out of life; she has passively accepted whatever has come her way. Possibly she has learned that nothing she does will affect her circumstances. If she is abused in late life, that too is accepted. It may also be that she is a repeat victim of violence. Walker (1984) studied battered women and reported that early and repeated sexual molestation and assault in childhood make a woman more susceptible to being battered in later life. Almost half of the battered women in Walker's study reported that they repeatedly had been sexually molested as children. This dramatic pattern of victimization raises the question whether the victim of elder abuse, who is usually a woman, may have been abused previously as a wife and as a child. She may have learned to be compliant as a coping style when, in fact, compliance may reinforce the instances in which aggression may occur (Tomita, 1988).

Some older people do not acknowledge abuse, or they accept it because they feel they are failures because of the way they lived their lives or because they have become dependent on others. It is only with great reluctance that older people resign themselves to being dependent on someone who once depended upon them for physical survival. Some older people do not report mistreatment because they are not aware of it or are incapable of realizing that they are being abused. Financial abuse can be well-hidden, sometimes for years. Some victims are too impaired mentally or physically to be aware of abuse. The old-old, the most frequent victims of elder mistreatment, are often impaired and disoriented in regard to time, place, and person; they are incapable of physically taking care of themselves (Wolf & Pillemer, 1989). Sometimes they simply don't know what's going on around them.

Finally, elder abuse victims do not report that they are being abused because there is always the hope that the abuse will somehow stop—just as children hope abuse will stop; just as battered spouses hope that battering incidents will stop.

## Role of the Alleged Abuser

Alleged abusers, too, refrain from reporting abuse. This may occur out of conscious self-interest. But generally speaking, alleged abusers tend to rationalize or minimize their actions and to deny that they have inflicted damage on the victim. The abusers may justify their actions, alleging that the victim provoked the abuse and therefore got what he or she deserved. They often excuse their behavior, blaming it on the stubbornness of the elder or behavior on the part of the elder that they view as demanding, aggressive, or embarrassing. Other alleged abusers may excuse their actions by claiming that they "lost it" under the influence of alcohol or drugs. They may complain of depression (Homer & Gilleard, 1990; Paveza, Cohen, Eisdorfer, Freels, Semla, Ashford, Gorelick, Hirschman, Luchman, Luchins, & Levy, 1992; Wolf & Pillemer, 1989). If abusers are repentant and remorseful after a battering incident, this period is short-lived, and the abuse begins anew, escalating in frequency and intensity (Sonkin & Durphy, 1982). Elder abusers commonly blame elderly victims for their injuries by saying that they fell or otherwise bruised themselves. Some elder abusers may literally not know that they are abusing, particularly if they are demented, suffer from a mental illness, are developmentally disabled, or are inebriated.

A stressed caregiver who suddenly and impulsively strikes out may feel too ashamed to ask for help or may feel that no help will be forthcoming even if it is requested. Also, a caregiver may not know where to look for help, or may ask for assistance in a way that precludes receiving help. For example, he or she may ask a practitioner for one service when in fact elder mistreatment is a hidden agenda (Block & Sinnott, 1979). The request for help may be too veiled or indirect, or it may be impossible for the agency to fulfill. The request may not be recognized as a call for help.

## Growing Old

Some of the reasons that we do not recognize elder abuse and neglect have to do with the isolation of the aged and how we think and feel about growing old ourselves. Those of us who work with the frail elderly may be especially prone to viewing old age as *solely* a time of dementia and dependency simply because that is the only part of the aging population we see in our daily work. If there are no healthy, robust elders in our private lives, we may come to think very negatively of aging. Ageist attitudes may be an occupational hazard for us (Breckman & Adelman, 1988).

The elderly, especially the frail elderly, are less invisible than other age groups. They are often not visible on the streets, and unlike children, they do not go every day to a school where abuse and neglect can frequently be detected by an observant teacher or school nurse. Frail elders do not go out of the house much; they tend to be more isolated than abused spouses, who may at least get to the supermarket and theoretically can walk away from an abusive situation. If an elder is bed-bound, the isolation may be complete. That elder may seldom if ever be seen by anyone other than family members or the caregiver.

Many people tend to shy away from the old, especially the elderly who are mentally or physically impaired, or both. These elders may seem frightening, and many people do not feel comfortable being around them. Visiting a nursing home for the first time can be traumatic: it can be overwhelming to see large numbers of extremely impaired dependent elders living in one place. The thought, "Is this what my old age will be like?" is inescapable and frightening. These frail elders are shunned by the general public. Many people find it difficult to know how to act in the presence of an elderly individual who is impaired, how much help to give, how to hold a conversation. Often there is a feeling of wanting to get away quickly.

The old are the only minority most of us hope to join, no matter how ambivalent we may personally feel about the aging process. But old age is rarely seen as the triumph of survival that it really represents. Myths and stereotypes about aging infect everyone. For instance, old people are not alike, despite the fact that they are all old. Chronological age does not determine impairment levels or emotional maturity. We each age at different rates and in uniquely different ways. In fact, we may become even more diverse as we age. This is especially true when there are generations among the old. It is now common to see parents who are in their nineties and older who have adult children in their sixties and seventies. Another myth is that we will all become "senile" or suffer from Alzheimer's disease. In fact, on the basis of a review of major studies on Alzheimer's disease, the prevalence rate for people 65 years of age and older ranges from 971 per 100,000 in Turku, Finland, to 10,300 per 100,000 in Boston, Massachusetts, or from approximately 1% to 10.3%. The age-specific rate increases with age, but still, not all elderly develop this disease (Mayeux & Schofield, 1994). Other myths include the concept that we all become more serene as we grow old, that we become unproductive, and that we all become resistant to change as we age (Butler & Lewis, 1982).

## EMERGENCE OF ELDER ABUSE

There has always been elder mistreatment, just as there has always been child abuse and neglect and woman battering. There are referrals to maltreatment of the old both in myth and in literature (Stearns, 1986; Reinharz, 1986). In Greek mythology, for instance, parricide—murder of parents—

is an essential component of the creation of the world; the young succeed to their parents' power by violently replacing them. It is the way to become an adult. In direct contrast to Greek mythology, the Bible speaks of respecting, obeying, and fearing the father in the form of God. The Bible does not mention parricide but does refer to sons outwitting their fathers and dreaming of besting them (Reinharz 1986). A form of parricide is documented in Fraser's work on rites and ceremonies (Fraser, 1900). He writes of the practice of regicide, the killing of a king who has grown old and perhaps is becoming demented, thereby endangering his subjects. According to Fraser, numerous types of euthanasia were practiced on aging kings, as well as priests (Fraser, 1900).

Family conflict noted in preindustrial times centered on the eagerness of the young to inherit the land and the fears of the old that they will be neglected in their old age. In addition, the burning of postmenopausal women at the stake as witches and the outright physical violence against older men are evidence that elder abuse and neglect existed in preindustrial times (Stearns, 1986). In primitive societies where resources are scarce, there may be traditions whereby failing elders voluntarily die either by permitting themselves to be abandoned or by asking to be killed so as to protect resources for the group, or out of weariness after a life of labor (Daly & Wilson, 1982). Some societies may encourage killing elders by justifying it in different ways, including a holding a belief that one will have a happier afterlife if one is killed than if one dies naturally.

Fairy tales and literature speak of the maltreatment of older people. Actual cases of parricide are known. In general, where adolescents kill their parents, there is a history of physical and even sexual abuse from the parents. Thus, there is an element of self-defense. When adults murder their parents, they seem to do so to gain wealth and power, which gives the appearance of motivation by greed (Reinharz, 1986).

At some periods in history, maltreatment of the elderly is not mentioned, possibly because the elderly themselves were not of interest (Stearns, 1986). This was true of the late 19th and early 20th century. However, the subject is resurfacing. The initial research and the congressional hearings in the late 1970s and early 1980s, where abused elders told their stories, sounded a warning of this "new" form of domestic abuse. That call fell on receptive ears because of previous work by dedicated researchers and clinicians involving other forms of domestic violence, i.e., spouse abuse and child abuse and neglect. Therefore, even though the discovery that old people also suffer domestic violence has been met with shock, revulsion, and some denial, it is not as unbelievable as it might have been had it emerged before other forms of domestic abuse and neglect. In fact, there has been unprecedented professional and public attention to the issue of mistreatment of the elderly in recent years (Wolf & Pillemer, 1989).

Government has taken an active role in dealing with elder abuse and neglect, although there has been more response on the state and local level than on the federal level (Wolf, 1990). All states now have some type of  reporting law, usually mandatory (American Public Welfare Association/National Association of State Units on Aging, 1986). Most of the laws require that the mistreatment be reported to adult protective services, although a few require reporting to the criminal justice system or other systems. Very few of the laws attached extra funding for the agencies dealing with elder abuse and neglect or the services that victims require. The laws vary widely in their definitions of abuse and neglect. They also differ in what types of abuse or neglect are to be reported, who is required to report abuse, and the penalties for not reporting.

Actual reports of elder mistreatment have increased, in part because of the reporting laws. In 1990, the U.S. House Select Committee on Aging surveyed Adult Protective Services in all 50 states and found that 70% of reported adult cases of abuse involved the elderly, whereas a decade earlier 60% of reported cases had involved the elderly. Ninety percent of the states reported that the incidence of reported elder abuse was increasing (U.S. House Select Committee on Aging, 1990). Wisconsin, which has had a voluntary reporting law since 1984 but which mandated development of a statewide system to address elder abuse and neglect in each of its 72 counties, reported a 14.3% increase in the number of reports in one year, from 1989 to 1990. Over 1 in 9 cases involved a life-threatening situation; in 15 of the 1,952 cases, death was the result of the abuse or neglect (Wisconsin Department of Health and Social Services, 1991).

In most of the states, reports of elder mistreatment to regulatory agencies have increased by 106% in 8 years. In 1986, 117,000 reports were made; in 1994, 241,000 reports were made. On the basis of the only prevalence study on elder mistratment conducted so far, it is estimated that only one in 14 cases are reported to the authorities (Pillemer & Finkelhor, 1988). Excluding self-neglecting elders, and given a substantiation rate of approximately 26% (Tatara, 1993), an estimated 818,000 elders became victims of other-inflicted elder mistreatment in 1994. In the 1994 reports, 21.6 percent came from physicians and health care providers; another 9.4 percent came from other service agency providers; an additional 1.9% of the reports came from family members and relatives. Others making reports included friends, neighbors, law enforcement personnel, clergy, financial institutions, and victims themselves. Excluding self-neglecting elders, the median age of the victims was 76.4 years. The majority of the victims were women (62.1%), and a little more than half of the abusers were women (52.4%). Adult children were reported as the most frequent abusers. Thirty-five percent of the substantiated elder mistreatment cases in 1994 involved adult children; 13.4 percent involved spouses (National Center on Elder Abuse, 1995).

Financial resources to combat elder mistreatment have been meager. In fact, at the same time that elder mistreatment have been increasing, states' budgets have decreased their funding for Adult Protective Services. In 1980, 6.6% of the states' budgets was allocated for Adult Protective Services; in 1989, that amount had decreased to less than 4%. This reality is even more striking in view of the growing numbers of older persons in our society, especially those who are "old-old" and in need of assistance, the elders most likely to be abused or neglected. (Wolf & Pillemer, 1989; U.S. House Select Committee on Aging, 1990)

Still another reason for the emergence of elder mistreatment is the public's increased awareness of old people, a result in part of their rapidly growing numbers. There is a new and genuine climate of concern. Basically, this society is more compassionate than it once was, and most people are aware that all is not well with old people or with the way we live out our lives. There is also an increased willingness by the state to intervene in family life. Beginning in the late 1960s, there has been enormous growth in the portion of the state bureaucracy dedicated to protecting people who are vulnerable, beginning with child protective services. Reporting laws reflect this concern, as do investigatory procedures and state custody, which serve to separate people from their families and provide them with more secure environments (Wolf and Pillemer, 1989). Less altruistically, there is great concern at many governmental levels about the enormous costs in seeing to the needs of the frail elderly. Medicare funding is always under siege, and Social Security—the single most important source of income for the elderly—is preserved only because older people ceaselessly advocate for it (U.S. Bureau of the Census, 1984). Politicians are acutely aware of older people because as a group, they are much more likely to vote than other age groups. Age-based organizations are common and some have millions of members.

# GRAYING OF AMERICA

In a way, the awareness of elder mistreatment has been thrust upon society because of the unprecedented growth in the number of older people, particularly those 75 and older, the age group that seems to be most vulnerable to abuse and neglect. This increase means enormous shifts in family roles, in public policy, and for elders themselves.

Never before in this country have so many middle-aged and young-old (aged 65–75) adult children had surviving parents or found themselves having to take care of the old-old, (75 and over), their aging parents. Put simply, there are more elderly people than ever before; they are living longer; and their disabilities and dependencies increase in severity with their age. For example, as shown in Table 1.1, a person born in 1900 could expect to live an average of 47 years (U.S. Bureau of the Census, 1992). A person born in 1989, however, can expect to live, on the average, to nearly 75.3— an increase of over 28 years. In addition, those who are already old have had years added to their lives by advances in medical technology. In 1990, people aged 65 had an average life expectancy of an additional 17.2 years; in 1980, it would have been 16.4 years (U.S. Bureau of the Census, 1984; American Association of Retired Persons, 1994). The fastest-growing segment of the population is the age group 75 and older, which means that more and more middle-aged adult children will have old-old parents and four-generational families will become commonplace. The group 85 and over is growing particularly rapidly, up by 38 percent from 1980 to 1990. Those over 100 more than doubled during the 1980s. In addition, the elderly population will become more racially and ethnically diverse over the years. For instance, in 1990, only 1 in 10 elderly people were races other than white. This could increase to about 2 in 10 elderly by the year 2050, with the most dramatic growth in the Hispanic groups (U.S. Bureau of the Census, 1992).

Clearly, dramatic shifts are taking place. There is every reason to expect that this "graying of America" will continue well into the next century. In 1990, the proportion of Americans 80 or older was 1 in 35, but by 2050 at least 1 in 12 could be 80 or older (U.S. Bureau of the Census, 1992). There is the strong possibility that even these figures are conservative because they cannot take into account immigration, continuing medical advances, and voluntary changes in health habits such as having a better diet and quitting smoking.

**Table 1.1  Life Expectancy at Birth and at 65 Years of Age, by Race and Sex: Selected Years, 1900 to 1989**

| Specified age and year | All races | | | White | | Black | |
|---|---|---|---|---|---|---|---|
| | Both sexes | Male | Female | Male | Female | Male | Female |
| At birth | | | | | | | |
| 1900[1,2] ............... | 47.3 | 46.3 | 48.3 | 46.6 | 48.7 | [3]32.5 | [3]33.5 |
| 1950[2] ............... | 68.2 | 65.6 | 71.1 | 66.5 | 72.2 | 58.9 | 62.7 |
| 1960[2] ............... | 69.7 | 66.6 | 73.1 | 67.4 | 74.1 | 60.7 | 65.9 |
| 1970 ............... | 70.9 | 67.1 | 74.8 | 68.0 | 75.6 | 60.0 | 68.3 |
| 1980 ............... | 73.7 | 70.0 | 77.4 | 70.7 | 78.1 | 63.8 | 72.5 |
| 1989 ............... | 75.3 | 71.8 | 78.6 | 72.7 | 79.2 | 64.8 | 73.5 |
| At 65 years | | | | | | | |
| 1900–1902[1,2] ....... | 11.9 | 11.5 | 12.2 | 11.5 | 12.2 | 10.4 | 11.4 |
| 1950[2] ............... | 13.9 | 12.8 | 15.0 | 12.8 | 15.1 | 12.9 | 14.9 |
| 1960[2] ............... | 14.3 | 12.8 | 15.8 | 12.9 | 15.9 | 12.7 | 15.1 |
| 1970 ............... | 15.2 | 13.1 | 17.0 | 13.1 | 17.1 | 12.5 | 15.7 |
| 1980 ............... | 16.4 | 14.1 | 18.3 | 14.2 | 18.4 | 13.0 | 16.8 |
| 1989 ............... | 17.2 | 15.2 | 18.8 | 15.2 | 19.0 | 13.6 | 17.0 |

[1]Death registration area only. The death registration area increased from 10 states and the District of Columbia in 1900 to the coterminous United States in 1933.

[2]Includes deaths of nonresidents of the United States.

[3]Figure is for "all other" population.

*Sources:* National Center for Health Statistics, *Health, United States, 1990.* Hyattsville, Md: Public Health Service, 1991, table 15. 1989 "At birth" data from Monthly Vital Statistics Report, Vol. 40, No. 8(S)2, January 7, 1992. 1989 "at 65 years" data unpublished final data from Mortality Statistics Branch. As it appears in U.S. Bureau of the Census (1992), Current population reports, Special Studies, Series P23-178. *Sixty-five plus in America.* Washington, D.C.: U.S. Government Printing Office.

## Impact on Families

Families, traditionally looked upon as the caregivers of frail elderly kin, are facing many changes because their old-old members live so long, especially if an elder becomes dependent in any way. The term "generational inversion" has been coined to describe the phenomenon whereby responsibilities, status, control, and dependency for survival are permanently inverted, and adult children assume the roles previously held by their parents (Steinmetz, 1983; Steinmetz, 1988b). This is typically an unforeseen and unwelcome situation for parent and child; often, no one envisioned that the parent would live to such an advanced age. More and more Americans are finding themselves in this position. The old-old often express amazement that they are still alive. During the course of a social service interview, one 94-year-old woman turned to her 92-year-old husband and said, "John, why on earth have we lasted so long?"

One very concrete result of longevity is that it becomes almost impossible to pass on an inheritance. The elder wants to give it, and most likely the adult child needs it. But the impaired elder ends up needing the money to purchase a variety of services, many of them health-related. Elders use medical services more than younger people: people aged 65 and over average nine physician visits for every five of the general population. In 1992, older people accounted for 35% of all hospital stays and 46% of all days of care in hospitals (American Association of Retired Persons, 1994). Most older persons have at least one chronic condition and many have multiple conditions. In 1987, those 65 and over represented 12% of the population but accounted for 36% of the total personal health care expenditures. About $1,500, or one-fourth of the average expenditure, came from direct ("out-of-pocket") payments by or for older persons (American Association of Retired Persons, 1994). Thus, needed services for the very old may consume the inheritance.

### *Dependency and Disability*

Most people understand that older adults may need some assistance. But being largely dependent over long periods of time, perhaps years, is not looked upon favorably either by old people or by those who must care for them. On the contrary, such dependency is often viewed with fear, dread, disrespect, shame, and disapproval. Needing others is not the American way. There is still a strong ethos in this country that says the most admirable people are those who are able to suffer without complaining, who can take care of themselves without the aid of others. Rugged individualism, no matter the cost or the circumstances, is more valued than dependency or even interdependency. We accept dependency in children because we understand that children need their parents for survival. But children grow up and gradually become less dependent. This is not true for those old adults who become dependent because of physical or mental impairments. These impairments are likely to worsen over time, given the nature of chronic illness. The older adult becomes progressively more dependent, and therefore more vulnerable to actions of others.

Types of dependence encountered in the process of aging can include economic dependence, as the individual moves from being a producer to being a consumer; physical dependence arising from waning physical strength and energy and diminishing ability to perform daily tasks; social dependence occurring if mobility becomes problematical or contemporaries die; and emotional dependence, often an outcome of the other forms of dependence (Cantor, 1991).

The kinds of dependence that come normally and gradually to many of the aged can be exaggerated by the mental and physical conditions that frequently accompany old age. As we age, the incidence of acute illnesses greatly decreases, but the incidence of chronic physical and mental disease increases, leading to permanent impairments, which take their toll on functional abilities. Most chronic health conditions are not disabling. With increasing age, however, they are much more likely to be associated with functional disability. The old-old, that is, those over 75, generally need more care and assistance than those under 75. For instance, among people under 65, only 2% need assistance with activities of daily living (ADL). But 9% of those age 65–69 need assistance, and the figure jumps to 45% of those 85 and over (U.S. Bureau of the Census, 1992).

The likelihood of spending one's life in a nursing home does increase with age. But contrary to popular belief, most older adults continue to live in the community whether or not they are impaired; only 5% of those over the age of 65 live in nursing homes at any given time (American Association of Retired Persons, 1994). This means that more impaired and dependent older people are living in the community and are dependent on others for assistance particularly as they reach advanced old age.

### Reactions to Dependency

Most families respond in caring and helpful ways to the dependence of elder members and do not abuse or neglect them in any way. And there are many families who exhibit amazing creativity, compassion, and heroism in their dealings with aged dependent family members. The reactions of the dependent elder are also a factor; some older adults are able to accept dependency with more grace and style than others. But for most people, it is a very difficult time, and not all families have the capacity to react to dependency in a constructive manner.

Some families react in ways that exacerbate the difficulties of dependence. Adult children may deny it because it is too painful to confront— too painful to acknowledge that a beloved parent or a powerful, forceful parent is losing strength and may no longer be the authority in the family; it means "growing up" and is a hint of the children's own mortality (Lustbader, 1991). It is also a forceful reminder that the parent will leave by dying, placing the adult child in the position of being in the "lead generation," next in line to face the terrors of old age and death.

Some adult children fail to acknowledge an aging parent's dependency because it frightens them and they don't know what to do about it. They become paralyzed. Some deny that their aged parent is failing because they don't wish to know and don't wish to help, sometimes for understandable reasons but other times out of selfishness or even cruelty. Some adult children rush their parents into complete dependency out of ignorance, or because it means gaining control, or because it is easier than coping with someone who is partially independent.

Older people may deal with dependency in ways that make it even more problematical. Some are able to adapt to each new limitation with astounding creativity and even verve. Others embrace dependency prematurely, even when they are still capable. This can anger adult children who are busy with their own lives and feel their parents could cope if only they tried. Other old people resist dependency, denying it verbally and struggling to maintain their former position of power, all the while having to accept more and more assistance from their adult children.

## *Losing Control*

Any one impairment increases the possibility (and in many instances, the probability) that the elder will lose the capacity to handle his or her own personal and financial affairs. With that profound loss comes an inevitable decrease in personal control, including loss in decision-making power. Someone else may be given the legal authority to decide such critical matters as who the elder's physician will be or if a lifelong home should be sold.

The elder may lose the ability to reciprocate when a caregiver performs a service. As a group, elderly people may have diminished social and economic power with which to make exchanges with younger persons (Dowd, 1975). People who are physically or mentally impaired usually receive more in goods and services than they can return. Generally speaking, there is a loss of power when one cannot reciprocate in kind. The balance of power shifts. Early on, exchange theory was used to explain elder mistreatment, assuming that those (caregivers) with the most goods (money), services, and capacities become the ones with the most power and are in a position to wield control over those (elders) with fewer goods, services, and capacities. Sometimes older people try to reciprocate by using what resources they have left as payment to the caregiver or by leaving real or personal property to the caregiver in a will. The agreement, it was thought, usually unwritten, goes like this: "You take care of me until I die. In return, I will leave you everything I have, including my house." This process may happen with or without legal documentation. When it happens with legal documentation, it is termed "life estate." Older people, alone and lonely, have been coerced into signing their homes over to a caregiver as a condition of being taken care of. This is a precarious situation for the older person, who can be removed from the house any time the caregiver chooses—the house no longer belongs to the older person.

The social exchange theory as used above is helpful in explaining elder abuse, but only to a point. It does not explain those situations where a financially dependent adult child mistreats the parent to obtain resources or to hasten the parent's death. Most dependent elders are cared for without any abuse or neglect whatsoever. Why some elders are abused and others are not is still unclear. It has been speculated that the alleged abusers view themselves as *powerless* and lacking alternatives to a frustrating situation; they then strike out at the perceived object of stress, the elder (Pillemer, 1985b). But this opinion has not yet been supported by studies. A more plausible explanation may be the lack of adequate controls to stop mistreatment within the home. The alleged abuser may be a very mild-mannered person to the outside world. The social cost of being abusive to a more vulnerable family member may be less than that of being abusive to someone in a work setting. This may be particularly true when the caregiving is unending; the elder will not or is unable to express appreciation, and there are no real rewards for the caregiver (Tomita, 1988).

It frequently happens that people in a position of trust, handling other people's resources (real property, bank accounts, stock portfolios), come to think of those resources as their own. This occurs particularly if the rightful owner of the resources is impaired and is incapable of understanding how the resources are being used, and if the impairment has extended over a long period of time. It is a cruel reality that there has always been maltreatment of those less able to take care of themselves, of those who have lost the power of personality, and of those who cannot fight back effectively. The more vulnerable and impaired an individual is, the more tendency there is for others to objectify that person, to "thingify" the person and to attribute fewer and fewer human characteristics to him or her until the frail dependent elder may not be seen as human at all but perceived simply as a source of frustration and stress.

Through the multiple losses of power that can come in old age, elders can come to feel that they are a burden—sometimes an accurate perception. Some older people react by becoming more compliant and obsequious, which in turn may be invite more abuse by a cruel or indifferent caregiver. Many older people come to believe that events are beyond their control, and feelings of impotence take root. The elder, helpless to change the maltreatment, stops trying to do anything and accepts whatever treatment is offered. This phenomenon was described by Seligman (1975), who termed it "learned helplessness." Seligman postulated that helplessness produces emotional disturbances. The motivation to respond to a situation is sapped if the individual feels nothing can be done to affect the outcome. Another person may perceive that a particular reaction will make a difference in a given situation. But the person afflicted with "learned helplessness" will not think of that solution. There is also an increased inability to perceive success. The elder may do something that does indeed change the situation for the better but may not be aware of the success or may not fully comprehend that his or her action made a difference. The individual cannot recognize success even when it is publicly acknowledged. In this way, even success begets failure. According to Segliman, perceived helplessness produces fear as long as the person is uncertain of being able to influence events, and then it produces depression.

Still other older people react to a loss of personal power by becoming resistive and verbally combative, as they try desperately to hang on to what little power they may still have. This too, may bring on abuse and neglect, as the caregiver becomes frustrated with an uncooperative elder.

## SUMMARY

Over the last two decades, elder maltreatment has been emerging as still another facet of domestic violence. In part, this is due to the rapidly increasing number of old people, especially those who are 75 and over and in need of assistance in daily living. This reality is affecting many people, especially families who have traditionally furnished the caregiving for elder members. It is also a dilemma for the elderly.

No one wants to be a burden. Most people want to live to a healthy old age until they come to the end of their days; then they want to die quickly, painlessly, and effortlessly with no fuss or trouble to those around them. Because of increased longevity and the frequency of health impairment and disability in late old age, fewer and fewer people are being granted that wish.

# CHAPTER 2

# Victims and Their Abusers

She had demanded nothing all these years, never doubting that he would be there when needed. She had carefully pruned his spirit only in the enclaves of her will, and she had willed so little that he had been tempted again and again over the last thirty years because his just being had been enough to satisfy her needs. *(Women of Brewster Place,* Gloria Naylor)*

This quotation reflects the strong bonds that can exist between a parent and child despite years of mistreatment. The following case illustrates much of what is known about elder mistreatment. Several forms of abuse are present, the profiles of the abuser and the victim are fairly typical, and the abuse is recurring. The case also describes the frustrations of the case practitioners, the complexity of the issues relating to mistreatment, and finally, the resolution of the situation through the tenacity, competence, and compassion of the practitioners.

## CASE HISTORY

She was 76 years old and totally helpless. Four years earlier, she had fallen and struck the back of her head. The blow was so hard that her brain had slammed into the front of her skull; it was badly bruised and bled profusely. Although surgery helped and the blood clots were removed, part of her shattered skull bone could never be replaced. To protect the brain, a plastic disk now sat where once there had been bone.

Though she was alive, she was confined to her bed. With effort, she could turn over. She had difficulty swallowing and had to be fed. She ate very

*"Mattie Michael," from *The Women of Brewster Place* by Gloria Naylor. Copyright © 1980, 1982 by Gloria Naylor. Used by permission of Viking Penguin, a division of Penguin Books USA Inc.

slowly. A tube carried away her liquid body waste. She was fragile and thin. She could not care for herself in any way; she was totally dependent on others for all her needs.

She spoke in a whisper and tended to drift off into a dreamlike state after a few sentences, which were usually not related to the subject at hand. She could not hold a real conversation. In fact, her brain had been so badly damaged that she was incapable of asking for anything—even a glass of water. Most likely, she didn't know where she was. She had lost her ability to think, to dream, to imagine, to reason. She smiled sweetly and often. She was helpless, mentally and physically.

She and her son Harry lived in a two-bedroom apartment in a "nice" part of town. The apartment itself was dirty, dank, dark, and extremely cluttered. There was no place to sit in the living room because papers and materials, probably articles of clothing, were piled several feet high on chairs and tables. Harry said that he was doing research and that the clutter was temporary. It looked permanent, though, even to the most casual observer.

Harry had dismissed all the household help and was taking care of the apartment and his mother by himself. He was 50 years old and unemployed. He said he had been a postal worker but had developed hypertension and resigned on doctor's orders. When he tried to qualify for disability payments, he had been found to be able-bodied.

Harry had been appointed by the superior court to handle all of his mother's affairs when she became disabled. He had done this on the advice of the doctor, who had told him that his mother would never be able to handle her own affairs again. Thus, Harry was his mother's conservator of person and estate and as such was empowered legally to handle her money and to determine the kind of care she would receive. Income to the household came from his mother's pension and social security checks. Harry had no income of his own; he depended on his mother for food, clothing, and shelter. He was an only child and had never married. There were no close relatives.

Visiting nurses had been involved since the original injury, and a nurse was still coming to the house because Medicare paid for the service. But the nurses were growing discouraged and feeling impotent. Despite their best efforts to teach Harry techniques of caring for his mother, he did not follow through. Worse, his mother was hospitalized every time she was eligible for Medicare hospital benefits. The diagnoses were always the same: dehydration and malnutrition. Often, bruises about the face were noticed. On one admission, the mother had a split lip that was swollen and bleeding.

Other patients in the hospital saw Harry strike his mother on the side of the face when he thought she didn't swallow fast enough. He admitted hitting her. "I have to," he said. "She is deliberately not paying attention to her swallowing. I have to get her attention. Otherwise, it would take forever to feed her. It has to be done."

The hospitalizations always coincided with Harry's trips to southern California to see his "spiritual counselor." Invariably, his mother would do well in the hospital. She would brighten considerably and regain physical functioning through rehabilitation. Just as invariably, she would then be discharged home to her son. He refused to place her in a nursing home even though a doctor had recommended that he do so. He said that she had cared for him in his youth and now it was his turn to pay her back.

Harry was always cheerful and affable. A tall man with a large protuberant stomach, he tended to intimidate people because of his bulk and his tendency to stand very close when holding a conversation—"too close for comfort."

One day, the visiting nurse noticed that the mother's arm was swollen, bruised, and misaligned. She spoke to Harry about it, and he told her what had happened. He had been feeding his mother a hamburger, he said, and she was eating very slowly. Out of frustration, he left the room. When he returned, he found that she had made a mess with the food. He reached over her to clean up the mess. It was then, he said, that she raised her arm to protect her face. In the following confusion, he lost his balance and fell on her. As he fell, he pushed her arm "out of the way" and he heard a distinct "popping noise" come from the arm. Harry called the doctor, who told him to wrap the arm but refused to treat the arm more than that. The visiting nurse finally persuaded the doctor to permit a portable X-ray machine to come to the house. The doctor was reluctant to do so because "she's old and it wouldn't be worth the effort to treat her." The X-rays revealed a broken arm and elbow. The doctor still refused to treat the arm, even though this was the mother's functioning arm, the one that had been the center of much rehabilitation attention in the hospital. Now all use of the arm was lost.

The nurse was horrified. She began to feel that the doctor was in collusion with the son. She called a practitioner from the adult protection agency, who went to the home and tried to work with Harry. The practitioner offered to assist Harry in getting household help to care for his mother and the house. Harry refused. The practitioner then offered to help Harry get vocational training; Harry refused that too.

At all times, Harry spoke with affection for his mother and denied that he was under undue stress in caring for her. Yet even as he spoke, his smiling eyes seemed to reveal hidden hostility. Practitioners who knew the case observed coyness and flirtation between the mother and son. One practitioner said it gave her the creeps; another said, "There's something unnatural about that relationship."

Harry continued to disregard suggestions about rehabilitation. He refused to stop smoking in his mother's room, even though he knew it increased her respiratory distress and aggravated her swallowing problems; he smoked incessantly while feeding her. Harry did not follow through on any of the treatment plans that had been devised by the rehabilitation team at the hospital. He would not help his mother turn in bed or reposition her and never even sat her up in her chair. Her condition continued to deteriorate.

The same doctor who was "sure" that Harry had nothing to do with his mother's original fall was now sure that Harry "pushed and pinched his mother." The physician, although positive that Harry caused the bruises and lacerations on the mother's face, had a hard time accounting for her multiple hospitalizations for dehydration and malnutrition. He felt that Harry did the best he could but that it must be very frustrating to deal with someone as helpless and dependent as Harry's mother. Yet, though the doctor questioned Harry's ability to care for his mother, he declined to actively help place the mother in a good nursing home. "Harry just won't pay for it," he said.

Then Harry said he wanted to visit his "spiritual counselor" in southern California, explaining that the doctor would cooperate by placing the mother in the hospital. That was when a fresh bruise appeared on the mother's chin. Harry said, "Maybe I had to help her close her mouth."

In sheer desperation, the practitioner from the geriatric home visiting team called the local superior court and asked the court investigator for the court's help in protecting the mother. Much to the practitioner's surprise, the investigator discovered that Harry was indeed his mother's legal conservator and thus responsible to the court for his mother's care and the administration of her finances. What had been a issue of care now became an official legal concern. A judge, upon learning the preliminary facts of the case, ordered a full-scale investigation and set a courtroom hearing in 5 days.

The court investigator who conducted the investigation talked to everyone involved in the case, reviewed all the medical records, and made several determinations. First, she concluded that the case properly belonged in the court, both because the court had appointed the son legal conservator and because community workers had already exhausted all other approaches. Second, she concluded that the mother was in need of 24-hour skilled nursing care. She said that the son could not possibly provide it, and that he was actually harming his mother. Finally, she recommended that the son be removed from his position as conservator of person and estate of his mother.

The hearing was held as scheduled. Testimony was taken from the doctor, the visiting nurse, and the practitioners from the adult protective services agency; from the geriatric home visiting team; from Harry; and from the court investigator. The judge rendered his decision from the bench at the end of the hearing. Harry's legal powers over his mother were terminated and, on the order of the judge, she was immediately removed from the apartment and placed in a nursing home known to have especially kind, loving, and competent staff.

It was the feeling of the judge and all the workers that the mother would be in jeopardy if she were in the apartment when her son returned from the court hearing. If the mother's arm could be broken "accidentally," maybe she could suffer a more serious "accident." Maybe she could die "accidentally." It would not take much. She would not be able to fight off a pillow over her head. In fact, maybe the original fall was not an accident.

Today, the mother continues to live in the nursing home. She has gained weight, she speaks more clearly, and her mental state is vastly improved. She no longer cringes when her son comes at mealtimes to feed her. He is carefully watched by the nursing staff whenever he spends time with his mother. He has never admitted any wrongdoing and continues to believe that he is doing "what is best for Mom."

Upon the judge's referral, the district attorney is now investigating the case; there is a possibility that Harry will be prosecuted for the physical and financial abuse of his mother.

## Discussion of Case History

This case history illustrates many facts of elder mistreatment. Several forms of abuse were present: physical, psychological, and financial. The physical abuse was obvious and ongoing; it escalated from bruises around the mouth to a broken arm and included the son's compromising the mother's respiratory and swallowing mechanisms by his incessant cigarette smoking in her room. There were strong indications that the son was deliberately withholding food and liquid from his mother in order to make her eligible for periodic Medicare-reimbursed hospitalizations, which in turn afforded him respite from caring for her. His failure to follow through on rehabilitation recommendations or to get his mother up in the chair can be seen as neglect, which may or may not have been intentional on his part. Although no evidence of sexual abuse was found, the coyness and flirtatiousness between mother and son suggested that theirs was an unusual mother-son relationship; one worker speculated that there may have been sexual contact between the two when the son was a child. Certainly their attachment was very strong; the son had never married and the two had lived together for a number of years.

The mother was incapable of speaking more than a few phrases of social amenities, so it was not possible to determine whether she felt psychologically abused. But psychological abuse can be inferred from the fact that the mother frequently cringed and cowered whenever her son was in the room, as was observed by the nurses and patients both in the acute care setting and in the nursing home. This behavior gradually stopped after the woman was placed in the nursing home where the nursing staff could closely observe the son whenever he visited her.

The financial abuse was clear. The son used his mother's money to support himself instead of using it to pay for homemaker and health aide services that would have benefited his mother—though as his mother's legal conservator, he was bound to use her money only for her. He refused to work and support himself. This is a common scenario in elder abuse and neglect when an adult child mistreats a parent.

This case illustrates the complexity of the issues when elder mistreatment is involved. It can take several months for practitioners to be certain that elder mistreatment is occurring, and then it may take just as long to find successful interventions. This can be very frustrating. There may be other practitioners involved in the case whose actions are questionable. In this instance, the physician appeared to be colluding with the abuser. The case was finally resolved only because the practitioners never stopped looking for solutions and refused to give up.

In this case, the profile of the "typical" abused elder resembles the description in the four germinal research studies (Block & Sinnott, 1979; Douglass, Hickey, & Noel 1980; Lau & Kosberg, 1978; O'Malley, Segars, Perez, Mitchell, & Kneupel, 1979). She is a widow over the age of 75 with significant mental and physical impairments and is dependent on an adult child with whom she resides. However, the earlier studies were based on clinical samples and anecdotal information and did not have adequate information to develop a profile of the abuser and of elders in the general population. Only after subsequent studies were conducted in the second wave of research did other characteristics of the victims and the abuser more clearly emerge, such as the finding that the abuser is often dependent on the victim, and not vice-versa.

## THE GERMINAL STUDIES

### First Wave of Research

The first public knowledge of elder mistreatment cases came in 1978, when Dr. Suzanne Steinmetz, a noted researcher in family violence, startled a congressional committee with her descriptions of "battered parents" (1978, 1980). She described elderly people who reside with their relatives, are dependent on them, and are battered by them. Dr. Steinmetz based her information on case studies and information gathered from social services, hospital social workers, and emergency rooms. At the same time, Rathbone-McCuan (1978, 1980) was also conducting case studies. The information obtained by the these groundbreaking studies formed the first works published on elder mistreatment and led to further research.

Lau and Kosberg (1978) conducted a retrospective case review of 404 patients over age 60 who were assessed during a 12-month period at the Chronic Illness Center, Cleveland, Ohio. Agency staff members were asked to identify cases of mistreatment from case documentation and from their recollections of individual patients. Thirty-nine patients, or 9.6%, were identified as victims of mistreatment. Physical abuse was the most common form of mistreatment, but this is in part because physical neglect was considered to be a part of physical abuse. Psychological abuse was the second most common form of mistreatment, with 33% of the victims experiencing verbal assault. Material abuse and violation of rights followed. Most of the clients suffered from two to five forms of mistreatment. These elders lived in the community and were dependent upon family or others for services to keep them in the community. Denial and resignation were the most common forms of response to the mistreatment, with only four elders seeking intervention. Lau and Kosberg found that 30 of the victims were women, and 58% of those were widows. About half (51%) of the elders could not walk without the assistance of another person or required a wheelchair; 18% were partially or totally incontinent; 10% had hearing difficulties; and 41% were either partially or totally confused or "senile." More than three-fourths of the abused elderly had at least one major physical or mental impairment. Twenty seven of the 39 abused elders lived with a spouse, a daughter, or another relative. Most of the abused elders were Caucasian (29); 10 were African American.

The study done by Block and Sinnott (1979) reflects data obtained from case reports from health and human service agencies and from elderly persons living in the area of metropolitan Washington, D.C. The participants were asked about their knowledge or experience with domestic neglect or abuse of the elderly. The researchers also mailed out questionnaires to three practitioner groups thought to have contact with abused elderly people: members of the American Psychological Association, emergency room physicians, and members of the Gerontological Society of America who live in Maryland. Of the 443 questionnaires mailed, 73 were returned; the response rate was 31% among the professionals, and 16% among the elderly. The number of mistreatment cases obtained was 26: 19 from responses from the professionals, 4 from agency case records, and 3 from the elder group. From this small sample, the researchers found that the abused elder was usually a woman (81%) over 75; the mean age in this study was 84. Impairment levels were significant: 94% of the abused elders were physically impaired (62% could not prepare their own food and 54% could not take their own medication), and 47% were moderately to severely mentally impaired. Regarding race, 88% of these abused elders were Caucasian; 12% were African American. Concerning religion, most of the abused group or 61% were Protestant; 8% were Catholic; 4% were Jewish; and in 27% of the cases, the religion was unknown. As to socioeconomic status, 58% of abused elders were middle class although 27% were retired on pensions. A significant percentage (46%) lived with their children, 32% lived with their spouses, and 39% lived with other relatives.

O'Malley et al. (1979) surveyed 1,044 medical, legal, police, and social work professionals and paraprofessionals in Massachusetts in March and April 1979; they received a total of 332 (32%) responses, which cited 183 cases of elder mistreatment occurring over an 18-month period. The findings generally agree with the other studies in this early phase of research as to the profile of the abused elder, although some of the numbers differ. In this study, the abused elder also tended to be very old (36% were over 80; 19% were aged 75–79), with a significant physical or mental disability that prevented the elder from meeting daily needs. Of the 183 reports of elder mistreatment, 80% involved female victims. The researchers noted that national census figures indicate that women account for only 58% of the population 60 years and older; therefore, women may represent a proportionately larger share of the abused elders than their numbers in the general population would suggest. The point is made by the researchers that women may seek assistance or report abusive behavior more often than men and that the client population of the professions surveyed may be composed largely of women or "very old" elderly or both. In three-fourths of the reported cases, the victim lived with the abuser, and in 84% the abuser was a relative of the victim.

The ethnic composition of the abused elders in this survey was: Caucasian (85%), African American (4%), Native American (7%), and Latino or Latina (1%), with the ethnicity of the remaining percentage not reported. As to religion, this study found that 37% were Catholic, 25% were Protestant, 3% were Jewish, and 35% were identified as "none" or "other" or "not applicable." Economic figures in the survey indicated that 27% of the households where elder mistreatment occurred had annual incomes of less than $5,200. But this last question appeared to be difficult for practitioners to answer—37% of those surveyed left this question blank. The average income of elderly women in the survey was markedly lower than that of men, leading the researchers to speculate that old women may be more financially dependent on their families—possibly one reason why there are more abused women than abused men.

Douglass et al. (1980) conducted 228 semistructured interviews with a variety of practitioners: lawyers, doctors, social service and mental health workers, police officers, coroners, and clergy in Michigan. They also included personal interviews with 36 people in 12 nursing homes and carried out a secondary analysis of both Detroit police data on crimes against the elderly and nursing home admission data. The authors of this study emphasize three issues: Does mistreatment of the elderly exist in the community? What are its characteristics? Why does it occur? Those interviewed reported a significant amount of mistreatment; most of the mistreatment was thought to be passive and neglectful, rather than active and abusive. The nurses and aides did not feel that elder mistreatment was a problem in the nursing homes, a finding that contradicted the results of other agencies' findings in the area. The study provided additional support for the findings of earlier studies regarding the profile of the abused elder; the typical victim is an older woman who is highly dependent and frail.

### Note: Limits of the Early Studies

These early studies focused on profiles of the abused and the abuser, incidence rates among clinical populations, and preliminary discussions of theories of causation, but they were fraught with problems. There were inconsistencies in defining the various forms of elder mistreatment, the age at which a person was considered elderly, and the method of obtaining information. For example, in one study, respondents were asked to recall a case of mistreatment that occurred within the last 12 months; in another, the time period was 18 months. Duplicate counts of cases may have occurred within some of the studies; and the results were descriptive in nature, with no comparison groups utilized. The samples did not represent the general population, which meant that the results could not be applied to the total population. The results of the studies reflected the opinions and recollections of professionals, with very little information obtained directly from victims. At the time, elder mistreatment was felt to be such a sensitive issue that it would preclude voluntary disclosure and sharing of information by victims.

Despite their shortcomings, however, these early studies identified elder mistreatment as a serious problem in need of further study, and confirmed that the problem was not based on media hype or sensationalism. In the 1980s, clearer definitions were implemented by reporting agencies and researchers (Godkin, Wolf, & Pillemer, 1989; Hudson, 1989; T. Johnson, 1986); practitioners developed detection and intervention techniques (D. Johnson, 1981; Fulmer, Street, & Carr, 1984); victims became priorities of agencies serving the elderly; training and education seminars were conducted, and mandatory and voluntary reporting laws were passed or updated in almost every state (Salend, Kane, Satz, & Pynoos, 1984).

## Second Wave of Research

Other studies have followed the first wave, some using more detailed investigative techniques and others addressing the shortcomings of the initial studies. Some of the second-wave studies included control groups, and others conducted interviews with the victims themselves.

Searching for predictors of elder mistreatment, Giordano and Giordano (1984), retrospectively studied cases reported to adult protective services between January 1976, and January 1982, in six counties in Florida. Each type of mistreatment was studied as a distinct category. Six hundred of 750 substantiated cases were compared with 150 randomly selected unsubstantiated cases. Giordano and Giordano were able to identify specific predictors for the different forms of mistreatment. The sample of 650 was divided into two groups for cross-checking. Victims of physical abuse lived with the abuser, either a spouse or a son, experienced more than one incident of abuse, and did not have severe illnesses. Those suffering from psychological abuse also lived with the abuser, either a spouse or a son, and experienced more than one incident of abuse. In addition, there was two-generation conflict in the home. The next category, multiple abuse, was predicted by a history of previous abuse and by the victim's living with the abuser, either a spouse or a daughter. For financial abuse, the victim was older, between 72 and 89 years old, widowed, and in relatively good health. He or she lived with the abuser, who was a nonrelative. Neglect was identified by physical illness and intellectual impairment of the victim, and by the victim's living with the abuser, a relative. In this study, elder mistreatment included spousal abuse and marital conflicts, which were recurring incidents. Psychological abuse was difficult to predict, whereas financial abuse was easiest to predict and had the greatest number of predictors. Some of the predictors are difficult to generalize, because in the cross-checking, the statistics were not reliable. For example, in psychological abuse, the figures for the two subgroups were not similar.

Sengstock and Hwalek's study (1983a; 1983b) through Wayne State University is somewhat similar, involving a comparison group to examine six types of mistreatment. Fifty cases of abused elders were compared with 47 nonabused elders from caseloads in nine social services agencies. Data analysis was conducted to reduce 203 original indicators of mistreatment to 93, then to 17, and finally to 9, which were 94% accurate in classifying the cases into the "mistreated" or the "nonmistreated" group. Three of the 9 indicators were questions asked of the elder: Has anyone taken money or property? Are your needs being met by others? Have you been threatened by someone? Two were characteristics of the elder: the elder is a source of stress, and the elder has symptoms with no illness-related cause. The last four were characteristics of the caregiver: the caregiver has an inappropriate awareness of the elder's condition; the caregiver is a persistent liar; the caregiver tried to get the elder to act against his or her own interest; and the caregiver is dependent on the elder for support.

During this second research phase, Phillips (1983, 1986) was the first to conduct hypothesis testing that was based on symbolic interaction theory. Symbolic interactionism describes a process between two individuals that takes place in three phases: the cognitive process, the expressive process, and the evaluative process (Phillips, 1986). In the cognitive process, each person assigns meanings to the encounter with the other person, and these meanings are based on prior encounters, belief systems, and current perceived roles. Sometimes the role that individuals assign to the other person is based on an idealized view of the other and on what they would expect of themselves if they were in the situation of the other. In the expressive phase, behaviors are based on improvised and imputed roles. Role synchrony and role asynchrony may occur, depending on the imputed roles chosen. The third phase, the evaluation process, consists of negotiations between the individuals, who sometimes alter their behaviors and their expectations for others in response to their own assessments of the situation. Applying this process to elder mistreatment, abuse may occur as a result of role asynchrony, when a discrepancy exists between the elder's and the caregiver's expectations for one another. This role asynchrony can lead to anger, hostility, depression, or dejection, which could then contribute to abuse. A blind interview technique was conducted with 30 abused and 44 nonabused elders from public health nurses' caseloads. Phillips hypothesized that the abused group would have greater elder–caregiver age differences, greater expected versus actual caregiver behavior differences, plus higher scores for stress, depression, anxiety, and anger. In addition, the abused group was predicted to have lower scores for their activities of daily living functioning, social networks, and perceived social roles. The results showed that there were no significant differences in role asynchrony between the caregivers and the elders in the abused and the nonabused group; the abused group had a higher depression score but none of the other hypotheses were supported. Elders who were impaired were no more abused than the elders who were unimpaired. Within the abused group, however, the elders had fewer friends to call by phone in times of trouble, perceived having less support from the individuals who were identified as being part of their social network but had more in-home help. Ultimately, these findings challenged the theory that social isolation is an important causal variable in elder mistreatment, and that dependency and high stress levels are associated with abuse. One limitation of this study is the subjectivity of the nurses who participated. It was difficult to classify 12 cases, and an independent judge had to assign them to one of the two groups.

## The Emergence of Abuser Dependency

Dominating this period were the reports that emerged from the Three Model Projects on Elder Abuse (Pillemer, 1985a; 1985b; 1986; Wolf, Godkin, & Pillemer, 1986; Wolf, Strugnell, & Godkin, 1982). Study sites in Worcester, Massachusetts; Syracuse, New York; and Rhode Island yielded 328 cases of mistreatment. Overall, 72% were victims of psychological abuse, 46% of physical abuse, 36% of material abuse, 36% of passive neglect, and 20% of active neglect. Most of the victims were female. 75% had some decline in their physical health and needed some help with their activities of daily living. Of note, the study found that while the victims had some limitations to their physical mobility—with about half using mobility devices—the majority, or 70%, were physically independent.

From this study on, physical abuse no longer predominates chiefly because active and passive neglect were removed from that category. In addition, with this study, the focus of interest shifted to the characteristics of abusers. Here, abusers were sons (28%), daughters (18%), husbands (18%), and wives (7%). Surprisingly, 68% of the abusers were dependent on the elder for financial support. Abusers who were husbands were declining in health, and within the couple dyad, they were having to shift from being dependent on their wives for household and other tasks to being caretakers as their wives became less functional.

At the Worcester site alone, the characteristics of 59 caregivers of 59 abused elders were compared with those of 21 caregivers of 49 nonabused elders who were served by the same agency. The caregivers of the abused were mostly men (71%) and had a poorer emotional status than the controls. One-third (31%) of abusive caregivers had had psychiatric hospitalizations, and more in the abusive caregiver group had a history of psychiatric problems (40.7% versus 5.3%), a history of alcohol abuse (33.9% versus none), and a recent decline in psychiatric status (45.8% versus 5%). This comparison study supported the data on abuser dependency from all three sites; here, 74% of the abusers were dependent on the elder, versus 36.8% in the control group.

Within the same population, Pillemer's matched-pair study (1985a) on physical abuse of 42 victims also confirms abuser, and not victim, dependency. On a six-point scale, the abused elders were *less* dependent than their controls, and the abusers were *more* dependent on the elders, especially for housing and money. No differences were found between the matched elders regarding life stress, and although more in the abused group felt socially isolated, it could be that the causal arrow is in the opposite direction; that is, the elders became isolated as a *result* of the abuse (Wolf & Pillemer, 1989).

In addition to focusing on abusers' characteristics, the Three Model Projects attempted to find support for the concept that the intergenerational transmission of violence was a factor in elder mistreatment cases (Wolf & Pillemer, 1989). Information on the families of 75 of the 328 victims showed that 32 had reported abuse or neglect as a child, and among 102 of the 328, 20 reported that they had come from unstable or nontraditional families in which violence occurred. In addition, among Pillemer's matched pairs, only one in each group reported physical punishment as a child or a teenager. Since much of the information is based on the professionals' interpretation, and abusers were not asked directly about their early histories, this information is inconclusive.

## The Prevalence of Elder Mistreatment

The only prevalence study thus far (Pillemer & Finkelhor, 1988) was conducted in the Boston metropolitan area soon after the Three Model Projects. "Abuse" consisted of one incident of severe violence since the victim had turned 65 years old, and 10 incidents of chronic verbal aggression within the previous year as defined by the Straus Conflict Tactics Scale (Straus, 1979b). "Neglect" was defined as 10 or more incidents within the previous year of failure to perform caregiving tasks on the Older Americans Resources and Services (OARS) inventory (Fillenbaum & Smyer, 1981). Telephone and in-home interviews (when necessary) of 2,020 elders or their proxies yielded 63 cases of mistreatment—a prevalence rate of 3.15% or 32 per 1,000 persons. The physical violence rate was 20 per 1,000 persons; the verbal aggression rate was 11 per 1,000 persons, and the neglect rate was 4 per 1,000 persons. When perpetrators' characteristics were examined, spousal abuse was most common, consisting mainly of wife-to-husband mistreatment (23/63, or 36.5%). Husband-to-wife mistreatment was the next most prevalent (14/63, or 22%), followed by son to parent (10/63, or 16%) and daughter to parent (5/63, or 8%). Perhaps these figures reflect the fact that men tend to live with others in late life and are more likely to be married or to remarry than their female counterparts.

The rate of physical violence may be relatively low when compared with rates of violence against children and spouses, as obtained by two national violence surveys, but is considerably higher than the prevalence rate of street violence, 1 per 100,000, indicating that regardless of age, in the United States people are much more likely to be harmed by a family member than by a stranger (Straus, Gelles, & Steinmetz, 1980; Gelles & Straus, 1988). The main problem with this survey is the limited definition of elder mistreatment: financial or material abuse, sexual abuse, abandonment, and some forms of psychological abuse were missing. Considering these omissions, it is likely that the prevalence rate is much higher than reported by Pillemer and Finkelhor.

In Canada, a similar prevalence study was conducted through a telephone survey of 2,008 elderly people living in private residences in British Columbia, the Prairies (central Canada), Ontario, Quebec, and the Atlantic provinces (Podnieks, 1992a). The elderly in these regions accounted for

99% of elderly Canadians living in private dwellings. Measuring physical abuse, neglect, psychological abuse as indicated by chronic verbal aggression, and financial exploitation, the study found 80 persons who experienced one form of mistreatment, and this translates into a prevalence rate of 40 per 1,000 elderly persons, or 4%. This is similar to the prevalence rate (3.25%) found in Pillemer and Finkelhor's Boston study. Whereas this Canadian study included material abuse, the Boston study did not. The elderly population of Canada is approximately 2,680,000, and so it is estimated that 84,000 to 132,000 elderly Canadians are abused and neglected nationwide. Material abuse was the most common form of mistreatment, amounting to 25 per 1,000 persons. This was followed by chronic verbal aggression, 14 per 1,000 persons; physical violence, 5 per 1,000 persons; and neglect, 4 per 1,000 persons. Physical abuse was lower than the prevalence rate of 20 per 1,000 found in the Boston study, probably reflecting the comparatively low overall lower violence rate in Canada.

With regard to the abusers, material abusers were distant relatives and friends or neighbors; those committing chronic verbal aggression and physical aggression were more likely to be spouses; and neglectful persons were spouses, daughters, daughters-in-law, or other caregivers.

## Recent Research: Facets of Mistreatment

Within this current phase, particular theoretical viewpoints have been examined, chiefly the popular causal explanation of "caregiver stress". Also emerging in this phase are studies conducted among different ethnic groups and on mistreatment in nursing homes.

### *Mistreatment by Caregivers*

In London, Homer and Gilleard (1990), interviewing 43 patients diagnosed with strokes, dementia, or other disorders, and 51 of their caregivers, found that 23, or 45% of their caregivers admitted to mistreatment as defined by Pillemer and Finkelhor (1988). Significant factors were alcohol consumption and depression on the part of the caregiver, and socially disruptive behavior and communication problems on the part of the elder. Service delivery, social isolation, and the levels of physical and mental disability of the elder were not associated with abuse. Instead, interactional stressors, such as the elder's socially disruptive behavior and poor communication, contributed to the mistreatment.

During this period also, Paveza and colleagues found a high rate of depression among caregivers in their study of 184 patients with Alzheimer's disease and other dementias and their caregivers (Paveza et al., 1992). The overall prevalence rate of severe violence as defined by the Straus Conflict Tactics Scale was 17.4% for either patient or caregiver, and 5.4% for caregivers alone. Computing odds ratios, the authors conclude that elders cared for by depressed caregivers and elders living with families without a spouse present are at three times greater risk of being abused. Paveza and colleagues surmise, by comparing their violence prevalence rate with the violence prevalence rate of elders interviewed by Pillemer and Finkelhor (1988), that persons with Alzheimer's disease and other dementias are at 2.25 times greater risk of being physically abused than those without such diagnoses (54/1000 versus 20/1000).

The third study on caregiver stress involved interviewing 236 caregivers of patients with Alzheimer's disease and other dementias from 13 medical centers and from referrals by neurologists and psychiatrists caring for this population (Pillemer & Suitor, 1992). Of the 236, 46 (19.5%) feared that they would become violent, and among these 46, 14 (5.9%) actually committed violent acts. The elders cared for by these 14 exhibited a higher rate of violent behaviors than those cared by the 32 who did not become violent. The violent caregivers were spouses who were older, with a mean age of 64.8 years. Two main points from this study are (1) that focus should be on interactional stressors as contributors to violence, not on frailty and concomitant caregiver demands; and (2) that the spousal violence reported by many of the studies in this latter phase could reflect weaker norms against spousal violence than child-to-parent violence. A discussion of how these third-phase studies fit in with causal concepts can be found in Chapter 4.

### Elder Mistreatment among Different Ethnic Groups

Among professionals, it is generally agreed that elder mistreatment, like other forms of domestic violence, is not a new phenomenon and is not confined to a few countries or to certain ethnic groups. Throughout history, parricide among different groups has been reported in South America, Africa, and Melanesia, and among Indo-Europeans and the Inuit (Eskimos; Reinharz, 1986). In one holocultural analysis, the majority of 60 societies practiced what was termed nonsupportive treatment of the elderly (Glascock & Feinman, 1981). In the United States, Anetzberger (1987) has mentioned "abusive enculturation," which would be defined by the general population as abusive behavior, among the Appalachian population.

In Brown's study of the Oljato Chapter of the Navajos in Utah, a large portion of the randomly selected elders were victims of various forms of mistreatment, some falling into a "vicious cycle of negative interdependency" (Brown, 1989). This study is a good example of focusing on the interplay of culture, social system, and personality. Brown applies commonly used research and diagnostic methods to a particular ethnic group, then studies the variations that may be attributed to their culture. Among these Oljatos, while neglect was as prevalent among the subjects as it has been reported throughout the United States, (American Public Welfare Association, 1986), Brown wonders if it is a more serious problem among the Navajo than in other groups. Both he and John (1988) report that generally speaking, Native American families are more interdependent, with the extended family including even far-flung cousins. They have a deep and abiding responsibility to and for each other. In contrast, mainstream Caucasian-American families tend to be more independent and see themselves as relying mainly on spouses and immediate family members. Among Native Americans, elders feel that it is their privilege and duty to help the less fortunate in their extended family, and that it is an unspoken expectation that their actions be reciprocated. Within this cultural context, Brown states, neglect is a serious problem, and elders may not realize that they are viewed by outsiders as victims of financial exploitation and neglect.

In a review of research conducted on violence against Native American women, Chester, Robin, Koss, Lopez, and Goldman (1994) note several problematic areas, which also apply to studies on elder mistreatment among different cultures. These areas include the lack of a working definition as to who is considered a Native American, the use of rating scales that do not capture the reality of Native American populations, and the use of interviewers who have little experience with the language or customs of the targeted population The authors also note that while alcohol use and abuse have been identified within the general population as a correlate of domestic violence, alcohol may play an even more integral role in female abuse among American Indians. Still, they caution:

A consistent theory of alcohol and battering is difficult due to heterogeneity of behaviors connoting both domestic violence and alcohol abuse among Indian people. Although there is scant reliable information concerning the relationship between alcohol abuse and wife battering among American

Indians, it has been suggested that extensive use of alcohol has accompanied a sharp increase in wife abuse among American Indian people (Wolf, 1982). There are, however, many factors in addition to alcohol that have accompanied the alleged increase in domestic violence in American Indian communities. These include removal of Indian people from their ancestral lands, prohibition against religious and spiritual practices, forced removal of Indian children into foster homes and boarding schools at a rate of 5–20 times the national average (May, 1987), rapid transition from hunting, gathering, and subsistence farming to a cash-based economy, and a 90% reduction of the American Indian population from the time of European contact to the establishment of reservations (Fleming, 1992). These cataclysmic changes in social, spiritual, and economic structure have drastically undermined traditional lifeways. In this context, both alcohol abuse and assault of women may reflect additional aspects of disintegration and disconnectedness within American Indian communities. (p. 254)

Carson (1995) notes that in order to understand the issues facing Native American elders, the basic tenets to which most tribal groups subscribe must be acknowledged. These are a strong spiritual orientation to life and living in harmony with nature, family and tribal interdependence and support, community responsibility and commitment to the welfare of others, respect for the elderly, group participation and cooperation over individual achievement, emphasis on the past and present more than the future, nonindividualistic competition, the unique value of children, humility, and avoidance of hurting the feelings of others. He then lists the risk factors in elder mistreatment among Native Americans, such as poverty and its concomitants, disintegration of family ties and lifestyles on and off the reservations, and the stress of trying to adapt to the dominant culture. Dependency and interdependency, common among the generations, combined with limited resources create a greater potential for conflict and elder mistreatment. Also, in some tribal groups, many elders are nonconfrontive and noninterventive in others' lives; knowing this, others may mistreat elders, feeling assured that negative consequences are unlikely.

The chances of being mistreated may be minimized by tapping those cultural strengths that have helped the families cope under difficult conditions. Where there is an emphasis on family and tribal interdependence and support, group participation and cooperation, and extended family, Carson notes, ". . . the collective liability for a family member's actions helps protect family members and regulate individual behavior by providing expected standards of behavior (i.e., by establishing a collective conscience and consciousness) and emphasizing individual responsibility for one's actions and how these reflect on the family and tribe" (1995, p. 31).

Krassen Maxwell and Maxwell (1992) examined elder mistreatment from a social-structural perspective among two geographically different reservations of Plains Indians—the Lone Mountain and the Abundant Lands reservations. Elder mistreatment in the form of physical abuse and neglect was more common at Lone Mountain, and on a community level was associated with high unemployment, little potential income from the land, and significant substance abuse. In contrast, in the Abundant Lands Reservation, where there is less elder mistreatment, residents had a housing improvement program and varied sources of income from agriculture, town-based employment, tourism, crafts, and firefighting. The differences in the treatment of the elderly in the two reservations were attributed to variations in economic opportunities for the younger residents.

Cazenave (1983), Crystal (1986), and Griffin and Williams (1992) note that the research on elder mistreatment among African Americans is sparse; it is largely a result of analysis of larger samples, which often lack sufficient numbers of African American elderly and do not explore the qualitative details of life of the African American elderly. Cazenave (1983) and Griffin and Williams (1992) have suggested various risk factors for elder mistreatment among African American families, including low income, poor health, and inverse generational family support. The importance of these factors is supported most recently by Griffin's exploratory study (1994), which examined ideas about mistreatment among African Americans in rural North Carolina. Griffin found through interviews of 10 victims and 6 of their abusers that financial exploitation was the most prevalent type of mistreatment. Physically abusing elders was unacceptable among rural African Americans; poverty was pervasive in the mistreatment situations; and African American perpetrators of elder mistreatment were involved in dependent, mutually beneficial relationships with elders. Korbin, Anetzberger, Thomassen, and Austin (1991), in a small case-study sample found that African American elders were more likely to seek legal recourse against their abusive adult offspring than were Caucasians. Last, comparing victims reported under Wisconsin state law, Longres, Raymond, and Kimmel (1991) found that African American victims were more likely than non-African American victims to be younger, experiencing a life-threatening form of mistreatment, and willing to use services offered; the alleged perpetrators were likely to be female and the daughters of the victims.

Moon and Williams's (1993) study explored African American, Caucasian American, and Korean American elderly women's perceptions of elder mistreatment using 13 scenarios as well as their help-seeking behaviors. All of the scenarios involved a female elder as a possible victim and a family member as a possible perpetrator. The respondents' perceptions varied significantly, depending on the scenario. For example, in one scenario a daughter or daughter-in-law, frustrated by an elder's embarrassing behavior when guests were invited to the home, gives the elder tranquilizers, falsely telling the elder that they were prescribed by a physician. Of the African American respondents, 63% perceived this scenario as elder mistreatment, compared with only 36% of Caucasians and 10% of Korean Americans. Overall, a smaller percentage of the Korean Americans (50%) than the African Americans (73%) or Caucasian Americans (67%) perceived the scenarios as mistreatment, leading the authors to conclude that they were less sensitive to or more tolerant of potentially abusive situations than the other two groups. The numbers who would have sought help had they been the victim in the scenario also varied depending on the scenario: on the average, approximately two thirds of the respondents who perceived the scenarios as abuse would seek help; and one third of those who did not perceive them as abusive would also seek help. Many in the Korean American group indicated they would be reluctant to reveal the abuse or neglect to others, out of shame or fear of creating conflict among their children and other relatives as a result of reporting the mistreatment. This corresponds with the cultural emphasis on community and family harmony, more than on individual needs or well-being, within some Asian cultures. For the African Americans, perhaps their higher response to certain situations may reflect a cultural memory of slavery and oppression. Generally speaking, for all participants, the intention of the person involved in the potentially abusive behavior was considered in deciding if a scenario was abusive; if the caregiver was perceived as having good intentions and if there was no other practical alternative to the behavior examined (such as restraining the elder in bed), the scenario was not judged to be abusive.

In another study, this time focusing on *ijime,* or bullying, of mothers-in-law by daughters-in-law in Japan, Kaneko and Yamada (1990) report that the most common manifestation of mistreatment was twofold: (1) no conversation, followed by making rude statements; (2) ignoring the other person. This use of silence and avoidance may be as emotionally devastating as physical abuse (Tomita, 1994). Over time, the consequences of contained anger and nonverbal cruelty are unknown; ill feelings may fester or mount over time, or silence and avoidance may cause the elder to want to die. Such behaviors are clearly not benign, and they have been categorized variously by other researchers: as aggressive (Foner, 1984), as nonviolent means of conflict management (Livens, 1989), and as forms of death-hastening or nonsupportive treatment of the elder (Glascock & Feinman, 1981).

In a study derived from a population-based sample of 2,812 men and women living in the community in New Haven, Connecticut, risk factors associated with referring 68 of these elders for an investigation for elder mistreatment were: requiring assistance with feeding, being a minority elder, being over age 75, and having a poor social network (Lachs, Berkman, Fulmer, & Horwitz, 1994). Stratifying by race, requiring assistance with feeding was associated with being referred for an investigation among minority elders but not among nonminority elders; but having a poor social network was more strongly associated with a referral for investigation among nonminority elders than minority elders. Unfortunately, the elders referred for any reason were pooled to improve the data's statistical power and maximize the number of outcomes available for study, so it is unclear how many elders were referred for self-neglect as opposed to suspicion of injury inflicted by others, and how many investigations resulted in the substantiation of the initial reasons for the referral. However, the study raises several important issues with regard to minority overrepresentation in the referrals, which should be considered when interpreting data such as these. Minority elders may be preferentially referred and investigated; they may not have adequate access to in-home and social services that would prevent the need for an investigation; and families of minority elders may care for elders so much longer before asking for help that the level of the elder's impairment is higher at the time of the referral.

## Mistreatment in Facilities

In addition to the emergence of studies on specific ethnic groups, elder mistreatment in facilities such as nursing homes and "board and care" has become a separate area of study. Patient aggression, along with staff "burnout" and conflict over daily living tasks appear as risk factors in one study of nursing home abuse (Pillemer & Moore, 1990). Nurses and nursing aides ($N = 577$) from 32 nursing homes reported that 81% had observed one or more incidents of psychological abuse; 41% had committed at least one type of psychological abuse; 36% had observed at least one incident of physical abuse; and 10% had committed an act of physical abuse. Staff-patient conflicts were over tasks such as eating, grooming, and using the toilet. The age of the staff and negative attitudes toward the elderly provided the greatest explanation for psychological abuse. Four-hour training sessions on responding appropriately to problem behaviors were provided in exchange for the staff's participation in the study, with positive feedback.

In a second study, Payne and Cikovic (1996) examined the characteristics, consequences, and potential causes of abuse of residents in nursing homes. A total of 488 incidents reported between 1987 and 1992 were derived from *Medicaid Fraud Reports,* a publication of the National Association of Attorneys General. These incidents, probably representative of the most severe cases in nursing homes, had been reported to states' Medicaid Fraud Control Units, the agency responsible for detecting, investigating, and prosecuting Medicaid fraud and patient abuse in facilities. Four factors were considered: (1) types of abuse, (2) occupation, (3) age and gender of the accused offender, and (4) gender and age of the victim.

Examining the data and conducting thematic and semantic content analysis of the reports, the study found that most of the reported acts were physical abuse (411/488 or 84.2%). Physical abuse included burning a resident on the chest with cigarette, pulling an elderly man out of bed by grabbing his nipples, and hitting a resident on the head with a hairbrush. The rest of the acts were sexual abuse (43/488 or 8.8%), duty-related abuse or acts in which the employee did not perform specific routines correctly (15/488 or 3.1%), monetary abuse (7/488 or 1.4%), and those that fell into an "other" category (12/488 or 2.4%)

Nurses' aides (302/488 or 61%) made up the largest group of abusers, which represents the fact that they make up the largest occupational group working in nursing homes and have more contact with the residents than other employees do. Male employees were responsible for the majority of the incidents (307/488 or 63%), while females were responsible for about one third (181/488 or 37%). In 307 of the cases, the victim's gender was known: over half of the victims were men (174/307 or 57%) and 43% were females (133/307). Forty percent of the acts were male-to-male, 16% were female-to-male, and 22% were female-to-female (the rest were not identified in this regard).

Of the 488 reported incidents, 335 resulted in criminal convictions, and 295 of the offenders received sentences, most commonly probation (67%). Twenty-three percent (68/295) were institutionalized in either jail or prison. Of the sexual abuse cases, over half (24/43 or 56%) resulted in a conviction. Of the 24 convicted, 6 received a prison sentence (6/24 or 25%). For all cases, a conviction was more likely if a witness had been present at the time of the offense.

The offenders attributed the mistreatment to efforts to control patients whom they judged to be uncooperative or uncontrollable. Examples of such acts included a nurse's aide who hit a resident on his back for turning on a call light, and a nurse's aide who hit a patient who was already restrained in a chair (this latter incident had been witnessed). The offenders justified the acts as responses to stressful situations in which they perceived they had been provoked. Suggestions to prevent such incidents include more stringent hiring criteria, training, and certification, as well as better enforcement of the mandatory reporting laws through staff education.

### Mistreatment by Nonrelatives

Financial exploitation by acquaintances and even social workers has not been a strong focus of research in any of the phases, but it should not be ignored. The following case of exploitation shows that being in good health does not necessarily exempt the elderly from being abused:

> At one time, he had been a scriptwriter for a famous comedian. Now he had grown old and lonely. He lived in a large city and dreamed of becoming active in show business again. He also wanted to pass his knowledge on to a younger person, to "help someone get started." One day when he was standing in line at a bank, he met a young man who said he was trying to break into show business. This is what the former scriptwriter had been waiting for, and he invited the young man to his room, where they "hit it off" and had several drinks. Soon after, the old man decided that he could best help the young man by giving him money; he offered to share his $20,000 bank account with him; and as proof of his offer, he signed a power of attorney with the bank, which gave the young man equal access to his bank account. The money soon disappeared, but amazingly enough, the young man did not; he continued to visit the old man. The elder said he "didn't blame" the younger man. "He needed the money," he said.

It may be tempting for workers whose job it is to protect the elderly to take advantage of financial opportunities:

> An APS worker went out to see an elderly woman who lived in a duplex. The old woman stated to the worker that she wanted a tenant for one unit of her duplex that was empty. The worker then moved in and negotiated a reduced

rent. Later, the elderly woman expressed concern about her own well-being and who was going to take care of her since she had no relatives or friends to care for her and she was getting increasingly frail. The APS worker offered to take care of the old woman and then somehow tried to buy her house at a greatly reduced market rate. This attempt was discovered by an employee at the title company who noticed how little the worker was paying for the house. The title officer called the worker's agency, which initiated an investigation. The APS worker was told he could buy the house but that he would have to pay the market value. Since he could not afford to do so, he did not buy the house. The worker was transferred to another area of the department where he would not have access to clients' finances.

## In Conclusion: Phases of Research

Initially, studies of elder mistreatment were based on questionnaires and surveys and were focused on the victim, with the elder described by respondents as impaired and as a source of stress. Abusers were thought to be daughters, since they were most likely to be the elder's caregiver. As more information became available from clinical samples and comparison studies, the "typical profile" was eliminated; the mistreated elder was found to be no more dependent than nonabused elders and could no longer be compared to the helpless child in studies of maltreatment of children. Distinct categories of mistreatment were created, and risk factors for each were studied. Abusers' characteristics—dependency, substance abuse, and psychiatric problems—were more explanatory of maltreatment than victims' characteristics.

The following case example illustrates the impossibility of identifying victims and abusers as belonging to a particular group. Some elders are mistreated by people who befriend them over time:

> The husband and wife lived in a downtown hotel, where they had moved after selling the house that had become too large for them to maintain; they were financially comfortable; their estate was over $200,000. After the husband died, the woman found herself entirely alone; her friends were far away or had died. Her only contact was her hairdresser across the street. She confided in him, and he in turn began spending more time with her, to the point of helping her bathe and dress when she became too confused to do those things herself. She would go to his shop every day to chat, and he began charging her estate for a manicure or a hair set, sometimes up to four manicures per

week and several hair sets. He also started taking her out to dinner at expensive restaurants together with a large group of his friends. She always paid. He said, "Well, she is so confused. I wouldn't enjoy myself at all if I didn't have some of my own company."

In the second and third phases, spouses emerged as a significant proportion of the abuser population, and in the prevalence study (Pillemer & Finkelhor, 1988), husbands appeared as more frequent victims than wives. However, Miller and Dodder (1988), focusing on the abused–abuser dyad, found that although males are receiving more attention recently as victims, the recent data substantiate that victims are most likely to be women. Among abusers, males are more likely to be perpetrators of physical abuse; females are most likely to be perpetrators of neglect. In the same vein, Filinson has warned that if neglect, threats, and financial exploitation are lumped together with physical abuse, females are (falsely) regarded as just as likely to be perpetrators as males. Such a grouping, "reject[s] the systematic bases for subordination in the family as well as the gender-based differences in power and the use of violence" (Filinson, 1988).

In the latter studies, some spouses were depressed, and some caregivers responded with violence when the demented elder was disruptive. As a separate component of victims' and abusers' characteristics, interactional stressors and dyadic dynamics (instead of caregivers' demands) are now emerging as important areas of focus. In addition, on the basis of the Boston prevalence survey, elders living with both a spouse and a child were at greater risk of abuse than elders living alone or with either a spouse or a child.

Many problems remain, in spite of the progressive improvements over the past 15 years in the conceptualization and design of studies. These problems include the lack of a uniform set of definitions and the lack of consistent data-gathering methods (as mentioned earlier), and the unavailability of adequate detection tools to identify and compare regional and cultural differences. Although a few studies have been conducted on certain ethnic groups, very little is known about how elder mistreatment is manifested in the different cultures and how victims cope and respond in these situations. Also, it is difficult to generalize information from studies which use the Straus Conflict Tactics Scale (Straus, 1979b); although this scale is a valid and reliable instrument, it measures only particular aspects of elder mistreatment and also falls short of capturing circumstances, motivations, or consequences.

# SUMMARY

This chapter has described the main studies conducted in the past 15 years that have eliminated the "typical" victim and abuser profiles. Since the research is not complete as to the exact nature of elder mistreatment, practitioners should maintain a high index of suspicion for elder mistreatment when working in any situation where older people are involved; it is likely that any one of these elders could be suffering from some type of mistreatment.

# CHAPTER 3

# Types of Elder Mistreatment

## INTRODUCTION

One of the first hurdles practitioners face when dealing with elder mistreatment is deciding exactly what constitutes mistreatment. Under the rubric of mistreatment, the terms *abuse* and *neglect* have been defined differently in the preliminary studies; and the two terms have sometimes been run together, leading to a great deal of imprecision and confusion.

Generally speaking, neglect has been viewed as being less serious than abuse with regard to the *intent* of the caregiver. Neglect is seen as an act of omission, of not doing something, of withholding goods or services, perhaps because of ignorance or stress on the part of the caregiver. This type of neglect has been referred to as *passive neglect*. Some observers have therefore concluded that it may not be deliberate and that supportive services and education for the caregiver would alleviate the problems. Other clinicians, however, have noted that neglect can be deliberate and malicious, resulting in no less damage to the elder than outright abuse; in such a case the perpetrator knows full well that he or she is being neglectful. This type of neglect is often referred to as *active neglect*.

Abuse is generally viewed as more serious. It is seen as a deliberate act of the caregiver, an intentional act, an act of commission. The caregiver means to inflict injury (Douglass & Hickey, 1983).

The intent of the caregiver is a critical subject as regards dealing with interventions and trying to decide how to approach a case. For instance, a practitioner may choose to arrange for respite care if he or she has concluded that the abuser unintentionally struck an impaired elderly person once out of extreme fatigue and is remorseful and frightened. A different intervention will be indicated when an abuser admits willfully hitting a dependent elder, has inflicted substantial damage, blames the victim for the abuse, and says that nothing can stop him or her from hitting the elder again. In the end, however, when defining the *effects* of the abuse or neglect, it does not matter if the act was deliberate—the elder is injured in some way. It may never be clear to anyone, not even the abuser, whether the elder was injured intentionally.

O'Malley et al. (1983) have suggested another approach to definitions which is nonjudgmental and is aimed at eliminating any sense that the caregiver is being blamed for the symptoms of abuse or neglect. They suggest that the terms *neglect* and *abuse* have accusatory implications and lead to lack of cooperation on the part of caregivers, who may decline to answer questions or may refuse further interviews if they feel blamed and threatened. O'Malley and colleagues propose that definitions be based on the *needs* of the elder for physical and financial support and suggest that the abuse or neglect stems from an abnormal expression of the caregiving role. They define neglect as the failure of a caregiver to resolve a significant need of the elder despite an awareness of available resources. Abuse is seen as an active intervention by a caregiver "such that unmet needs are created or sustained with resulting physical, psychological, or financial injury." In this model, the practitioner focuses on the *unmet needs* of the elder and aims to resolve them regardless of what might be causing them. The label *abuse* is used only where a noncaregiving family member exhibiting pathological behavior is involved. O'Malley et al. argue that defining abuse and neglect in terms of unmet needs enables practitioners, specifically those who work in the medical arena, to remain nonjudgmental and to focus on treating the abused person without labeling the caregiver.

A nonjudgmental attitude is imperative when investigating cases of suspected elder mistreatment. A great deal of time and effort must be expended before it can be determined that mistreatment of an elder has occurred. If prejudgments are made and are acted upon by the practitioner, the treatment plan may be aborted or may be sabotaged by the client, the caregiver, or both. The client and the caregiver could decide to collude to keep the worker out of their sphere. Of course, in emergency situations such as those described in Chapter 7, the practitioner must quickly judge and act.

What are we to do, then, about definitions? Fortunately, there is some agreement among the studies and articles in journals as to the types of mistreatment: physical abuse and neglect, psychological abuse and neglect, financial abuse, and violation of rights. The types of abuse and neglect may be defined a bit differently or measured in different ways, but there is some common ground. As research proceeds, investigators will have to decide if they are measuring the *intent* of the caregiver or the *effects* of the abuse or neglect. Decisions will have to be made as to whether the maltreatment will be measured by acts of omission or commission. For the purposes of this text, the terms *abuse* and *neglect* will be used as they specifically relate to the *effects* on the elder—how elders look and act as a result of actions by others (or, in the case of self-neglect, by themselves). Often an elder is the victim of several forms of mistreatment at the same time; these forms are ongoing, that is, they are not limited to a single incident (Block & Sinnott, 1979; Lau and Kosberg, 1979; O'Malley et al., 1979). Most likely, some professions see one type of abuse more often than another. Medically trained practitioners, police, caseworkers, and mental health workers are more likely to see physical abuse and neglect whereas lawyers and judges are more familiar with financial abuse and neglect (Douglass et al., 1980).

## ⚡ PHYSICAL ABUSE

The outcome of physical abuse is bodily harm, which can range from bruises and scratches to death. Figure 3-1 shows the range of conditions, many of which can be observed by practitioners in any setting. These conditions are not in themselves diagnostic of inflicted abuse; rather, they are clues and thus helpful in assessing the client's total situation. (Refer to Chapter 6 for more information on physical assessment of the elder.)

Bruises over soft tissue areas are frequently signs that an elder has been grabbed or hit. Many older adults have fragile skin which bruises easily and may even tear with the slightest trauma. If there are healing bruises and new bruises at the same time, the practitioner should be alert to the possibility that abuse is occurring and is repetitious (Tomita, 1982). To explain bruises, abusers will frequently say that the elder fell, but the alert practitioner who is familiar with patterns of bruising will be able to assess whether or not the sustained bruises could be due to an accidental fall. Scratches, cuts, and burns can also be recurrent and can appear in various stages of healing. Rope burns and bruises or pressure sores around the ankles and wrists and under the armpit area may indicate that the elder is being confined to a bed or a chair for long periods of time. (Chapter 6 gives more information on indicators of physical abuse).

Death
Murder

Paralysis
Injuries from
   attempted
   murder

Detached retina
Hematoma
Pressure sores
Fractures
Choke marks
Dislocation

Veneral disease
Swollen genitals

Sprains
Punctures
Pain on
   touching

Welts
Scalp injury
Gag marks

Cigarette burns
Rope burns

Scratches
Cuts
Bruises

*Source:* Tomita and Quinn, 1996.

Figure 3-1    Indicators of physical abuse.

Depriving an elder of aids such as eyeglasses, a hearing aide, or a walker may also be abusive. In one case, an attorney reported that his client was being abusive in this way:

The Court Investigation Unit received a call from a concerned attorney who stated that a nursing home was telephoning him continually about a patient who was being deprived of a wheelchair by her conservator, who was the attorney's client. The patient was an elderly woman who suffered from diabetes; both her legs had been amputated as a result of poor circulation. Her conservator was an old friend. An investigator contacted the conservator, who admitted that she was not supplying a wheelchair. She said, "If I supply a wheelchair, she'll only go out and sit in the hall like all those other old goofy people. That's no life." The conservator also refused to buy powders or lotions for the woman, saying that they weren't necessary; and she declined to buy the woman a television set, saying, "There's never anything good on anyway." The conservator was also delinquent in paying bills from the pharmacy and the nursing home. The investigator interceded; all items were purchased and the bills were brought up to date. It was later learned that the conservator was the sole beneficiary of her longtime friend's will, and the question arose whether the conservator had been saving her friend's money for herself.

Permanent damage can result from physical abuse. In the following case, the elder suffered the loss of an eye:

An 89-year-old woman was both physically and financially abused by her grandnephew, who had lived in her home for approximately 14 years. The house was literally falling down around the occupants, but the grandnephew said that it wasn't bothering him, that he had no plans to do anything about it, and that it was "just a matter of lifestyle." The grandnephew had no income and had never held a job. He paid the bills out of his aunt's savings, but the real estate taxes were delinquent and there was no insurance. He planned, when the aunt's savings got low, to get a power of attorney from her and to begin cashing in her bonds. He fancied himself a scientist or an artist who could "make a million if I wanted to."

The grandnephew admitted hitting his aunt to "get her to shut up." When her eye injury was mentioned by the practitioner, the grandnephew expressed amazement that her eye had been surgically removed but said it was simply a result of an injury in the home. According to him, she had fallen off a stool and hit the side of her head, injuring her eye. She had not received medical treatment for over a week. The elderly woman either did not recall how the injury happened or was covering up for her grandnephew; she said that "something flew in the window and got in my eye." All the professionals involved in the case felt, but could not prove, that the grandnephew was responsible for the eye injury. His explanation for the injury was suspicious and implausible. He did not visit his aunt when she was hospitalized and did not want her to return to the home following the hospitalization. He relented only when reminded by the staff that it was legally her house. A week after the woman was discharged from the hospital, when no one answered the phone or the doorbell, concerned practitioners called the fire department and forced entry into the house. They found the woman lying in a bed of human excrement. Her grandnephew had not cared for her in any way, although she was frail and disabled. He had not permitted in-home attendants into the house. She was rehospitalized and then placed in a board and care home. A conservator was appointed to prevent further financial abuse and to handle her financial affairs, including her house. The conservator also arranged for the grandnephew to receive public benefits and for alternative housing.

The elderly woman continues to think of her grandnephew as a wonderful scientist and wants to return to her home. It is impossible to return her to her home because she does not have enough money to make the house fit for human habitation. The grandnephew occasionally visits his aunt and has been found sleeping in vacant rooms or closets of the facility.

## Sexual Abuse

Sexual abuse—as distinguished from physical abuse—constitutes less than 1% of reported cases of elder mistreatment (Tatara, 1993). Still, sexual abuse should be considered when an elder reports being sexually victimized or when there are symptoms that are commonly associated with sexual victimization (Ramsey-Klawsnick, 1993). For instance, one elderly woman who seemed demented was admitted to an emergency room because she had suffered a mild stroke. She asked one of the nurses if she could be pregnant. The nurse took her seriously and decided that the woman might be disclosing something in code. A pelvic examination was performed, with further testing. It was discovered that the woman was suffering from a venereal disease. It was later discovered that her son suffered from the same unique strain of venereal disease.

Signs and symptoms of possible elder sexual abuse include genital or urinary irritation, injury, or scarring, and intense fear in reaction to a particular individual or to procedures which might involve the pelvic area such as bathing or cleansing after incontinence. Other signs and symptoms include: actual observation of sexual activity, usually in an acute hospital or care facility; overt and covert disclosures of activity with possible sexual comments and threats; actual trauma in the pelvic region; or a history of the perpetrator denying access to the elder or having a history of sexual offending (Holt, 1993).

In some cases, financial abuse accompanies sexual abuse:

A 78-year old widow, severely mentally impaired from dementia, had always lived with her adult son. He was described as a "Charles Manson type" in appearance. Her two daughters, both capable women, had for years tried to encourage their mother to live with them, because they frequently noticed bruises on her arms and legs and because she and her son lived in squalor. The mother refused to move, saying, "I want to be with Jimmy." The son had never held a formal job or filed an income tax return. He dissipated a trust that had been left to his mother, lived on her Social Security, and induced her to put his name in joint tenancy on her home.

One daughter finally took action and filed a petition to become the conservator after the mother was hospitalized with serious injuries. The mother had been brought to the emergency room by the son, who said she had fallen. Her injuries were inconsistent with the type of fall he described. She had a head injury so severe that it caused massive blood clots on the left side of her brain. Her head and body were covered with contusions, and there were wounds on her neck resembling human tooth marks. Severe bruises were noted on the lower part of her abdomen. Surgery was performed to remove the blood clots. The son's behavior toward his mother after the surgery was such that he was never permitted to be alone with her. He had been discovered trying to get into bed with his mother on one occasion, and on another occasion he was observed with his hands under the sheets manipulating his mother's genitals. The mother, whose mental status was confused under the best of circumstances, frequently referred to her son as her husband.

The mother was well enough to attend the hearing for the conservatorship, at which time she reviled the daughter for seeking the conservatorship and said, "I gave her life. Isn't that enough? What more does she want?" She spoke of her son in glowing terms. At the conclusion of the hearing, the son came up to the mother, and it was apparent to observers that he physically yearned to be with her. There was a feeling of "unnaturalness" in the air. Initially, the mother did not recognize her son because he had changed his appearance before coming to court. His shoulder-length hair, which apparently hadn't been cut for years, was now short, and he had put on a suit. The daughter was appointed to serve as conservator of the person and estate of her mother.

The profile of the typical sexual abuse victim is far from certain. For instance, Ramsey-Klawsnik (1991) found that the most typical victim was a woman in her seventies, suffering major impediment in her self-care, and that the majority of victims were female with male abusers. In a study done in Great Britain, there were a significant number of male victims whose abusers were men. Alcohol dependence, mental illness, and drug dependence were relevant factors (Holt, 1993). Elder sexual abuse is perhaps the most hidden of all types of elder abuse and neglect. It is also likely to be the most distasteful and difficult type of abuse for practitioners to acknowledge and to treat.

## Death

Death can occur from physical abuse. In one instance, a petition was filed in a superior court by the daughter of an elderly woman who had been struck on the head by her 37-year-old son. Before the petition could be investigated, the woman died. The son was later held on murder charges. In another case that made newspaper headlines, a New York socialite was found guilty of first degree murder for having persuaded her teenage son to murder her millionaire father. She was quoted as being obsessed with the fear that her father would cut her out of his will. In still another case, a 20-year-old woman was arrested by homicide officers for arson and murder in connection with a fire that had killed an 85-year-old invalid. The young woman had visited the elder—a bedridden patient—and they had argued over money. As she left the apartment, she contemptuously flicked a lighted cigarette into an open closet. The smoldering butt apparently burst into flames, and the elderly man died from smoke inhalation.

## PHYSICAL NEGLECT

Neglect has been defined as a state in which the basic needs of an elder exceed what is being provided. It results from difficulty in obtaining, maintaining, and managing the necessities of life independently (Rathbone-McCuan & Bricker-Jenkins, 1988). Those necessities include personal care, nutrition, medical attention or medication, and a safe, well-maintained environment (Dubin, Garcia, LeLong, & Mowsesian, 1986). Neglect may be active or passive: that is, it may be intentional or unintentional (Fulmer & O'Malley 1987). In active neglect, the withholding of basic necessities of life and physical care is willful; in passive neglect, the withholding is usually due to a lack of experience or information. Figure 3-2 shows that neglect can lead to death just as abuse can (Quinn & Tomita, 1996).

Death

Failure-to-thrive
syndrome
Malnutrition and
dehydration

Untreated medical
conditions
No food or spoiled
food
Vermin in home
Animal or human
droppings in home

Numerous neglected
pets
Pressure sores
Abnormal blood chemistry

Hypothermia or
hyperthermia
Utilities turned off
Client unclean; environment
and clothing
unclean

Unexplained rashes
Body odor
Matted hair

Clothing inappropriate for
weather
Untreated sores
Serious maintenance
problems in home

Always same clothing
Ingrown nails
Decayed or missing
teeth

*Source:* Quinn and Tomita, 1996.

Figure 3-2    Indicators of physical neglect.

## Neglect by a Caregiver

In a survey of 29 states in 1990 and 30 states in 1991, neglect by others accounted for nearly half of the substantiated reports made to regulatory agencies (Tatara, 1993). It may be difficult to sort out who is to blame for the neglected elder's state—the caregiver or the elder. In some instances, though, it may be clear that it is the caregiver who is responsible for neglecting a dependent elder:

> Two elderly sisters slowly starved to death while living in a board and care home that was under the supervision of the Department of Social Services, Adult Protective Services division. The operator had given good care for a number of years, but after her divorce from the women's nephew, she locked both sisters in a room and stopped giving adequate care. At one point, an ambulance was called to the home and both elders were taken to a university medical center. Although the ambulance personnel made efforts to let all concerned know that the elderly women lived in squalor and were found in their own excrement, no one, including the doctors who examined the two women, made a diagnosis of elder neglect. The women, who were severely demented, died from malnutrition and dehydration. Each weighed less than 80 pounds at the time of death.

In cases where it seems clear that the caregiver is responsible for the neglect, the caregiver may offer one of the following explanations: (1) It was an accident; it was not intentional. (2) This is the type of care that the elder wanted. (3) The caregiver did not understand what would happen to the elder as a consequence of that particular situation. (4) The caregiver had no legal duty to the elder to perform caregiving. (5) Someone else was responsible or said he or she would take care of the victim (Heisler, 1994). Recurrent cases of neglect by a caregiver may not be intentional but may rather be attributable to stress, ignorance, apathy, or the caregiver's own frailty and advanced age. Victims of such neglect typically require a high level of care, and they tend to be mentally and physically disabled. The caregiver or the elder, or both, may be unwilling to accept or pay for services or resources, or community resources may not be available. There may be a link between repeat cases of caregiver neglect and financial exploitation, especially when the caregiver is dependent on the person for whom he or she is providing care. In most states, gross cases of caregiver neglect are referred to the district attorney or attorney general for prosecution (Simon, 1992).

## Self-Neglect

Historically, self-neglectful elders have been the subject of opera, literature, and folklore. Self-neglecting elders have been depicted variously as hermits, witches, tramps, and recluses, who are mentally ill, able to call upon fearful supernatural powers, or interested in hoarding "treasures." This stereotyping continues as self-neglectful elders live on the margins of our communities, psychologically and physically (Fabian & Rathbone-McCuan, 1992).

Self-neglect has sometimes been called the "Diogenes syndrome," referring to the fourth-century Greek philosopher, who reportedly admired lack of shame, outspokenness, and contempt for social organization (Clark, Mankikar, & Gray, 1975). The term has been used to describe elders who are thought to be grossly neglectful of themselves and their environment, who seem to be unashamed of their situation, and who are contemptuous of, or at least uninterested in, the recommendations of neighbors, family, health care providers, or the community.

The National Association of Adult Protective Service Administrators adopted from Duke (1991) the definition of self-neglect as, "the result of an adult's inability, due to physical and/or mental impairments or diminished capacity, to perform essential self-care tasks including: providing essential food, clothing, shelter, and medical care; obtaining goods and services necessary to maintain physical health, mental health, emotional well-being and general safety; and/or managing financial affairs."

Self-neglect is the most controversial form of elder mistreatment because there is some question whether it should be included at all when elder abuse and neglect are being considered. In child neglect, parents benignly or malevolently withhold care and services that the child needs for survival. However, it is widely acknowledged that parents are legally responsible for their children. The reverse is not true. In general, adult children are not legally required to provide for their elderly relatives unless there is a specific legal relationship such as trustee, guardian, or other fiduciary arrangement or unless the children are providing caregiver services for the parent or other family member (California Civil Code Sections 206, 242; Penal Code Section 270c, 1995). Thus, older adults are considered to be responsible for themselves unless and until they are declared incapable or incompetent by a court of law. Therefore, if elders neglect themselves, it may be a matter of informed choice. Salend and colleagues point out that "one man's self-neglect may be another's exercise of free judgment" (Salend, Kane, Satz, & Pynoos, 1984).

Not only is self-neglect the most controversial form of elder mistreatment; it appears to be the most common. Nearly half of all elder mistreatment cases reported to Adult Protective Services are self-neglect. Not only that, self-neglect makes up half of all the repeat cases reported to Adult Protective Services (Salend et al., 1984; Sharon, 1991; Deets, 1993).

Self-abuse and neglect mean that an individual is failing to provide the necessities of life for himself or herself, such as food, clothing, shelter, adequate medical care, and reasonable management of financial resources. It ranges from poor grooming and poor eating habits to disintegration of the body through lack of medical care, and to death.

With the elderly, self-neglect is usually associated with the increasing severity of mental or physical impairments, but it can also be part of a lifestyle, as is frequently seen with alcoholism or drug abuse. It can include a filthy and unhealthy living environment with animal droppings in the house, or dissipation of bank accounts or other assets. Some elders in this category isolate themselves from those who would care for them. They show physical signs of self-neglect, such as dirty, matted hair, layers of disheveled clothing, clothing inappropriate to weather conditions, lack of food in the refrigerator, or food that is decayed and moldy. Some older people who cannot cope are abandoned by their families, or they live too far away for their families to be of assistance. Some simply have no family; they are the last to survive. In one case, the Public Guardian petitioned the court to become the conservator of an elderly woman whose daughter lived nearby but had become alienated from her for unknown reasons:

The referral for conservatorship had been received by the Public Guardian's Office from the Geriatric Home Visiting Team, who had been contacted by the gas and electric company when the woman had failed to pay her bill for several months. The team made several visits to the woman, explaining that the bill needed to be paid. Initially, she said that she was unaware that the bill was past due and then began to fabricate excuses such as, "A man hit me over the head, and that's why I forgot to pay." She would always agree to pay but never did, and the team became increasingly concerned about her because winter was setting in. Her mental impairment was obvious. She thought the year was 1941, and that her mother was still living, although she herself was in her mid-eighties. Her ankles were grossly swollen, but she denied that there were any problems; she said her ankles had always been that way and that she would go to a doctor if she really needed to. She was always very pleasant. She had a dog whose hair was falling out because he was truly flea-bitten. Large areas of his pink skin were showing through his meager hair and there were large bumps on his skin. He scratched himself incessantly. This did not seem to disturb the woman, who said that there were no problems with the dog, that sometimes he had hair and other times he didn't. There was also a scruffy cat. The woman never took the animals outside; as a result, the upholstered furniture had semicircles on the legs where the animals had relieved themselves. Her house was neat, but it was permeated by an extremely foul, dank odor. The practitioner found herself retching if she breathed through her nose. The kitchen floor was covered with animal feces, and when the woman was asked about it, she said, "Why, my goodness, someone must have come in and put that there when I was out shopping." The ceiling of the kitchen had been severely rain-damaged and was collapsing. When that was pointed out, the woman said, "Oh, that must be new." The kitchen sink was backed up with smelly, dirty water, and the woman seemed surprised about it. She seemed genuinely concerned about the sink but could not think what had to be done about it or how to go about getting it fixed. It was very apparent that she could not mobilize her resources to get anyone into the house to repair it.

## Etiology of Neglect

Neglect may arise out of a number of situations. For instance, it may be an outcome of acute or chronic alcoholism; bereavement; loss of self-care skills and capacities due to mental functional impairment; drug reactions; isolation; or a lifelong pattern of chaos on the part of the caregiver, the elder, or both. Neglect is frequently associated with psychiatric and personality disorders, including depression, late-life adjustment disorders, bipolar disorder, and focal neurological disorders ("small strokes"). Physical problems that can lead to neglect include: anemia; delirium; nutritional deficits; anorexia; poor eating habits; problems associated with swallowing; lassitude and fatigue associated with chronic illness, which lead to interference with appetite; sensory deprivation, leading to poor appetite; dehydration associated with less fluid intake due to incontinence and lack of mobility; malnutrition; social isolation; and poorly fitting teeth. Neglect may also be associated with health and medical problems, such as vitamin deficiencies and chronic obstructive lung disease, which interfere with brain function. The cause of neglect can be hard to diagnose because it can be a combination of factors (Vickers, 1992). Moreover, many of the symptoms may appear to be thought of as a natural part of the aging process, when in fact the symptoms could be treated with proper nutrition and fluid intake.

# Faces of Neglect

Using data from the Wisconsin Elder Abuse Reporting System, Longres (1995) compared substantiated cases of self-neglect with substantiated cases of elder mistreatment committed by others. Living arrangement was the most likely predictor of self-neglect, with self-neglecting elders more likely to be living alone. Like a study by Dubin and colleagues (1986), the Wisconsin study found varying scenarios. Some self-neglecting elderly people were social isolates with no formal social network; others had relatives who lived far away or had relatives with whom they had no close relationships; and some had a dysfunctional caregiving system (Longres, 1995).

In an effort to further understand situations that give rise to elder neglect, Dubin and colleagues (1986) examined 84 cases of confirmed neglect that had been reported to an adult protective services agency, usually by other professionals. The issue of *who* (elder or caregiver ) was to blame for the neglect was sidestepped because the researchers were more interested in describing situations than in pointing fingers.

Most of the reports of neglect came from social service practitioners who had observed the situation firsthand. Of the 84 people studied, 45 percent were men and 55 percent were women. They ranged in age from 70 to 89. Five profiles of neglect were found: (1) overwhelmed caregiving system; (2) elder who refused assistance, (3) self-interested caregiver; (4) dysfunctional caregiving system; and (5) elder alone.

## *Profile 1: Overwhelmed Caregiving System*

In profile 1, there were people who were concerned about the elder, but they were unable to meet the needs of the elder. The elder may or may not have lived with the caregiver. It may have been a situation where the adult child lived out of town, came to visit periodically, and tried to arrange for services, but the services simply were not enough. Or it may have been a situation where the elder refused to consider nursing home placement despite the need for heavy, extensive care. In an effort to please the elder and abide by his or her wishes, the caregiver kept trying to supply care in the home. Possibly the caregiving system was adequate at an earlier time, but as the elder became more frail or had a stroke or a fall, more care was needed. Other situations include those where the elder was home alone all day while other household members worked, and those where people were not aware of agencies that could provide services. Some families and elders denied that the needs of the elder had increased, and therefore did not act. Some families in this category had always been on the edge of survival; with the onset of chronic illnesses, they could not cope at all.

### Profile 2: Elder Who Refuses Assistance

In profile 2, which characterized 13 percent of the cases, elders refused care. A caregiving system composed of family and friends existed, but the elders did not want it. These elders refused medical care and medication; they did not want their homes cleaned; at times they even refused food. In some instances, the elders, very old and frail and aware of impending death, wanted to die in peace at home and did just that. Other elders were disabled, were possibly alcoholic, and preferred to be left alone to die even though they were not close to death. In a situation where the elder, usually a woman, had been the dominant force in the family, no one in the family could confront her with her failing health or suggest possible remedies. Some of the elders refused help because they did not want their circumstances altered or because they did not want the "state knowing their business." Some elders went without services rather than divulge their financial status. Some found their situation familiar and secure and feared alternatives. Elders in this category had the highest mortality rate.

### Profile 3: Self-Interested Caregiver

Profile 3 accounted for the smallest number of neglect cases in the research study. In this profile, the caregiver was more interested in the financial resources of the elder than in the actual care of the elder. The elder may have been aware of the exploitation but still preferred the situation to a nursing home. In these cases, the elder was removed from the care of the self-interested caregiver. Frequently, nursing home placement followed. Initially, these caregivers were hostile to workers, but eventually they complied, with some pressure.

### Profile 4: Dysfunctional Caregiving System

In profile 4, the elders had difficult personalities, or there were long-standing conflicts and estrangements between family members. In some instances, the elders were violent; often, alcohol was used by the elder, the caregiver, or both. The elder may have been violent with family members previously. Family members wanted nothing to do with these difficult people, who also drove away household help. These are the elders who end up being evicted by nursing homes. Bonding may have always been weak in the family or may have become weakened over time or because of distance or too many years of caregiving. In some instances, the elders had abandoned their children decades before.

### *Profile 5: Elder Alone*

In profile 5, the elders had no one to rely on at a time when they needed assistance. Family members and friends had died, leaving no one at all or only people who themselves needed assistance. Elders in this category may have been divorced or widowed and had no children. These elders did not know where to turn, had low energy, and were depressed. Some were always loners, perhaps preferring the company of animals to people. Sometimes the situation consisted of an elderly couple, neither of whom was capable of being a caregiver. These elders were reported to Adult Protective Services by the police or by neighbors. Some had avoided doctors because of the expense or because they feared what the doctor might tell them. They were resistant out of fierce independence and mistrust, or a fear of the alternatives, or out of despair.

Given these five categories, it is difficult to generalize about neglectful situations. Interventions for elders in each category were not similar. Instead, specific circumstances—such as an elder fiercely defending his or her independence; or an overwhelmed caregiver—determined what interventions by agency workers would be successful.

## Signs and Symptoms of Neglect

Signs and symptoms of neglect include poor hygiene: body odor; decayed teeth; concentrated urine or lack of feces due to low liquid and food intake; grimy clothing, bed linens, environment, and skin; vermin and feces in the house. The neglected elder may have untreated medical conditions or be improperly medicated. The residence of the neglected elder also shows signs of neglect: windows are broken; plumbing or electricity does not functio; roof leaks; the house is badly in need of painting; utilities have been turned off. There may be numerous pets who have been neglected. A look into the refrigerator reveals no food, or moldy food or jars, or only beer and bottles of condiments. In addition, two other major syndromes can also be a sign of neglect: *failure to thrive* syndrome and *compulsive hoarding* syndrome. These are discussed in the following sections.

## FAILURE TO THRIVE

Dehydration and malnutrition are widespread among the elderly for a variety of reasons. When accompanied by abnormal blood chemistry values, pressure sores, and malnutrition and dehydration, a diagnosis of "failure to thrive" syndrome may be made. Practitioners familiar with child abuse and neglect will recognize the term, which is usually applied to infants who fail to gain weight or to grow normally owing to lack of proper nutrition. In elders, this syndrome can occur in dependent living and independent living. The following cases illustrate home situations that were discovered by practitioners:

An elderly woman was mute and unresponsive when admitted to an acute care hospital. She had been living in subsidized senior housing and had a full-time attendant who was being paid by the county Department of Social Services. When the woman became more disabled, the attendant took her to her own home with the permission of the social work practitioner, who had no reason to doubt that the woman would receive good care. The attendant was the elderly woman's representative payee for her Social Security and she continued to receive a salary from the Department of Social Services—the total monthly income was $1,200. Visiting nurses were coming regularly, and over time they noticed that the elderly woman was always tied to the bedside commode. She was becoming more and more lethargic, and pressure sores were developing underneath her buttocks. Finally, the nurse and the social worker called an ambulance and—over the protests of the attendant and her very large, threatening boyfriend—had the woman taken to the hospital. On admission, the woman was found to be filthy and unkempt. There was evidence that she had been left lying on one side at all times—there was a great deal of swelling over the entire left side of her body. She was diagnosed as being acutely dehydrated and malnourished, with profound elevation of blood sodium and blood sugar. The attendant lobbied to have the woman returned to her care and was outraged when this was not permitted. The woman was placed in a county chronic care hospital which enjoyed a reputation for providing excellent nursing care.

Two sisters, one 85 years old and the other 92, were being cared for by the son of the younger woman. The son, a former priest with no known income, removed his mother from a convalescent hospital in order to save money, took possession of both women's bank accounts, and refused to hire adequate help in the home. Both women were bed-bound and incontinent of bowel and bladder. The son seemed incapable of understanding what must be done to care for the women. Over a period of 6 months, they were repeatedly hospitalized with pneumonia, pressure sores, severe dehydration and malnutrition, and abnormal blood chemistry due to the malnourishment. On one admission, the mother's temperature was 92 degrees and she was covered with human excrement. Adult protective service workers removed the women from the abuser's care after determining that he was incapable of properly caring for them or accepting assistance. Application was made to the Public Guardian's Office for joint conservatorships so that the women's funds could be used for their care.

## Malnutrition and Dehydration in Failure to Thrive Syndrome

In dependent living, malnutrition and dehydration occur when elders are incapable of preparing food for themselves or even reaching for a glass of water and the caregiver neglects to encourage fluid intake or spend the time necessary to feed them. Some impaired elders can take up to an hour to eat when being fed. Few caregivers think to keep track of how much an elder eats and drinks, although more and more nursing homes are now doing so. If intake of food and liquid is not monitored, no one knows if an elder is getting adequate nutrition. Elders may fail to eat properly because a caregiver does not adapt meals to their preferences or culture or because the food does not have the right consistency. When normal intake is not adequate, supplements such as vitamins and commercially prepared liquid nutrients are needed, and if these are not utilized, still further malnourishment will result (Anastasio, 1981). Some caregivers withhold liquids when an elder is incontinent of bladder so that they do not have to change the clothing or the bedding as frequently.

Elders in nursing homes and hospitals are considered to be living in dependent situations. Some studies estimate as many as 85 percent of those elders are malnourished. The outcome of poor nutritional status is further fatigue, greater confusion, increased risk of infections, and poor wound healing. The protein and calorie malnutrition commonly caused by famine in developing countries can appear in institutionalized elderly people who take in too little protein, too few calories, or both, for too long. Signs of nutritional deficiencies are less clear in elders than in younger people and can be difficult to measure; disease, medications, and aging itself can alter biochemical measures used to evaluate nutritional status. The single most useful and most readily available indicator of nutritional status is body weight. A guide is to consider "significant" weight loss in elders as 5% of body weight in 1 month, 7% in 3 months, or 10% in 10 months. Prolonged hospitalization and surgery are two conditions that predispose elderly people to protein-calorie malnutrition. Anemia due to malnutrition is a bigger problem in women than in men and can be measured by hemoglobin and hematocrit blood tests, which measure iron status (Yen, 1989). Low levels of serum (blood) albumin may be caused by long-term malnutrition (Ebersole & Hess, 1994). There may be significant changes in blood levels of vitamins (Braun, Wykle, & Cowling, 1988).

A high level of sodium in the blood may be a sign that the elder has become dehydrated as a result of low liquid intake. Also, specific medications such as lithium and diuretics dehydrate elderly patients easily. Coffee, which has a diuretic effect, calls for increased liquid intake. Other situations that affect liquid intake are hot weather, fever, upper respiratory infections, and gastrointestinal influenza when there is vomiting and diarrhea (Reedy, 1988). Gaspar (1988) studied fluid intake in nursing home patients and found that as age increased, fluid intake decreased; there is a possibility that as people age, their thirst decreases. Other factors found to influence intake were gender, functional ability, speech and visual impairment, opportunities to obtain water, and the time that water was within reach. Those who were functionally dependent were better hydrated than those who were independent or semidependent, perhaps because they were offered fluids at regular intervals. Elderly people may decrease fluid intake to avoid having to get up at night to urinate. Dehydration can cause mental confusion due to electrolyte imbalance.

Elders who live independently are also subject to malnutrition and dehydration, sometimes to the point of actually starving themselves. There may be an acute or chronic decrease in the quantity and quality of food, or alcohol intake may be replacing meals and causing nutritional deficiencies. Common causes of nutritional neglect and abuse in independent living are diminished appetite secondary to depression, isolation, or decreased taste acuity. Bereavement is a frequent cause of a poor appetite in the aged. Loss of appetite can often be traced to the onset or increasing severity of a chronic illness. Also, financial constraints impel some elderly people to purchase and eat less food. Sometimes the actual process of eating may be difficult. As elders grow older, their gums tend to shrink—hence the term "long in the tooth," which is a way of saying that someone is old. Those who have dentures must have them relined periodically to make them fit properly. As a result, many older people have dentures that do not fit, and they are unable to chew their food well. Eating becomes a problem. Elders who have mobility or transportation problems may find it difficult to get to a grocery store. Some may simply not take their nutritional needs very seriously. Medical conditions, therapies, and medication may affect the appetite or the ability to prepare and eat foods. Some medications have unpleasant side effects such as nausea (Anastasio, 1981). Elders who are demented may simply forget to eat or may be unable to keep track of when or if they have eaten.

Signs and symptoms of malnutrition and dehydration include sunken eyes and cheeks, extreme thirst, loss of weight unrelated to an illness, and a gaunt appearance (such as that found in victims of starvation or concentration camps), although it should be noted that obese people can also be malnourished. Practitioners may be able to determine if an elder is malnourished simply by putting an arm around the elder's shoulders; in a malnourished elder, the bones may be so prominent that the skin seems like thin tissue paper stretched over a frame. Elders who are malnourished and dehydrated may also be confused and apathetic and may suffer from hallucinations:

> One elderly woman, who was seeing black and white faces coming at her from the television set and hearing her upstairs neighbor's voice talking to her through her radio, lived alone and was found to be suffering from malnutrition. A homemaker was hired to purchase food and prepare meals for her. Once the elderly woman was eating properly, the visual and auditory hallucinations vanished.

## Pressure Sores in Failure to Thrive Syndrome

Pressure sores, frequently termed *decubitus ulcers* or *bedsores,* are another symptom of failure to thrive syndrome. They are due to sustained pressure on soft tissues which deprives the tissues of proper blood supply. The blood is squeezed out when the skin is under heavy pressure and the soft tissues in between a bone and a surface do not receive the nourishment that a good blood supply furnishes. Pressure sores usually occur over bony parts of the body such as the sacrum ("tailbone"), elbows, heels, and hips. The most common site for a pressure sore is under the sacrum because most bed-bound people spend a great deal of time lying on the back. Many conditions predispose an elder to pressure sores; diabetes, circulation problems (common in the elderly), anemia, nutritional inadequacy, certain drugs, and breakdown of the skin caused by lying in urine and feces. The first sign of a pressure sore is a reddened area. If the pressure continues, the skin blisters and opens, exposing tissues underneath the skin. In the next stage, the open wound widens and deepens and the bone underneath becomes visible. Surgery to remove dead tissue may be required, and it may become necessary to graft skin over the wound. When pressure sores on limbs will not heal, amputation may become necessary. Pressure sores are notoriously difficult to heal and call for exemplary nursing care (Kennedy, Graham, Miller & Davis, 1977). The cost of pressure sores in human suffering and dollars is enormous. Expenditures for the treatment of one pressure sore can range from $5,000 to $34,000 (Blom, 1985). Death can result from pressure sores when they become infected and cause systemic problems.

## Hypothermia and Hyperthermia in Failure to Thrive Syndrome

Hypothermia and hyperthermia account significantly for deaths among the elderly; in fact, elderly people are the group most susceptible to accidental hypothermia and heatstroke. These conditions may be part of failure to thrive syndrome, especially if an elder is dependent. They are preventable. In general, more women die from excessive heat while more men die from excessive cold. This gender difference is thought to be due to the disproportionate numbers of men who are homeless and therefore more exposed to cold. Fatal conditions can develop in just a few hours. Elders are very vulnerable to temperature changes, owing to diminished perception, impaired ability to regulate internal temperature, and reduced ability to detect temperature changes. Impaired nutritional status can also be a factor. Moreover, many elders try to save money on heating and electric bills; their houses may be older and therefore less insulated, so that there is a greater loss of heat as well as of cool air from air conditioning. Hypothermia is more common than hyperthermia and is the sixth leading cause of death in the elderly. The numbers may be low because hypothermia may not be listed as a cause of death on certificates of death (Macey & Schneider, 1993).

### Deprivational Behavior in Failure to Thrive Syndrome

Deprivational behavior, common in elder failure to thrive syndrome, shows up when elders are hospitalized, when they begin day care, or when they are admitted to long term care centers. These elders gobble up food and refreshments; eat triple-portion meals for weeks, and take food from others. They may have a "flat personality," seemingly incapable of showing emotion; they may be depressed. They may be in a state of psychological and biological "giving-up" which has been described as making a conscious decision that life is not worth holding onto (Stenback, 1975). They may also express desperation and panic at times; they may cling to nursing staff and "whine" and may unnecessarily take up the time of the staff, especially authority figures.

## OBSESSIVE-COMPULSIVE HOARDER'S SYNDROME

She saved bits of old string, empty cans and bottles, paper——trash of every description.

"Why don't you get rid of some of this junk?" and he would move destructively toward it.

"No you don't, Mr. Gant!" she would answer sharply. "You never know when those things will come in handy." (*Look Homeward Angel,* Thomas Wolfe)*

Obsessive-compulsive hoarding is only now beginning to be recognized and described; it is not clearly understood. No one knows how common it is or if it can be effectively treated. It appears to be characterized by the saving of all types of items: clothing, no matter what condition it is in; food, no matter how old or rotten it is; garbage; and even bodily waste. While those who hoard may initially be able to exert some self-control over their behavior, perhaps aided by family members, the "collections" can eventually become overwhelming, to the point that there are only small pathways through the house, with items piled on either side of the pathway. The person may need to sleep in the car or garage because there is no room in the house. Nothing is thrown away.

*Reprinted with the permission of Scribner, a Division of Simon & Schuster, from *Look Homeward, Angel* by Thomas Wolfe. Copyright 1929 by Charles Scribner's Sons; copyright renewed © 1957 by Edward C. Ashwell, Administrator, C.T.A. and/or Fred W. Wolfe.

Hoarders forage at garage sales or garbage dumps and are frequently secretive and defensive about their behavior. Some feel shame and embarrassment; others are paranoiac and let no one into the house. They resist psychiatric treatment and have limited insight into their behavior. Paradoxically, young people who hoard are often quite personable and function well in their community; their grooming and self-presentation are entirely acceptable.

Hoarding does not seem to be a function of poverty; it has always been a part of society and it appears to cross socioeconomic lines (Greenberg, 1987; Conklin, 1993). Some hoarders regard the items they collect as "having a use someday." Hoarding may be a symptom of fear of theft, of disorganized personality traits, or of a belief that everything in the universe is in short supply. Some hoarders appear to believe that miserliness is a virtue. People who hoard cannot bear to think of anyone taking anything away, become extremely threatened when family or authorities suggest culling items, or work hard at replacing items that are being removed. Hoarders can be violent when people try to throw out their belongings (Greenberg, 1987).

Hoarding has long been recognized as a feature of dementia. The gathering of familiar objects may compensate for confusion or the loss of loved ones. Hoarding may be the result of fatigue, cognitive impairment, or an inability to look after oneself (Greenberg, Witztum & Levy, 1990).

Compulsive hoarding is usually discovered by neighbors because it is producing a stench or vermin, and is then generally reported to public health authorities. The hoarder may also be self-neglectful and neglectful of his or her environment. The main interventions that seem to curtail the hoarding are some psychiatric medications, social pressure, and legal processes (Greenberg, 1987). In extreme cases, hoarding can contribute to death:

A disabled elderly woman, believed to be in her eighties, was trapped inside her burning home and died. Firefighters found a foot and a half of paper debris, consisting of junk mail, newspapers, and other paper, stacked throughout the residence. Cardboard boxes, which were stacked up on top of a floor heater, had apparently caught fire and started the blaze. The firefighters noted that the cluttered living room ignited like a ready campfire. A passerby saw the blaze in its early stages and contacted the Fire Department, which quickly put out the blaze and rushed the woman to the hospital where she died from extreme third-degree burns. A firefighter said, "I suppose she hated to live that way, with all that junk in her house, but she just couldn't help herself. For years, everything went into that house and nothing came out."

## PSYCHOLOGICAL ABUSE AND NEGLECT

Psychological abuse includes name-calling, saying unkind things about the elder within earshot, and mocking. Psychological neglect may consist of ignoring and isolating the elder and excluding him or her from activities. Manifestations of psychological abuse and neglect are seen in the actual behavior of the elder and can range from shame and passivity to severe anxiety, "nervous breakdown," and, theoretically, suicide. They can include confusion and disorientation, fearfulness, trembling and fidgeting when talking about certain subjects, changing the subject frequently, cowering in the presence of the caregiver, and referring all questions, even basic ones, to the caregiver. Figure 3-3 details the range of behaviors. Some elders report that psychological abuse hurts the most or that it is the worst thing that can happen to them (Anetzberger, Korbin & Tomita, 1996; Seaver, 1995).

Psychological abuse is difficult to prove, and practitioners are cautioned to proceed slowly. Some families have always spoken in loud voices or even yelled at each other as a matter of course, and they may consider it normal behavior. In addition, some of the behaviors listed in Figure 3-3 commonly occur with the various types of dementia or other chronic diseases, such as Parkinson's disease.

Most likely, psychological abuse is an integral part of the other types of abuse. Victims often report being threatened with nursing home placement if they protest physical abuse or if they threaten to tell someone outside of the family or if they refuse to hand over money. Living with constant threats can be very debilitating. Some elderly people find themselves physically impaired, living alone and with no one to help them. They may become dependent on attendants who are hired from agencies. The attendant may exploit the situation by playing on the fears of the elder:

An 83-year-old woman who was alert and oriented lived alone and was confined to a wheelchair. She had been a waitress, she said, and a "damn good one." Her hair was dyed bright red but was growing out gray from her center part. She had recently been hospitalized. When she came home from the hospital, she contacted a reputable home health agency, and a housekeeper was sent out to clean her house, do the cooking and shopping and help her with bathing.

At first, the housekeeper was attentive and did a good job. Then she began eating at the elderly woman's house, pleading hunger and citing the poor wages she was receiving. She began bringing her granddaughter to the woman's house, and the granddaughter too began eating the woman's food.

Suicide

"Nervous
breakdown"

Fearfulness
Depression
Helplessness
Hopelessness
Severe anxiety

Disorientation
Confusion
Anger
Agitation
Hypervigilance

Cowering
Lack of eye
contact

Evasiveness
Isolation
Trembling
Clinging

Passivity
Denial
Mild anxiety
Nonresponsiveness
Implausible stories

Ambivalence
Deference
Obsequiousness
Shame

*Source:* Tomita and Quinn, 1996.

Figure 3-3    Indicators of psychological abuse and neglect.

The elder felt trapped: She was angry and knew she was being taken advantage of, but she felt weak and sick, and she was afraid of being alone.

The subject of finances came up. The housekeeper suggested that the elder change her will and make her (housekeeper) the main beneficiary. When the woman demurred, the housekeeper insisted and said, "You know you need me. You can't do by yourself. You help me and I'll do for you. Otherwise, I'll have to leave you. What would you do then?" The elderly woman became desperate. She had no close relatives except her son, a "no-good" who had not contacted her in years. She signed a new will that was drawn up by the housekeeper's attorney. Over the next weekend, the elder decided that it just was not right. She called the home health agency on Monday morning and told the supervisor what had happened and said she "never wanted that woman in my house again." She also contacted an attorney and eventually changed her will back to its original form. The housekeeper came to the house to pick up her things. She screamed at the elderly woman, gave her a hand gesture and told her to " go do it to yourself." The housekeeper took some of the woman's new clothing and $200 in cash and then left, slamming the door. The woman was terrified that the housekeeper would come back "with some of her people" and kill her. "It's just not right," she said. "People like me are fair game. There's other people just waiting to move in on us. Now I know what old people mean when they say they don't want to go on. I'm a fighter, but I'm getting tired. I'm sick and I'll never be well again."

Clinging may be a sign that affection is missing from the elder's life or that it is being deliberately withheld. Prejudice against the aged who are impaired can lead others to deny that they have emotional needs.

The court visitor interviewed a 90-year-old woman who was living in a nursing home in a three-bed ward. Her estate was worth well over $300,000, so the visitor talked with her about luxuries such as having her own room. At that point, the woman began crying and said, "If I didn't have these other two women for companionship and if I couldn't visit with their company, I would be totally alone. All my friends are dead and I've outlived most of my relatives. I have no children and what relatives I do have live on the East Coast. Please don't have me moved." As the court visitor prepared to leave, the woman grasped her arm and said, "Please say you'll come back soon. I need people."

In reviewing the court file, the court visitor learned that the woman's long-time attorney was her conservator. The court visitor wrote a report describing what she had seen and related that, according to nursing staff, the woman had no visitors. She also said that she was aware that the attorney was very busy and that she knew of compassionate gerontologists who could provide the personal attention and care the elder woman needed and craved. She offered to help the attorney-conservator make the arrangements.

No sooner had the attorney received the report than he was on the phone to the court visitor. He was furious. He said, "Why, I go there every month for a few minutes just to make sure she is all right. I never bother to talk with the nurses at the desk. If someone was hired, it would mean that it would cost money, and her apartment house might have to be sold." The court visitor knew there were enough liquid assets to cover the cost of a gerontologist, and she wondered why the attorney raised the question of selling the apartment house. She also thought to herself: Even if the apartment house has to be sold, so what? It belongs to the woman, it is her money, and why shouldn't it be used to bring her happiness. The court visitor speculated that the attorney might be a beneficiary of the woman's will.

Sometimes, a nursing home can be a haven, especially if being in one's own home means being abused. In the following case, an elder chose to leave her home:

An attorney went to a judge complaining that an 84-year-old woman was being held in a nursing home. The judge ordered an investigation. It was discovered that the elderly woman had been placed in the nursing home when her attendant, who was also her conservator of person, went on vacation. The elder was very happy in the nursing home and did not want to return to her own home and the care of the attendant who, she said, was abusing her psychologically by cursing at her and insulting her on a regular basis because she was unable to walk. She said she was kept in one room all the time and was not permitted to use the rest of her house. The woman was alert, drug-free, and oriented. She had made friends at the nursing home and wished to remain there. The judge honored her wishes and removed the attendant as the conservator. It was later learned that the attendant had induced the elderly woman to sign over stocks and to give the attendant and her family "gifts" of over $80,000.

Undue influence, a legal concept in many guardianship laws, is a form of psychological mistreatment. It can be defined as the substitution of one person's will for the true desires of another. It may be accompanied by fraud, duress, threats, or different types of pressure on people who are particularly susceptible, such as dependent or impaired elderly people (Grant & Quinn, in press). It can happen to older adults who would otherwise be considered competent. Here is one case of psychological mistreatment:

An elderly woman gave a neighbor $14,000 as partial payment toward a new boat and, according to the neighbor, promised to give more money to finish paying for the boat. The neighbor had promised to "take care" of the woman "if anything happened." The woman was alert and oriented, but it was clear that this was a case of undue influence because she was extremely parsimonious. She had never contributed any money to anyone or to charity. She hated boats. The judge, upon hearing the case and learning of the woman's attitude toward money, agreed with the court-appointed attorney that undue influence had been used by the neighbor who had promised life care to the woman. The judge ordered the neighbor to give the money back, which he did.

## *Note: Depression and Suicide*

Depression is found throughout the life cycle, but it is the most common emotional illness in old age (Butler & Lewis, 1982). It can resemble dementia and in fact is often confused with dementia. A further source of confusion is the fact that in the beginning stages of dementia, depression is frequently present, particularly if the elder is aware of the dementia (Heston & White, 1983). Burnside (1976) has noted that depression in the elderly may go unnoticed because it differs from depression in the young. The main characteristic is apathy. Irritability, common with depression at any age, may be dismissed as "cantankerousness" in the old. Biological signs of depression in the old are common and may be the presenting complaint to the physician. These signs can include constipation, slow movements, and insomnia. When depression is obvious, it can include feelings of helplessness and hopelessness, a frequent sense of guilt, loneliness and despair, fear of death, loss of interest in sex, and loss of appetite, which can result in loss of weight. Hypochondriasis and somatic symptoms are frequently evident. Depression may follow the diagnosis of a chronic illness or the death of a loved one. It can occur as a side effect of medication. It can result from a loss in status in the community, such as retirement—which brings a fixed income (Butler & Lewis; 1982; Heston & White, 1983; Ostrovski, 1977). It has been estimated that 15 percent to 20 percent of elderly patients living in the community have either a major depression or a significant degree of dysphoria (Blazer, 1989).

Suicide is common among the old, although its relationship to elder abuse and neglect is still unknown. The highest rate of suicide occurs in white men in their eighties. Suicide in the elderly is more than double the average for all ages (McIntosh & Hubbard, 1988). Suicide remains one of the 10 leading causes of death in this country and, even so, is probably underreported because of religious taboos. People over 65 are extremely "successful" at suicide; their attempts rarely fail, particularly among men.

Rates for women, especially older women, are rising around the world (Butler & Lewis, 1982; U.S. Senate Special Committee on Aging, 1984).

## FINANCIAL ABUSE

The term *financial abuse* means that the assets of the elder are misappropriated. Financial abuse can range from stealing small amounts of cash from impaired elders or shortchanging them at a store to inducing them to deed over a house. In one study in the United States, financial abuse was found in one third of the cases of elder mistreatment. The victims in these cases had significant cognitive and physical impairments (Wolf, 1986). A random sample study in Canada found that financial or material abuse was the most common type of elder mistreatment (Podnieks, Pillemer, Nicholson, Shillington, & Frizzel, 1990). This type of mistreatment had a prevalence rate of approximately 25 cases per 1,000 elderly persons in private dwellings or about 2.5 percent of the survey sample. The single most common form of financial abuse (it was found in over 50 percent of the cases) was an effort to persuade the victim to part with money. In many instances, financial or material abuse is a crime (Heisler & Tewksbury, 1991). Elders who are financially abused may complain of not understanding recent changes in their financial status such as checks bouncing. Some elders may state that they are giving cash as gifts to housekeepers or newspaper delivery people or that they are simply very confused about their financial status.

There are several indicators of financial abuse:

- There is unusual activity in bank accounts. Accounts may be changed from one branch of a bank to another, or there may be several withdrawals in one day for large amounts of money.
- Bank statements and canceled checks no longer come to the elder's home.
- The caregiver disappears suddenly or without explanation.
- There is activity in bank accounts that is inappropriate to the older adult: e.g., drastic changes in types and amounts of withdrawals or withdrawals from automated banking machines when the elder cannot walk or get to the bank.
- Documents are drawn up for the elder's signature, but the elder cannot understand what they mean. These documents might include a

power of attorney, a will, joint tenancy on a bank account, or a deed to the elder's house. The elder may say that he has been signing "papers" but does not remember what they were.

- The care of the elder is not commensurate with the size of the estate, or the caregiver refuses to spend money on the care of the elder, or there are numerous unpaid bills (such as overdue rent, utilities, and taxes) when someone is supposed to be in charge of the elder's money.
- There is a lack of amenities—e.g., television set, personal grooming items, or appropriate clothing—when the estate can well afford it.
- The caregiver expresses unusual interest in the amount of money being expended on the care of the elder and asks the practitioner only financial questions, not questions about the care of the elder.
- Recent acquaintances express gushy, undying affection for a wealthy older person and may suddenly begin living with him or her.
- Caregivers show exaggerated defensiveness or excessive concern for the elder.
- Personal belongings such as art, silverware, jewelry, or furs are missing.
- A housekeeper tries to isolate the elder from his or her family by saying that the family does not care. The housekeeper then tells the family that the elder does not want to see them and later induces the elder to sign over assets by saying, "I am the only one who cares for you. After all, I am the one who takes care of you."
- A caregiver or a recent acquaintance promises the elder lifelong care ("I'll keep you out of a nursing home") in exchange for the elder's deeding all property and bank accounts over to the caregiver.
- The signatures on checks and other documents do not resemble the older person's signature.
- The older person cannot write, but there are "signatures" on documents.
- The caregiver has no visible means of financial support.
- There are no solid arrangements for financial management of the elder's assets. The caregiver is evasive about his or her sources of income.
- There are implausible explanations about the elder's finances by the caregiver, the elder, or both.
- An eviction notice arrives when the elder thought he or she owned the house.

Other indicators of financial abuse include inducing the elder to change his or her will to benefit strangers or newly arrived and considerably younger companions or suitors, and persuading an elderly person to part with valuable personal property such as jewelry or to sell real property at much less than its market value (Gordon, 1992).

According to Blunt (1993), certain predictable types of cases have emerged. The common denominator is that someone whom the elder trusts is handling the finances of the elder with or without formal authority. The first type of case is the elder who is a "financial prisoner." The elder is physically and perhaps psychologically dependent on the primary caregiver and is isolated by that person. The caregiver handles the assets. The elder literally loses the ability to say "no" to the caregiver and may even ratify suspicious transactions after the fact. Typically, these abusers have strong personalities, "tell a good story," and can be quite convincing. Practitioners may initially feel that the victim and the alleged abuser should not be separated because that is the only relationship the elder has. In some situations, the handling of the assets can be taken out of an alleged abuser's control and the suspected abuser will still remain in the relationship with the elder, even though someone else is now involved in the elder's life and is controlling the assets. In other situations, a suspected abuser abandons the victim when another person assumes authority over the elder's assets and the flow of money is cut off. The victim may grieve over the loss of the relationship but may very well have the capacity to form new relationships with caregivers who are not abusive.

The second type of case involves elders who are "slipping" and whose ability to handle their financial affairs has been lost owing to physical impairments. Someone else gradually assumes responsibility for the handling of the elder's affairs, but the responsibility is informal and the elder has little or no understanding of what is happening or its consequences.

The third type of case involves elderly widows and widowers. In these instances, the deceased spouse handled the financial affairs of the couple, and the surviving spouse simply does not know what to do. Typically, these elders are relieved when someone comes on the scene and helps them with their finances (Blunt, 1993). They are incapable of determining if that person is trustworthy.

A fourth type of case is the situation in which an elder adamantly refuses help and financial advice from responsible, trustworthy people who may or may not be relatives. This elder is suspicious and even paranoid and typically ends up placing control of his or her assets in the hands of a stranger, with the feeling that "at last I have found someone I can trust." That individual may be very charming and may abuse the elder terribly.

Financial abuse can be difficult to detect, investigate, and prove. Practitioners may not be accustomed to asking clients questions about money. An elder may be reluctant to divulge the location of bank accounts or may swear that the $20,000 he or she gave a new acquaintance was a "gift." It can be difficult to check the nature of bank accounts because banks have strict confidentiality guidelines which prohibit them from sharing information with practitioners. Forgery can be very hard to prove. Accurate statistics regarding financial exploitation may be hard to come by because the abuse is reported to the police but not to the agency mandated to receive elder abuse reports, or because banks, lawyers, and judges, who traditionally are aware of financial abuse, are not mandated to report it (Salend et al. 1984).

The following cases illustrate situations practitioners can encounter in working with financial abuse:

An 84-year-old woman and her 81-year-old brother were the victims of two separate incidents of financial abuse. The abusers were a corner grocer, who systematically robbed the woman of thousands of dollars; and a bank official, who withheld trust money to which the brother and sister were legally entitled. The elderly woman was severely demented. She was persuaded to give the grocer power of attorney over her finances and to name him as sole beneficiary in her will. He subsequently transferred $220,000 of her savings to a bank account in another county. When the fraud was discovered, there was some evidence that the grocer was acting with others who planned to defraud the elderly woman and then murder her and her brother. During the same time period, a bank officer—who visited the elderly pair in their home—refused to release money from a $573,226 trust fund held in their names because he thought the brother was "funny." The brother was receiving Social Security and Supplemental Security Income because he had no other resources. The court ordered a conservatorship established for the sister and brother, and the trust fund was eventually distributed to them, with the conservator acting as the fiduciary.

A 90-year-old widow who had lived in her neat-as-a-pin home for more than 50 years was induced to deed her home, worth $120,000 at the time, over to a bogus contractor. He was eventually forced by authorities to deed the home back to the woman, but by that time, it carried a $70,000 lien from a loan the "contractor," had taken out. Cash and stocks worth approximately $92,000 vanished after the elderly woman met the "contractor," leaving her to get by on $200 a month in Social Security and her $8,000 savings. The district attorney felt she was too mentally impaired to testify against her abuser, so charges were not brought against him. A conservator was appointed, and he filed a civil suit against the abuser, seeking to recover the $70,000 plus punitive damages. Several other elderly people, most of them unable to testify because of mental impairments, were defrauded by the same perpetrator and his partners.

An 84-year-old widow was bilked out of approximately $50,000 by her sister and brother-in-law, who arrived from the Midwest 2 months after her husband had died. The elderly woman had assets totaling nearly $500,000 in investments and income property. She suffered from dementia and was confused and disoriented. Aided by his wife, the brother-in-law put pressure on the elderly woman to give him money, to sell her property, and to make out a will naming him and his wife as sole beneficiaries. The actions of the brother-in-law raised the suspicions of the widow's tenants and friends, and bank officials, who alerted authorities. The court established a conservatorship and ordered the brother-in-law to return the $20,000 they could prove he had taken. He is believed to have taken an additional $30,000. On the witness stand, the perpetrator denied wrongdoing and said, "I'm just a country boy."

An elderly woman who lived in a pleasant residential home for seniors wanted very much to live in a private home. She made friends with one of the employees of the home and asked her to get an apartment so the two could live more comfortably. After a few months in the apartment, the former employee began to talk about getting a house and bringing her family to the United States. A house was rented, and gradually the entire family of the former employee was brought into the country. Initially, the elderly woman was being charged $1,000 a month for the care she received but when other family members were brought into the household, the charge skyrocketed to $2,000 in one month's time. The elderly woman was paying one third of the utilities, rent, and food even though the household consisted of six adults and one 2-week-old baby. By this time, the elderly woman was significantly impaired by Parkinson's disease. A conservator was appointed to protect her after her accountant became alarmed over the money that was going out. The conservator bargained with the caregiver, keeping in mind that there was a relationship between the caregiver and the impaired elderly woman and that the only alternative for the elderly woman would be a nursing home. On the recommendation of the court investigator, the judge reduced the monthly charges to a sum which was consistent with community standards and included all personal care, food, and utilities.

A 20-year-old legal secretary in a small town called the district attorney's office when she became aware that her boss, an attorney, was embezzling funds from an elderly client. An investigator went down to the seedy hotel where the elderly woman lived in order to see if she was all right and if she needed anything. The investigator never saw the woman, because she would not answer the door; but she could be heard talking to herself in the room, using many different voices. Neighbors reported that the elderly woman looked well-nourished and that she carried groceries into her room, apparently cooking against hotel regulations. Whenever the woman left her room, she nailed it shut with very large nails.

The investigator telephoned the attorney, who told her that the elderly woman had originally had $60,000 but that her fund was now down to $800 after only a few years. The investigator feigned confusion and said, "Well, I know you've been sending her $600 per month for expenses and that includes a $200 Social Security check. At current interest rates, her funds should have lasted much longer—in fact, several years." The attorney acknowledged that the investigator might be right. The following day, the legal secretary telephoned the district attorney's office and reported that the attorney had deposited $52,000 into an account with the elderly client's name on it.

# VIOLATIONS OF RIGHTS

The Select Committee on Aging of the U.S. House of Representatives noted in its 1981 report, *Elder Abuse: An Examination of a Hidden Problem,* that all Americans have certain inalienable rights under the Constitution and federal and state laws. These include the right to personal liberty; the right to adequate appropriate medical treatment; the right not to have one's property taken without due process of law; the right to freedom of assembly, speech, and religion; the right to freedom from forced labor; the right to freedom from sexual abuse; the right to freedom from verbal abuse; the right to privacy; the right to a clean, safe living environment; the right not to be declared incompetent and committed to a mental institution without due process of law; the right to complain and seek redress of grievances; the right to vote and exercise all the rights of citizens; the right to be treated with courtesy, dignity, and respect.

An examination of the case examples throughout this text will reveal that these basic rights have been violated in almost every instance of elder mistreatment. Violations of rights can range from not being permitted to open one's personal mail to being totally divested of all civil rights. Some observers have noted that convicted criminals have many more due-process protections in this country than do elders facing incompetency hearings. Chief among the protections *not* accorded to most elders in these situations is the right to have an attorney represent them. In some states, merely being old is reason enough to have a conservatorship or guardianship imposed.

A client whose rights are being violated may complain of not being permitted to vote or go to a house of worship. In one instance, a son who was his father's conservator directed the board and care operator not to permit his elderly father to receive visits from church members because he feared that the father would change his will and leave his considerable estate to the church. In another instance, an elderly woman was deprived of her personal liberty and her right to assembly by her housekeeper:

A retired schoolteacher had a bank acting as her conservator of estate, but no one was checking on her physical well-being. The bank had contacted a home health agency, which provided an attendant. The attendant forced the woman to stay in her bedroom by saying that she was weak and needed to rest. The attendant then removed the television from the woman's bedroom and put it in the living room so that she herself could watch it without the interference of the elderly woman. The attendant also pinned all the curtains shut, saying that the woman "didn't need to look outside." She took all the pictures off the walls and substituted her own pictures. She refused to give the woman her mail, instead telling her that there was no mail. When the elderly woman's friends called, the attendant would tell them that the woman was not well enough for them to stop by; or she would make an appointment for them to visit, but when they arrived she would tell them that the woman was too sick to have company. She also refused to bathe the woman. The elderly woman was rescued from this situation only because the attendant dropped dead from a heart attack. A new attendant arrived, and the first thing she did was to bathe the woman and give her a permanent. She also threw open the curtains, and put the woman's pictures back on the wall. She found the woman's address book and called all the woman's friends and urged them to come over and visit. She reinstated all magazine subscriptions and made sure that the woman got her mail. She took the woman to the doctor and initiated a medical regimen. In effect, she saved the woman's life.

Here is another instance:

A son who lived out of state was appointed to be the conservator of person of his wealthy 86-year-old father, at the father's request. The son refused to hire in-home care and immediately proceeded to confine his father to a nursing home, despite the fact that the father was alert and oriented and complained that he was "going crazy" in the nursing home. The son said, "Well, we all have to put up with things in life that we don't like." In effect, he violated his father's right to personal liberty and privacy. The court carefully monitored the situation because the son lived out-of-state and because he did not seem interested in his father's care. Even so, the father was returned to his own home only after threatening to change his will and disinherit his son.

In some cases, the professionals who are placed in charge of the care of a helpless elder may be abusive. In the following case, a woman thought she had done everything possible to protect her older sister and could not bring herself to believe that there had been any abuse. She violated her sister's right to adequate, appropriate medical treatment until the court stepped in.

A woman in her mid-eighties, and in the end stages of dementia, could not care for herself in any way. She was alert but disoriented as to time, place, and person. She was not capable of complaining about inadequate care; she seldom spoke. She was living in an apartment in a multilevel care facility run by a church group. She had private duty nursing around the clock, which was costing her estate $6,000 per month. Over a period of time, the nurses refused to permit any-one from the facility see the woman, and in fact developed an adversarial rela-tionship with the facility's staff. A doctor would visit occasionally, but he never examined the woman completely because the nurses always told him that she was "the same," and he trusted their opinion. Finally, the administrator of the facility instructed the director of nurses to go into the apartment and examine the woman. The director of nurses found 13 pressure sores, some of them far advanced, with necrotic tissue, and some so deep that bone was exposed. The conservator could not bring herself to believe that the nurses she had hired could possibly be mistreating her sister; and she refused to permit her sister to be hos-pitalized until the administrator called in an investigator from the court, who threatened to get a judicial order if the conservator did not hospitalize her sis-ter. It was later determined that in addition to having pressure sores, some of which required surgery, the woman had been oversedated by her nurses.

## INDICATORS OF ABUSE OR NEGLECT
## BY THE FAMILY OR THE CAREGIVER

Frequently, practitioners sense that something is "not quite right" in the life of an elder, but it may be difficult to pinpoint the exact nature of the problem.

Often, there are clues in the behavior of the family or the caregiver which are suspicious or unsettling. Detecting elder abuse and neglect is frequently a matter of "putting all the pieces together" and coming up with a definite diagnosis. In those tragic cases where death has resulted from abuse or neglect, hindsight may reveal that a practitioner missed clues or did not follow up on "gut feelings." Practitioners who are alert to the following indicators of abuse and neglect will be in a better position to detect maltreatment:

- The elder is not given the opportunity to speak for himself or herself or to see others without the caregiver being present.
- The family members or the caregiver have an attitude of indifference or anger toward the elder.
- The caregiver fails to provide the proper assistance or necessary mechanical devices for the frail elder.
- There are too many "explained" injuries, or explanations are inconsistent over time.
- A physical examination reveals that the client has injuries that the caregiver has not divulged.
- The client or caregiver has a history of "doctor shopping" and utilizing several different medical practitioners over a period of time.
- There is a prolonged interval between a trauma or illness and presentation for medical care.
- The caregiver or family withholds security and affection from the elder, or teases him or her in cruel ways, or uses nursing home placement as a threat.
- There are conflicting or implausible accounts regarding injuries or incidents. The physical findings are either better or worse than the accounts would lead the practitioner to believe.
- There is flirtation or coyness between the elder and the caregiver which may indicate a possible inappropriate sexual relationship.

## HIGH-RISK SITUATIONS

There are some situations that seem to be particularly dangerous for elders. This is when the practitioner should be especially alert and monitor the case carefully, remembering that some elders have been permanently injured and others have died while under the care of others.

A caregiver may have unrealistic expectations for older people or ill people and consequently feel that they should be punished if they do not do what the caregiver thinks they are capable of doing. Some caregivers feel that elders are incontinent on purpose or are faking when they say they cannot walk. Others are overconcerned about correcting what they see as "bad behavior" in an elder. If a family has a history of domestic abuse or a family member has an uncontrollable temper, that is a potentially unsafe situation for a dependent elderly person. In such families, hitting each other on a regular basis may be acceptable as a way of "correcting" unwanted behavior.

Some caregivers are incapable of taking care of dependent elders because of their own problems. Some are young and immature and have dependency needs of their own. They cannot possibly take care of a frail elder, particularly if the elder is demanding or needs a great deal of personal supervision. The risk for abuse and neglect of elder members is also high if the caregiver is mentally ill or has problems with alcohol or drug abuse.

Other high-risk situations include those where the caregiver is forced by circumstances to take care of the elder or where the care needs of the elder exceed or soon will exceed the ability of the caregiver to meet them. A caregiver who is also ill may be under further stress and be unable to adequately care for an elder. In those instances, the caregiver may be unwilling or reluctant to plan for or to implement the care of a dependent elder and he may therefore refuse services, thus placing further stress on himself or herself and inevitably on the elder as well.

Situations where the caregiver is dependent on the elder for financial support are also high-risk circumstances. Frequently, these are situations where a middle-aged child has never left home. Clinicians have noted that these caregivers tend to be evasive about financial and care arrangements for the elder and frequently are angry and resentful if they have to take care of the elder. There may show contempt for the elder, who was formerly powerful and in charge of the household but now is less able to defend himself or herself physically or even verbally.

Sometimes, elders unknowingly create a high-risk situation by tempting their heirs with money or possessions either through gifts while they are living or through a will. These elders may change their wills regularly, according to whim and depending on the behavior of their heirs. This kind of erratic behavior has the effect of breeding resentment and bringing out greed in everyone associated with an elder. Shakespeare depicts this phenomenon in *King Lear*. In his old age, Lear decides to relinquish his vast holdings to his three daughters. He is mistakenly certain of their affection and demands that they publicly declare their love for him. The elder daughters, Goneril and Regan, give obviously insincere protestations of love for their father, which he believes, and they are rewarded handsomely with lands and money. The younger daughter, Cordelia, gives a simple forthright statement of love which her father misinterprets to mean that she does not love him. She receives nothing. Thereafter, the two greedy older daughters turn their frail elderly father out of what is now their property and effectively deprive him of food, clothing, and shelter.

## SUMMARY

There are several types of elder mistreatment, and each has indicators. Additionally, there are certain situations that should raise the suspicions of the practitioner. At this stage of knowledge, practitioners must be investigators, carefully searching for clues and answers to puzzling situations. Detecting elder mistreatment requires the practitioner to realize that it exists and know the forms it takes. If practitioners are not alert for indications and clues, they will not be able to "see" abuse and neglect.

# CHAPTER 4

# Why Elder Mistreatment Occurs

What causes elder mistreatment? Does it represent a random striking out by the abuser? Is it a way of venting anger or frustration? Or is it deliberate, part of a chain of mistreatment that extends over months, or sometimes years? Are there families who have always, as a matter of course, settled conflicts and arguments by hitting each other or by abusing each other verbally? Is abuse a way of "getting even" with an elderly parent for real or imagined wrongs that happened decades earlier?

And what about financial abuse? Is it motivated by opportunism and greed? Does the caregiver, suddenly given access to a frail elder's bank accounts, and knowing that the older person is too impaired to realize that funds are being misused, act impulsively? How much plotting goes into defrauding an elderly relative out of a home or valuables?

Are large numbers of old people really being placed in nursing homes against their will? Are families abandoning their elders to the care of strangers when they no longer wish to be bothered?

Self-neglect and self-destructiveness raise other, slightly different questions. The issue here is whether these behaviors are long-standing, part of a lifestyle, or whether they are evidence that physical and perhaps mental impairments have overtaken the older person's ability to reason and to make sound judgments.

These and other questions arise in trying to understand elder mistreatment. Some tentative answers will be explored in this chapter. Recent studies and the current literature offer a place for beginning to consider general theories of causation.

Preliminary hypotheses regarding the causes of elder mistreatment that were based on case reports and early studies were reviewed by O'Malley et al. (1983). They were:

1. Those focusing on the victim's dependency: that is, on physical and mental impairment of an older adult.
2. Those emphasizing the effect of stress on the caregiver.
3. Those concerned with the influence of families who have learned to solve problems by being violent with one another.
4. Those which focus on the individual problems of the abuser.

To these four categories a fifth was added:

5. Effects of a society which casts older adults in the role of nonpersons through ageism, sexism, and destructive attitudes toward the disabled and toward those who are perceived to be unattractive. Greed is also a part of this category and cannot be discounted where financial abuse is present.

As a result of more recent studies, modifications have been made with regard to the concepts of dependency and the stressed caregiver. Although still important, characteristics of the elder alone are insufficient explanations for the various forms of mistreatment; characteristics of the abuser and the abuser-elder interaction, some stemming from elder impairment, are emerging as interesting theoretical explanations. Further studies will determine which will be the strongest explanation. It may be that specific explanations apply to certain subgroups of the elderly but not to the general elderly population. In the following sections, each of the five explanations will be discussed in turn.

## 1. THE DEPENDENT ELDER CONCEPT REVISITED

As noted in Chapter 2, during the first phase of research on elder mistreatment, several researchers observed that the majority of victims of elder mistreatment were impaired—physically, mentally, or both (Block & Sinnott, 1979; Douglass et al., 1980; Steinmetz, 1978; Steuer & Austin, 1980). The inability of impaired older people to carry out the activities of daily living (ADL)—such as personal grooming, dressing, using the toilet, shopping for food and preparing it, handling money, and other vital activities—makes them vulnerable and dependent on caregivers' actions and, perhaps literally, puts them at the mercy of their caregivers (O'Malley et al., 1979; Hickey & Douglass, 1981).

Second-phase research found that the dependency of *abusers* rather than elders was a stronger explanatory variable for elder mistreatment (Hwalek, Sengstock, & Lawrence, 1984; Phillips, 1986; Pillemer, 1985a, 1985b; Wolf & Pillemer, 1984, 1989). Hudson (1994) conducted a study among laypeople to determine if they agreed with professionals about the definitions of the various forms of elder mistreatment. Of 104 participants, 72% did *not* agree with the statement, "In order to be abused, the elder has to be dependent on the person who does the abuse." In addition, 90% felt that healthy elders can be abused; 80% felt that professional help is needed in elder mistreatment situations; and most felt that early intervention is needed in these situations. These findings support taking an inclusive rather than exclusive and narrow approach to elder mistreatment because any elder, frail or independent, may be mistreated and may be desirous of professional intervention.

Along with the idea of elder dependency, a good deal of the early literature on elder mistreatment contained the basic principles of exchange theory: that people tend to maximize their rewards and minimize or avoid their costs or punishments; and one's power is equivalent to another's dependency (Blau, 1964; Cook, 1987; Cook & Emerson, 1978; Emerson, 1972a, 1972b, 1987; Homans, 1974). Early on, concepts from exchange theory had tremendous appeal in explaining elder mistreatment, because it seems logical that caregivers would become angry and at times abusive if they were denied their just rewards. But as a result of more recent data that identify abuser dependency as a stronger explanatory variable than elder dependency, exchange theory has not been mentioned as often as before, perhaps because elderly victims are not perceived to be more powerful than dependent perpetrators. If only the simple concepts based on exchange theory are used—such as maximization of rewards, the withholding of rewards as a cause of anger, and dependency as a determinant of power—they cannot be applied to elder mistreatment. The elder who rewards the perpetrator with money and housing does not minimize the chance of mistreatment, nor does withholding rewards such as money guarantee that the perpetrator will stop the mistreatment . In some cases, compliance may in fact promote further abuse, and some abusers may be "bottomless pits": No matter how many goods or services they take, they will never be satisfied.

To some researchers, it is the perceived power deficit, not the other's dependency, that contributes to abusive behavior in domestic settings (Pillemer, 1985a, 1985b; Pillemer & Finkelhor, 1985). Finkelhor (1983), identifying common causes of family abuse, noted that abusers of women and children frequently *perceive* themselves as being powerless and that the acts of abuse serve to compensate for those feelings. Although this concept is purely speculative, it may be true also of elder mistreatment, especially because adult children who are dependent and abusive know in some way that by remaining dependent on a parent, they are not fulfilling the expectations of society. Striking out or abusing in some way becomes an equalizing act through which the abuser again feels potent.

## 2. THE STRESSED CAREGIVER

To the lay public, the notion of an exhausted caregiver suddenly and impulsively striking out at an impaired elder after years of frustration is probably the most popular of all the theories of elder mistreatment. It is important to realize, however, that although this theory of causation is the easiest to identify with, it is *not* necessarily the right one. Nearly everyone has, at one time or another, experienced the *feeling*, however fleeting, of wanting to strike out at a dependent person who needs a great deal of help with activities of daily living. Most of us have at times felt impatient or intolerant of an older person who walked slowly in our fast-moving world, who yelled at us, who had trouble assimilating new information, who told the same stories over and over, or who incessantly ruminated over lost opportunities.

The hypothesis of the stressed caregiver has received a great deal of attention from researchers and clinicians, not only because it is the most readily acceptable explanation, but because if fits with interventions that have been pioneered by those working in the field of domestic violence, particularly in child abuse and neglect. Those intervention models include peer groups which provide emotional support and information about resources and normal growth and development, respite care enabling a caregiver to have time for herself, telephone hot lines to help in times of crisis, and in-home services to lighten the load of the caregiver. With the finding that abuser dependency is a significant factor in elder mistreatment cases, the stressed caregiver concept has lost favor among those researching the problem. Yet, stress is still a vulnerability factor thay may contribute to elder mistreatment. In this chapter, the recent literature on abuser-elder interaction is reviewed, and its role in the stressed caregiver concept is considered.

## The Original Concept of the Stressed Caregiver

### *Families and Caregiving*

The family has traditionally been expected to provide care and support for impaired elderly members. To this day, the great bulk of impaired older people are in the community and are dependent on their family, friends, or others for assistance with daily living (American Association of Retired Persons, 1994). For a variety of reasons, nursing home placement is usually a last resort for families and elders. The public image of the nursing home industry, which grows more "corporate" every day, has not been generally favorable. Although new laws regulating the operation of nursing homes go in effect each year, there are still bad nursing homes that give substandard care. For many people, the existence of such homes makes this an unattractive option for an aging parent. Nursing homes that do give competent, kind attention seldom receive public notice. In addition, nursing homes can be expensive; currently, the average cost of a nursing home in an urban area can range from $100 to $250 per day excluding doctors' bills, medications, and special treatments such as physical therapy. At this rate, even a frugal elder's resources would be rapidly dissipated. There also may be community or family pressure for adult children or spouses to care for the elder in his or her own home or take the elder to live with them. Adult children may have promised their parents never to put them in a nursing home. Often, spouses make a similar promise to one another, a promise which is kept even when circumstances have drastically altered:

> A 71-year-old woman, described as a "sweet little old thing" by police, pleaded guilty to voluntary manslaughter in the death of her 92-year-old husband. Her husband's pajama-clad body had been found on the couple's bed when the coroner arrived. The coroner had been called by the crematorium society, which in turn had been called by the woman. The woman told the coroner's investigator that her husband had died in his sleep. But the investigator was immediately struck by a line around the dead man's neck: From the line down, the body was the color of a normal dead body; but above the line, the face was reddish-purple. When the investigator told

the woman that something was not right, she showed him to the telephone and he called the police.

Neighbors indicated that the couple had been very close. They said that the husband's memory had begun failing about 8 years before; he had also suffered several strokes and was afflicted with arteriosclerosis, emphysema, and severe hearing loss. He would be found wandering the neighborhood and would get lost even on the way to the bathroom in his own home. After their eldest son committed suicide, the husband became much worse. The wife refused to hire any help because she had been a nurse and had reared three children. She refused to place her husband in a nursing home because the couple had promised one another that neither would put the other in a nursing home. She kept thinking she would be able to handle it. Two weeks before the death, she broke down in the arms of a friend and said, "I just can't take this."

Some families take their elders in because they fear what others will say if they do not at least attempt to care for the elder in a home setting. Other families have traditionally cared for their impaired elderly members in their homes. For some adult children, taking care of an impaired elder relative in the home is perceived as the last chance to resolve negative feelings left over from the past. Few anticipate that the situation will impose further stresses which may make it impossible to perform the needed care (Hayes, 1984). Also, the role of caregiving is not satisfying to everyone and may not fulfill the adult child's fantasies of what it would be like.

Caring for an elderly parent is rapidly becoming a "normative" adulthood life event (Brody, 1985), and it has been called an "unexpected career" (Aneshensel, Pearlin, Mullan, Zarit, & Whitlatch, 1995). For older persons themselves, care from family and friends is the first choice; care from friends and neighbors is the second choice; and care from formal agencies and organizations is a last resort (Ory, 1985). Although it may be reassuring to learn that elders are not being abandoned in institutions, family care should not be idealized or romanticized. Some families care for an elder because of their own pathology and their inability to take advantage of formal and informal support. Others are psychologically unable to place a severely impaired elder in a nursing home even though the entire family is severely deprived by the caregiving. And in some instances, caring for the elder involves a search for parental affection and approval, a search that by this time is fruitless. This type of caregiving can be called "excessive caregiving" and may be due to pathology, not heroism or love (Brody, 1985; Brody & Spark, 1966).

## Pressure of Caregiving

There are undeniable pressures on middle-aged children to care for frail elders at home, even though the burdens can be enormous and can extend over a long time. Dementia, which is the most common cause of mental impairment among older people, has a long course, sometimes 7 to 10 years, and the period of total physical care (feeding, bathing, coping with bladder and bowel incontinence) may extend over several years (Aronson, 1984). One study noted that the *average* length of caregiving was 7 years (Aneshensel et al., 1995). With time, many physical and mental conditions become even more disabling, requiring higher levels of care. The result is increasing isolation for caregivers, who must focus more and more on meeting the survival needs of the elder and forgo time for themselves. Vacations, a career, education, and friendships may go by the wayside. In a study of support groups for relatives of functionally disabled older adults, feelings of severe isolation and entrapment were reported as the foremost concern (Hayes, 1984). Zarit, Reever, and Bach-Peterson (1980) studied 29 caregivers who were responsible for the care of demented persons and found that the heaviness of the burden experienced by the caregivers was directly related to the number of visits from other family members to the household. The more the visits, the less burdened the caregiver felt. Surprisingly, the weight of the burden was *not* related to the level of physical or mental impairment of the elder, or to the duration of the illness, or to behavior problems of the elder.

Caregivers are under other stresses too. Frequently, the caregiver—"family"—is one person, usually a middle-aged woman, who does the caregiving with no respite and very little understanding from her spouse, her children, or her family of origin (Steinmetz, 1983). In fact, her immediate family members may subtly increase their demands on her in order to balance out the attention she is giving to the impaired elder, especially if they do not like the elder (Schmidt, 1980). Sommers (1985) estimates that 85 percent of caregivers are women. Until the advent of the women's rights movement, it was assumed that middle-class women would stay in the home and care for all dependent members, including the frail elderly. However, this has changed in recent years. Just as women with small children are juggling careers and family, women who have elderly relatives in need of assistance are trying to balance competing demands. The idea of a "Superwoman," who has a career and a family and "does it all," creates pressure and conflict for women of all ages.

If there is disharmony in the caregiver's family of origin, those family members may feel free to criticize the primary caregiver for the type of help given to the elder, and for the time and money being spent on the elder's care. Old patterns of sibling rivalry can flare up when a parent becomes dependent. Some clinicians have observed an inverse relationship between the amount of complaining done by siblings and the level of contribution they make to the care of the elder: the more complaining, the less contribution. It often happens that the adult child who is doing the most work gets the least credit or is even blamed by the elder, while the sibling who does virtually nothing receives praise from the aged person for the slightest contribution. This seems to be true particularly when a daughter is the primary caregiver and the aged parent favors a son who is doing little to contribute to the caregiving. Generally speaking, caregivers receive little or no recognition for the ceaseless work they do. There may be a Mother's Day, but there is no Caregiver's Day.

People who are taking care of their impaired partners, in addition, have to take on household duties that the partner performed previously. The prospect of a life happily shared in old age dissolves as the workload increases. If the partner is demented, there are personality changes which irrevocably alter and diminish the couple's relationship. Some caregivers have noted that they feel as if they are in a state of perpetual mourning for a "lost partner" who is still living.

Fitting and Rabins (1985) report that there are differences between men and women when it comes to caregiving. They base their findings regarding gender predominantly on spouse caregivers because among studies of adult children as caregivers, few sons were available for inclusion. In a study of 28 male and 28 female caregivers (55 of these caregivers were spouses; 1 was a sister), Fitting, Rabins, and Lucas (1984) found that there were minimal differences between men and women as to feelings of burden, family environment, psychological adjustment, and social contacts. However, the women had significantly more symptoms of depression than the men. Traditionally, women have had less societal power and therefore have internalized their anger. In contrast, men have had more freedom to act it out. This may account for the overrepresentation of males among reported abusers, given that most caregivers are women.

Interestingly, the men tended to hire help more than the women did, possibly as a result of having been in the world of work and learning the value of delegating tasks. Presumably, men are also more accustomed to having a woman in their lives take care of household tasks and naturally seek to re-create this kind of support for themselves. Younger caregivers were found to resent the caregiving role more than older caregivers, possibly because of other family and career obligations (Fitting et al., 1984).

There is some evidence to indicate that caregiving is experienced differently by partners and adult children. Partners as caregivers often appear to be suffering from greater objective burdens, but adult children have a greater sense of being burdened, possibly because caregiving means more disruption in their lives (Ory, 1985). Adult children may be more likely to seek physical and emotional distance from their mother or father as time goes on. Partners tend to be more emotionally involved and more distressed by the changes wrought by disease, finding themselves caught up further in the relationship as the dependency deepens (Johnson & Catalano, 1983; Zarit, 1985). A couple may increasingly withdraw from social involvement as the caregiving needs compound, especially if there is no one to help. If the caregiver's heath collapses, immediate institutionalization may result for the impaired spouse. In many instances, adult children will insist on placing their ill parent in an institution when the other parent's health has broken down as a result of caregiving.

### Lack of Knowledge as a Contributor to Stress

Distinguishing between "normal" aging and changes considered to be treatable pathology has been a challenge to practitioners, researchers, families, and clients (Kane, Ouslander, & Abrass, 1994). Indeed, recent discoveries showing that much of what has been considered normal aging is in fact pathology have not been publicized sufficiently. This lack of information results in confusion as to whether a given condition is treatable or should be accepted as chronic and inevitable.

Techniques for dealing with disabilities, particularly the behaviors associated with dementia, have not been widely disseminated. Some caregivers feel that if they physically discipline an impaired elder, this will give them control over their problems with the care. They simply do not know what to expect, or which behaviors are not deliberate on the part of the impaired elder.

### Obstacles to Caregiving

A caregiver faces many obstacles in trying to provide responsible, competent care: Doctors and other medical practitioners may not offer the desired assistance or information. Caregivers may be too intimidated by physicians to press their concerns. Physicians may not take the time to explain medical conditions adequately, leaving the caregiver with an imperfect understanding of the situation. Community resources such as respite care and in-home services may be sparse in the caregiver's geographic area, or the caregiver may not know how to find or use these resources.

A further difficulty is a lack of adequate role models or mentors for caregivers of the elderly, because widespread longevity is relatively new. It is not uncommon for stressed caregivers to express bewilderment at the quantity and complexity of the work entailed in taking care of a frail elder, wondering aloud, "Why didn't someone tell me?"

## Elders as a Source of Stress

The dependent elder himself or herself can be overwhelming for the caregiver. In one study, 63 percent of abusers reported that the elder was a source of stress because of the high level of physical and emotional care required (O'Malley et al., 1979). With demented elders, there are a number of behaviors that can be worrisome and disconcerting for caregivers, such as wandering, primitive eating habits, attacking caregivers physically and verbally, leaving stove burners on, insomnia, and disrobing in public. There is fear that elders will hurt themselves or others. In fact, it is this *emotional* burden, rather than the physical work, that seems to put the greatest strain on caregivers. Doing household tasks, grooming, and transporting an impaired elder are reported by caregivers to be time-consuming but not stressful, whereas the strain of dealing with elders who have emotional problems or severe memory problems creates tension for the caregiver (Steinmetz, 1983, 1988b). Aneshensel et al. (1995), on the basis of their longitudinal study of 555 caregivers referred by the Alzheimer's Disease and Related Disorders Association (ADRDA), note that troublesome behaviors keep the average caregiver in a constant state of vigilance. "Role overload" and "role captivity" were found to be associated with high levels of troublesome behavior, and role captivity intensified when disruptive behaviors worsened. These problematic behaviors were not predictable from the duration of an illness, although cognitive impairment and ADL dependencies did predictably worsen over time.

## Other Stressors

Other stressors have to do with the emotional history of the caregiver and the elder. Old battles can come back to life when the elder and the adult child are thrown together. Conflicting ideas about such things as politics, love relationships, raising children, and the conduct of one's work life can arise once again, resulting in renewed anger and resentment on both sides. Character traits which the parent always disliked in the child may provoke "guilt trips." Not all caregivers can control their anger, modulate it, channel it, or understand it. In addition, some parents do not learn to let go of their adult children, failing to perceive them as adults with rights and responsibilities. A parent may berate adult children for what they are not or for what they could have been, or may compare them unfavorably with other siblings. With the onset of dementia, an elderly parent may become disapproving, unable to give the warmth, appreciation, and support that is much needed in the situation. Paranoia may set in, leaving suspicion where once there was respect and regard. The demented elder may become accusatory, putting extra stress on a caregiver already chronically fatigued and doing everything possible to keep the elder comfortable.

## Revisiting the Concept of the Stressed Caregiver

Not all older dependent people are abused. The question then becomes: Why some and not others? There are probably two factors other than dependency that must come into play before mistreatment occurs. First, there must be an individual who, for some reason, abuses or fails to take necessary action. Second, there must be a triggering event—a crisis of some sort which precipitates the incident of abuse (O'Malley et al., 1983). It may be that the onset of the elder's impairment or the worsening of health problems creates a crisis leading to the mistreatment, or the mistreatment occurs when the need for assistance exceeds the caregiver's capacity to respond appropriately (Steinmetz, 1980). Elders may have been fairly independent, but then their need increases, and they turn to an adult child for help. Sometimes, parents expect that an adult child will take them in, perhaps in spite of the fact that they have never had an amiable relationship. The elder may see it as the child's obligation, and the child may see it in the same way or may capitulate out of guilt or fear of being judged harshly by friends or family. Some adult children take their elderly impaired parents into their homes too quickly, without considering other viable alternatives or without planning how they will go on with their own lives. The elderly parent and the adult child may have had a good relationship until the dependency began, but the parent's care needs may change the relationship by shifting the balance of power.

## *"Double Direction" Violence*

Early on, Steinmetz suggested that abuse was related to interactions between the caregiver and the elder (1981, 1988a). Studying 60 adult children who were caring for a dependent elderly parent, Steinmetz found strong evidence that parent and child tried to control one another. She called this "double direction violence." The most common form of control was screaming and yelling, but hitting and slapping also occurred. Caregivers who slapped an elder often gave the same reasons for their behavior as child-abusing parents, saying that the slapping or hitting was done to discipline the elder and to ensure his or her safety (see Tables 4-1 and 4-2).

## *Recent Studies on Caregiver-Elder Relationships*

Homer and Gilleard (1990) support Steinmetz's observations of two-way violence. Interviewing 51 caregivers and 43 patients with dementia and other illnesses who received respite care in a geriatrics program in a London hospital, they found that 23 (45%) caregivers admitted to committing some form of mistreatment. All of those admitting to mistreatment lived with the elder. Factors most significantly associated with the mistreatment were alcohol consumption by the caregivers and abuse toward the caregiver by the patient. This finding is similar to that in a study by Anetzberger et al. (1994) in which abusing caregivers were more likely than nonabusing caregivers to use alcohol, to become intoxicated, and to be identified as having a drinking problem.

In the study by Homer and Gilleard, triggers of physical abuse were reported by the caregivers to be physical abuse or threats of violence by the patient, incontinence, or both. The abusers identified the elder's behavior as the main problem—not physical impairment, financial problems, social isolation, or emotional strain. The abused patients were considered to have more communication problems and to be more socially disturbed than those who were not abused. They were not more physically dependent than the nonabused patients. The caregivers who admitted to physical and verbal abuse scored higher on the depression scale than the nonabusive caregivers.

NOTE: QUALITY OF RELATIONSHIP PRIOR TO IMPAIRMENT. With regard to the relationships in Homer and Gilleard's study, the caregivers in the dyads involving verbal abuse and physical neglect rated their previous

**Table 4-1    Methods Used by Adult Children
to Control Their Elderly Parents**

| Methods | Percent |
| --- | --- |
| Scream and yell | 40 |
| Use physical restraint | 6 |
| Force feeding or medication | 6 |
| Threaten to send to nursing home | 6 |
| Threaten with physical force | 4 |
| Hit or slap | 3 |

*Source:* Reprinted from S.K. Steinmetz. (1981, January–February). Elder abuse. *Aging,
315–316,* 7.

**Table 4-2    Methods Used by the Elderly to Control their Adult Children**

| Methods | Percent |
| --- | --- |
| Scream and yell | 43 |
| Pout or withdraw | 47 |
| Refuse food or medication | 16 |
| Manipulate, cry, or use physical or emotional disability | 32 |
| Hit, slap, throw objects | 22 |
| Call police or others for imagined threats | 10 |

*Source:* Reprinted from S.K. Steinmetz. (1981, January–February). Elder abuse. *Aging,
315–316,* 9.

relationship as poorer than those in the nonabusive dyads. They were more
likely to have had a history of verbal abuse prior to the caregiving relationship. For those in the dyads involving physical abuse, however, there
was no prior physical abuse. The authors conclude that alcohol consumption by the caregivers, disruptive behavior on the part of the victim (not
cognitive impairment), and the quality of the previous relationship were
most closely related to mistreatment. Some may argue that this is hair-
splitting because disruptive behavior is often a result of cognitive impairment and should not be separated from a client's characteristics.

## *Frequency of Violence*

Paveza and colleagues, also recognizing that caring for persons with Alzheimer's disease and related disorders can be stressful enough to lead to violence, studied the frequency of violence and risk factors for violent behavior in the caregiver-patient dyad (1992). In their study, 184 patient-caregiver dyads were selected from an Alzheimer's disease registry. The general prevalence rate of severe violence committed either by the caregiver or by the patient, as measured by the Conflict Tactics Scale (CTS; Straus et al., 1980)—including hitting, kicking biting, punching, and threats with or use of a weapon—was 17.4%. Within the dyads, 15.8% of the patients were reported by the caregivers to have exhibited severely violent behavior toward caregivers in the year since diagnosis; 5.4% of the caregivers reported that they were violent toward the patient. Two-way severe violence was reported among 3.8% of the dyads.

NOTE: RISK FACTORS FOR VIOLENT BEHAVIOR. In the study by Paveza et al. (1992), two variables were statistically associated with the violent patient-caregiver dyads: the caregiver was depressed, and the patient was residing with relatives other than a spouse. Cognitive and functional impairments were not predictive of violence among the dyads. This finding supports the findings of earlier studies that impaired elders were no more likely to be abused that those without impairments (Phillips, 1983; Pillemer, 1986). The finding of depression on the part of the caregiver is similar to what was found by Homer and Gilleard (1990). Caregivers who scored high on the depression scale were at three times greater risk for violence than caregivers who scored below the cutoff score. Likewise, patients who lived with relatives other than a spouse were at almost three times greater risk for violence than patients who had other living arrangements. Paveza et al. further observed that severe violence expressed toward a caregiver is not rare, and that although abusive behaviors by a patient do not justify violent reactions by caregivers, it is necessary to understand how both sides contribute to violent interactions.

### *Elder Impairment as a Measure of Caregiving Demands*

Findings of the study by Pillemer and Suitor (1992) were similar to those of Homer and Gilleard (1990) and Paveza et al. (1992). Focus was on risk factors for fear of becoming violent and for violence actually committed among caregivers and their elderly relatives who had been diagnosed with Alzheimer's disease or some other nonreversible dementia within the previous 6 months. A total of 236 caregivers were asked about (1) their own characteristics; (2) interactional stressors, such as disruptive behaviors exhibited by the recipient of care and his or her aggressive behaviors toward the caregiver; (3) the caregiving context, indicated by social isolation and by the structural relationship, that is, whether the caregiver was a spouse or a child of the recipient; and (4) caregiving demands, measured by the client's ADL status, and the amount of time the caregiver spent helping the recipient.

The results showed that 46 (19.5%) caregivers feared that they might become violent; 14 (5.9%) stated that they had actually engaged in violence. Fifty-seven percent of those who reported violent feelings had experienced violence from the recipient of care while only 17% of those who did not report violent feelings had experienced violence. Those who feared becoming violent cared for relatives who had the most disruptive behaviors; these elders were more functionally impaired and needed help with a greater number of activities. This finding differs from those in previous studies indicating that abused elders were no more impaired than those who were not abused (Phillips, 1983; Pillemer, 1986). Regarding caregivers' characteristics, those who reported fear of becoming violent were also slightly older, had lower self-esteem scores, and were more likely to live with the recipient of care.

In addition, data analysis indicated that two interactional stressors—violence by the elder and disruptive behaviors such as incontinence and wandering—were related to the caregivers' fears of becoming violent. Qualitative data confirmed that some caregivers were frustrated by an elder who refused to cooperate with their attempts to provide care. This construct runs the risk of blaming the elder for behavior that is in fact related to impairment.

Elsewhere, caregivers have cited poor communication, incontinence (Homer & Gilleard, 1990), and the elder's lack of cooperation or inability to understand the ADL task in progress (Payne & Cikovic, 1996; Pillemer & Moore, 1989) as triggers of abuse or violent feelings. In Pillemer and Suitor's study, interactional stressors and caregiving demands are another way of labeling the elder's cognitive and functional status. Since caregiving demands in this study are equated with the elder's ADL status, the elder's degree of impairment prevails as an important factor to consider in examining contributors to caregivers' stress and potentially to elder mistreatment, as earlier research has suggested.

NOTE: ACTUAL VIOLENCE.   In Pillemer and Suitor's study, a further exploration of the differences between caregivers who actually became violent (14/46 or 30%) and those who feared becoming violent but did not become violent (32/46 or 70%) found that violence by the caregiver was related mainly to initial violence by the recipient toward the caregiver. This scenario appears to be similar to the "double direction violence" described by Steinmetz (1981). There were no differences in mean disruptive behavior scores between the two groups. Spouses predominated among those who actually committed violence (9 out of 14), a finding which is consistent with Pillemer and Finkelhor's (1988) finding that spouses were more likely to engage in physical abuse than other relatives. Pillemer and Suitor speculate that norms against spousal abuse are weaker than norms against abuse of a parent by an adult child. Thus, spouses can engage in violence more freely than other relatives.

The source of the care recipient's violent behavior deserves exploration. Some confused and frightened elders who are incapable of mediating verbally and who fear being harmed may strike out at those who are closest to them, their caregivers. In some cases, an elder's impairment may contribute to interactional stressors, which in turn lead to violence by the caregiver. While the elder's ADL status alone does not explain violence or the fear of becoming violent, it is not possible to abandon entirely the causal concepts related to elder impairment that were popular earlier. Calling a confused elder's striking out and a caregiver's hitting back "interactional behaviors" renames what happens when an impaired elder's condition causes stress in a caregiver. An impaired elder's communication difficulties may produce socially disturbing behaviors toward which caregivers have negative reactions.

### Potential for Abuse

Bendik (1992) evaluated the effects of personal and situational variables on coping and mood and the potential of caregivers to mistreat. In this study, 110 Caucasian caregivers over age 55 in private residences in California were recruited and interviewed (all recipients of care in the study were elderly).

Mood disturbance was the strongest predictor of the potential to abuse; but perceiving one's situation as stressful was *not* associated with the potential to abuse. Deficits in physical health and social supports, inadequate income, an external as opposed to an internal "locus of control," and not using self-blame as a coping mechanism but using fantasy instead—combined with mood disturbance—accounted for 46% of the variance in abuse potential. Although this study deals with stress as a potential explanatory variable, it cannot be compared with the studies mentioned above, because Bendik considered only the potential to mistreat as measured by a modified HALF scale (Ferguson & Beck, 1983), not actual mistreatment.

## In Conclusion: The Stressed Caregiver

In the early 1980s, frailty and dependency of the elder were cited as a cause of stress that in turn contributed to abuse. Wolf and Pillemer (1989) noted that more recent studies did not support this concept; no direct correlation can be assumed between the dependency of an elder and abuse. Yet stress as a factor cannot be dismissed totally if aggressive behaviors of the elder are considered to be stressors as well. The question for researchers and practitioners remains: Does the "stressed caregiver" concept still hold for elder mistreatment if the elder's aggressive behaviors, currently known as an "interactional stressor," are acknowledged as stemming from his or her own impairment and dependency? A more useful statement of the concept of the impaired elder may be: Impaired elders are not more likely to be abused because they are unable to protect themselves and are easier targets of abuse; instead, impaired elders who are provocative and disruptive within a caregiving context are more likely to be abused. "Disruptive behaviors" and "interactional stressors" seem to be new labels for the formerly popular explanation "elder dependency and impairment." Care must be taken when using the term "caregiver demand," because it can approach victim-blaming and steer away from holding an abuser accountable. Findings from these studies of the caregiver-elder relationship compel practitioners to ask caregivers about depression, lowered self-esteem, and fear of becoming violent as well as assisting them in finding ways to alleviate their symptoms. Discussing "double direction" violence with the caregiver in a matter-of-fact manner may uncover actual incidents and provide an opportunity for appropriate intervention.

## 3. LEARNED VIOLENCE

This section discusses another popular concept, learned violence. This third theory of how elder mistreatment occurs draws on research and clinical work that has been done in recent decades regarding child abuse and neglect as well as spouse abuse. Although it remains for future researchers to find specific relationships between these types of domestic abuse and elder mistreatment, a brief review of the issues relating to domestic violence is important to the understanding of learned violence as a causal concept.

### Domestic Violence

#### *Background*

Child abuse and neglect have been defined as such only within this century. Historically, children were viewed as the possession of the male head of the household and were considered his property to do with as he chose. It was thought that children needed to be trained and that it was the parent or guardian's responsibility to see that they learned their duties. Some young noblemen had whipping boys so that they could escape being punished personally (Radbill, 1968). This harsh treatment of children has been controversial, with an increasing number of voices objecting and drawing attention to the rights of children. The current wave of concern is the result of advances in X-ray technology. In 1946, Caffey published findings that called attention to the common association of subdural hematomas with abnormal X-ray changes in the long bones of children (Caffey, 1946). Later observers corroborated these findings, and it was gradually realized that these injuries had been willfully inflicted. In 1961, the American Academy of Pediatrics held a symposium on the subject, which by then had been had been called, by Kempe, the "battered child syndrome" (Radbill, 1968). Gradually, government agencies became interested and funding was supplied for research grants. Currently all of the 50 states have mandatory reporting laws, and services for both parents and children are widespread. Nevertheless, practitioners in the field point to the need for better understanding and more programs. Only since the 1980s has the hitherto taboo subject of sexual abuse of children begun receiving national attention.

Concern about spouse abuse has arisen only since the 1970s, stimulated by the book *Scream Quietly or the Neighbors Will Hear,* which was published in 1974 by the English author Erin Pizzey. That book was followed in 1976 by Del Martin's pioneering book, *Battered Wives.* Women too have been historically viewed as the property of the male head of the household and therefore subject to his control. Wife beating has been condoned for centuries and encouraged as a way of preserving control. It has been sanctioned by church authorities as a form of instructional discipline for actions on the part of women which their husbands found unacceptable. Martin (1976) notes that at least one society issued instructions detailing the circumstances under which a man might most effectively beat his wife. Actual murder of women, femicide, has not always been viewed with concern. There are still many societies that look upon women as second-class citizens or as the legal possessions of the head of the household. Wife battering remains common.

Very little evidence is available to describe what happens when the battered woman grows old. However, one descriptive study (Gesino, Smith, & Keckich, 1982) verifies some observations similar to those for younger battered women, and Wolf and Pillemer's (1995) recent comparison of 22 cases of abused older wives and 53 abused mothers provides some insights. Two different profiles emerged from Wolf and Pillemer's study. The abused wives were more likely to be victims of physical abuse, with slapping being the most common form of physical abuse; they were more apt to feel lonely, to need assistance from the abuser with their activities of daily living, and to be dependent on the abuser for companionship. In contrast, the older abused mothers were subjected to verbal abuse, such as insults and swearing, and were more likely to be abused financially. As had been found in previous studies, the abusive grown children were more likely to be dependent on their parents for housing and money. These abusive children were more likely to have problems with alcohol and substance abuse than the abusive spouses. Wolf and Pillemer conclude that for these two distinct groups, different intervention approaches are needed. The abused spouses may benefit from the services commonly available for spousal abuse and domestic violence in general: legal protection, criminal prosecution, incarceration, and battered women's shelters. For the abused parents, interventions may be more abuser-focused, including mental health services, job counseling, treatment for substance abuse, and housing.

Gesino, Smith, and Keckich (1982) studied two older women—one age 73 and married for 37 years, the other age 76 and married for 47 years—

who had been admitted to an adult psychiatric ward with diagnoses of depression. Both women were described by their children as having been physically and psychologically abused for most of their married lives. The authors note that both women "became depressed as a result of the loss of the familiar pattern of relating, and the shift from a submissive role to a dominant one." Neither woman would discuss the abuse she had received; according to both, abuse was not a problem. The women did not feel it was proper to share the intimate details of their marriages with others. Divorce was not an option for either of them, and each felt that her husband could not control his behavior—neither man was held accountable for his actions. Each women accepted the man as the authority in the house and had no social life other than what he permitted. In fact, these women had no friends of their own. Both women demonstrated a strong sense of loyalty to their husbands.

The women had different reasons for staying in the marriage, besides the stigma of divorce. One felt that it was her responsibility to stay and make the marriage work, and the other felt that her primary role in the marriage was to fulfill her husband's demands. The latter also felt that she was not a good person, and the abuse served to confirm her feelings. Both women had low self-esteem, understandably limited social skills, and a passive interpersonal style, which was probably adaptational. Both showed vegetative signs of depression, such as eating disturbances and declines in personal care and sleep. Both responded to long-term inpatient treatment, which included individual and group psychotherapy, socialization, medication, and electroconvulsive treatments.

### Incidence of Domestic Violence

Two nationwide studies on domestic violence have been conducted so far. The results of the first study were published in *Behind Closed Doors: Violence in the American Family* (Straus et al., 1980), those of the second study were published in *Intimate Violence: The Causes and Consequences of Abuse in the American Family* (Gelles & Straus, 1988). For the first survey, the researchers studied 2,143 intact, mentally healthy families who were selected randomly. The second survey consisted of 6,002 telephone interviews. Children under the age of 3 were not included. Neither were elders. For both studies, violence, defined as "any act carried out with the intention or perceived intention of causing pain or injury to another person," was found to be widespread in the United States. Most incidents were minor assaults such as pushing, slapping, or shoving. But more severe violence—including kicking, biting, hitting with a fist, battering or trying to batter with an object, threatening the other with a knife or gun, or actually using a knife or a gun—were quite common. Approximately 6 out of every 100 married couples in the first study admitted to being involved in one of these acts. Twenty-eight percent of the spouses also reported having engaged in at least one act of violence during their marriage.

In the first study, the incidence of wife beating was 3.8%; but it dropped to 3% in the second survey; the incidence of husband beating was 4.6% in the first survey and remained about the same in the second, 4.4%. The higher rate for husband beating probably represents retaliation on the part of the wife or violence by both parties. Other studies have noted that men engage in more violent actions than women, and they inflict more serious damage. Walker (1984) found that women may strike back at the men who batter them, but their efforts to stop the abuse are usually futile and the harm they inflict on the men is minimal, although the net effect may be that the severity of their own injuries is lessened. The women in Walker's study tended to be less violent when they were not living with a violent man.

For children, the figures on violence are higher; for the first survey, 14 out of 100 children age 3 to 17 were the victims of severe violence in a given year, which meant that 6.5 million children were victimized during the survey year. Because many people consider hitting a child with a belt or a hairbrush to be acceptable, the researchers separated that action out from the category of severe violence. They then found that 36 out of every 1,000 children were victimized each year; 1.4 million children faced being kicked, bitten, punched, or beaten up by a parent, or threatened or actually attacked with a knife or a gun. In the second survey, the figure for parents using abusive violence dropped from 36 to 19 per 1,000 children. This translates into 700,000 fewer children being victimized in 1985 than in 1975.

Given that the rate of street violence is 1 per 100,000, the family is where most people learn to act in violent ways. There is a greater chance of being assaulted in one's own home than on even the most dangerous of city streets. One argument against the claim that child and spousal abuse have declined is that the findings were inaccurate, owing to the differences in methodology between the two surveys. The telephone survey method of 1985 failed to capture the habits of those without telephones, 5% of households. Another explanation for the decrease is that after 10 years there was a greater reluctance to report mistreatment because of increased public condemnation of abuse. In spite of these arguments, Gelles and Straus (1988) contend that the rates of violence have declined in one decade and could be due to changes in five areas: (1) family structure, including later age at marriage and later onset of childbearing, leading to fewer children per family; (2) an improved economy; (3) more legal and environmental alternatives for battered women; (4) greater availability of treatment programs for abusers and victims; and (5) more widely publicized deterrents from the criminal justice system.

## Intergenerational Transmission of Violence

Many observers have concluded that domestic violence such as child abuse and neglect and spouse abuse is learned in the home and passed from one generation to the next (Ackley, 1977; Hotaling & Sugarman, 1986; Kempe & Kempe, 1978; Martin, 1976; Pizzey, 1974; Rosenbaum & Maiuro, 1990; Roy, 1982; Sonkin & Durphy, 1982; Straus, 1979a; Straus et al., 1980, Walker, 1979, 1984).

Walker (1984) interviewed 435 women who volunteered to talk about the physical violence they had suffered at the hands of their men and found that the men tended to be generally violent people with a high incidence of other violent activity. Men who abused their partners tended to have more arrests and convictions and to be involved in more incidents of child abuse than nonbattering men. Sonkin and Durphy (1982), who have treated battering men, found that 65% of male abusers came from homes in which they saw their father abuse their mother or where they themselves were abused. These men have learned that physical violence against others is a legitimate way to deal with anger, stress, interpersonal conflict, and frustration. The best indicators as to whether a man will be violent in a relationship seem to be past incidents of violence either in his home or toward pets, a previous criminal record, or longer time spent in military service where specific training for violence takes place (Walker, 1984).

In the first national survey on family violence, Straus et al. (1980) found that men who have seen their parents attack each other are three times as likely to hit their wives than others, and the statistics are roughly the same for women. On the other hand, people whose parents were never violent toward them had the lowest rate of spouse abuse—2 percent, the researchers found. One third of parents with teenagers reported hitting them; 37.3% had been hit by their own parents when they were teenagers. Adults who had received most punishment as teenagers had a rate of spouse beating four times greater than those whose parents did not hit them. Age was also a factor in spouse abuse. People under 30 were more active in every form of domestic violence. Also, a low income was found to be correlated with spouse abuse.

As in the national survey, Walker (1984) found in her study that most wife batterers had always lived in homes filled with violence: spouse or child abuse had occurred in 81% of their childhood homes, as compared with 24% of the nonviolent men's homes. The majority of the abusive men (63%) saw their fathers beat their mothers. In 61% of the homes, the men were battered by their fathers, and in 44 percent they were battered by their mothers; in some cases both parents battered. Victims of spouse battering also reported battering in their backgrounds. Over 66% of battered women came from homes where battering occurred (Walker, 1984), though another study reported a figure of only 35% (Roy, 1982). Walker (1984) found more than half of spouse abusers also beat their children, and that battered women were more likely to discipline their children physically when living with their batterers.

The death of children from child abuse may be directly related to incidents of spouse abuse. Weston (1968) reported on a study of 23 children who came to a hospital or medical doctor in a terminal condition or postmortem. The average age of the children was 24 months. In cases where the mother was the assailant, several mothers said they had been beaten in childhood and also in the weeks and months prior to the death of the child.

Given this abundance of research, it is widely believed that children who observe violence in the home or who are victims of violence grow up to be abusive or violent. Yet this explanation of transmission does not explain why *most* children who experience or witness violence do *not* exhibit violent behaviors as adults. Citing other colleagues' works, Gelles and Straus estimate the rate of intergenerational transmission of violence to be about 30 percent. While 30% is a minority, it is at least 10 times greater than the average rate of abusive violence for the general population, which is less than 3% (Gelles & Straus, 1988). Hunter and Kilstrom (1979), studying parents who did *not* repeat the cycle of abuse, found that they shared the following characteristics: They had more social supports, fewer ambivalent feelings about their pregnancies, and healthier babies; they also had one parent who was supportive if the other was abusive; and they were more free in their expressions of anger about the abuse.

## *Application to Elder Mistreatment*

While the concept of intergenerational transmission of violence is almost as popular as the concept of the stressed caregiver, it has not been supported by the research on elder mistreatment. In the Three Model Projects, when the victim's child was the abuser, the elders were asked about their method of punishment when their children were young. Only one person in the abuser group and one in the comparison group mentioned physical punishment, with most saying that no physical force, or no punishment at all, was used (Wolf & Pillemer, 1989). At this time a paucity of information makes it impossible to form conclusions on the use of this concept. Although abusive behaviors could be passed on generationally, different dynamics could be taking place; that is, the abusive child may harm the elder for retaliatory and not imitative reasons (Korbin, Anetzberger, & Eckert, 1989; Wolf & Pillemer, 1989) . Homer and Gilleard (1990) report anecdotally that one of the caregiving sons reported that his father had always been sadistic and the son was now paying him back. Instead of focusing on childhood treatment of the abuser, it may be beneficial for future research to focus on how the abusive child's parents treated the grandparents and whether the abuser had a history of observing parent-to-grandparent mistreatment during childhood and adolescence.

In a comparison of physically abusive children of elder parents ($N$=23) and physically abusive parents of children who were 2 to 5 years old, ($N$=21), Korbin, Anetzberger, and Austin (1995), utilizing the Conflict Tactics Scales, found that the elder abusers and the child-abusing parents did not differ significantly in their overall experience of violence as children. However, the child-abusing parents were significantly more likely than the elder abusers to have experienced, as children, the more severe forms of violence listed in the Conflict Tactics Scales, including being kicked, bitten, or hit with a fist; hit with an object (or subjected to an attempt to hit them with an object); being threatened with a knife or a gun; or being beaten up by their parents. Although the authors conclude that intergenerational transmission of family violence is a construct more applicable to child abuse than to elder abuse, they note that some of the results of data analysis cannot be ignored. Approximately one third of the child-abusing parents did not report abuse as children, and one fourth of the elder-abusing adult children reported physical abuse during their childhood by their now elderly parents.

## Comparison Between the Various Types of Domestic Abuse

The theory that violence is learned behavior, taught in families and perpetuated through generations, is convincing. Astonishingly, elderly people have for the most part been ignored by the major studies on domestic violence. It is almost as if domestic violence vanishes when a family member turns 65, no matter how violent the elder may have been throughout life or how much he or she may have been victimized. This is, of course, highly unlikely. The evidence with regard to learned violence is overwhelming and should be a red flag to geriatric practitioners. Questions about family violence should be woven into every interview situation with older adults and their caregivers. This includes caregivers who are not family members. Given the high rate of family violence, it is obvious that many nonfamily caregivers have grown up in violent homes and may look upon violence as a way of shutting up a complaining elder. Added to this is the reality that many nonfamily caregivers and their elderly charges form familylike relationships and may transfer old family patterns of interacting onto any intimate situation.

The problems confronting practitioners are greater with elder mistreatment because of the complexity of the needs of elders, especially their physical needs. Leaving the home where the abuser is the sole caregiver presents many problems, especially if the elder owns the home. The question of who should leave becomes an issue, and so does the question of who should do the caregiving. Currently, nursing home placement is the most widely used and probably the most feared alternative. Recently, more assisted living facilities are being built and have provided a better alternative. Shelters for abused women have traditionally shied away from taking in older women, because they did not have the necessary resources to care for elderly victims, but the situation is changing (Vinton, 1992). Recently several groups have been funded by the Administration on Aging to provide comprehensive services to battered elders, including shelter care. An exploratory study by Salamone and Berman (1995) in New York state examined the use of domestic violence shelters by elder mistreatment victims. Through a questionnaire, the study found that elderly victims were assisted rarely. Each shelter assisted an average of 7 victims who were 60 years old or older. Some of the directors of these shelters noted that they were unprepared to serve elderly victims adequately because of the older victims' physical limitations and mental impairment, and because of age differences. Staff training on gerontology and the elimination of physical barriers were cited as areas in need of attention.

One aspect of elder abuse and neglect is different from other forms of domestic violence. Elderly people are more likely than children or younger women to have money and to own property. In 1993, of the 20.9 million older persons who were heads of households, 77% were owners and 23% were renters. Older male householders were more likely to be owners (85%) than were females (67%) (American Association of Retired Persons, 1994). These homes were acquired at a time when home ownership was economically feasible and expected; many older people have lived their entire adult lives in the same house. Over the years, the homes have increased greatly in value, and they represent security and safety to their elderly owners, who may not be aware of their market value. The inflated value of the homes makes them a target for fraudulent practices on the part of the unscrupulous strangers, "friends," and family.

## 4. THE IMPAIRED ABUSER

The theories in this fourth category focus on the role of the abuser as the sole factor in elder mistreatment. The abusers are seen as having profound disabling conditions: addiction to alcohol or other drugs, a sociopathic personality, serious psychiatric disturbances, dementia, mental retardation, or chronic inability to make appropriate judgments about the care of a dependent elder. In cases of domestic violence that end in death, one study found a strong likelihood that autopsies and other postmortem tests will reveal use of alcohol and other drugs by the perpetrator, the victim, or both at the time of the fatal incident (Slade, 1990; Slade, Daniel, & Heisler, 1991). What is still unclear, however, is whether there is a causal relationship between substance use and domestic violence, and the direction of the causal arrow, if one exists.

In the early phases of research on elder mistreatment, substance abuse was mentioned in a few publications as a major correlate (Douglass et al., 1980; Lau & Kosberg, 1979) and targeted as a risk factor in assessment instruments (Breckman & Adelman, 1988; Fulmer & O'Malley, 1987; Tomita, 1982). An evaluation of the data based on 328 cases of elder mistreatment from the Three Model Projects on Elder Abuse by Wolf et al., (1986) confirmed alcohol abuse as a strong correlate of physical and financial abuse. In addition, comparing 42 physically abused elders in the project who were matched with 42 nonabused elders, Pillemer found that the abusers were more likely to be identified as alcoholics (45.2 % versus 7.1%). Bristowe and Collins (1989), comparing 29 abusive situations with 39 "appropriate care" situations, also found an association between alcohol use by the caregiver and elder abuse.

More recently, in a comparison group study of abusing and nonabusing caregivers, Anetzberger et al. found that the abusers were more likely to use and abuse alcohol, to become intoxicated, and to be identified as having a drinking problem (1994). While the differences between the two groups were statistically significant, the data are not generalizable to abusing and nonabusing adult children, since the subjects were limited to those receiving services from agencies or hospitals. An important thought for future research, based on a paradigm by the anthropologists MacAndrew and Edgerton (1969), is offered in this study. Alcohol consumption is used as an excuse for normatively unacceptable behavior, including elder abuse; that is, the abuse is attributed to the effects of the alcohol, freeing the abuser from blame or from being regarded as willfully malicious.

Wolf and Pillemer (1984) call attention to the many cases they found in their research which indicate that a large number of abusers are dependent on their victims financially, emotionally, and for housing. They called this phenomenon a "web of mutual dependency." Pillemer (1985a, 1985b) focused on 42 cases of physical abuse from the above research and found that 64% of the abusers were financially dependent on their victims, and 55% were dependent on their victims for housing. In general, Pillemer found that physical abusers were frequently heavily dependent people. Psychopathology of the individual was found to be one of the main causes of mistreatment in a national survey of elder mistreatment in Canada as well (Podnieks, 1992a, 1992b). Over half (56%) of the abusers had mental or emotional problems and almost three fourths (70%) were dependent on their victims for financial support:

> An elderly stroke victim was living alone and recovering well. The van came every day and took her to a rehabilitation center. Her son was divorced, allegedly because his wife could no longer stand the beatings he administered. After the divorce he came home to live with his mother because he had no financial resources. He immediately began interfering with her treatment plan, first by forbidding her to go to the rehabilitation center and then by telling her that the only therapy she needed was to go out into the backyard and pull the weeds, which were nearly 4 feet high.

With time and further research, it is possible that this category of impaired abusers will be smaller than others, but there will always be situations where it applies. Within the broader field of domestic violence, in which research has been conducted for a longer period, it is now considered to be a myth that abusers are mostly psychotic or mentally ill. All demographic groups are represented among perpetrators and victims of domestic violence (Sonkin, Martin & Walker, 1985). Gelles and Straus (1988) estimate that at present only 10% of abusive incidents are attributable to mental illness.

Citing the works of colleagues in the research on batterers, Walker reports that a set of typologies of batterers has been developed: (1) those who batter at home, motivated by power and control needs; (2) those who have serious psychological problems; and (3) those who have committed crimes outside the home as well as within the home. Even though the behaviors involved in domestic violence are similar, she cautions that, "the psychological and physiological processes may be so different that different treatment methods are necessary to avoid escalating the violence" (Walker, 1995, p. 267). Given this and applying such findings to batterers of elders, it could be that there are representatives of all three typologies who cohabit with elders and who claim to be caregivers.

These abusers can be the most difficult for practitioners to work with. They may not respond to traditional or even innovative interventions. They may be cavalier in their treatment of a frail elder and blithely ignore the elder's basic needs, such as food, clothing, shelter, and medical care, despite repeated interventions by the practitioner. Often they fail to see any connection between their actions and injuries to the elder. They cannot or will not exercise judgment, even if given new information and followed over a long period of time by an experienced and sympathetic practitioner. Some give elaborate and preposterous explanations for their abusive behavior. Frequently, the practitioner is hard put to it to find genuine concern for the elder in the abuser's attitude (Ramsey-Klawsnik, 1995).

The abusers who have sociopathic tendencies or personalities may totally disregard conventional mores and may offend or even violate cultural standards—for example, they may have served time in prison. They are unable to form meaningful relationships or identify with others, and they exhibit a remarkable lack of conflict, guilt, anxiety, and insecurity. They do not seem to profit by experience and seem unable to control their impulses (Brantley & Sutker, 1984). Often they appear intellectually intact, even

bright, but they are incapable of following through on a practitioner's recommendations even when they promise to do so. This can be very confus-
ing for the practitioner, who is accustomed to associating intellectual
functioning with appropriate actions. Some abusers have extremely charming and magnetic personalities, while at the same time demonstrating an
emotional immaturity and callousness that can be shocking. People with
sociopathic tendencies or personalities often cheat, lie, or steal, even when
there seems to be no particular advantage to doing so (Manfreda &
Krampitz, 1977). Some clinicians have noted that the cases involving the
most damaging physical abuse—cases which also involve sexual abuse—
are frequently associated with sociopathic sons and their elderly mothers.
The adult sons live at home, because they never achieved the maturity necessary to leave, because they came home to live with a widowed mother
after a failed marriage (which may have been marred by spouse battering),
or because they couldn't function in a competitive society. Some of the sons
have sustained severe and permanent brain damage from indiscriminate and
prolonged use of street drugs or alcohol. These sons, who seem outside the
mainstream of society, and oddly different from their peers, may have failed
to complete an earlier stage of psychosocial development (Ostrovski, 1979).
In one case, the mother was able to report what happened:

> She and her son had lived together for a very long time. He had returned
> home after failed efforts at employment and was living off her money. In fact,
> he invaded a trust fund that was meant for a mentally disabled sister. During
> this time period, he was having sex with his mother. She reported that he
> would hold pieces of her good china and would throw them to the floor and
> break them until she consented to have sex with him.

A study focusing solely on adult offspring as abusers (Anetzberger,
1987) outlined three major categories of abusers: (1) those who were hostile, (2) those who were authoritarian, and 3) those who were dependent
(Anetzberger, 1987). The first group, the "hostiles," had long-term relationship problems with the parent and considered the parent to be a "mental case." They seemed to prefer the elderly parent to be passive or even
dead. In this group there was a history of the abuser having been abused as
a child by the parent. The abusers in the "hostile" group were the best educated but saw themselves as underachievers and blamed their lack of success on the parent. They found caring for the parent extremely burdensome
and were the most abusive of the abusers, but they felt that they had to take

care of the parent, that it was expected by others in the family. They also felt that they were the only ones who could do it.

The second group, the "authoritarians," consisted of those who were married and leading lives that would be well accepted in any community. However, they were also rigid, punitive, intolerant of ambiguity, and domineering to subordinates, while at the same time servile to superiors. They had a need to control and were inflexible with respect to household routines and other standards. They were not mentally ill, but they were rigid in their expectations for themselves and their parents, sometimes to the point of disregarding the impairments the elder was suffering. They punished the elder and described the elder as having been authoritarian with them when they were children. In fact, they tended to infantilize the elder and were particularly resentful if the elder spoke to "outsiders" about family business.

The third category of abusers were described as "dependent." These abusers were financially dependent on their elderly parents and in most cases had lived with the parent for the entirety of the last 2 years. They seemed to represent the "losers" in life. They were poorly groomed, seemed quite immature, and never achieved the emotional, economic, or social status expected of American adults. They were attached to the parent in a childlike fashion and seemed to have no desire to alter their circumstances. They were unmarried, poorly educated, and unemployed, and had low incomes. Of the three groups, they were the most isolated and the most likely to admit to inflicting harm on an elderly parent.

Some adult children may be actively abusing chemical substances. On one geropsychiatric unit, the staff noticed that the daughter of a severely demented man visited her father an average of once a month. Gradually, the staff realized that the daughter, an obvious heroin addict, was coming to the unit the first week of every month and bringing her father's Social Security check so that he could sign it over to her. She would then cash the check and keep the money to support her habit. The staff remedied the situation by finding a responsible party to serve as the representative payee for the checks. In another drug-related situation, an elderly woman who was mentally impaired was found sleeping on municipal buses night after night. A bus driver finally reported the situation to his supervisor, who called social services. It was discovered that her son, a drug addict, had gained title to her house and had sold it to an innocent third party. The mother literally had no place to go until she was placed in a board and care home and public benefits were instated. She was not only demented; she was psychologically in shock.

Some caregivers were once institutionalized themselves. Beginning in the early 1960s, the treatment and custodial care of developmentally disabled people and chronically ill psychiatric people began shifting from large rural facilities to "the community"—a euphemistic term for urban board and care homes where the staff has minimal training. Typically, there were (and still are) few community resources for these emotionally and cognitively impaired people. Some went to live with their aging parents. (Others had always lived with their parents because their parents fought to keep them out of an institution or because they were unable to separate themselves from the impaired child.) There may be no other siblings, or if there are, they leave the family home and go on to their own careers, perhaps relocating in other states. This leaves the impaired sibling to do the caregiving should the parent become dependent.

A caregiver who suffers from dementia is most likely to be a spouse. The elderly couple live together and have become isolated. The demented spouse is physically healthy, while the physically fragile spouse is mentally intact. Together, they make "one whole person." As the demented spouse's illness progresses, so do the mate's physical incapacities, until there is a severely demented caregiver and a bed-bound invalid. Abuse becomes a possibility. Often both individuals need a protected setting, and they may consent to being placed in the same facility and sharing a room. It should be noted, however, that not all aged married couples want to live in the same room or even in the same facility. A physical illness or mental impairment may bring about a separation that the partners have long desired but did not know how to initiate.

Sometimes, those handling the affairs of others become incapable themselves.

An 81-year-old woman who had been a yeomanette in World War I became emotionally depressed and unable to function in the 1950s, when her job was phased out in a corporate merger. She admitted herself to a Veterans' Hospital and took up residence there. She was ambulatory, alert, and oriented. She had her hair done weekly, attended luncheon parties, and engaged in other social activities associated with a leisurely lifestyle. She also visited her brother in a convalescent hospital. He had been her guardian until he became incapacitated and turned her affairs over to his law partner. The law partner, an elderly man, was for several years very faithful in sending her $200 monthly allowance, but gradually he began to forget to do it or sent it so late that the woman was greatly inconvenienced. From conversations with other people, the woman ascertained that the law partner was "slipping" and came to believe that he was "senile." She asked the court's help in terminating the guardianship. A public defender was appointed to represent her, and she was restored to capacity after it was learned that her pension checks could be sent directly to Patient Accounts at the VA hospital; she would then have direct access to her funds, and the accounting department would have a supervisory role. The retired yeomanette gained a great deal of self-confidence and felt even more independent once she was able to have control of her funds.

## 5. SOCIETAL ATTITUDES AS CONTRIBUTORS TO ELDER MISTREATMENT

There are several societal attitudes that contribute to elder mistreatment. While not causes in themselves, these attitudes create an atmosphere that paves the way for maltreatment of the elderly. Among these attitudes are ageism, attitudes toward the disabled, sexism, and plain old-fashioned greed.

### Ageism

Myths and stereotypes about the old and the process of aging are widespread and contribute to a pervasive prejudice against elders. This prejudice is called *ageism* and is defined as:

> a process of systematic stereotyping of and discrimination against people because they are old, just as racism and sexism accomplish this with skin color and gender. Old people are categorized as senile, rigid in thought and manner, old-fashioned in morality and skills. . . . Ageism allows the younger generations to see older people as different from themselves; thus they subtly cease to identify with their elders as human beings (Butler & Lewis, 1973).

In our fast-moving technological society, older people are often seen as having nothing to offer, as being in the way of "progress," or as having no future. In fact, they are shunned and avoided, especially if they are impaired. The old are frequently removed from the mainstream by placement in segregated institutions such as nursing homes and retirement communities. Aging or infirmity has become a stigma. The unique set of personality characteristics; the yearnings, triumphs, and strengths which make up a life; the knowledge gained from overcoming personal handicaps and surviving tragedies and fears; the growth achieved through loving others and one's own imperfect self—these have little value when measured against the visual reality of graying hair, arthritic joints, facial wrinkles, and minor memory losses. Old age has become synonymous with loss of personal power, disability, and lack of control over one's own life. When aging is seen in that light, it is little wonder that there is so much ambivalence about growing old, and it is understandable that ageism has arisen as a way of distancing ourselves from and fending off old age. Ageism serves to protect younger generations against thoughts of growing old and impaired, and especially against death. But the respite is temporary. With each advancing year, and particularly in late middle age, the realities of physical aging become apparent. Ageism is a time bomb of the most personal nature because most people hope for a long life and, if they get their wish, will end up as part of the very group toward which they have always harbored prejudice. They become targets of their own internalized myths and stereotypes about aging. Ageism is alive and well, and is a real potential in everyone.

There are many false beliefs about growing old: "Everyone ages at the same rate." "Aging lowers productivity and leads to a desire to disengage from life." "Older people are inflexible and less adaptable to change than younger people." "Old age inevitably brings senility." "The older people become, they are more likely to become forgetful" (Butler, 1975).

The myths about memory loss may be the most damaging of all. While some forgetting is common in aging, pathological memory loss occurs in only a small percentage of older adults. Less serious forgetting occurs throughout the lifespan. We are likely to forget things that are too unpleasant to remember. For example, the pain involved in giving birth to a child or the details of a traumatic event such as a divorce tend to fade with time. We also forget when we are distracted, in a hurry, or under a great deal of stress. And yet, after a certain age, the explanation most people seize upon for minor lapses of memory is that the person "must be getting old" or—more recently—that "Alzheimer's disease must be setting in."

For some people, anxiety about forgetting prompts even more memory lapses, until they lose all confidence in their power to remember. They may feel that this is the normal course of events. After all, "Doesn't everyone become senile with age?" This, in fact, is one danger of stereotyping; the victim comes to believe the myths and to act accordingly. The myths are also reinforced by others who believe them. Snyder (1982), who has investigated self-fulfilling stereotyping, noted that when prejudiced people deal with the objects of their biases, they often elicit the behavior they expect.

In fact, they tend to selectively notice and remember the ways in which a person reinforces their biases and to resist evidence contradicting the stereotypes. Thus, those who harbor negative attitudes toward the aged may actually cause an elder to act in a negative or powerless way, or in a way which reinforces myths and stereotypes about aging. Prejudice is learned at an early age and is deeply held, perhaps sometimes at an unconscious level. It is difficult to dislodge.

Ageism shows up in the use of language. Most of the adjectives or adverbs used to describe aging are negative. Aged wine, cheese, or lace may be looked on with respect and valued, but this is rarely true with aged people. Nuessel (1982) notes that positive attributes descriptive of aging— mature, mellow, sage, veteran—are sparse. He lists 75 terms he considers ageist, including *battle-ax, decrepit, fogy, goat, old-fashioned, obsolete, over the hill, second childhood, toothless,* and *wizened.* Many of these terms become even more denigrating if the word *old* is placed in front of them. Medical professionals reveal their negative attitudes in the terms they often use to describe the elderly, referring to old people as *crocks, codgers, hypochondriacs* or, for women, *douche bags* (Brown, 1978).

Ageism is also apparent in social policy and government funding patterns. For instance, there has always been more public funding for child protective services than for adult protective services, clear evidence that children are more valued than elders and that there is more interest in the future than in the past. Studies of family violence, though well researched and documented, have always excluded the elderly, for reasons that are not entirely clear. It may have been inconceivable that elderly parents would ever be abused because of the religious imperative found in many faiths which instructs children to honor their parents. Or perhaps the idea was just too painful to contemplate.

Many people, even lawyers and physicians, still assume that all impaired older people belong in nursing homes and should be under conservatorships. In fact, in many states just being old is reason enough to have a guardianship or conservatorship imposed, regardless of functioning or abilities. Ageist attitudes are as common in the legal system as anywhere else. One lawyer, referring to a severely mentally impaired woman, called her a "fruitcake," a "vegetable," and a "slab of meat." Social workers dealing with the case were puzzled by the attorney's use of food images to describe the client, but it was clear to them that he did not regard the elderly woman as human.

Medical practices tend to be ageist in part because medical students receive little, if any, training in gerontology. Conditions which produce

temporary symptoms of confusion and disorientation are often misdiag-
nosed as dementia. Thoughtful and meticulous assessment of the complex
medical problems of the elderly is only now beginning to take place.
Ageism can show up in subtle ways. One nursing home house physician
routinely places all residents on salt-free diets, saying, "Well, it can't hurt
them." In fact, those who do not need a salt-free diet are deprived of more
tasty food and eat poorly as a result.

What does ageism have to do with elder mistreatment? Are the two
related and, if so, how? Again, specific research is lacking, but speculations
can be offered.

Through myths and stereotyping, older people come to be seen as nonpersons, as less than human. They are taken less seriously than younger
people and are less valued as human beings by themselves and others. As
a result, mistreatment of the elderly may be viewed as less important than
mistreatment of younger people. Jensen and Oakley (1980) believe there
is sufficient evidence to suggest that the appearance and behavior of old
people was at one time a deterrent to physical attack by others. But appearance is no longer effective and, in fact, may be a stimulus for aggressive
behavior on the part of others. Jensen and Oakley urge older adults to
become more assertive, and to take an active "mastery" approach to their
problems, whether political or personal.

Block and Sinott (1979) note that attitudes, misperceptions, and distortions
may be heavily implicated in abuse, calling for more research into the role
of ageism. They suggest that the old may view abusive treatment as deserved
or unavoidable because they internalize society's negative stereotypes.

## Attitudes toward the Disabled

Negative attitudes toward the disabled may also play a part in elder mistreatment. Many older adults are disabled, and our society has traditionally
viewed disabled people as unproductive and as not contributing to the economy. They are seen as a drain on society and as undesirable. According to
studies by English, nearly half of the nondisabled population hold primarily negative attitudes toward the disabled (English, 1977, 1980). Other studies have indicated that children's stories and comic books often portray evil
characters as having some type of physical abnormality or disability or as
being very unattractive. Butler and Lewis (1982) have noted that there
seems to be a human propensity for hostility toward the handicapped, perhaps based on aversion and revulsion, but possibly also based on the fear

of becoming disabled. Many primitive societies do not permit disabled people to live and put them to death at birth or as soon as disability becomes obvious. This is also true for the aged.

As with other stigmatized groups, the disabled must fight stereotyping by others as well as their own internalized prejudices against their disabled state. The disabled are seen as dependent on the charity of others, and they come to view themselves that way (Johnson, 1983). Thus, there is a self-image that facilitates feelings of helplessness, hopelessness, and vulnerability in disabled people of all ages.

## Sexism

A disproportionate number of victims of elder mistreatment are women. This suggests that sexism may play a part in the maltreatment of elderly women. Over the past two decades, the women's rights movement has documented the ways in which all women lack the power to control their lives. Where older women are concerned, the issue of powerlessness is clear and dramatic, surfacing in such areas as low income, poor health, and negative societal attitudes toward older women.

All women suffer from sexism, whether or not they acknowledge it. Most women (80%) continue to be clustered in a small range of low-paying employment categories, working in jobs which have no potential for potential and pay only 65% of what most men make (Axinn, 1989).

With advancing age, sexism and ageism link and work together to create a poisonous climate for many women. The traditional emphasis on physical beauty as a way to attract a man and to "hold" him screens out the old. Divorce is becoming more and more common after 30 and 40 years of marriage, not always because it is desired by the woman. Older women, particularly the old-old (over 75), are rarely described as attractive or vital or sexually appealing. On the contrary, they are called "hags," "old bags," or worse. Many authors have called attention to the imprisoning roles of adult women: first as partners to men, then as childbearers, and finally as nurses to their ailing husbands in their final illnesses (Brown, 1978; Butler & Lewis, 1982; Pedrin & Brown, 1980; Rathbone-McCuan, 1982). Widowhood, a common condition for old women, who tend to outlive their husbands, contains no ready-made roles for women, although being a grandparent might bring such roles. But the role of grandparent can become attenuated in a world where the nuclear family is often impermanent and people move around the country.

Elderly women are frequently viewed as being in the way or as problems if they are dependent because of their disabilities. With few exceptions, older women are not taken seriously and, in fact, are encouraged to remain passive and invisible. Many older women internalize these negative attitudes and refer to themselves as "useless," especially when they become impaired. It is not uncommon to hear an older woman say, "I have nothing to contribute," or, "I've done all the work God sent me to do," or, "Why am I still here? I just take up space." One elderly woman, newly widowed, said, "Why don't I just die?" Older women often view their economic and health problems as the result of their personal failings. They are not aware that there are other old women who are struggling with the same issues (Brown, 1978; Sommers, 1984).

Many older women are unnecessarily lonely, because they reject close relationships with other women in their age group as unsatisfying (Butler & Lewis, 1982). Often they feel that something is "not quite right" if they are not in the company of a man. This attitude can become more of a problem with age, because fewer and fewer men are available. Elderly women outnumber men three to two. For the oldest women, this inequality is even more pronounced. In 1993, among the older population—people 65 or older—there were 19.2 million older women and 13 million older men, a ratio of 147 women for every 100 men. The ratio increases with age, from 122 women to 100 men for ages 65–69, to 256 women to 100 men for ages 85 and older (American Association of Retired Persons, 1994).

Being old and female in the United States is frequently synonymous with being poor. In 1993, older women had a higher poverty rate (15%) than older men (8%). In addition, 4 of 10 (44%) African American women 75 and older who lived alone were poor, or had incomes less than $6,930 a year, in 1992 (American Association of Retired Persons, 1994). Only 4% of women over age 60 compared with 31% of men receive money from a job, a pension, or any income other than Social Security benefits (Axinn, 1989).

In part, women are excluded from survivor benefits because a husband can choose to have pension benefits paid out only during his own lifetime. Monthly payments are then higher during the husband's lifetime, but they stop when he dies. In some pension plans, men can make this choice without informing their wives. In those cases, although income is sufficient while the husband is alive, poverty descends suddenly on the unsuspecting newly widowed woman. Widowhood can extend over many years. The average age when women become widows is 56 years (Gottlieb, 1989), and a woman who becomes a widow at age 65 lives, on average, another 19.1 years (American Association of Retired Persons, 1994).

Most women who marry will be widowed. In 1993, almost half (48%) of all older women were widows. There were nearly five times as many widows (8.6 million) as widowers (1.8 million), and older men (77%) were nearly twice as likely to be married as older women (42%). These facts reflect the fact that women usually marry men who are older than they are and usually outlive their husbands. Also, men who are widowed or divorced frequently remarry, often to a woman younger than 65. Widows are much less likely to remarry, either because they choose to remain single or because the pool of available men is so small. This means that most women will be single in old age whether or not they were married at one time. It also means that they are more likely to be poor. Older women who are married or living in multigenerational housing have higher incomes than women who live alone. Four of 10 (4%) older African American women who lived alone were poor in 1993 (American Association of Retired Persons, 1994). And of course, if older women become poor and disabled and are forced to live alone, they quickly become dependent on the good graces of others.

Even when a woman is left with what appear to be adequate resources, medical bills can quickly consume them, reducing the woman to poverty. The myth of the rich widow is just that: a myth. Elderly men are much more likely to be wealthy than their female counterparts. The median income of older persons in 1993 was $14, 983 for men and $8,499 for women. Older women had a higher poverty rate (15%) than older men (8%) in 1993 (American Association of Retired Persons, 1994).

This disturbing financial picture is further complicated by the fact that many women have been taught to leave financial management to the man even if that man was not competent financially or did not want financial responsibility. First their husbands managed their finances; then, when they became widows, they relied on their sons or other male relatives or on male lawyers and bankers. Thus most older women are ignorant and virtually helpless when they are eventually forced to handle their own money and as a result become dependent on the good intentions and good judgment of others.

Some elderly widows, lonely and with no male relative to help them with financial affairs, fall prey to male strangers who offer help. In one urban area, for example, a smooth-talking contractor succeeded in ingratiating himself with several mentally impaired elderly women and persuaded them to sign over the title to their homes. He did this did either by outright fraud (having them sign legal documents and not telling them what they were) or by promising to take care of them for the rest of their lives. He then placed the women in nursing homes or otherwise abandoned them. Newspaper accounts noted that in each of these cases, the victims were from a generation in which women were encouraged to rely on the male in the family to make decisions. The contractor sometimes endeared himself to his victim by developing a mother–son relationship. With others, he took the role of the gigolo. Through the diligent efforts of authorities (and because one woman was capable of testifying), the contractor was apprehended, tried, and convicted. He was sentenced to 3 years in connection with the one case. Several of his victims were too mentally impaired to testify, and so the man could not be tried for defrauding them.

With regard to living arrangements, the proportion of elderly people living alone has remained constant, at 30%, since the 1980s. In 1993, 9.4 million of all noninstitutionalized elderly lived alone, with women outnumbering men by over three to one (7.4 million women versus 2 million men). These figures represent 41% of all older women and 16% of all older men (American Association of Retired Persons, 1994). The trend toward living alone in old age is probably due in part to the false value American society places on independence, on not needing anyone to help out with daily living activities. As a result of this attitude, many elderly people feel humiliated and shamed when they finally must accept help because of their infirmities. Few elderly women live in intergenerational households, with children or with other relatives in the home. But as age increases, the number of women living with others increases, suggesting that the women are taken in by their relatives when they can no longer meet their personal needs in their own homes. Often, a medical emergency, such as a stroke or a fractured hip, precipitates the change in living arrangements, and the elder is taken into the relative's home upon discharge from an acute-care hospital. Discharge planners and physicians can help elders and families plan realistically during this time by encouraging them not to make hasty or permanent decisions solely on the basis of crisis situation.

## Greed

Human greed is another societal attitude implicated in elder mistreatment. Anyone in a position of trust is in a position to commit elder mistreatment. A caregiver may wish that a dependent elder would die and "get out of the way" so that the inheritance can be passed on. Some caregivers, trusted by impaired elders, have proceeded to expropriate their funds or property, rationalizing their behavior by saying, "I know she would want me to have it if she were in her right mind," or, "Dad said he wanted to pay for the kids' college education," or, "I need the money now and there is a lot left over after her care is paid for. Why shouldn't I have it now? She's taken care of, and besides, I'll always take care of her if she runs out of money."

These rationalizations ignore the fact that an elder's resources legally belong to him or her and do not revert to the heirs until the elder dies. One grandson could not wait:

A Court Investigation Unit got a call from a convalescent hospital adminis-trator. The administrator was concerned because the grandson of a longtime resident had come in and asked for a list of nursing homes which would accept Medicaid patients. The grandson told the administrator that he had been advised by an attorney to transfer all his grandmother's assets (two parcels of real property plus a substantial amount of cash) into his name and to place his grandmother on public benefits. He quoted the attorney as say-ing that no one would ever check. The administrator knew that the grandson was his grandmother's legally appointed conservator.

When the Court Investigator arrived at the convalescent hospital, she found other matters to be concerned about. The activities director told her that the grandson had confided in her too. He told her that while his mother had been alive and serving as coconservator for his grandmother, she had taken money from the conservatorship estate "anytime she wanted." That was why, he said, his mother had often been delinquent in paying the convalescent hospital's bills. Now that his mother was dead, the grandson felt justified in taking money from the estate himself. He and his wife had recently returned from Hawaii, and he implied that he had used his grandmother's assets to pay for the trip.

The grandmother's clothing was in poor condition; she wore hand-me-downs donated to the nursing home. Personal items such as lotions and pow-ders were provided to her by charitable organizations and by donations from private individuals at Christmastime. The hospital staff had shamed the grand-son into buying one blue dress for his grandmother. However, the grandson regularly claimed reimbursement for clothing in his accountings to the court. The investigator wondered if that was how he had financed his trip to Hawaii.

No rental income was listed for either of the parcels of real property. The grandson occupied one of the parcels but appeared to be paying no rent to the estate. Further, he charged his grandmother's estate for maintenance and repair of the property.

Upon completion of her investigation, the court investigator wrote a polite but pointed letter to the grandson, asking questions regarding the management of his grandmother's estate. When he did not reply, she referred the matter to the court, and the grandson was ordered to come to court and make an accounting directly to the judge in open court.

## SUMMARY

Throughout this chapter on theories of causation of elder mistreatment, the focus has been on probable causes. As O'Malley et al. (1983) note, these hypotheses about the causation of elder mistreatment are not mutually exclusive. For instance, a stressed caregiver could have come from a home filled with violence but could also be mentally ill and trying to cope with an elderly relative whose behavior is disruptive. Such combinations are probably more common than one "pure" causative factor. Elder mistreatment is probably the result of a multiplicity of factors.

The theories described in this chapter have arisen from preliminary research and exploration on the subject of elder mistreatment. Other research, such as the more mature studies on domestic violence, have also contributed. The field of gerontology, too, has much to add to the understanding of elder mistreatment. No doubt further research will refine, confirm, or take issue with some of these theories. But for now, they provide a logical framework which can help practitioners understand the phenomenon of elder mistreatment.

# 'agnosis and Intervention

Systematic and realistic interventions can lead to satisfactory results, even with difficult cases. The purpose of Part Two is to present components of the Elder Abuse Diagnosis and Intervention (EADI) Model. This model, which takes an eclectic approach in treating elder mistreatment, is the result of having examined various assessment and intervention strategies in different disciplines: geriatric nursing, medicine, social work, public health, psychiatry, and psychology.

The EADI Model consists of two phases. The Diagnosis Phase consists of taking the referral, preparing for the assessment interview, and conducting the assessment. Specific protocols and questions are offered to assist practitioners in identifying elder mistreatment in their practice.

The Intervention Phase offers crisis intervention and counseling strategies that can individualize intervention with the elder and the abuser. Termination issues for each of these strategies are also considered. Termination in the Intervention Phase depends on the chosen intervention strategy. A referral to other agencies and plans for follow-up and monitoring procedures may be made. In some cases, termination consists of the practitioner rehearsing with the client and family some future problem scenarios and solutions.

The first stages of the EADI Diagnosis Phase are described in Chapter 5. Issues that arise when the practitioner accepts a referral are presented. People refer suspected cases of elder mistreatment for a variety of reasons, not always out of concern for the elderly client. From the moment a referral is received, the practitioner begins to gather information and develop strategies. Suggestions are made on how to prepare for initial contact and how to obtain access in order to interview the client.

Chapter 6 describes the rest of the Diagnosis Phase, presenting the assessment protocol that is used to diagnose elder mistreatment. Signs and symptoms that may alert the practitioner to elder abuse and neglect are listed. The methods for conducting the functional assessment and the physical examination of the client are described in detail. The specific questions and strategies to be used when interviewing the alleged abuser may alleviate some of the practitioner's anxieties in this difficult period of the assessment process.

Chapters 7, 8, and 9 then discuss the Intervention Phase. The first half of Chapter 7 discusses the factors that affect the choice of intervention method. Among them are the client's capabilities and cooperation as well as the degree of the abuser's pathology. The second half of Chapter 7 describes how the practitioner can utilize crisis intervention strategies to handle medical and financial emergencies. In crisis situations, treatment begins immediately, and the practitioner often functions as a case manager, organizing other practitioners and institutions to save the elder from further harm.

In Chapter 8, the focus of treatment with the victim and the abuser is on problem resolution, with an eye to the future. Since many victims of elder mistreatment will choose to remain with the abuser, it is necessary to work with them as a unit without taking sides. Environmental change, reality orientation, and education can help to prevent and eliminate abusive incidents. In practice, it may take several months for the practitioner to sort out alternatives and options before the appropriate mix of services is in place. Motivations of the elder and of the abuser are also factors. Long-term treatment in the form of group therapy or monitoring activities may be more appropriate when abuse is long-standing; this kind of treatment is also appropriate for elders who respond to a more gradual intrusion of change.

Chapter 9 describes legal intervention, ranging from the least restrictive to the most restrictive legal options that are available to the practitioner and the abused or exploited client. Highlighted are remedies that do not require court involvement, such as helping the client with the direct deposit of his pension check to a bank or obtaining a protective payee. Also highlighted are remedies that require court involvement, such as guardianships or conservatorships. Criminal proceedings are also described. In addition, this chapter gives practitioners suggestions on how to have impact on the judicial system and how to give court testimony.

Part Two ends with Chapter 10, an epilogue in which thoughts for future research, practice, and training are provided.

# CHAPTER 5

# Diagnosis Phase

## I. Preparation for Assessment

### THE EADI MODEL

The Elder Abuse Diagnosis and Intervention (EADI) Model is the result of a desire to present practitioners with a consistent and coherent set of principles and methods for treating elder abuse and neglect. Since resources and the amount of time that is available for a practitioner to carry out a treatment plan vary with agencies and settings, it is sensible to take an eclectic approach. The different treatment approaches that were studied all have the goal of changing, modifying, or improving the client's situation, but the manner in which the goals are accomplished differs among the various approaches (Simon, 1970; Strickler & Bonnefil, 1974).

The EADI Model is an amalgam of different approaches and consists of two phases. The first phase, the Diagnosis Phase, utilizes the traditional psychosocial casework approach (Gambrill, 1983; Lowry, 1957; Simon, 1970); crisis intervention (Aguilera, 1990; Golan, 1978, 1979, 1987; Parad, 1971; Parad & Parad, 1990; Rapoport, 1962, 1970); and psychiatric diagnostic techniques (Folstein, Folstein, & McHugh, 1975; Fillenbaum & Smyer, 1981; Goodwin & Guze, 1984; Kahn, Goldfarb, Pollack, & Peck, 1960, Katz, Ford, Moskowitz, Jackson, & Jaffe., 1963). The nonvoluntary client, a person who does not initiate the request for help but finds himself or herself face to face with a practitioner, may present with ambivalent feelings and with behaviors commonly labeled "resistant." Mitchell (1973), Wasserman (1979), Murdach (1980), and Butler and Lewis (1982) provide suggestions that will engage the client in the helping process, making the transitions from "doing to and for" to "doing with."

The second phase, the Intervention Phase of the EADI Model, is composed of two main sets of strategies: crisis intervention and problem-focused counseling. Ideally it is the need of the client that determines the type and length of treatment. However, various other factors intervene: agency mandate and budget, availability of resources, and the amount of time the practitioner has to provide treatment. Treatment modalities that are utilized in this phase are rich and varied: the psychoanalytic approach as applied to a geriatric population (Butler & Lewis, 1982); cognitive-behavioral therapy (Breckman & Adelman, 1988); learning theory (Carkhuff & Anthony, 1979; Cormier & Cormier, 1985); sociology's neutralization theory as it is applied to the treatment of both the client and the abuser (Tomita, 1990); learning theory as it is clinically applied for the treatment of batterers (Ganley, 1981; Roberts, 1984; Roy, 1982; Sonkin & Durphy, 1982; Sonkin et al. 1985; Star, 1978; Walker, 1979, 1984, 1987, 1991, 1995); pragmatic approaches that are used to diminish and prevent child abuse and neglect (Kempe & Kempe, 1978; Steele & Pollock, 1968); environmental therapy (Butler & Lewis, 1982); group therapy techniques (Burnside, 1976; Ebersole & Hess, 1981, 1985, 1994; Foster & Foster, 1983); and family therapy techniques (Herr & Weakland, 1979).

Having a variety of options allows the practitioner to take a flexible, creative approach. None has a goal of "curing" the client or treating every problem presented to the practitioner. In many cases the focused and individualized treatment plans that are developed by the practitioner may be a combination of two or more treatment approaches. Legal issues weave in and out of all of the suggested intervention strategies, and a separate chapter—Chapter 9, "Legal Intervention"—is devoted to them.

The present chapter describes in detail the role of the practitioner in the first half of the Diagnosis Phase: Assessment. In this period, an assumption is made that "forewarned is forearmed." Cautious collection of available information and the formulation of a tentative treatment plan prior to making the first contact are compatible with crisis-intervention guidelines.

## THE REFERRAL

The purpose of the assessment process is to obtain information and an understanding of the client and the client's situation that will predict and guide the practitioner's intervention. It also marks the beginning of an individualization process that continues until termination (Simon, 1970).

The assessment process usually begins with an initial phone call to the practitioner. From the moment the practitioner receives the phone call he or she must function as a first-class strategist and use all available resources, internal as well as external. That is, the practitioner must use all five senses and rely on intuition as well as use concrete agency resources. In this phase, the practitioner's actions are guided by three assumptions:

- To treat elder abuse and neglect successfully, practitioners of different agencies need each other.
- People who report elder abuse and neglect may themselves be abusive, or they may use a referral as a means of retaliation or revenge. The practitioner cannot assume that reports are made solely out of concern for the elderly.
- In general, people who report elder abuse and neglect expect prompt action on behalf of the victim.

Referrals may come from practitioners, relatives, friends, neighbors, or concerned citizens. Each of these referring groups presents different problems or issues, and the practitioner must take them into consideration during the initial phone call. Regardless of who makes the referral, demographic data and patient information should be obtained:

1. Client's name, address, phone number, age, gender, ethnic background.
2. Client's close relatives and friends and their phone numbers; collateral agency contacts and their phone numbers.
3. Alleged abuser's name, address, and phone number; physical description and knowledge of the abusive behavior; relationship to client; and length of relationship.
4. Description of abuse and neglect, suspicions, and evidence obtained to date. Dates of prior contacts, action taken, and by whom are very helpful.
5. Physician and other known practitioners and their phone numbers.
6. Referrer's name and contact phone numbers; description of referrer's involvement in the case to date; how long referrer has known client.

Bergeron (1989), writing about the process of referral to APS agencies, notes that while reports come from professionals who are often well aware of protective services reporting requirements and the symptoms of elder mistreatment, the lack of an integrated procedure on reporting and responding to reports has resulted in referrers' remaining anonymous and not preparing the client for the investigation or the follow-up activities. Not preparing the client often results in a situation where the APS practitioner faces a suspicious, frightened client who does not accept any services. Instead of keeping the referral from the client, it may be helpful to tell the client that out of concern, a report is being made and that the main purpose is to explore with the client programs and services for which he or she may qualify. At this point, clients may be reminded that their right to self-determination will be maintained, and that once the assessment is conducted, the initiation of services may not occur without their permission (Ostrovski-Quinn, 1985; Quinn, 1985).

## Referral by Practitioners

Practitioners who refer cases may be colleagues in the same agency, employees of another agency, or people in private practice in the community. Table 5-1 shows that health care professionals, including physicians, make up the third largest category of reporters, following service providers and a category that includes all others who do not fit in any of the other categories (Tatara, 1993). This may be due to the fact that over the years, health care practitioners have raised others' awareness of the physical abuse and neglect they have discovered in their everyday work. They were among the first to train their colleagues about treating elder abuse and neglect. Medical associations have distributed pamphlets and brochures on the subject on a local and a national level (e.g., American Medical Association, 1992). Some may be mandated to report elder abuse and neglect; others may call for different reasons. The practitioner must clearly understand the purpose of the referral, which may be one of the following:

- The practitioner is to assume care of the client after the referral is made; the case is transferred permanently.
- The practitioner is asked to do a one-time-only assessment and refer the case back to the referring practitioner or agency.
- The practitioner is asked to function as a consultant, to give advice or suggestions by telephone or in the company of the referring practitioner during the investigative contacts.

**Table 5-1   Categories of Reporters of Domestic Elder Abuse:
Reports for 1990 and 1991**

| | Percentage of reports made | |
|---|---|---|
| Reporter category | 1990 (N=29)* | 1991 (N=25)* |
| Service provider | 28.1% | 26.7% |
| All other types | 18.7% | 21.0% |
| Physician/health care professional | 17.0% | 18.0% |
| Family member/relative | 14.9% | 15.0% |
| Friend/neighbor | 8.8% | 8.2% |
| Elder victim | 5.6% | 4.6% |
| Law enforcement | 4.3% | 4.3% |
| Unknown/missing data | 2.2% | 2.0% |
| Bank/business | 0.2% | 0.2% |
| Clergy | 0.1% | 0.1% |
| | 99.9%** | 100.1% |

*Number of states that provided data.
**Due to rounding errors, the total is not exactly 100.0%.
*Source:* Reprinted from T. Tatara (1993). Understanding the nature and scope of domestic elder abuse with the use of state aggregate data: Summaries of the key findings of a national survey of state APS and aging agencies. *Journal of Elder Abuse and Neglect, 5*(4), 35–57, p. 42.

- The practitioner is asked to collaborate on a case and assist in the development of an assessment and treatment strategy that is to be mutually agreed upon by the referrer and the practitioner accepting the referral.

At first contact, lack of clarity about the role of the agency or the delineation of the task may result in poor or missed communication, mismanagement of the case, and—most important—frustration on the part of the practitioners involved. For example, if the referrer assumes that the practitioner will function as a consultant who will be asked for advice but the practitioner expects to be the client's primary practitioner or case manager, the practitioner may become upset or frustrated if the referrer rejects his or her advice and selects a different intervention option. Practitioners must fully understand the limitations and boundaries of their role, especially when these

are defined by the referrer. In some cases, it may be possible or even necessary for the practitioner to state conditions or prerequisites for becoming
involved. The practitioner may want to think about five kinds of questions
before making a decision to accept or reject a referral:

1. *Choice:* Do I have a choice about accepting this case? Is my agency
   mandated to accept all referrals and act on them?
2. *Time:* Do I have the time to devote to this case? How many contacts
   am I able to handle? Will my involvement result in a worse outcome
   than if I did not become involved?
3. *Fees:* Practitioners in private practice may ask, Do I want to be paid
   for my services and expenses incurred? How much shall I charge?
   Will I see this client at no charge if no one can pay for my services?
4. *"Role comfort":* Will I be comfortable as a consultant even if I disagree with the intervention option or options selected by the other
   practitioner?
5. *Agency policies:* Do agency policies mandate specific types of intervention? Can I remain within the confines of agency guidelines and
   accommodate the referrer at the same time? Will the agency support
   me even if boundaries are transgressed?

Bergeron (1989) notes several common misconceptions about the reporting process, one of which is that the reporter's responsibility ends once he
or she files a report. In reality, the reporter and the person working for the
agency that received the report usually end up collaborating on the case,
especially when budgetary constraints create staff shortages. The referrer
can smooth the way for the investigation, and in many cases a referrer has
accompanied the APS practitioner to the first visit. In any case, a collegial
relationship, with open communication and cooperation, is most likely to
promote a satisfactory working environment.

## Referral by Relatives

Family members or relatives account for approximately 15% of all referrals made (Tatara, 1993). As with referrals from practitioners, it is important to understand clearly the purpose of the referral when a relative calls:

- The relative may feel that another relative is being abusive or neglectful and would like an investigation.

- The relative has been accused of being abusive or neglectful and would like an investigation to prove his or her innocence.
- The relative is a stressed primary caregiver of an elderly person and would like help to prevent an abusive or neglectful situation.

The practitioner should be aware that motivations for reporting a case vary among relatives. A relative could be upset about the contents of an elderly person's will or may be engaged in "sibling rivalry" with another relative and feel compelled to "turn in" the other relative. To clarify the nature of the referral, the practitioner may ask three questions:

1. *How did you hear about our program or agency?* Relative's possible response: "I read about your program in the newspaper. I want you to come to our home to do an investigation and prove to them I'm innocent."
2. *Why are you calling now as opposed to a month ago or a year ago?* Relative's possible response: "Well, I thought my brother was going to take good care of my father, but lately I've seen him change. He's been yelling at him more often."
3. *What are your expectations about our program?* Relative's possible response: "I want you to help me with my alcoholic brother. He comes over to harass me and my father. He shoved me around last week, and I am wondering if I should press charges against him. I want him to stop this behavior."

A case may be inappropriate for the agency or the type of practice in which the practitioner specializes. At this point, the practitioner may refer the caller to another agency. In the case of a referral by a relative (unlike a referral from another practitioner) the practitioner must make it clear that this referral does not exonerate the relative or excuse him or her from being investigated and interviewed in the same manner as those he accused of being abusive or neglectful. To convey neutrality, the practitioner may say:

"Mr. Smith, I'm glad you are concerned enough about your mother to call and make this referral. I want you to know that our assessment process involves interviewing everyone, including yourself and the alleged abuser. We do not presume anyone's innocence or guilt and will defer judgment until our investigation is completed."

## Referral by Others

A survey by the Alliance/Elder Abuse Project of the reporting data of adult protective services agencies in 17 states revealed that nonmandated reporters generated the largest number of referrals (1983). More recently, information from 29 states in 1990 and 25 states in 1991 indicates that service providers, or nonmandated providers, were still the largest group of reporters to regulatory agencies—slightly more than one fourth of all reporters (Tatara, 1993). Workers in this group provided homemaking and chore services and home health, personal care, and other in-home services.

The next largest category, "all other types," included neighbors, utility workers, apartment managers, friends, concerned citizens, and anonymous callers. Friends and neighbors, categorized separately, were 8 to 9% of the reporters in the survey. These referrers often have known the elderly people for many years and may have observed their steady mental or physical decline. Sometimes these referrers have observed an apparently abusive or neglectful relationship between the alleged abuser and the elderly person over a period of time and feel compelled to report the situation because they can no longer remain passive observers. They may report the situation also because of a recent newspaper or television report on a situation similar to the one they have observed.

The anonymous caller presents a challenge. The practitioner should accept all information in an objective manner and not press for the caller's name. Without knowing who the referring person is, the practitioner is reduced to guessing the purpose of the call and deciding how to proceed without jeopardizing the safety of the elder or the outcome of the case. Fear of reprisals could be the main motivation for remaining anonymous. Some professionals may choose anonymity in order to protect another frail elder, for example, who may have been a witness to an abusive act in a board and care home, and who fears retaliation. The practitioner may inform the referrer about the protection offered by the state's elder abuse reporting law, if one exists. The referrer should be informed that confidentiality is practiced in the agency to the extent possible and that state law provides for immunity from civil and criminal liability for reporting the abuse or neglect, and for giving court testimony. Callers may say they do not want to testify in a case, and the practitioner cannot guarantee them that they will never be subpoenaed. However, the practitioner can reassure such callers that cases seldom come to trial and it is highly unlikely that they will ever have to testify. Although confidentiality can be offered, no practitioner can guarantee a "fail safe" system, since most cases of elder abuse and neglect involve communication among practitioners from several agencies. Mistakes do happen, and the primary practitioner cannot monitor everyone's actions. The public has become better educated about elder mistreatment and has learned about agencies to which people can turn with trust and hope, and this has resulted in a tremendous increase in the volume of reports (Tatara, 1993). It is important to acknowledge the referrer's concern and courage, and to thank him or her for picking up the phone, dialing, and finally completing the referral, sometimes after months of deliberation.

## PREPARATION FOR INITIAL CONTACT:
## CASE PLANNING

Successful intervention is a result of adequate planning and anticipation of problems that the practitioner must be prepared to handle, should they arise. At this point, the following steps may be useful to follow.

1. *Make collateral contacts promptly to assess the seriousness of the situation.* The practitioner should determine whether the case that is referred requires immediate attention. On the basis of the nature of the presenting problem, the practitioner should decide whether the client should be seen immediately or whether contact can be deferred for a few days. For instance, in one county, the protective services supervisor rates each call on the basis of the type of abuse reported. Cases involving sexual abuse, physical abuse, and abandonment are assigned the highest priority and are dealt with immediately. Cases involving neglect and self-neglect are the second highest priority; cases involving financial abuse are accorded a third priority. The rating scores may be amended, depending on additional information received (K. Burge, personal communication, September 1995). Chapter 7 discusses crisis-intervention techniques in greater detail.

Quick phone calls to collateral contacts or people who have recently seen the client can help the practitioner make this decision. Whenever possible, the practitioner should call the client's physician, home health nurse, or medical group to ask what the plan of action should be if the practitioner finds the client in need of immediate medical care. Sometimes it is difficult to contact medical practitioners by phone on short notice. Nevertheless, to reflect careful planning, the practitioner's notes should indicate that an attempt was made to contact them. If a medical practitioner is consulted and placed on "standby" status during this care planning phase, the practitioner will later save precious time and be able to act promptly and institute the agreed plan of action. If the medical practitioner is unavailable, it may help to leave a detailed message explaining the importance of the call. Sometimes medical practitioners will respond promptly if they realize that the practitioner is waiting to consult them before proceeding with an assessment.

Practitioners seem to be divided on the issue of making collateral contacts without the client's consent. Some practitioners feel that it is unethical to call a client's medical practitioner and obtain confidential medical information, while others feel this is a prudent step to take. Practitioners who are mandated by state law to investigate reports of elder abuse and neglect, and mental health professionals who must assess a client for involuntary commitment, usually are permitted to obtain confidential information. One way to handle this issue is to call the medical practitioner and to give, not obtain, information. For example:

> "I am aware that you (a nurse, a doctor, a hospital) are providing care to Mr. Smith. There has been a complaint of abuse or neglect and he has been described as being listless and unable to get out of bed. I am considering a home visit soon and want to know what you would want to do if I find him to be in need of medical care."

It is up to medical practitioners to share information or to provide suggestions for treatment without breaking confidentiality. They may merely state that if necessary, a client should be transported to a specific hospital where they have hospital privileges, or they may ask to be contacted from a client's home or after a client has been seen. Sometimes medical practitioners will readily provide information on a client's current health status and medications if they feel that the situation warrants it.

2. *Become familiar with available information.* Valuable information may be obtained from other practitioners who have had previous contact with the client or the alleged abuser. Some agencies have statewide computers that can inform the current practitioner if the client's case is active in another unit or office. For example, in Florida, an automated statewide information system quickly determines whether prior reports have been made on an alleged victim, and within 1 hour of the time a call is received through a 24-hour toll-free hotline, the case is relayed to the appropriate

local office, where it is assigned to an investigator (Simon, 1992). Previous reports or charts, if they are available, should be studied. One city has a formal agreement with the police department that allows its state agency to receive information regarding an alleged abuser's criminal record.

People known to have been threatened by an alleged abuser should be interviewed in order to determine what the safest approach for completing the assessment is. For example:

An attorney assigned as the guardian *ad litem* in a difficult guardianship process called the hospital social worker involved in the same case. He asked her how she had handled the male friend of the allegedly incapacitated person, an elderly female. This client was easily swayed by the friend, who was demanding and verbose. The social worker described the friend's personality and made suggestions on how to approach him and to obtain his cooperation in completing his investigation.

In another example:

A protective services practitioner who had not checked on the alleged abuser's background made a home visit alone to interview a client who lived with an abusive man. She found no one at home. Later, she found out that this man had been convicted of rape and murder in the past and had a record of assaulting women. Given this information, she realized that she should not have made the home visit alone and decided that on her next visit she would go with another worker or ask that the interview be held instead at her agency.

3. *Document a tentative plan.* Once information has been obtained from collateral contacts and available reports, the practitioner can document a tentative treatment plan. The plan can serve as evidence to anyone who may criticize the practitioner's intervention. A plan that reflects planning and forethought may prove to be valuable later if the practitioner is accused of being capricious or sloppy, or acting mostly on emotions (Gambrill, 1983).

4. *Be familiar with the protocol questions, and gather forms and equipment for the interview.* It may be helpful to memorize the questions to be asked in the interview or to be prepared to read them from a printed sheet. The practitioner should bring appropriate forms, such as release of information forms for interagency communication, or consent forms to obtain services and to be photographed.

5. *Rehearse intervention options and have them ready.* The practitioner

should anticipate the need to introduce intervention options to develop the client's belief in interventions. It is helpful to have in mind a range of services available specific to the client's situation. A brochure containing resources the client may use can serve as a calling card and can be slipped under the door. Practitioners are at a disadvantage if they are unprepared to "sell" themselves in the first few minutes of the initial interview.

Rapoport (1970), in formulating short-term treatment techniques utilizing the crisis intervention approach, states:

> The primary need of the client is to experience in the first interview a considerable reduction in disabling tension and anxiety. One way in which this is achieved, which may be specific to brief treatment approach, is by the worker's sharing tentative hypotheses and structuring a picture of the operating dynamics in language that makes sense to the client. This enables the client to get a manageable cognitive grasp of his situation, and usually leads to a lowering of anxiety, trust in the worker's competence, and a feeling of being understood. (p. 288)

6. *Develop a prompt sheet or card listing backup contacts and strategies.* In work with elder abuse and neglect, many contacts are adversarial in nature and can be stressful. It is at times helpful to "feed" oneself by using a prompt card that lists ways to get through a stressful interaction (Gambrill, 1983), and phone numbers of backup people. The card can read:

> "These people can use my services."
> "I have dealt with angry people successfully."
> "I can get backup help if I need it."
> "Don't panic; count to three and try another approach."

7. *Do not work alone.* Before contacting a client or an abuser, it is helpful to spend 15 minutes reviewing a case with a colleague or a worker from another agency or discipline. The practitioner can discuss the tentative treatment plan and ask for comments, additions, and suggestions. Invariably, practitioners with different areas of expertise who are farther removed from the situation can clarify the practitioner's goals or add options missed by the practitioner. Furthermore, their support will give the practitioner the confidence and emotional backing that are necessary to investigate a difficult case.

# FIRST CONTACT

Having gathered whatever information is available, through review of written documents or through contacts with professionals and people familiar with the situation, the practitioner initiates the first contact.

## Settings for First Contact

1. *In the home: Drop-in visit versus visit by appointment.* There are both advantages and disadvantages to either dropping in on a client or visiting by appointment. The method of choice depends on the practitioner's perception of the acuteness of the client's condition, the client's ability to consent to the interview, and the perceived cooperation of the alleged abuser. Dropping in on a client is chancy. The client may not be in, and time is then wasted, especially if many miles have been driven. However, if the case is presented as an emergency or life-threatening, or if the practitioner is unable to contact an elderly client by phone and feels that it would take too long to send a letter asking for an appointment, then a drop-in visit may be justified. The practitioner may also feel that visiting an elderly client unannounced will provide a realistic picture of the client's functional and environmental conditions and prevent any cover-up of signs of abuse or neglect. However, drop-in visits are disadvantageous because they can alienate both the client and the alleged abuser and put them on the defensive if they feel the visit was meant to "catch them in the act." The practitioner is perceived as a threat, with the client and others feeling a loss of control over their own situation (Wasserman, 1979). The resentment and defensiveness that are developed from an initial drop-in visit can hinder future contacts and prevent the development of an ongoing relationship, especially when the client is ambivalent about receiving services. In most cases, an accurate portrayal of the home situation may be obtained without dropping in, through the administration of the elder abuse protocol as described in Chapter 6.

Whenever possible, the practitioner should call the elderly client to arrange the visit and state the time and date of the appointment. Regardless of who made the referral—an agency worker, a relative, or an anonymous person—it is necessary to speak to the client directly. When the referral is from another agency's worker, the practitioner should elicit this colleague's help to call and prepare the client for the impending visit. When the referral is from a relative, it is not possible to assume that the client will be told about the visit. On the phone, the practitioner may say,

> "Please put your father on the phone; I want to introduce myself and let him know I'll be visiting him."

When the client comes on the line, say,

> "Your son has asked me to come by to discuss some services for which you may qualify. I would like to come by tomorrow at 2:00 P.M."

It is important to be positive and firm. It may be necessary to compromise on the appointment time or another detail, but a rejection can be avoided by preparing the client and others for the visit. Formally establishing contact directly with the elderly client conveys many things: for example, that the practitioner does not intend to use the referral person as the sole means of obtaining information from or giving information to the elderly client; and that the practitioner respects the elderly client and assumes that he or she wants time to prepare for the visit. Also, a practitioner who is expected to visit and does not barge in will be met with less resistance when he or she is in the home and attempting to engage the client in conversation.

Sometimes clients are prisoners in their own home. In such cases, the caregiver may field telephone calls by using an answering machine or may attempt to prevent the practitioner from contacting the client by saying that the elderly person is sleeping or cannot come to the phone right then. Even if the client is perceived as being in need of immediate contact, the practitioner should attempt to call first. If there is no answer, the practitioner can later justify the drop-in visit by saying that an attempt was made to contact the elderly client by phone. Another method is to call 1 to 2 hours before visiting an elderly client. Within that short period, everyone involved will be alerted to the visit and the practitioner will not be perceived as dropping in unannounced. If a client has no phone, or simply to save time, the practitioner may want to drive to the client's home and say,

> "I was in the neighborhood and in order to save time, I thought I'd stop by to see if you had time to see me. If this time is inconvenient, I would like to make an appointment with you."

2. *"Neutral territory" setting.* The practitioner may wish to consider interviewing an elderly client outside the home if the client has difficulty speaking up because of interruptions or lack of privacy. For instance, in the case planning phase the practitioner may have found out that the client has been attending a day center for adults. Instead of a home visit, the practitioner may wish to approach the client in that setting without letting others know. The staff of the center must agree to maintain confidentiality. Prior to meeting the client at a place where others may observe the interview, the practitioner can ask that a private room be set aside for a specific time period. Staff members are to refrain from talking about the visit with other people who use the center. It is better if no explanations about the practitioner's presence are given. It is up to the client to respond to inquires himself or herself.

Other neutral settings may be a coffee shop or a car. The practitioner can interview the elderly client as he or she is transported to a medical appointment or a grocery store. The client's ambulation and mobility should be taken into consideration. Because clients in cases of elder abuse and neglect are often frail and vulnerable, it is doubtful that practitioners will be able to interview them while they are participating in activities requiring strenuous movements or walking great distances.

3. *Agency or clinic setting.* Clients very rarely seek help for elder abuse and neglect; they often present themselves to agencies and clinics for resolution of other problems. If elder abuse and neglect are suspected, the practitioner must seize the opportunity to assess the situation. Precautions must be taken to maximize privacy and confidentiality, for it is not uncommon to discover during an assessment that the person accompanying the elderly client to the interview is the alleged abuser. A terrible mistake can be made by interviewing the person accompanying the elderly client before the client is interviewed and by stereotyping him or her as a "normal" caregiver. Elderly clients may become more reluctant to disclose important information when they quietly observe the practitioner befriending a person from who they are trying to seek protection.

In a medical clinic, a physician who suspects elder abuse or neglect, but lacks the time to do the assessment, may say to the elderly client that he or she will be seen by another practitioner to determine what services may be required, being careful not to mention the word *abuse*.

4. *Hospital emergency room.* Hospital settings are assumed to be among the safest places—to be havens that can, at least temporarily, protect an

elderly client from an alleged abuser. Unfortunately, not all hospitals have staffs trained to detect and deal with elder mistreatment. Therefore, the onus is on the practitioner to prepare the hospital staff. When taking a client to a hospital, it is best to call the emergency room ahead of time and speak to the triage nurse or social worker. A summary statement may save the client hours of waiting (see Chapter 7 for format of statement). The statement may be filed in the chart for others to read, especially if a decision is made to admit the client, and a different staff will treat the client on a hospital floor. Carefully prepared written work and clear verbal communication add credibility to the practitioner's presence in the emergency room. The practitioner's self-assured style may have a calming effect on staff members who are uncomfortable with cases of elder mistreatment. Furthermore, the practitioner is less likely to be perceived as someone "dumping" the client in the emergency room or manipulating the staff to examine the client for problems that are not serious.

A hospital practitioner who suspects elder abuse and neglect or who is approached by an agency practitioner as described above has the role of hospitalwide advocate. That practitioner should find a private setting to interview the elderly client and inform the staff about the special nature of the case. Certain equipment should be ready for the assessment: camera, consent forms, tape measure, sketch sheet, note paper, and pen. The hospital practitioner should be prepared to explain the institution's procedures and to serve as liaison, since hospitals can be an intimidating setting for the client, the client's advocate, and nonhospital practitioners.

## Gaining Access to a Client's Home

Gaining access to an elderly client's home is more difficult than approaching a client in an agency, hospital, or medical setting. In most cases the practitioner has no authority to enter without the property owner's consent. Legal remedies such as police involvement or a court injunction are used as a last resort. States laws vary with regard to the criteria for the protective services practitioner to obtain court permission to enter a home to complete an investigation. Practitioners can assume that they will gain access if they approach the home visit with the goal of being perceived by the client and others in the home as someone helpful and friendly, able to provide services at no or low cost, or able to alleviate problems for the entire family. Several experts in the field of crisis theory stipulate that the goal of the initial contact is alleviation of tension and anxiety (Aguilera, 1990; Golan, 1978; 1979; Parad, 1971; Parad & Parad, 1990; Rapoport, 1970).

The practitioner's car should be parked in front of the client's home in case additional help is required. An ambulance driver or a law enforcement officer who is called to the home will then be able to identify the correct house easily. At the client's door, proper identification is necessary, preferably with a photo of the practitioner, especially if the visit is unexpected. The elderly client should not be expected to open the door to just anyone. A practitioner who anticipates difficulty with access may ask a friend or neighbor of the client to be present, or a member of the client's religious group, or an apartment manager. The client may open the door if a familiar, trusted voice is heard.

Home health nurses and public health nurses are rarely denied access to elderly clients' homes. O'Malley et al. (1983) state that "access is gained most successfully by nursing personnel who are nonthreatening, have the reputation of being helping professionals, and emphasize the effects of illness on the ability of the elderly person to function (p. 1003)." Nonmedical practitioners may have more clout if they are perceived as part of a medical team. Some protective services workers have learned how to take pulses and blood pressures as a way of assisting their clients and gaining acceptance. If a client's condition requires skilled nursing services, it may be helpful to ask a home health nurse to make the initial contact to the home and discuss other agencies' services that the nurse feels may be helpful to the family. An effective approach used by some home health agencies is to have their nurse and social worker visit the client as a team. Sometimes pairing up with another agency practitioner works. In one case, a public health nurse, an adult protective services practitioner, and a hospital social worker made a home visit together with good results.

### Conflict Situation versus Treatment Situation

The practitioner must remember that access is dependent on the ability to convince the client that suggested options have merit (Gambrill, 1983). Not all clients welcome practitioners' offers of help. The term *treatment situation* means that a client is cooperative and that the practitioner is able to proceed with the assessment and treatment plan. Conversely, a *conflict situation* is one in which an involuntary client has not consented to intervention, and bargaining and persuasion must be used to obtain the client's cooperation (Murdach, 1980).

Bargaining can be seen as a process with several phases:

1. Introduction.
2. Discovering the "bargainable," which consists of defining bargainable objectives, the range of disagreement, and possible areas of agreement.
3. Establishing areas of agreement. This is easier if objectives are quantifiable and the process does not involve basic moral or ethical commitments.
4. Critical bargaining, during which proposals and counterproposals are offered. This is the stage of compromise and concessions.
5. Public presentation of results, when the cementing of the agreement is marked by public display. (Mitchell, 1973)

Initial steps during the assessment phase may take the following form:

- *Step 1: Introduction.* Tell the client, the caregiver, or both who you are in a nonthreatening manner: "I am a counselor from (agency). Here is my card. I am here because our agency received a call of concern about you."
- *Step 2: Discovering the bargainable.* Put forth some service options that the client may consider: "Your doctor has asked me to come by to see if there are any services for which you may qualify. I would like to show you a list of services available to senior citizens. It is a part of my job to make these services available to as many senior citizens in the city as qualify. One of the outcomes of today's interview may be in a plan that may include delivery of 'meals on wheels,' chore work, housekeeping services, or more monthly income. You (your son) and I could work together to discuss and develop a plan like this."

Once the client exhibits signs of willingness to participate further in a discussion, the practitioner can proceed to the other phases of the bargaining process in the ensuing assessment phase.

### Continuum of Approaches

Sometimes the practitioner will be met at the door by a caregiver who does not wish to be bothered. If the friendly, diplomatic approach does not result in access, a more authoritative stance may be utilized. The following approaches may be used to gain access, and they are listed from (1) least confrontational to (4) most confrontational:

1. *Offer services.* "I am here to see whether you and your father need services. Your father requires increased care since his stroke, and it is difficult for one person to do all the work." The caregiver should not be faulted or put on the defensive.
2. *Offer to be an advocate for the caregiver.* "I'm here to do whatever I can to help people realize that you are doing your best. Many people do not realize how much work is involved in caring for a frail elderly person. Will you please take me through a typical day so I can understand your role?"
3. *Use ascribed authority.* "Before you slam the door on me, I want you to know that as a representative of my agency, I must obtain certain information on the client. I'll have to keep returning till I do. I want to work with you. I have been doing this type of work successfully for the past five years and know how to get the job done. Cooperate with me and I will leave as soon as I complete my assignment. I may have to call for assistance from the pay phone."
4. *Call for assistance.* "Our agency has received information that abuse has taken place. I want to spell your name correctly so I can give it to the police. I want you to know that you are quoted as saying, 'Shove it,' to me (the practitioner writes as she talks). All you are demonstrating is that the concerns seem valid. I want you to know that I will be back soon with the police."

Practitioners should use their own level of fear as a barometer for the level of danger in the situation but at the same time should not be intimidated by hostile behavior. If weapons are in sight, it may be best to leave and return with a law enforcement officer. The practitioner is in control of the situation, just as would be true if the setting were his or her own office. The practitioner is on a mission to rule out elder mistreatment and to determine whether intervention is necessary. Threats should not be made by the practitioner unless they can realistically be carried out. Practitioners must remember that they have an obligation to obtain access to the client and that they have the ability to bargain with a client or caregiver in order to get beyond the first few minutes of the introductory phase and be permitted to proceed to the assessment phase. The following words represent rules that may produce a successful introduction phase:

- *Tactics:* The practitioner should have bargaining and persuasion tactics well rehearsed, should carry proper identification, and should have service delivery options ready for presentation.
- *Tact:* The practitioner is to use diplomacy with perseverance, and avoid confrontations if at all possible.
- *Talk:* The practitioner should avoid pauses in the conversation, should speak in a calm manner, and should not give the client or caregiver the opportunity to deny access.
- *Time:* The client and caregiver should be allowed time to feel comfortable with the practitioner.

Lowry (1957) discusses the hazards of working within a time limit or a limited number of interviews in the context of short-contact casework. The practitioner is warned that if time is limited, overdirection in the interview may result, with too many questions being asked in an effort to obtain information quickly. The practitioner's anxiety may inhibit creative and accurate assessment of the client's situation:

> Because of the sense of being pressed by time, we may yield to the impulse to move along in the interview at a pace which we ourselves set. This may result in a loss of valuable understanding that might have been achieved had the other person been allowed to move more nearly at his own pace, particularly in the early phases of the interview. It is true that there is a need for discriminating direction of the interview on our part, but this direction should stem from our perceptions and thought processes rather than our feelings of urgency. (Lowry, 1957, pp. 53–54)

The practitioner is reminded that significant material may emerge spontaneously after attention is paid to the establishment of a relationship and some of the client's feelings of ambivalence and threat are addressed. Questions should be spaced sensitively and should be related to the client's immediate concerns. Sometimes it takes 20 to 30 minutes to put a client at ease or to let a client or caregiver become familiar with the practitioner. Accepting a cup of coffee may help to break the ice. Practitioners may want to disclose bits of information about themselves to diminish feelings that they are a threat. In the first interview, if an understanding has been established about the reason for the home visit, that in itself is a goal accomplished. Sometimes obtaining access and alleviating fear are the main goals of the first interview, and the practitioner may want to return at another time to proceed with the assessment.

## SUMMARY

Careful assessment of a case of elder mistreatment and successful interventions depend on meticulous planning prior to the initial contact with the elder and the alleged abuser. At times contacting others who are already involved will save the practitioner time and ensure the safety of both client and practitioner. Chapter 6 addresses the assessment process in detail.

# Diagnosis Phase

## II. Assessment

### A PROTOCOL FOR INTERVIEWING

Assessment of a client for elder mistreatment may require several contacts over a period of time, and can be very time-consuming process. This chapter describes the use of a written protocol which will help the practitioner focus efficiently, thus conserving time and energy. A concise, easy-to-use form for the protocol is given in Appendix A. It consists of guidelines for interviewing the elderly client and suspected abuser individually to identify and assess the possibility of mistreatment. The assessment protocol has four sections: (1) assessment of the client's functioning; (2) a physical examination of the client; (3) interview of the potential abuser; and (4) collateral contacts.

### Rationale

Originally written in 1981, the protocol was designed to be used by health care professionals in many disciplines, including nursing, social work, physical and occupational therapy, psychology, and medicine (Tomita, 1982; Tomita, Clark, Williams, & Rabbitt, 1981). It was developed after reviewing protocols used to assess child abuse and neglect and other forms of domestic violence, such as sexual abuse and assault and battered women syndrome (Anderson, 1981; Johnson, 1981; Klingbeil, 1979; Klingbeil & Boyd, 1984). The protocol assumes that in order for health care professionals to detect, intervene in, and prevent cases of elderly abuse, three major barriers must be overcome (Rathbone-McCuan & Voyles, 1982).

One barrier is denial by many health care professionals that elder mistreatment exists within their own client populations. For example, it may be difficult to believe that an 80-year-old woman who is seen regularly for therapy at a hospital with bruises on her upper extremities is being physically abused by her caregiver. For fear of being too intrusive, the practitioner may be reluctant to inquire about the bruises, or may not know what to do if the abuse is recognized or acknowledged by the client.

The second barrier is absence of written procedures for case detection (Rathbone-McCuan & Voyles, 1982). Few health care professionals are aware of or have routine materials that outline reporting or intervention procedures for domestic maltreatment of the elderly. Practitioners will be more likely to inquire about an elderly patient's bruises if they have training in detecting abuse and neglect and feel comfortable with a protocol that has been made available to the entire staff in their agencies.

The third barrier is lack of service and support options for the abused elderly person, the abuser, and the family. Practitioners are more likely to get involved in cases of elder abuse if they feel that treatment options exist for all involved.

The protocol is necessary because older adults may not report elder mistreatment just as they often may not report a complaint to a medical practitioner until the condition has reached an advanced state. Underreporting may be due to cultural and educational backgrounds. Also, some elderly people may believe that illness goes hand in hand with aging (Kane et al., 1994) and may similarly view mistreatment as part of being older (Nuttbrock & Kosberg, 1980). Williamson et al. (1964) found that among 200 patients over age 65 who were examined for physical and psychiatric disabilities, the men had an average of 3.2 disabilities, with 1.87 of these disabilities unknown to their family physician. The mean number of disabilities for women was 3.42, with 2.03 of these disabilities unknown to their families or to their physicians. The study found that physicians practicing in a metropolitan area were less aware of patients' difficulties than were physicians who lived in small, close-knit communities and who perhaps knew their patients better because of the communities' cohesiveness and informal communication network. Any general practitioner who relies on self-reports of illness is likely to be seriously handicapped in meeting the needs of old people. If elder mistreatment could be considered a disability that can be reported too late, then the need for periodic medical examinations, which would include a protocol to assess and treat elder mistreatment, is supported. The protocol can also be adapted easily for use in the client's home by social workers and home health nurses.

## Methodology and Technique

Each case and each interview session has its own "personality," with a unique tone, feeling, process, and pace. The practitioner should anticipate that things will inevitably go wrong during the process, and that the ideal 1-hour interview does not exist. At times, signs and symptoms will elude the practitioner because false assumptions have been made and attention has not been paid to important details.

The following basic tools will be required in conducting any assessment:

- Sketch sheet or trauma graph (see Figure 6-1)
- Ruler or tape measure
- Camera, film, and flash attachment
- Paper and pen
- Consent and release of information forms

The sketch sheet and camera are used to document injuries or other evidence of elder mistreatment. A tape measure or another measurement tool is needed to measure injuries accurately. The practitioner will need to record verbatim both the elderly client's statements and the alleged abuser's statements. Discrepancies between the two may point to elder mistreatment. The practitioner should anticipate which consent forms the client will need to sign and have them in hand. They may include forms consenting to intervention by a practitioner representing a particular agency, allowing exchange of information between agencies involved in the client's care, or allowing photographs to be taken of the client's injuries. These forms should either be gathered together in a packet and taken along on each home visit or be kept on file in the health care or service agency.

It is important to conduct the interview in a nonjudgmental manner. Personal feelings should not be allowed to interfere with giving the best possible care. Although having a high index of suspicion is important in ruling out elder mistreatment, the client should not be diagnosed prematurely as being a victim. Nor should the suspected abuser be told about treatment plans until all the facts are gathered. Special attention should be paid to trauma, nutritional status, recent change in physical and mental condition,

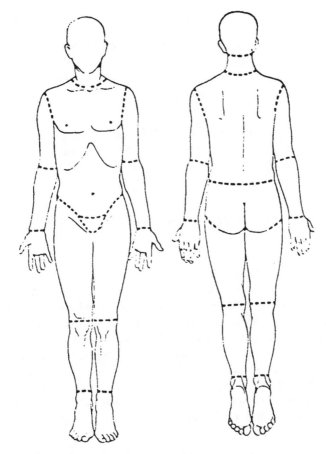

Figure 6-1  Sketch sheet to document physical injuries.

and the client's financial status and home situation. A good way to remember the essentials of interviewing techniques is to think of them as the "five P's" (Villamore & Bergman, 1981):

1. Privacy
2. Pacing
3. Planning
4. Pitch
5. Punctuality

## *Privacy*

Interview the client alone, with no one else present. Sometimes consider-able energy is required to negotiate privacy with the client, especially when the caregiver is reluctant to leave the client alone with the practitioner. The caregiver may offer a variety of justifications, such as:

> "I have an appointment elsewhere in an hour and you are going to make me miss that appointment. We can do this faster if you interview us together." Or, "My mother doesn't know what she's saying half the time. I'll tell you what you need to know."

The practitioner may emphasize the need for privacy by saying some-thing like this:

> *In a home setting:*   "Our agency insists on preserving clients' confidential-ity. I need to speak with your mother alone. I'll talk to her first in that room. After I'm done, I would like to talk to you so you can tell me how things have been here. Are you able to take a walk outside or go somewhere while I'm interviewing her? I'll take around 45 minutes with each of you."
> *In a clinic or agency setting*:   "Thank you for bringing your mother to this clinic. I will interview her first and would like you to wait in the waiting room; or, if you'd like, you can go get a cup of coffee. It will take approxi-mately 45 minutes. Then I would like to talk to you and ask you some ques-tions about your mother's home situation."

The interview setting should be a room with four solid walls and a door, where there is the least chance of being interrupted or eavesdropped on. Failure to take these precautions may result in a less successful interview. For example:

> A hospital social worker conducted her elder mistreatment interview of a 68-year-old woman in the patient's two-bed hospital room. The patient's room-mate was away, attending a physical therapy session. The interview was proceeding smoothly, and the patient was beginning to disclose information, when the roommate returned earlier than expected. The patient then became noticeably withdrawn and tried to avoid being overheard by speaking very softly. With only a fabric partition separating the two patients' bed spaces, the social worker belatedly realized she should have conducted the interview in a private office down the hall.

If privacy is not available in the home, the practitioner should consider interviewing the client elsewhere. For instance, a client might be interviewed in the car while being driven by the practitioner to a doctor's appointment, or the practitioner may arrange to meet the client in another setting. The practitioner needs to bear in mind that he or she is the one responsible for the physical setup of the interview. Being in someone's residence requires that the practitioner respect both the person and his or her property. At the same time, both client and suspected abuser tend to perceive the practitioner as someone who has expertise in interviewing people and who will provide gentle guidance and structure to help them feel secure. The practitioner may feel uncomfortable about "calling the shots" in a client's living room. But it may be necessary to ask the client to turn off the television and to sit down to talk. After conducting several elder mistreatment assessments, the practitioner will become more comfortable with these techniques and have an easier time "directing" clients and suspected abusers in their homes.

### Pacing

It is important to pace the interview evenly, while at the same time providing support to the client and to the suspected abuser. In spite of time restraints, questions should be worked into the conversation in a relaxed manner. Clients should never be rushed, even though they may respond to important questions in a tangential manner, or with metaphors, or in such a way that the practitioner is forced to read between the lines. While talking or listening, the practitioner should be attuned to a client's nonverbal behavior: posture, facial expressions (particularly those revealing emotions), and vocal tension. Lowry (1957) states:

> As case workers we really need four ears: one with which to listen to *what* is being said; one to attend to what is *not* being said; one to hear *how* it is being said; and one to heed the feelings *unexpressed*. (p.55)

### Planning

As it was noted in Chapter 5, it is important to have a goal or behavioral outcome for each case and each interview, and this requires memorizing preplanned statements and responses. It may be helpful to use prompt cards or written reminders of ways to cope in a tense or difficult situation. Before going to a client's residence, the necessary forms should be gathered, to avoid having to return for a signature at a later date.

### Pitch

It is helpful during an interview to speak in a well modulated tone of voice and to avoid sounding excited or surprised. A friendly tone of voice and facial expression will help the client develop confidence and trust in the practitioner.

### Punctuality

If an appointment has been made, it is important to arrive promptly. This shows respect and can help to develop trust. Some elderly clients will wait all day for the practitioner, worrying that they may have been forgotten.

## Suspicious Signs and Symptoms

On first contact, it is necessary to watch for signs and symptoms possibly indicating that the client is being abused or neglected. These may include the following.

*The client is brought to a hospital emergency room by someone other than the caregiver, or the client is found alone in the home.* For example, if the client is brought into the emergency room by a law enforcement officer or a neighbor after having been found wandering outside, or if the client dials an emergency number but is unable to answer the door when help arrives, it may be that the client has been abandoned or has been living in an unsafe setting for long periods of time.

*There is a prolonged interval between injury or illness and presentation for medical care.* Suspicious injuries may include week-old bruises and gangrenous feet. The practitioner should think about why the client or the caregiver waited so long to seek treatment for the client's injuries. The assumption cannot be made that all caregivers mean well. Failure to seek help in a timely manner may be the result of the caregiver's desire not to spend money on medical care, of ignorance, or of a need to minimize the severity of the client's problems until they no longer can be ignored.

*There is a suspicious history.* If the client is new to the medical clinic or agency, the practitioner should wonder whether the suspected abuser or the client is "doctor hopping" or "agency hopping" in order to hide previous injuries. The practitioner's suspicions should be aroused if the description of how the injury occurred is inconsistent with the physical findings, if the client has a history of similar episodes, or if the client has too many "explained" injuries or offers explanations for injuries which vary from time to time.

*There is noncompliance with prescribed medications.* A check of the client's pharmacy profile or medication bottles may indicate that medications are not being taken or administered by the designated caregiver as prescribed.

## INTERVIEWING THE CLIENT

### Functional Assessment

The guidelines for conducting a functional assessment are part of the protocol in Appendix A. The purpose of the functional assessment is to find out with whom the client interacts frequently, and on whom he or she depends for social, physical, or financial support. This may be accomplished by obtaining a detailed account of the client's typical day and by making an assessment of level of independence. In this section are compiled specific questions, which should be asked in the order listed. The people mentioned by the client during this assessment will form the pool of people who must be considered as possible abusers.

It is important to begin with more general, nonthreatening questions and to leave more emotionally laden questions until later. This method of assessment requires writing the client's responses down verbatim to the extent that note-taking is possible. Some practitioners may be reluctant to write during the interview, fearing that it will inhibit the client. If it would disrupt the interview process, practitioners may decide not to take notes at the time. Upon leaving the interview site, they can, for instance, drive a few blocks away, stop, and write down everything they can remember, especially quotes. Later, they may be able to check with victims and abusers for confirmation of certain facts. These notes may be required for later use in a legal proceeding and will help practitioners recall actual statements made by clients during the contact. A practitioner can explain the necessity of note-taking to the client by stressing the need to remember important information and to avoid repeating questions. Tape recorders can be used if a client is comfortable with the technique and has been assured of confidentiality. In many cases, however, tape recording is a time-consuming process which involves listening to the recording, transcribing the tapes or finding someone to transcribe them, and then reviewing the transcriptions before they can be used.

1. *Collect pertinent data.* The interview begins with the practitioner asking easy questions which will help to put the client at ease. It may be helpful to ask about services the client has already obtained and to collect information to determine whether the client qualifies for a service. Sample questions include:

"What is your correct address?"
"How long have you lived in your apartment?"
"Do you live alone?"
"Do you have a bus pass?"
"Do you receive meals on wheels?"
"What is your current income?"

Some clients may feel that questions about their income and savings are insulting, but it is necessary to obtain financial data to determine the client's eligibility for programs such as chore services and transportation. It is also important in ruling out financial abuse.

2. *Ask the client to describe a typical day.* Finding out how the client spends a typical day allows the practitioner to determine the degree of dependence on others and to find out who the client's most frequent and significant contacts are. Sample questions include:

"I would like you to tell me what a typical day is like for you. For example, what do you do from morning to night on any given day?"
"What time do you get up in the morning?"
"Do you need help getting out of bed?"
"Are you able to walk to the bathroom by yourself?"
"Who helps you?"

While the client responds, the practitioner should take down what he or she says verbatim. The notes might look like this:

Client states she wakes up by self around 7 A.M. daily; lies in bed and waits for spouse to help her out of bed. Some mornings he is late in helping her.

States, "I just lie in bed and wait till he comes." As she is sight-impaired and needs assistance with walking to the bathroom, she sometimes wets the bed. Breakfast is eaten at 8 A.M. and consists of . . .

It is important to go through the entire day, from the time the client awakens until bedtime, and to ask who helps or is supposed to help the client, who the client relies on, and how often these helpers are in contact with the client. The client invariably will mention significant others in her life, i.e., her spouse, children, friends, household help, or neighbors. At this point in the interview, the practitioner should obtain their names and phone numbers if possible. Usually, an abuser is known to the client. Thus anyone mentioned as a helper or contact may be an abuser.

3. *Assess the client's ability to perform activities of daily living (ADL).* Several excellent checklists—such as the Index of ADL by Katz et al. (1963) in Appendix D and the Older Americans Resources and Services (OARS) instrument (Fillenbaum & Smyer, 1981)—are available for assessing the client's ability to deal with daily living activities. Basic living skills that require assessment are the clients' ability to groom themselves, to dress, to walk, to bathe, to use the toilet, and to feed themselves. While taking down the client's answers, the practitioner should be thinking about what kind of help the client would require in order to remain independent.

4. *Ask the client about his or her expectations regarding care.* Sometimes there is a discrepancy between what the caregiver and the client expect of each other. Abuse can, at times, be the result of these unrealistic expectations, so it is important that the practitioner compare the client's statements with those given by the suspected abuser.

Gradually, the practitioner may begin to explore the subject of abuse more specifically.

5. *Have the client report any recent crises in family life.* At this point, the client may be willing to tell the practitioner about major problems in the home, or reveal that he or she has concerns about a certain family member.

6. *Ask about alcohol problems, drug use, illnesses, and behavior problems among household or family members.* In the data from the Three Model Projects on Elder Abuse, elder mistreatment was strongly correlated with the abuser's history of substance abuse and psychiatric problems (Godkin et al., 1989; 1986). Some questions the practitioner may ask here include:

"Is there anyone you know who has problems with alcohol, drugs, or with controlling his or her temper?"
"Is there anyone who has been having a particularly bad time lately?"


7. *The practitioner should next begin to ask the client about abusive incidents.* This part should include questions about whether the client has ever been shoved, shaken, or hit, tied to a bed or chair, or left locked in a room for long periods. The practitioner should also ask whether the client has been yelled at or threatened. If the response is yes to any of these questions, the practitioner should ask when it happened and where the client was hurt. Ask the client to point to parts of the body that were injured and to demonstrate how he or she was struck (e.g., with open hand or closed fist; how often). Ask how long the client was restrained and when it happened. The practitioner should narrow the focus of the interview to the specific incident or incidents mentioned by the client and should obtain more detail (e.g., what seem to be the factors precipitating the abuse and how often the abuser repeats these incidents).

Walker (1987) suggests that practitioners ask open-ended questions about possible abuse or neglect. If the patient makes no admission initially, the practitioner may ask how the patient and other family members express their anger at each other. Most important, she cautions practitioners that some victims do not trust neutrality. They see others as being either for or against them. Therefore, she suggests that practitioners initially align themselves with the victim by providing constant support, emphasizing a belief in the victim's story, and stating repeatedly that no one deserves to be treated abusively.

In the course of the assessment, covert as well as overt forms of mistreatment must be ruled out. Some clients dread being isolated, and consider being made to feel burdensome and being excluded from social interactions forms of psychological neglect (Anetzberger, Korbin, & Tomita, 1996; Tomita, 1994). If clients express feelings of being ignored or being a burden, additional questions may include:


"How often do your children/family talk to you (eat with you)?
"When was the last time you did something together?"
"Describe for me what it is like to be ignored."
"What do they do to make you feel that you are a burden?"
"Are you telling me that you hardly talk to anyone in the course of a week?"

At this point in the assessment, clients usually respond to direct questions with at least a "yes" or "no," and they often elaborate, as long as they perceive the practitioner to be trustworthy. Very few clients refuse to answer specific questions about elder mistreatment if they are asked in the right way. These questions must be asked, even if the client is perceived as confused or has been labeled "demented." Despite some memory loss, clients still may recall recent abusive incidents and begin to describe their profound loneliness. Some forms of mistreatment may be subtle and so long-standing that elders may not realize they are being victimized. Some elders may recall only incidents which occurred in the remote past and may say they have not been abused recently. Some clients may admit readily that they are victims of mistreatment but may refuse to name the abuser. It is possible, however, to determine who the abuser is likely to be from the pool of names obtained during the "typical day" assessment, and from clues the client gives inadvertently. For example, the client may say, "I don't want to tell; she might get mad at me." The practitioner will want to be alert for abuse by a female, possibly someone the client has named earlier in the interview.

It is helpful to prepare clients for these delicate questions by putting them at ease and by allowing time for practitioner and client to get to know each other. This is why the "typical day" assessment should ordinarily be conducted first. Some clients will deny mistreatment, but this should not deter the practitioner from asking specific questions. The practitioner is never able to determine mistreatment without giving the client an opportunity to speak on the matter.

Questions regarding financial abuse should be asked in the same manner as those related to physical abuse. The determination of financial abuse may be made by asking the following questions:

"Have you signed any forms or documents lately that you didn't quite understand?"
"Has anyone asked you to sign anything without explaining what you are signing?"
"Is anyone taking your checks?"
"Has anyone accompanied you to your bank and had you withdraw money for his or her use?"
"Who owns this house? Is it in your name?"
"Do you suspect that anyone is tampering with your savings or your other assets?"

To rule out sexual abuse, Ramsey-Klawsnik (1993) suggests discussing the practitioner's role, stating the following:

> "I work for the Department of _____. My job is to talk to older people to find out if they are okay. Some seniors are hurt by sexual abuse, when another person forces them into a sexual act against their wishes. When I find out that something like this is happening, I work very hard to make the hurting stop. Has anything like this happened to you?"

If a client refuses to respond, the practitioner may say that he or she will return in a few days to provide another opportunity to talk. A practitioner should also assure clients that they have a right to be safe and free from sexual assault. For persons with speech and language limitations, cards printed "Yes," "No," "Pass" may be used for the client to point at in response to specific questions. Drawings of the front and back views of the body and anatomically correct dolls have been found to be useful as well (Ramsey-Klawsnik, 1993).

When a victim discloses sexual assault, the disclosure may elicit strong feelings, which the practitioner may share with a supervisor or a colleague, but not with just anyone. Disgust should not be displayed toward the offender. The victim may love the offender and not wish that person any harm or retribution (Ramsey-Klawsnik, 1993).

In addition to the questions listed above, clients should be asked whether they are getting enough to eat and drink, and whether their medications are being given on time. The practitioner should also ask whether clients have been yelled at or threatened. In order to determine how they cope with the abuse, clients should be asked how they respond in abusive situations or when they are left alone for long periods of time. Clients' responses to these questions may range from, "Oh, I just expect her to have her way all the time so I don't fight back," or, "I don't say anything; I just cry when I'm alone," to "I hit her back and told her no one pushes me around like that."

Because some clients may be victims of multiple types of abuse, the practitioner must be sure to ask questions regarding all possible forms of abuse.

8. *Determine the client's current mental status.* The purpose of conducting a mental status exam at some point during the interview is to add credibility to the client's report of elder mistreatment and to counter attempts by others to dismiss the client's allegations with statements such as, "Oh, she made up the story," or, "She's senile. She doesn't know what

she's saying." Evaluation tools such as the Mini Mental State Exam (Folstein et al., 1975), Dementia Scale (Kahn et al., 1960), and Symptoms of Depression (Goodwin & Guze, 1984) are easy to administer and to score (see Appendixes B, C, and E). If clients do poorly, on the other hand, it may indicate that they are incapable of caring for themselves, or of giving consent for intervention. The practitioner's case plan may later need to include finding someone to assist the client (Brownell, 1994).

## Assessing Injuries

Practitioners who are not in the health care field are sometimes uncomfortable about examining for injuries. They may feel they lack training, or they may have been schooled to assess clients only verbally. Nevertheless, it is possible to review clients physically while at the same time protecting their modesty. While still in the client's home, the practitioner should ask to take a quick look at the client's scalp, arms, and legs, to make sure he or she is all right. For example, the practitioner might say:

> "Mrs. Smith, I would like you to roll up your sleeves for me so I can take a peek at your arms."
> "Will you please let me look at your neck and feel your scalp?"
> "Do you hurt anywhere in particular? Show me."
> "Would you mind rolling up your pants so I can look at your legs?"

If the client does not mind complying with the request for this examination, the practitioner should proceed and then ask to be allowed to look at the back and chest. The practitioner should say:

> "I'd like to look down your collar for a second, look at your back."
> "Will you please unbutton your front so I can look at your chest?"

In a medical setting, it is necessary to examine patients after they are undressed and gowned. Symptoms of abuse and neglect may be overlooked unless the entire body is examined carefully. Begin the examination from either the head or the feet, methodically proceeding up or down, looking for injuries on the head, including behind the ears, then the neck, trunk, thighs, legs, feet, and finally, both arms and hands. All findings should be recorded on a sketch sheet or trauma graph (refer back to Figure 6-1).

Document the following:

1. Size of the injury
2. Color of the bruise or injury
3. Its shape
4. Location of injury

Record the injuries in relation to several fixed anatomic landmarks (Adelson, 1974). For example, "Light-brown round bruise 2 inches directly below left nipple," or "Two- by 3- inch wound above right heel, some dried blood present." On an inpatient hospital floor, part of the assessment of elder mistreatment requires that documentation be made in detail in the patient's chart. Often, a nurse and social worker may interview the patient together, with one asking the questions and the other diagramming and recording their findings. If the patient is supine and unable to get out of bed, examine the anterior or front aspect of the body first, then turn the patient to one side to examine the back and arm on that side, then move to the other side of the bed to turn the patient in the other direction and examine the other half of the back and the other arm.

Findings should be described explicitly, and the patient's statements should be recorded in quotes. Suspicion should be aroused if a patient's version of how he or she was injured is different from the suspected abuser's. The patient's trunk and extremities should be sketched, and bruises, lacerations, or other injuries drawn according to size, color, shape, and location to call attention to the seriousness of the problem. The sketches should be signed and dated by the practitioner. Such eye-catching sketches in the chart have been very important for future reference and intervention as well as for staff education. For example, a suspected abuser may state that a patient's bruises are from repeated falls. If the physical therapist, after several sessions, finds that the patient ambulates independently with no assistance, does not fall, and has a normal gait, then it is necessary to consider possible elder mistreatment. In another example, a patient with organic brain syndrome may be admitted to the hospital with bruises of unknown etiology. If the suspected abuser says that the patient bruises easily, the nursing and physical therapy staff can observe how easily the patient actually bruises. If the patient develops no new bruises from routine handling such as being turned or transferred from a walker, or from being restrained with wrist or waist restraints and belts, and if bruises presented upon admission fade away during the patient's hospital stay, then the patient should be viewed as a possible victim of elder mistreatment.

If an injury is from an accident, the way the injury occurred should be determined. When a client says that he or she fell, it is not enough just to note that the client fell. The client should also be asked, "What were you doing when you fell?" "Was anyone with you at that time?" "Show me how you got this bruise or cut." The client's responses should then be recorded.

The client should be assessed for injuries to the head, scalp, or face. Bruises and hematoma that are distributed bilaterally, on both sides of the body, or that are symmetrical should be noted on a sketch sheet. A hematoma is a mass of blood confined to an organ or an enclosed area, such as the spleen, a muscle, the chest, or the head. A hematoma that is located in an arm or a leg causes increased girth or swelling of that extremity. The practitioner may see an accompanying bruise or discoloration in the adjoining skin area. The bruises may be shaped like the object that was used to inflict the injury. Some hematomas are not diagnosed by visual exam. For example, a subdural hematoma which creates pressure on the brain is detected by computerized axial tomogram (CAT scan). A "spongy" scalp, or one that is very soft to the touch, may be a result of hair-pulling. If round bruises are found on both upper arms or near both shoulders, the client may have been held by the shoulders and shaken.

The sketches shown in Figures 6-2, 6-3, 6-4, and 6-5, and 6-6 are examples of documentation of clients' injuries. In the case of Figure 6-2, the medical resident remembered the patient's bilateral arm bruises while discussing the case with the social worker after the patient and his daughter left the emergency room. The resident subsequently sketched the bruises and included the sketch as an addendum to the initial assessment. The sketch was extremely important in involving adult protective services to investigate the patient's home situation.

Each sketch should contain the client's name, the date of the exam, and the signature of the examiner. Later, such sketches can be used as evidence in a court hearing, such as a guardianship proceeding or when a protective order is needed.

While sketches are useful, photos taken during the examination are preferable. Photos of injuries should be taken during the physical exam, assuming that the client has given consent to be photographed by signing a release form. If the client is unable to give consent because of illness or inability to comprehend the request, pictures may still be taken. It may be necessary to find a substitute who can later give permission to use the

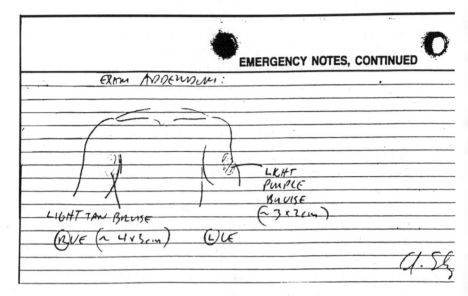

Figure 6-2　Case example A.

photos. Some state laws permit protective service workers to take photographs. Some law enforcement personnel will also take photographs when called to the scene. They usually must be notified to bring a camera with them in advance.

Cameras with film that develops instantly are practical because retakes are possible if the photos are under- or overexposed. However, instant-development film can distort color, depending on the camera's angle or lighting. Therefore, it is advised that a color guide be placed next to the subject for future reference. Placing a coin next to injuries will give the viewer an idea of the size of the injury. Close-up photos of the injury are not enough. It is advisable to take a full-length photo of the elderly client which includes the face and the injury, in case anyone attempts to challenge the veracity of the photos.

In a potential case of elder mistreatment, photographs should be taken as soon as possible. Regrettably, this has not always happened, often be-

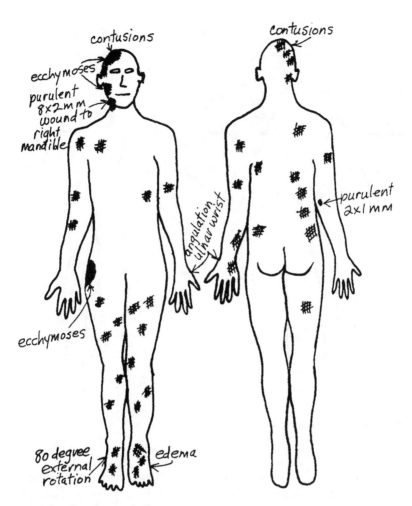

Figure 6-3    Case example B.

cause practitioners hesitate to act, out of disbelief or doubt that the mistreatment did occur (Matlaw & Spence, 1994). Unless photos are taken or injuries are documented at the beginning of the assessment, practitioners will be unable to counter the abuser's accusation that the injuries such as bruises did not exist prior to the visit with the practitioner, implying that the practitioner or health care team was responsible for the injuries while handling the client. In one case, a 78-year-old man was brought to the emergency room of a hospital from home by an aid car, suffering from

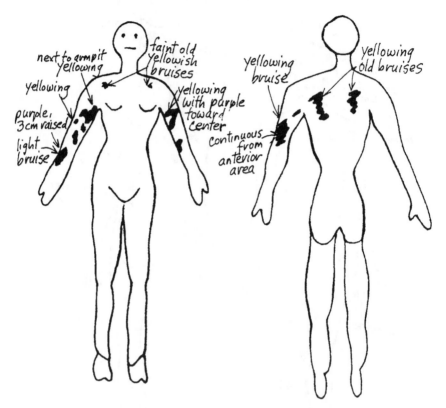

Figure 6-4    Case example C.

severe heart problems. While he lay in the intensive care unit, the nurses and social worker noted unusual marks on his chest. There was agreement that some of the marks were due to medical procedures conducted after the admission, but the majority of the marks were unaccountable. The social worker conducted a thorough psychosocial assessment and discovered that the patient lived with his wife and their mentally ill daughter, who, just prior to the admission, had attacked the patient from behind and had clawed her father's chest while she stood behind him. By the time the etiology of the injuries had been determined, it was too late to take the photos, since injuries inflicted by the daughter had been obscured by the marks caused by the medical procedures.

Suspicious bruise sites include the upper arm and thigh, and the inner arm and thigh. Bruises which are clustered, as if from repeated striking, or

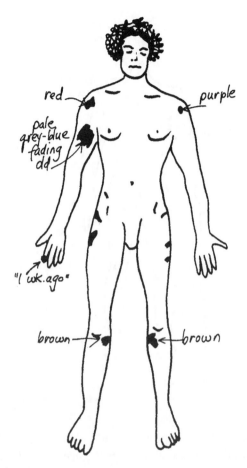

Figure 6-5   Case example D, front view.

which are shaped like thumbprints or fingerprints, are also suspicious. If new and old bruises are present at the same time, as if from repeated injury, or if injuries are present which are at different stages of resolution, elder mistreatment must be considered. Table 6-1 (page 171) will help to determine the age of bruises.

If bruises are noticed after a client has changed health care practitioners or after he or she has had a prolonged absence from a health care agency, the practitioner should consider and take steps to rule out elder mistreatment.

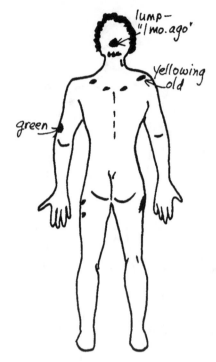

Figure 6-6    Case example D, rear view.

Besides bruises, other symptoms should also be noted. Marks around the wrists, around the ankles, and under the armpit may indicate that restraints have been used. Very pronounced marks under the armpit or in the axilla area may be due to the client's being restrained and then slipping lower in the chair. If the client has joint contractures—that is, the knees or hips are stiff from lack of use or movement—it may indicate neglect. Contractures and poor muscle tone may also be a sign that the client has been tied down or confined to a bed or chair for long periods of time.

Abrasions and lacerations differ from bruises and may be due to accidental falls or to falls resulting from being shoved or pushed; bruises similar to the shape of an object are sometimes inflicted by someone else. Abrasions, due to the scraping of the skin and the removal of superficial layers—for example, from fingernail scratches or from being dragged on a carpet or the ground—may cover a large surface area on the skin. Dry-

**Table 6-1 Dating of Bruises**

| Time | Description |
|---|---|
| 0–2 days* | Swollen, tender |
| 0–5 days* | Red-blue |
| 5–7 days | Green |
| 7–10 days | Yellow |
| 10–14 days | Brown |
| 2–4 weeks | Clear |

*0 = less than 24 hours

ing of the scraped areas results in color changes over time: the scraped area changes from pale yellow-brown while oozing tissue fluid, to dark-brown, and then to black. Lacerations are tears produced by blunt trauma or from falls. The appearance and depth of lacerations due to blunt trauma are determined by the force and the direction of the force. An equal undermining on all sides of a laceration is evidence of a perpendicular impact on the body, such as a blow by a hammer or another instrument (Adelson, 1974). Lacerations from falls may cover one side of the body, that is, if a person falls to the right, skin tears may appear over the outer and upper rims of the right eye socket and on the right cheekbone, sparing the eye and eyelid. The right lower jaw may also be injured. A minor laceration or abrasion may be the only external evidence of a more serious internal injury.

Death of an elderly person from subtle though fatal mistreatment may resemble death by natural causes. Henson (1987) writes, "Many elderly victims of abuse are just as helpless as victims of child abuse. Because of their age, however, death from abuse may be even less frequently detected in the elderly than in children. . . . Sudden, unexpected deaths of younger people are likely to be investigated, but those of older people are treated more routinely. As more and more cases of elder abuse by adult children of the victims come to light, deaths of the elderly may be scrutinized as closely as infant deaths." Given that victims may be stuck when they are helpless, investigators of elder mistreatment must consider assisting the elder with accessing proper medical treatment in a timely manner.

Senile purpura may be mistaken for injuries inflicted by another person. Often purple or dark-red in color, with jagged edges, senile purpura are hemorrhages in the skin of the elderly following minor injury, and are due to the fragility of small blood vessels. They also resemble steroid purpura caused by long-term high doses of steroids. Senile purpura often appear on the forearm, where the skin is thin and inelastic, and on areas commonly bumped (Andres, Bierman, & Hazzard, 1985). Collagen loss creates transparent, parchment-like skin that is vulnerable to purpura development even with the application of minimal pressure (Schier, 1982).

A neurological exam may be conducted if changes in the client's mental status are evident since a previous examination.

In a medical setting, diagnostic procedures, as indicated by the client's history, may include the following:

- Radiological (X-rays) screening for fractures
- Metabolic screening for nutritional, electrolyte, or endocrine abnormalities
- Toxicology screening for over- or undermedication
- Hematology screening for a coagulation defect when abnormal bleeding or bruising is documented
- Computerized axial tomogram (CAT scan) for major changes in neurological status or head trauma that could result in subdural hematoma
- Gynecological procedures to rule out venereal disease from sexual assault

Sexual abuse and sexual assault are unreported and underdetected partially because of societal attitudes that stereotype the elderly as being sexually inactive and unlikely to be victims of sexual assault. Symptoms of possible sexual abuse include evidence of a sexually transmitted disease; genital irritation or injury; extreme upset when being changed, bathed, or examined; and a reaction of jumpiness or fear to certain individuals or to people in general (Ramsey-Klawsnik, 1993). One health care team in a women's clinic stumbled across a case of elder sexual abuse by finding sperm in a urine sample. In cases such as these, owing to the client's love for and attachment and loyalty to their abusers, they may resist reporting the abuse until it becomes overt, for example, when an abuser progresses from discussing sexual exploits in detail with the elder to masturbating in the elder's presence while discussing sexual activities (Ramsey-Klawsnik, 1993). Practitioners must pay close attention to the client's statements and questions, which may provide hints or a coded disclosure that sexual abuse or assault has occurred. For example, in a case referred to one of the authors, an 80-year-old woman called a rape crisis line to inquire if she could become pregnant. Further inquiry revealed that she was being forced to engage in sexual acts with a neighbor who began to visit her regularly soon after her husband died. Such questions are indirect means of asking for help and should not be laughed off or dismissed as absurd.

## The Client's Concerns: "You Won't Tell, Will You?"

After finishing the interview with the client and before interviewing the suspected abuser, the practitioner needs to pay special attention to the concerns of the client. Regret, fear, and anxiety may surface after the client has admitted to being a victim of elder mistreatment. These feelings may show up in fearful questions such as those posed by one of the authors' clients, "You won't tell, will you?" "Now what are you going to do?" The client may fear reprisals if the suspected abuser finds out what has been disclosed. Clients may also have ambivalent feelings toward a suspected abuser. They may be upset about being abused but may sacrifice their own needs in order to keep the abuser from getting into trouble or being arrested and jailed. Clients may also be frightened if they think a practitioner is considering removing them from their own home, regardless of the reason. Sadly, in more than one instance, a victim of elder mistreatment has been removed from the home for reasons of safety, only to have the abuser move into or take charge of the now vacant house.

After completing the interview with the client, then, the practitioner should be straightforward and reassuring. He or she should give the client an example of what will be said to the suspected abuser. Taking a family systems approach, the practitioner may say:

> "We need to collect more data or information about your situation. I am going to talk to your daughter to see what her concerns for you are. I will not tell her what we discussed, even if she asks me what we talked about. For example, I will not say to your daughter, "Your mother just told me you've been hitting her (taking her money, etc.). I am going to have you arrested.' Instead, I will say to your daughter, 'I'm trying to determine what services your mother may require and would like your perception of how she has been doing.' I will not say anything that will get you in to trouble, OK? I will attempt to work with both of you to help you improve your situation."

## INTERVIEWING THE SUSPECTED ABUSER

Without sufficient knowledge, interviewing a family member or caregiver who is suspected of being abusive or neglectful can be anxiety-provoking or uncomfortable for the practitioner. This section of the evaluation is probably the most difficult to complete because the practitioner is faced with someone who is, or may be, dangerous to the client *and* the practitioner. It is difficult to predict a suspected abuser's response to specific questions because abusers come in all sizes, shapes, and colors. For instance, known abusers at one agency have included a perfectly coiffed, pleasant-looking daughter who worked as a nursing home aide; a tall, thin, articulate son who expressed a desire to take good care of his father; and a dapper, white-haired elderly male who appeared for his interview in a double-breasted suit. It is very important to interview the suspected abuser immediately after the client is interviewed. The suspected abuser will not have a chance to collude with the client or ask the client what was discussed earlier. A primary method of uncovering elder mistreatment is to find inconsistencies in stories or reports given separately by the client and the suspected abuser. When such inconsistencies are uncovered, it is then necessary to proceed with a longer investigation, including prompt collateral contacts.

It is advisable to stick to the format of the protocol—it can provide a "security blanket" for the practitioner during a very emotion-laden interview. It is best to maintain a friendly disposition and to speak in a well-modulated tone of voice, so as not to excite anyone. The practitioner should matter-of-factly record the suspected abuser's responses verbatim. If it is not possible to document every statement verbatim, practitioners may write key words that may trigger their memory later as they review their notes. Some clients may look nervous about the practitioner's note-taking and have difficulty focusing on the questions asked. Rather than quit taking notes, the practitioner may acknowledge the client's apparent concerns by stating, "It is difficult for me to remember everything that you said. I need to record what you say so I don't make mistakes. You can read my notes before I leave if you would like to."

The suspected abuser may resist being interviewed by the practitioner. If the protocol is introduced as a standard part of the exam, however, and is read by the interviewer, the suspected abuser may be less defensive and less likely to feel singled out or unjustly accused of wrongdoing.

The interview with the suspected abuser may include the following questions and statements:

"Thank you for waiting while I interviewed your mother. Now it's your turn. I need your help—I am doing an (psychosocial) assessment of your mother's current functioning and situation, in order to determine what services are appropriate at this time. I would like to spend some time with you and have you tell me your perception of how things are here."

"Tell me what you want me to know about your mother."
"What is her medical condition? What medicine does she take?"
"What kind of care does she require?"
"How involved are you with your mother's everyday activities and care?"
"What do you expect her to do for herself?"
"What does she expect you to do for her? Do you do those things? Are you able to do them? Have you had any difficulties? What kind?"
"Please describe how you spend a typical day."
"How do you cope with having to care for your mother all the time?"
"Do you have supports or respite care? Who and what?"
"Are there other siblings who help?"
"What responsibilities do you have outside the home? Do you work?"
"What are your hours? What do you do?"
"Would you mind telling me what your income is?" (If this question seems touchy to the suspected abuser, the practitioner might say, "I just wondered if your family can afford the pills she needs to take.")

The practitioner should assess the suspected abuser's degree of dependence on the elderly client's income, pensions, or assets through the following question:

"Is your mother's Social Security check directly deposited in the bank?"
"Who owns this house? Do you pay rent? Whose name is on the deed?"
"If you help your mother pay her bills, how do you do it? Is your name on her account?"
"Do you have power of attorney? Does it have a durable clause? When did you get it?"

Questions will seem less provocative if the suspected abuser perceives them to be client-centered and perceives the practitioner as someone who wants to make a detailed assessment of the client's situation rather than focusing on the suspected abuser's behavior or actions. All or most of the above questions serve that purpose. If the suspected abuser seems suspicious or slightly defensive, repeat the fact that he or she is being helpful by providing this information and that services for which the client may be eligible may benefit the suspected abuser as well. The practitioner needs to be assertive, and to use the bargaining and persuasion tactics that are helpful when working with involuntary clients. These tactics are described earlier in Chapter 5 and may help to keep the suspected abuser talking while the practitioner assesses the client's condition and physical surroundings.

When the suspected abuser presents with a serious physical or mental condition, even more delicate questions must be asked; it is best to save these questions for the end of the interview, when most of the necessary information has been gathered and a defensive response from the suspected abuser can be risked. Elder mistreatment must not be assumed. The burden of denial must be placed on the suspected abuser. The following appropriate questions can be asked to determine the suspected abuser's responsibility in causing the elder's condition:

"You know those bruises on your mother's arms (head, nose, etc.)? How do you suppose she got them?" (Document response verbatim. If possible, follow up with a request that the suspected abuser demonstrate how the injury may have happened.)

"Your mother is suffering from malnourishment and/or dehydration." Or "Your mother seems rather undernourished and thin. How do you think she got this way?"

"Is there any reason you waited this long to seek medical care for your mother?"

"Caring for someone as impaired as your mother is a difficult task. Have you ever felt so frustrated with her that you pushed her a little harder than you expected? How about hitting or slapping her? What were the circumstances?" (Document response verbatim.)

"Have you ever had to tie your mother to a bed or chair or lock her in a room when you go out at night?"

"Have there been times when you've yelled at her or threatened her verbally?"

At one hospital, many abusive caregivers interviewed denied or minimized their responsibility for the elderly client's injuries or precarious situation. When interviewing a suspected abuser, the practitioner's primary goal is to gather information and to document the information accurately. It is not to argue, to dispute, or to challenge the responses of the suspected abuser. In the intervention phase, after all information is gathered, the practitioner may decide to be confrontational, but the goal in this phase is to gather information.

The questions listed above provide the suspected abuser with an opportunity to admit frustration, stress, loss of control, or any "wrongdoing." This admission may be sincere ("I just lost it; I couldn't take one more night of her whining, and I'm sorry"), or it may be insincere, that is, the admission or apology is made only to get the practitioner "off my back." At this point, practitioners must make a judgment about whether they are faced with a sincere, stressed caregiver who needs assistance or with a pathological abuser who feels he or she has been "caught in the act" and so must cooperate with the practitioner. The suspected abuser's affect while discussing the abusive situation may help the practitioner assess sincerity. Furthermore, verification of the suspected abuser's specific response may be obtained by interviewing others who know both the client and the suspected abuser, such as neighbors, friends, relatives, and personnel of agencies involved in providing care to the client.

## COLLATERAL CONTACTS

Collateral contacts must be made promptly, before the suspected abuser attempts to collude with others. The number of contacts made by the practitioner may range from 2 to 20 people who have knowledge of both the client's and the abuser's behavior, and who are good sources of information. Concerned people who possess important information are usually reluctant to become involved if they anticipate having to appear in court or having to face the suspected abuser at a later date. To aid the client and to ensure confidentiality, the practitioner may need to appeal to them as "good Samaritans." When possible, collateral contacts may be made even before interviewing the client and the suspected abuser. The suspected abuser and client may be asked, "Who else should I talk to?" "Who can tell me more about your mother's condition?"

## SUMMARIZING THE INTERVIEWS

Summarizing may be done separately with the client and the suspected abuser. After completing the interviews with them and the collateral contacts, the practitioner should give the client a summary of what has occurred. The practitioner might say, "On the basis of what you're telling me, you would like some help with household chores. It must be difficult to have to rely on your daughter to do everything for you." Findings are stated in a factual manner: "On the basis of what you've revealed, your daughter mistreats you. You are frightened of your daughter and yet you love her. As frightened as you are of her, you are also saying you feel safe when she is around and are glad when she comes to your home, talks to you, opens your mail, and fixes your meals." Next, the client is informed that only with her permission will intervention or treatment options be explored. In the initial interview and throughout the treatment process, besides reducing tension and anxiety, a major goal is to provide the client with a feeling of hope for improvement and relief. A feeling of hopelessness can serve as a barrier to motivation and change. Hope or optimism is directly related to the practitioner's degree of therapeutic enthusiasm. The practitioner must play an active role in conveying to the client that change is possible, that the client can obtain some improvement in the situation (Golan 1979; Rapoport 1970).

When summarizing with the suspected abuser, the practitioner should thank him or her for cooperating and contributing. The practitioner should *not* disclose plans or strategies for intervention. Very often, suspected abusers begin to develop their own strategies when they realize that the practitioner is concerned about the client's current situation. The urge to confront the abuser should be resisted. Instead, the practitioner may inform the abuser that he or she will proceed at a cautious pace and, with the client's permission, develop an individualized treatment plan. The practitioner may feel that this is deceptive but should remember that the client's safety is at stake, and that the status quo should not be disrupted until better conditions can replace or improve it.

## DIAGNOSIS

After reviewing the client's history, the physical exam, the suspected abuser's history, and information from collateral contacts, the client may be given a tentative diagnosis. This may be one of the following:

1. No evidence for elder mistreatment
2. Suspicion of neglect

3. Suspicion of abuse
4. Positive for abuse, neglect, or gross neglect

## SUMMARY

Elder mistreatment is typically a hidden phenomenon. The first phase of the EADI Model provides a protocol to systematically determine whether elder mistreatment exists. Occasionally a situation will be characterized by the need for immediate action on the part of the practitioner, and the assessment phase must be collapsed and combined with treatment on first contact. Chapter 7 describes immediate actions the practitioner can take in crisis situations.

# Intervention Phase

## I. Considerations and Crisis Treatment

Owing to the variety of situations presented to the practitioner regarding elder mistreatment, the second phase of the Elder Abuse Diagnosis and Intervention Model provides several approaches for intervention: crisis intervention, and counseling with the victim and the abuser. This chapter describes factors that influence the practitioner's choice of intervention and then describes crisis intervention. The practitioner is provided with options that may be initiated immediately and do not require prior legal action. (Interventions that do require prior legal action are described in Chapter 9.)

### FACTORS INFLUENCING INTERVENTIONS

#### Client's Capabilities

After the practitioner has interviewed the client and the alleged abuser, the next task is to determine if the client is capable of consenting to treatment and deciding what should be the course of treatment. Specific assessment tools will enable the practitioner to determine the client's general level of physical and mental capacities. If the client is not oriented to time, place, and person, or has a low score on a mental status exam, and does poorly in assessment of activities of daily living (ADL) and advanced living skills, then finding a surrogate decision maker should be considered. The practitioner should bear in mind that these assessments may require several contacts in order to be completed. Practitioners from different disciplines are sometimes consulted, and these assessments can be carried out simultaneously with other intervention options.

In hospital geriatric evaluation units, an elderly client's workup to determine capabilities includes:

1. "Dementia" workup to rule out reversible illness:
   a. Laboratory tests
   b. Chest X-ray
   c. Urinalysis
   d. Computerized axial tomogram (CAT scan)
   e. Electroencephalogram (EEG)
   f. Skull X-ray
2. Administration of a mental status exam to determine mental capabilities (see Appendix C)
3. Assessment of basic and advanced living skills to determine functional capabilities (see Appendix D)
4. Neuropsychological tests, when indicated
5. Administration of an questionnaire to rule out depression (see Appendix E)

Conditions that are reversible or arrestable include nutritional and metabolic disorders, vascular diseases such as multi-infarct dementia, neurological diseases such as Parkinson's disease, depression, normal pressure hydrocephalus, infections, drug interactions, and tumors (Kane et al., 1994). Laboratory tests are conducted to detect any nutritional, electrolyte, or endocrine abnormalities. A geriatric nutrition screening panel may include blood levels of albumin, prealbumin, vitamin C, vitamin E, retinol, folate, and zinc. There is a tendency to prematurely label an elder as having Alzheimer's disease; instead, exploration of other causes of dementia and confusion must first take place. In addition, sight and hearing impairments resulting in insufficient sensory stimuli may contribute to mental status test scores below the norm. (Uhlmann, Larson, Rees, & Koepsell, 1989).

Neuropsychological testing performed by a clinical psychologist is indicated if the client's mental status exam shows capabilities in some areas but not in others and there is no clear explanation for these differences. Psychological tests can more clearly pinpoint the client's "pocket of deficiencies." For example:

A sociable and conversant client hospitalized with a broken hip was alert and oriented on admission and initially perceived as capable of caring for herself. Later, she was perceived by the staff to be uncooperative in grooming, dressing, and ambulation activities. Psychological testing showed that the client was losing some ability to digest and retain new information and that she was not capable of remembering everything that the physical therapist told her in previous sessions. The treatment plan was subsequently modified to add written cues to the verbal cues to help the client progress in her recovery.

It is necessary to perform an assessment for depression because some people may look and act "senile" or "demented," but may in fact be suffering from a depression that may be reversible with medications. Factors to consider when assessing for depression are listed in Appendix E.

The practitioner may feel uncomfortable about using the aforementioned tools, thinking that one needs to be a specialist to use them. However, case managers, social workers, and nurses have utilized these tools with no problems during home visits for a preliminary assessment. Being familiar with these tools will enable the practitioner to refer the client for a further workup to the appropriate agency. Time and again, a client has been too quickly labeled "competent" or "incompetent" without adequate information that justifies these labels. The practitioner's assessment of the client's capabilities has to be done carefully in order to establish an appropriate treatment plan and to hold up in a legal proceeding. With adequate information, an assessment team can recommend with confidence someone other than the abusive caregiver to be the limited or full guardian of the elderly client when it is necessary. In some instances the abusive caregiver has obtained legal counsel and contested the guardianship that was initiated on behalf of the client by the practitioner or others. Assuming that the guardianship will be challenged, the practitioner must be prepared to defend the reasons for declaring the client incapable and must be prepared to make a court appearance. In these cases, information must be gathered in depth, and all contacts, observations, and statements must be documented carefully and accurately.

After all specified assessments are completed, the client will fall into one of the following main categories:

- *Capable and consenting.* The client scores high in the dementia and functional assessments, and manifests the ability to integrate information, and consents to treatment.

- *Capable and nonconsenting.* The client scores high in dementia and functional assessments, understands his or her circumstances, but does not consent to treatment or services, for any of a variety of reasons.
- *Incapable and consenting.* The client scores low in the assessments yet requests assistance or services.
- *Incapable and nonconsenting.* The client does poorly in the assessments, is incapable of giving consent for treatment or services, refuses services, and requires surrogate representation.
- *Emergency client.* The client is in danger of irreparable harm to self or property, as a result of an acute medical condition, unsafe environmental conditions, or sudden and rapid loss of finances or property.

## Client's Cooperation

It is easy and often pleasurable to work with capable, consenting clients because they are motivated toward change and often express gratitude for the practitioner's time and concern. On the other hand, it is frustrating to work with capable, nonconsenting clients. They are aware of being victims of abuse or neglect but choose to remain in the abusive situation. Clients' willingness to consent to treatment and their degree of involvement can depend on several factors, such as their motivation to change their behavior or environment, their capacity to engage in a treatment relationship, and opportunities and resources available to effect change. Before becoming angry at clients or feeling that they are foolish to remain in the role of victim, the practitioner should examine factors influencing the choice. These clients may choose to remain in an abusive situation because of fear, hope, love, low self-esteem, financial dependence, emotional dependence, isolation, duty, lack of proper help from outsiders, and the fact that the abuse is not severe enough to make them want to leave (Star, 1978; Elliott, 1983).

Ambivalence is a concept that is acknowledged by practitioners but is not dealt with adequately. It is an inherent part of the beginning phase of treatment. Any practitioner working with abused elders has been told more than once, "No, I don't want your services," and has felt frustrated. It may be liberating to the client to hear the practitioner address the ambivalence, saying, "Perhaps you are having some thoughts as to whether or not you want a stranger like me to help you." Attending to ambivalent feelings early in the treatment period will decrease the chance of conscious or unconscious sabotage by the client (Wasserman 1979).

Gambrill (1983) cautions practitioners to refrain from labeling a client "resistant." When clients fail to comply with a practitioner's expectations and do not talk about issues the practitioner feels are important, they may not be "resistant" but instead may be struggling with discomfort, possibly due to a previous negative relationship with a practitioner or because they have never related to a practitioner under similar circumstances. These clients may also be struggling with having to take responsibility for their own actions. All new situations can threaten an elder, and the worker can show awareness of these feelings by saying to the client, "Perhaps you are wondering what I'm doing here; You must be wondering if I'm going to ask you to leave your home"; or, "Getting to know a new person takes time" (Wasserman 1979).

Cormier and Cormier (1985) define resistance as "any client *or* therapist behavior that interferes with or reduces the likelihood of a successful therapeutic process and outcome." They state that most, if not all, clients display resistive behavior at some time during therapy. Not only involuntary clients but also voluntary and self-referred clients can be resistive. Resistance may occur when an elder lacks necessary skills or knowledge, has pessimistic expectations, or has anxious or negative thoughts. Discussing their situation with a practitioner may require change on the part of such clients, something they may not yet feel prepared for. Sometimes the clients may seem uncooperative because they may want to avoid painful topics and may have ambivalent feelings toward change and toward the abuser.

Variables having to do with the practitioner also affect resistance. Sometimes practitioners label a client as resistant to explain their own failures. As a result, Cormier and Cormier (1985) suggest that practitioners avoid taking a client's resistance personally and be accepting of themselves. Practitioners can also help by encouraging the client's participation in the therapy and by acknowledging their own anxiety and discomfort about their competence. Rather than viewing the client as uncooperative, practitioners should view this period as an opportunity to examine how their behavior and attitudes could be influencing the client's participation (Bookin & Dunkle, 1989).

Butler and Lewis (1982) describe why some elders resist mental health treatment. These reasons may be applied to any "helping" situation. Elders may be resistant because they desire independence, taking pride in their perceived self-reliance. They also hold on to what they have because they fear change and the unknown. They may not seek treatment because they fear certain diagnoses. They may have symptoms of a condition of which a deceased friend or spouse died and may not realize that the state of the art has advanced and the condition can be treated. Low self-esteem, mentioned earlier, may be due to having absorbed society's negative attitudes toward aging. Other factors contributing to low participation by a client may be anxiety, low motivation, lack of information or misinformation, interfering beliefs and attitudes, distractions, interfering life circumstances, poor rapport, lack of participation in choosing the treatment procedures, and lack of social supports for participation. Physical and mental impairments also contribute to low participation (Gambrill, 1983).

## Pathology of the Abuser

Some abusers as well as elders may seem resistant but are on guard because they fear being misunderstood and labeled forever as mean and awful; they also fear they will not have an opportunity to tell their story. Others, however, are obstructionistic. The effectiveness of an intervention often depends on the abuser's willingness and ability to stop the abusive behavior. Guilt-ridden, overburdened caregivers who recognize that their abusive behavior is unacceptable may be more receptive to intervention than severely disturbed caregivers who deny any wrongdoing or feel that their behavior is justified. Sometimes an abuser will take responsibility for the abuse only after legal interventions, such as a protection order, have been initiated. The less cooperation abusers offer, the more drastic interventions against them are likely to be.

It is imperative that the practitioner determine early in the assessment and intervention phases the severity of the abuser's pathology and whether the client is in a life-threatening situation. This is especially important if a client chooses to remain with a pathological abuser. Joint sessions in which feelings such as anger, resentment, and jealousy are aroused may lead to an abusive episode after the interview when no witnesses are present (Star, 1978). Family systems therapy is not recommended initially in the treatment of some batterers and victims (Walker, 1995). Abused people who have not made the transition from "victim" to "survivor" may not appreciate the neutrality necessary in family therapy: they may perceive the therapist as siding with the batterer if the therapist does not "choose sides." Also, if the victim's fear of future violence has been minimized or trivialized by others earlier, the victim may not participate fully in the sessions. Walker and many of her colleagues believe that family therapy is appropriate only after the perpetrator has accepted responsibility for the violence, has stopped obsessive and stalking behaviors, has learned "anger management" skills, has addressed "family of origin" issues, and has learned the appropriate patterns of roles and socialization. With these cautionary statements in mind, it is suggested that the practitioner not provoke the abuser, but instead carefully plan the intervention steps and take no drastic action in opposition to the abuser unless the client *clearly* supports the intervention.

Very often, court-mandated treatment for a spouse or child abusers is necessary because of their own denial, minimization, externalization, and impulsivity (Ganley, 1981). An abuser with these characteristics will not voluntarily seek help. Because the study of elder mistreatment is in its nascent stages, special programs have not yet been developed for courts to mandate abusers of the elderly to seek treatment, and it is not yet known whether abusers of the elderly can be treated together with batterers of women and children in existing programs. In one state, a group solely for elder abusers is now being formed.

## Severity of the Situation

The severity of the situation dictates the type of intervention and how quickly intervention should occur. For example, if someone is removing large sums of money from a client's bank account in a short period of time, immediate intervention is necessary. If, however, a client is able to defend himself or herself in a neglectful or abusive situation and is not in immediate danger, the practitioner will probably have time to make a full assessment of the situation, make collateral contacts, and carefully develop a treatment plan.

## Quality of the Practitioner-Client Relationship

The development of a positive therapeutic relationship between the client and the practitioner will maximize the chance of mutual cooperation and a positive treatment outcome. Villamore and Bergman (1981) note that "an ongoing semi-therapeutic relationship may have greater long-term benefits than any specific service." Traditional intensive psychotherapy is not necessarily the sole or the most effective treatment modality for elderly clients who may be reluctant to go to mental health clinics or private practitioners.

Stone (1979) notes that on average, one third to half of clients in a medical setting do not follow treatments prescribed for them, even when instructions are clear. It is the quality of the interaction between the practitioner and the client that influences the degree of compliance. The practitioner may feel angry and may be tempted to terminate the relationship if a client seems uncooperative and consumes precious time. The practitioner might justify terminating the relationship by citing a heavy caseload, but it should be remembered that the ambivalent client can benefit from regular contacts and eventually may choose to accept the practitioner's suggestions and offers of help. For example, many hospital emergency rooms offer intervention options to a woman diagnosed as a victim of battering. If she chooses to return to the battering situation rather than go directly to a shelter or to a supportive person's home, she is informed that battering usually escalates to more serious forms and that she is free to return for help in the future. Such victims have returned three or more times before requesting active intervention. Victims of elder mistreatment are similar in their reactions; it may take repeated offers of intervention such as those listed in Figure 7-1 (American Medical Association, 1992), and additional incidents of mistreatment, before the elder accepts active intervention.

Having described influential factors in the intervention phase, we will next discuss the use of crisis intervention in elder mistreatment.

## CRISIS INTERVENTION

### Crisis Theory

A crisis is "an upset in a steady state." This definition was developed by Caplan in 1960 (Rapoport, 1962; Parad & Parad, 1990). Crisis theory is a combination of different theories and practices in the behavioral sciences. The study of crisis theory originated with Lindemann and Caplan and has been expanded by Rapoport (1962, 1970), Parad (1971), and Golan (1978, 1979, 1987). It has also been applied to therapy with groups and families in crisis (Aguilera, 1990; Langsley and Kaplan, 1968; Parad & Parad, 1990; Parad, Selby, & Quinlan, 1976; Roberts, 1996; Umana, Gross, & McConville, 1980). During the past 20 years, it has been applied to social casework, and practitioners who work with elder mistreatment can utilize this approach, especially when time constraints prevail.

# Interventions

↓

Coordinate approach with Adult Protective Services as mandated in your state

↓

**Patient is willing to accept voluntary services**

**Patient is unwilling to accept voluntary services or lacks capacity to consent**

↓

- Educate patient about incidence of elder mistreatment and tendency for it to increase in frequency and severity over time

- Implement safety plan (e.g., safe home placement, court protective order, hospital admission)

- Provide assistance that will alleviate causes of mistreatment (e.g., refer to drug or alcohol rehabilitation for addicted abusers; provide education, home health, and/or homemaker services for overburdened caregivers)

- Referral of patient and/ or family members to appropriate services (e.g., social work, counseling services, legal assistance, and advocacy)

**Patient lacks capacity**

↓

Discuss with adult protective services the following options:

- Financial management assistance

- Conservatorship

- Guardianship

- Committee

- Special court proceedings (e.g., orders of protection)

**Patient has capacity**

↓

- Educate patient about incidence of elder mistreatment and tendency for it to increase in frequency and severity over time

- Provide written information on emergency numbers and appropriate referrals

- Develop and review safety plan

- Develop a follow-up plan

---

Figure 7-1    Intervention options. Case management should be guided by choosing the alternatives that least restrict the patient's independence and decision-making responsibilities and fulfill state-mandated reporting requirements. Intervention will depend on the patient's cognitive status and decision-making capability and on whether the mistreatment is intentional or unintentional.

*Source:* American Medical Association (1992). *Diagnostic and treatment guidelines on elder abuse and neglect.* Chicago: Author, p.14.

There is a difference between a problem and a crisis. With a problem, an elder does not require new methods of coping; his or her current coping mechanisms are adequate to overturn the situation. In a crisis, the client must readapt to the situation and learn new methods to decrease feelings of anxiety and helplessness. The practitioner treating elder mistreatment, therefore, should be armed with specific sets of practice techniques that clients will wish to use, given their discomfort.

Crisis theory provides guidelines and techniques for intervention and has been used extensively in medical settings, mental health centers, and crisis clinics. Golan (1978) summarizes the basic tenets of crisis theory, which can be applied to elder mistreatment:

1. Crisis situations may occur episodically. They may be initiated by a hazardous event, may be finite, and may be the result of external or internal stressors. Crises may be composed of a single occurrence or a series of mishaps, which may build up to a cumulative effect.
2. A crisis is a disturbance in homeostatic balance and puts a client in a vulnerable state. To regain equilibrium, the client first uses a customary repertoire of problem-solving mechanisms, with an accompanying rise in tension. If the client is not successful in regaining equilibrium, then utilization of new, emergency methods of coping will be observed.
3. If the problem continues and cannot be resolved, avoided, or redefined, tension mounts, resulting in disequilibrium and disorganization. This period is called the state of active crisis.
4. A client may perceive the initial and subsequent stressful events as a threat, a loss, or a challenge. A threat may result in feelings of anxiety. Loss may result in feelings of deprivation or depression, or a state of mourning. A client who feels challenged by a crisis may experience a moderate increase in anxiety, but also hope and expectation.
5. A crisis is not to be equated with illness. It is not an illness or a pathological condition. Instead, it reflects a realistic struggle in the individual's life situation. It may reactivate earlier, unresolved, or partially resolved conflicts so that the client's response to the current crisis may be inappropriate or exaggerated. Given this, there is an opportunity for the client to resolve his or her present difficulties and also to rework a previous struggle and to break the linkage between past events and the current situation.
6. Each particular type of crisis follows a series of predictable stages, which can be mapped out and plotted. It is possible to anticipate

emotional reactions and behavioral responses at each stage. If clients
fixate at a particular phase or omit a phase, that may provide clues to
where they are "stuck" and what lies behind their inability to do their
crisis work and master the situation.

7. The active state of disequilibrium is time-limited, commonly lasting
   from 4 to 6 weeks. Parad (1971) reports that a specific number of
   interviews are part of a crisis-oriented treatment contract. Interviews
   range from 1 to 12, with the average number of contacts being 6
   (Aguilera, 1990; Parad, 1971; Parad & Parad, 1990). These interviews may take place daily within 1 week, or be spaced out over 1
   month.

8. During the resolution of the crisis, the individual tends to be amenable
   to help. It is during this period that the client is more open to outside
   influence and change. If intervention occurs during this period, a minimal effort can produce a maximal effect.

9. The last period in a crisis is the reintegration phase, when the client
   may emerge with newly learned adaptive styles. If help is not available during a crisis, clients sometimes adopt inadequate or maladaptive patterns, which can weaken their ability to function adequately in
   the future.

In a crisis situation, the practitioner is a participant, an observer, and a
change agent (Parad, 1971; Parad & Parad, 1990). It is a period when
immediate therapeutic contact and precisely articulated diagnostic formulation occur. It does not lend itself to systematic history-taking. Rapoport
(1962, 1970) and Parad (1971) emphasize the need for an unencumbered
method for intake. There should be no waiting list to obtain help, and there
is no separation between study, diagnosis, and treatment aspects of the case.

Capitalizing on the client's readiness to trust during this period of confusion, helplessness, and anxiety, the practitioner must work fast and be
actively involved. The practitioner in a crisis will be able to operate quickly
because of a past clinical experience, knowledge of personality organization, and ability to appraise the significance of the client's behavior on the
basis of overt communication and marginal clues (Golan 1978). The
emphasis of crisis intervention is on cognitive restructuring and accom-
plishing tasks in order to achieve a positive resolution of a specific crisis
(Rapoport 1970; Roberts, 1996). However, even cognitively impaired people can benefit from this model because the emphasis is on restoring comfort and safety. For example:

A 95-year-old man was referred by a neighbor to an outreach agency for older adults after he was observed to be a captive in his own apartment. Two young men, described as large and threatening, had moved into the man's apartment and claimed to be his caregivers. When the worker made his initial visit, he found an extremely frightened man who slept on the living room sofa. The younger men had taken over his bedroom, and the apartment was extremely dirty and cluttered. The worker immediately assessed the man as in need of a medical exam and as cognitively impaired in certain areas. While the man was aware of the goings-on in his apartment, he could not provide information about his income and was obviously intimidated by his "caregivers." In a brief moment when the worker and the client were alone, the worker whispered, "Do you want me to get you out of here?" The frightened man nodded yes emphatically. Focusing on the client's need for a medical checkup and not antagonizing the younger men, the worker left to work on a planned admission to a local hospital. After he obtained the cooperation of the client's physician and nurse, the worker returned to the apartment the next day, accompanied by several law enforcement officers as a safety measure, and transported the client to the hospital. Within a short period, the client was relocated to a safer apartment, was assigned a limited guardian for his estate, and began enjoying a tension-free life.

This example shows that the treatment structure in crisis situations does not rely on the quality of the relationship developed between a practitioner and a client. Instead, treatment relies on the client's readiness to accept help—a readiness stemming from discomfort and anxiety to regain a sense of autonomy or to reestablish equilibrium (Strickler & Bonnefil, 1974; Aguilera, 1990).

## Steps in Crisis Intervention

Professional intervention in crisis situations can be broken down into three steps: (1) formulation, (2) implementation, and (3) termination (Golan, 1978). Formulation includes establishing contact with the client, finding out what is going on, determining whether or not a crisis exists, and setting up a working contract for future activity. Implementation includes identifying and carrying out tasks, as well as organizing and working over data to bring about behavior change. The third phase, termination, involves arriving at a decision to terminate, reviewing progress made in the treatment situation, and planning for future activities.

## *Steps 1 and 2: Formulation and Implementation*

At the time of the initial contact with a possible case of elder abuse, the practitioner's first task is to determine if a crisis exists, how urgent the client's plight is, and if immediate action is needed. In many instances, referrals will be presented to the practitioner as if they are emergencies, but upon closer examination, the practitioner discovers that the situation is ongoing and not even at a crisis point, although the referrer perceived it as a crisis.

An emergency is defined as a situation in which either the client or the client's property is in danger of irreparable harm and immediate action is required (Villamore & Bergman, 1981). Treatment begins on first contact because there is not enough time for a formal and separate study. Two common types of emergency situations the practitioner may face are:

1. Medical-physical emergencies in which the client requires prompt medical attention.
2. Financial emergencies resulting from sudden withdrawal of funds from the client's bank account or other financial misconduct.

In these hazardous events, the client may feel a threat to his or her life, security, and assets. Fear, anxiety, helplessness, and confusion may accompany the stressful situation. The client is more likely to be open to the practitioner's intervention at this time.

MEDICAL-PHYSICAL CRISES.    Immediate intervention or action by the practitioner may be required in any of the following situations:

1. The client is alone and is unable to get up to let the practitioner in.
2. The client is unresponsive and, when finally aroused, is confused and disoriented.
3. The client shows a "failure to thrive" and is found
   a. Lying in urine and feces
   b. Unable to obtain nourishment or fluids
   c. Dressed inappropriately for the weather
   d. With untreated sores or injuries
   e. Unaware of or unable to explain the above conditions

If, upon arriving at the client's residence, the practitioner can see through the window that the client is unable to open the door, he or she should search for a neighbor or apartment manager and attempt to obtain an extra key or assistance in entering the residence. It may be necessary to call a law enforcement officer, who can suggest ways to gain entry, or call for additional assistance, if it is needed. A forced entry is justified only when the situation is perceived as an emergency. Chapter 9 describes in greater detail the involvement of law enforcement personnel in these situations.

When the practitioner reaches the client, the next step should be to make sure the client is oriented in regard to person, place, and time. This can be done by asking:

"What is your name?" (*Person*)
"Where are you?" (*Place*)
"What year is this?" (*Time*)

If the client is unable to answer any or all of these questions, further medical evaluation may be required. Disorientation can be a result of lack of food or an acute medical condition such as a stroke or overmedication. It does not necessarily indicate a psychiatric disorder.

Untreated sores, wounds, or other medical conditions may go undetected unless the practitioner is alert for telltale signs. A client lying under blankets or wearing heavy clothing and socks may have hidden injuries. The practitioner can gently ask the client to remove the covers or ask the client's permission to look under the covers. A quick look takes only a few seconds and does not require that the client fully disrobe. If the client and practitioner are of opposite sexes, awkwardness may be eased if the practitioner is comfortable with the situation, maintains eye contact, and proceeds slowly, explaining at each step what is being done. A strange or foul odor may be a clue that the client requires medical attention. One adult protective services worker reported missing the seriousness of a client's situation because she concentrated on the verbal interaction and did not use her senses of sight and smell:

"I went to see a man who was lying in bed with a blanket up to his neck. He smiled throughout the interview and assured me he was fine. I left after he refused all of the services I offered. Later our office received another call about him. When I interviewed him the second time, I removed his blanket and found a huge pressure sore on his back."

Although it will probably not be possible at this time to complete the written protocol in Chapter 6, attempts should be made to gather as much information as possible. If the caregiver is present, an interview should be conducted to determine his or her knowledge and awareness of the situation, and the practitioner should try to obtain an explanation of how the condition or conditions evolved. The client, the caregiver, or both may be asked:

> "When was the last time you (your mother) went to the bathroom?"
> "You are (your mother is) soiled. Are you aware of this? Can you (she) clean yourself (herself)?"
> "What did you (your mother) eat for breakfast this morning? What did you (she) drink, and how much?"

The practitioner should document *verbatim* the responses to the questions asked. Discrepancies, inconsistencies, and "holes" in the explanations offered may be helpful in detecting elder mistreatment. For example:

> An 84-year-old woman was brought to the emergency room unresponsive and malnourished with bruises on her face, arms, and right thigh. Upon questioning, her male friend, with whom she resided, stated that earlier in the day he had dragged her to the dining room table and sat her up. He stated that she then ate meatloaf, mashed potatoes, and peas by herself. The staff had difficulty believing that the client was recently able to do anything for herself, much less sit up at a table and hold a utensil to feed herself. The staff began to suspect abuse.

Having determined the client's current status, the practitioner moves quickly from the formulation phase to the implementation phase, determining the availability of internal, intrafamilial, and community resources that can be mobilized quickly to restore a degree of equilibrium (Rapoport 1970). When appropriate, the practitioner should let the client know that a "checkup" at a hospital or clinic will be necessary. Chapter 5 emphasized the importance of calling the client's physician before the home visit to develop a plan of action should the client need immediate medical care. A plan which includes having key people on standby will help the practitioner to obtain assistance quickly and efficiently. If the client is unable to give consent, the caregiver, if present, must be informed that the client may require treatment outside of the home. The practitioner may say:

> "Your mother isn't well, and we need to help her. I am going to call her doctor (or the nearest emergency room, a consulting nurse, etc.) to discuss her

condition. She may need to be seen by a doctor today, and I will probably need to call for an ambulance."

In cases of suspected abuse, neither family members nor the alleged abuser should be relied on to transport the client to the treatment site. An ambulance or cabulance may have to be called. Because the client or the client's health plan will be billed for private transportation services, consent should be obtained. Transportation by a law enforcement officer is not billed but may not always be available. It is helpful to inform the ambulance company ahead of time (if possible) of the client's approximate height and weight, and whether a stretcher or wheelchair will be required. If the client is overweight or immobile and in a upper-floor bedroom or a basement room, two or three people may be required to transport the client up or down the stairs.

The practitioner should accompany the client to the treatment site and exchange information with the treatment staff. It is best to speak directly to the medical practitioner when conveying a suspicion of elder mistreatment and the need for the medical practitioner to document findings in detail. Not all emergency room personnel or other medical professionals have been trained in assessing and detecting elder mistreatment. To expedite the care, the practitioner should prepare a referral note on a sheet of paper large enough not to be lost or misplaced. The referral note should contain the following information:

- The practitioner's name, title, agency, and phone number.
- The client's physician or treatment agencies and their phone numbers.
- Names and phone numbers of the client's significant others.
- Names and phone numbers of the client's neighbors.
- Information gathered so far on circumstances surrounding the injury or illness.
- The practitioner's concerns, suspicions, and warnings regarding physical abuse, neglect, or financial exploitation of the client.

Valuable time and information can be lost if the agency practitioner provides only oral information to the admitting clerk, assuming that it will be forwarded to the examining practitioner. Taking a few minutes to write the referral note or asking to speak to the examining practitioner—or both—will promote a careful assessment.

If the client is admitted to a hospital, the agency and medical practitioners must maintain contact with each other and develop a discharge plan together.

FINANCIAL CRISES.   Certain financial situations can be as serious as medical crises. Some elderly clients have suffered financial or material abuse which has taken their entire life savings, their pension checks, their real estate, or their valuables, causing them irreparable harm. Others have had to spend large amounts of money to recover their assets through the legal system. To intervene successfully in financial abuse, a practitioner must assume that the client's report of financial loss may be correct and that abuse may have occurred. Emotional signs of a crisis in a client may include anxiety, tension, shame, hostility, depression, and guilt. Cognitive confusion may also be observed (Rapoport, 1970). Practitioners should take prompt action and must have a thorough knowledge of the options available in financial emergencies. When the practitioner is suspicious or disbelieving of the client's report, the delay may allow the financial abuser to further dissipate the client's assets and to escape accountability for these actions. Chapter 9 presents additional legal remedies.

Financial abuse can take many forms. Acquaintances, friends, or relatives may add their names to the client's checking and savings account, claiming that this will make it easier to pay the client's bills and to assist the client in the event of illness or accident. When there are unexplained withdrawals from a client's account, prompt action is necessary. Consider the following example:

> A 75-year-old woman was hospitalized after suffering a stroke and was visited by an 80-year-old sister who lived in another state. The sister brought with her a joint account signature card from the client's bank and asked the client to sign it. The sister's name was added to the account. The sister immediately withdrew $7,000 and returned to her home state. The abuse was discovered accidentally when a close friend of the client happened to meet the hospital social worker one evening and asked if the staff were aware of the sister's actions.

Sometimes a caregiver or friend may forge a client's signature to withdraw money, may alter a signed check, or may ask a client to sign a blank check. In these instances, the practitioner has several options.

1. *Call the bank to place an alert on the account.* The practitioner may need to find out the name and branch of the client's bank. The practitioner can call and ask to speak to the bank manager, identifying himself or herself and the agency and explaining the purpose of the phone call. Banks vary in how much information they will give a practitioner. Some banks will indicate only if there are sufficient funds to cover a check for a certain amount; others will answer yes or no to general questions that are asked by a practitioner. For instance, the practitioner might inquire if the client's account balance is in four figures and if the amount is a high or low number. Most bank managers appreciate calls of concern, and while they are unable to provide detailed information by phone without the client's written consent, they will take information and alert tellers and other bank branch offices to be alert for unusual activity in the client's account.

2. *Transport the client to the bank to discuss the incident with the manager.* When possible, the practitioner should consider taking the client to the bank, where the bank manager can speak directly with the client. A client in a nursing home or a hospital may be allowed to go out of the institution on a pass granted by a physician. The practitioner should call to prepare the bank manager for the visit. It will be necessary to go to the client's home or institution early enough to prepare the client emotionally and physically for the visit. If the practitioner's agency forbids the use of personal vehicles, other transportation options include senior escort services and public or volunteer transportation. Some practitioners who occasionally choose to transport a client in their own vehicles have arranged with their insurance agent to increase their coverage at a nominal fee. A folding wheelchair may be necessary if the client is unable to walk long distances or to stand for long periods of time. In order to be free to aid the client, the practitioner should consider using a taxi or having someone else do the driving. At the bank, the practitioner should explain the purpose of the visit and allow the client to express his or her concern.

3. *Help the client close the current account and open a new account that is inaccessible to others.* In the case described above:

> The hospital social worker, once alerted, asked the client if she had let her sister put her name on her checking account. The client nodded yes. The worker then asked her if she was aware that $7,000 had been withdrawn from her account. The client became visibly upset and said "no." She indicated she wanted her sister not to withdraw any more money. The worker took the

client to the bank. The bank manager knew her well and had visited the client at her home in the past to complete other transactions. The manager recommended that the woman close the current joint account and transfer her money to a new account to which her sister would not have access. Phone calls to the client's sister made prior to the bank visit indicated that the sister had left the state with the client's checkbook and had been writing checks on the account. Everyone involved later agreed that the immediate transportation of the client to the bank had probably prevented additional thousands of dollars from being withdrawn from the account.

4. *Bring bank personnel to the client's home.* If a client is unable to go to the bank because of illness or impairment, or if the practitioner feels that a bank visit may be too exhausting or upsetting for the client, the practitioner may ask a bank representative to visit the client in the home or institution. During the visit, it is important to ensure privacy and to make sure that the conversation is not overheard. The bank representative can then ask if the client was aware of the unusual activity on the account, and in cases of forgery, ask if the client wishes to take legal action. Banks may be particularly concerned about forgery because in some instances lawsuits have been filed against banks when signatures were not checked and forged checks were cashed.

5. *Obtain a consent form or letter from the client to inquire about his or her account.* If a bank representative is unable to visit the client, an alternate plan is to request information on the client's behalf through a release of information form or a letter requesting that the bank provide the practitioner with specific information. It is helpful to know the client's account number and bank branch. The letter might read:

October 15, 19—

Dear Bank Manager of _____ Bank:
I am unable to go to the bank myself, so I am asking Mr. John Smith, Case Manager for the Division on Aging, to obtain for me my current bank balance. I am concerned that someone is taking money from my account. My phone number is 555-4469. Please call me if you require more information.

Sincerely yours,

_____

(signed) Jane Doe
Account # 000-00-0000

The practitioner should be prepared to present proper identification along with the letter. Copies of the letter should be made for the client and the practitioner.

Generally speaking, bank representatives are helpful to clients and their advocates when presented with adequate information and documentation. Elders in Los Angeles, California, are fortunate to have the Los Angeles Police Department's Elder Person's Estate Unit, which was formalized in 1992 within the Bunco-Forgery Division (Nerenberg, 1995). In operation since 1987, with a goal of safeguarding seniors' assets, the Unit has worked very closely with the staffs of adult protective services, public guardians, and ombudsman agencies. The Unit has targeted entire estates that are at risk, usually worth over $200,000, and owing to its fast and creative intervention, it has recovered $31 million in homes, vehicles, and life savings. Although law enforcement agencies do not usually become involved with abuses related to civil actions such as power of attorney and quitclaim deeds, this Unit reframed these "civil mirage" cases as serious and criminal acts against the elderly, and took action. Its detectives would suggest that an administrative hold be placed on a possible victim's account to prevent further exploitation.

### Step 3: Termination

In crisis intervention, there is no separation of diagnosis and treatment activities. Treatment begins in the first session. Termination in crisis intervention is also combined with these other two activities; it is not a separate and distinct phase. During termination, practitioners review the progress made during the course of their contact with the client. They can discuss future strategies such as whom and to call for help, and when. It is hoped that by this time, the client has developed a realistic awareness of the stressful situation and can move to a level of mastery over a short time.

An important goal in termination is to develop a method for monitoring the client. The client should be left with the knowledge that he or she may return for services. It is helpful to routinely build in a method for following up with a client. This could be done in person within a few months, or by a telephone call. In addition to restoring the elder's emotional equilibrium, a major goal of crisis intervention is the development of foresight. Before closing the case, the practitioner may utilize role rehearsal and anticipatory guidance to prepare the client for similar future incidents. For example, the practitioner may want to list names and phone numbers of agencies and people clients should call if they are not getting their medications regularly, if they are feeling ill, or if, say, they are again pressured to sign over their Social Security checks to someone else. At the time of termination, the client should have developed new ties with persons and resources in the community (Golan, 1979).

## SUMMARY

This Intervention Phase of the EADI Model can be considered a process during which the client and the abuser may reveal a variety of conflicting feelings. The client's capabilities and willingness to cooperate will affect the intervention outcome, as will the abuser's pathology and the severity of the situation.

In cases of elder mistreatment, medical and financial crises can arise at any time, and practitioners need to be alert to the possibilities in each and every situation. Prompt action can mean the difference between life and death or between financial comfort and poverty. Chapter 8 describes a variety of interventions that the practitioner can utilize when no emergency situation exists.

# Intervention Phase

## II. The Many Forms of Treatment

Some elder mistreatment situations, such as those described in Chapter 7, are best treated by crisis intervention strategies. Others benefit from treatment methods of a longer duration. Focusing on short-term treatment, ongoing monitoring, and collaborative intervention, the present chapter provides a context in which some acts of mistreatment can be interpreted and the related interventions can be utilized.

Practitioners in the field of elder mistreatment have been somewhat stymied when developing treatment techniques for victims who refuse help and for abusers who deny elder mistreatment. Current theories on elder mistreatment do not explain why such denial occurs. For this reason, some of the sociological literature on deviance and social control is reviewed, and an attempt is made to apply neutralization theory to the problem of elder mistreatment. Neutralization theory attempts to explain acts of denial and rationalization and may contribute to the development of more appropriate and efficacious interventions for victims and their abusers. Additionally, an explanation of how the victims' and the abusers' cognitive and behavioral processes relate to societal norms may help practitioners face these difficult cases with greater understanding. In the first part of this chapter, issues related to short-term treatment are discussed. The next part of the chapter gives an explanation of neutralization theory* as a context in which specific interventions are used. The next parts of the chapter will

---

*An earlier version of the section on neutralization theory was published as Tomita, S. K. (1990). The denial of elder mistreatment by victims and abusers: The application of neutralization theory. *Violence and Victims, 5*(3), 171–184.

describe intervention techniques, on the individual level and the community level, to assist the victim and the abuser. The remainder of the chapter will discuss ongoing clinical interventions: group therapy, environmental therapy, and prevention and awareness programs.

## SHORT-TERM INTERVENTION

### What Is Short-Term Treatment?

In short-term treatment, the concept of "cure" is abandoned. It is essential that goals be limited and that the practitioner genuinely accept this limitation. This may be difficult for the practitioner, especially when clients present with a multitude of problems and situations which will not be resolved within a short time.

Short-term treatment involves immediate problem solving and the restoration and enhancement of the client's functioning. It also focuses on removing or reducing specific symptoms to the extent possible; but reconstructing the personality is not the goal. In short-term treatment, the practitioner must be regarded as a likable and reliable person who takes a more active role than in traditional psychotherapy. Some of the procedures used in brief intervention are reality testing, intellectualization, reassurance and support, and increasing the clients' self-esteem (Aguilera, 1990). In this method, goals are concrete and specific, marked by the use of referrals to other agencies. These goals are determined by what the practitioner considers to be the "useful next step" (Rapoport, 1970).

The practitioner is not necessarily the ongoing worker, but refers the client for case management. Practitioners make plans that do not necessarily include themselves. For example, a practitioner may come into contact with the client only during the assessment phase; he or she may be the practitioner responsible for ruling out elder mistreatment—by actually making the assessment or by requesting a geriatric evaluation in the home or at a clinic, and working with other professionals. Sometimes a short hospital stay or repeated home visits are necessary to assess a client and to develop a case plan. A client with medical problems such as malnourishment, dehydration, or pressure sores may be admitted to a hospital from home. The hospital staff should be alerted to check for signs of elder mistreatment during the client's inpatient admission. A practitioner who does not have time to follow a client for a long period (for example, beyond 3 months) may conduct the diagnostic assessment and then refer the client to another agency for long-term follow-up.

In short-term treatment, there is less emphasis on developing a relationship than there is in long-term treatment. The short-term practitioner stays involved until plans for long-term care and monitoring are developed. Emphasis in brief treatment is on the development of foresight through educational techniques and anticipatory guidance. Brief treatment often is not by purpose or plan; but is labeled retrospectively.

In terms of time, short-term treatment may involve up to a dozen interviews spaced over 3 to 6 months. Assessment and treatment are often combined, which means that the treatment goals and strategies may change from time to time as new facts emerge. Short-term treatment is a *different* method of intervention, rather than simply less treatment. It is attractive to many practitioners, for it is one way that they are able to see as many clients as possible within time and fiscal constraints. In many communities, this treatment method is used by practitioners in protective service agencies.

Short-term treatment is not for psychiatric clients who are in a chronic state of crisis, who have continually erupting crises, or who require services over an indefinite period of time. These clients require indefinite case management, structure, and ongoing care and may need to be referred to agencies such as community mental health centers where they can be cared for adequately.

The major limitation of short-term treatment is the lack of time to develop the positive therapeutic relationship that often is required before change can occur. Rapoport (1970) suggests that the focus should be on the client's motivation to seek relief from discomfort—which short-term treatment can accomplish—rather than on the client's motivation to make permanent behavior changes.

While tools for detecting and assessing elder mistreatment are now being developed in greater quantity than they were 10 to 15 years ago, specific counseling techniques for victims and abusers have only recently been developed and are still scarce. A few helpful counseling guidelines now exist (Breckman & Adelman, 1988; Ramsey-Klawsnik, 1995; Rathbone-McCuan, Travis, & Voyles, 1983; Tomita, 1990; Villamore & Bergman, 1981). Methods used to work with victims of child abuse and domestic violence, and their abusers, have been reviewed, and their applicability to elder mistreatment is being explored. Neutralization theory, taken from the literature of deviance and delinquency and elaborated on later in this chapter, has been used to develop short-term intervention techniques (Tomita, 1990). The following suggestions are the result of a review of literature on crisis intervention, counseling, child abuse, and domestic violence, in combination with direct field experience. These are general guidelines and in no way represent proven methods for treating all aspects of elder mistreatment. They are subject to modification as more knowledge is gained from new research and practitioners' experiences. A wide range of interventions are presented because the types of clients and abusers are so diverse.

## Client Advocacy, the Abuser's Accountability, and Other Issues in Short-Term Treatment

Professionals currently are divided on whether it is possible to fulfill the role of advocate for both abuser and victim with impartiality. Many professionals are "pro-victim," and have difficulty with the concept of being "pro-abuser." They feel that the abuser is not deserving of their attention and should be left alone or punished. These practitioners often feel anger, which distances them emotionally from the abuser and lead them to view the victim as the sole client. This stance in part can be influenced by the practitioner's schooling, which may have emphasized individual therapy; by the agency's philosophy and mission; and by a lack of practitioners who could be role models for treating both victim and abuser.

Practitioners may become frustrated in their efforts to find successful interventions with either the victim or the alleged abuser (Quinn, 1990a). The intervention most frequently chosen by practitioners when dealing with a pathological abuser is physical separation of the abuser and the elder, especially when other interventions have failed or when the elder's life is endangered. Often this means that a frail elder will be placed in a nursing home—usually a painful step, because most elders want to remain at home, even if they are being abused and even if they are physically or mentally impaired. In spite of the greater availability of assisted-living and other group settings, most elders, and indeed most of the general population, view the nursing home as a house of decay and death and as a last-ditch alternative—the sole alternative to living at home.

The effect of separating the abuser and the victim remains an unsettled issue in both child abuse and spouse abuse. For cases of elder mistreatment, the reality of the situation should guide the practitioner: cases that require permanent separation of the client and abuser account for only a small percentage of all cases. Most cases of elder mistreatment involve a victim who chooses to remain in an abusive situation, and this results in provision of services to a dysfunctional or stressed family.

Counseling techniques addressing the needs of both victim and abuser should be offered. Factors influencing the practitioner's ability to maintain concern for the abuser as a person include the practitioner's knowledge of formal and informal resources, an ability to refer, and support received from the agency (Rathbone-McCuan et al., 1983). Many agencies do not have a staff adequate to treat both client and abuser and therefore may emphasize contacts with clients alone.

Ganley (1981) argues in favor of treating both the client and the abusive or neglectful caregiver. Rather than being a supportive counselor to both in the traditional sense, the practitioner becomes an advocate for the client and a monitor of the abuser's behavior, making the abuser accountable. The goal of such joint counseling is to stop the battering. It is based on social learning theory, which holds that behaviors are learned from one's family of origin, culture, and prior experiences. If these behaviors are learned, then they can be unlearned and replaced with acceptable alternatives.

## Counseling Methods in Short-Term Treatment

### *Choice of Style*

The practitioner has a choice in selecting a counseling style. Szaz and Hollander (1956) discuss three models of the physician–client relationship that may be applied to working with elder mistreatment: (1) activity–passivity, (2) guidance–cooperation, and (3) mutual participation.

Short-term treatment often requires model 1, in which the practitioner is active and directive, while communicating concern and authenticity (Rapoport, 1970). The practitioner will choose to be active when the client is in an emergency situation or is incapacitated. Szaz and Hollander caution the practitioner not to use this model unless absolutely necessary, and to examine whether the active role is chosen to maintain the practitioner's feelings of authority and superiority. With regard to this point, Stone (1979) suggests that if the patient is incapacitated and immediate action is not crucial, a guardian must be found to consent to treatment.

The guidance–cooperation model—model 2—dominates present medical care delivery and may be the one most frequently chosen by practitioners responding to elder mistreatment clients. The client is suffering from pain, anxiety, and fear and wants help. The practitioner presents options and facts, gently guiding the client toward the treatment plan of choice. Szaz and Hollander (1956) again serve as the practitioner's conscience, asking practitioners to examine whether their active guidance is due to their own need for superiority and mastery over the client.

The third model of mutual participation, the contractual model, is one in which the client has control in decision making. Here the practitioner and the client have equal power, are interdependent, and relate in a mutually satisfying manner. The model is not appropriate for children or for clients who are cognitively impaired, poorly educated, or profoundly immature. While it may be difficult to accept the fact that a client may choose to disagree with a treatment plan, some comfort may be had in knowing that options have been presented and that the practitioner did his or her best to educate the client about the situation. Szaz and Hollander (1956) offer reminders that to an effective practitioner, the therapeutic relationship is a process, one in which the client may progress from being passive to becoming cooperative and ultimately to being a partner in care management. The practitioner must have the ability to recognize these changes and respond to them accordingly, rather than labeling the client as "difficult" or "uncooperative."

### *Countering Resistance*

Cormier and Cormier (1985) discuss many specific techniques that the practitioner can utilize when working with a resistant or involuntary client. For example, they suggest that resistance may stem from a client's lack of necessary skills or knowledge. Resistance may also be due to fear, and in these instances, the provision of informative details and skills training may help to counter those fears. For example, when elders have pessimistic expectations for the treatment relationship, instead of countering with statements of optimism, the practitioner should acknowledge their pessimism. Instead of saying, "You don't sound hopeful that I'll be able to improve this situation, but I will do my best to work this out successfully," the practitioner may instead say, "Let's move slowly. Let's assume that things will not improve right away, and that we may not make any headway with your son for a while."

When clients have negative or anxious thoughts, Cormier and Cormier (1985) suggest providing support and exploring their fantasies, expectations, and fears in detail. The elder may have inaccurate beliefs that should be countered, such as, "If people find out I'm being beaten by my son, they'll wonder what I did to deserve this." To this, the practitioner may start with, "Tell me how you came to that conclusion," followed by, "Blaming yourself is a common reaction in situations like this one; right now we need to help both of you as a family, and to stop the abuse." Also, to combat the elder's fear of failure, the practitioner may want to give tasks that are easily handled before suggesting a larger task that may seem overwhelming and discouraging. Last, practitioners are advised to place little emphasis on their own role in any changes the client has made and to focus on the client's contributions instead: "We couldn't have made this change happen if you hadn't taken the plunge and agreed to . . . Give yourself credit for being so brave."

## *Courtesy and Respect*

Being courteous and respectful also helps to improve the elder's willingness to work with the practitioner. For example, the client should be alerted in advance to the practitioner's impending absences and other disappointments. If the practitioner anticipates being late for an appointment, even 15 minutes late, it is respectful to stop and phone the client. Some clients peer out their windows regularly as they wait for appointments, worrying that the practitioner has forgotten about the meeting. The client may take a while to trust the practitioner but then may count on the regular contacts. To avoid later feelings of rejection and lowered self-esteem, the practitioner should inform the client at the beginning of the relationship how long the relationship is likely to last. Another basic courtesy is for a student practitioner to explain that he or she will be on vacation between quarters. Similarly, a practitioner who anticipates absences from agency work should explain that to the client.

## *Establishing and Maintaining Trust*

It is necessary to build a relationship of trust with a victim before confronting him with the reality of the abuse. The practitioner should carefully consider how that confrontation should be done or if it should be done at all. It may be possible to resolve a situation without a flat-out confrontation. Many older adults are uncomfortable with direct confrontations but may be willing to work with the practitioner to eliminate the abuse. This may be true of the caregiver or the abuser as well as the victim. If clients are treated against their will or promises made to them are broken, they may experience ambivalence and an inability to trust the next practitioner. If the current practitioner experiences difficulty establishing a relationship with a client, exploring the client's past experiences with other practitioners may reveal a fear of being betrayed again, of being misunderstood (particularly with regard to fears), of being stripped of rights, of being let down as in the past. Unfulfilled promises may be more harmful than no promises. Since trust builds slowly, it is necessary that each client be assigned to one practitioner on whom that client can rely and with whose style he or she can become familiar. The main practitioner can serve as the case manager, orchestrating collaborative activities among agencies.

## Privacy

The practitioner should counsel the client in privacy. In the assessment phase, emphasis is placed on maintaining privacy to promote disclosure of painful and sensitive information. Having entered the intervention phase, the practitioner must continue to interview the client in private settings, including the client's home if interruptions are not anticipated, as well as offices, medical clinic examining rooms, and quiet public areas. Later on, as treatment progresses and the client believes that the practitioner sincerely wants to help the abuser too, joint sessions may be possible.

## Acceptance

The practitioner should allow for the clients' need to talk and their desire to be in charge of their own situation. Clients may take months or even 2 to 3 years to finally end an abusive relationship. During that period, they may need a friendly visitor to simply talk about their doubts, anxieties, frustrations, and ambivalence. They may ask for active intervention later, when they feel the time is "right." That "right" time may not jibe with the practitioner's time frame.

The expression and management of a client's feelings can lead to a discharge of tension—a goal in itself in short-term treatment. The practitioner then validates the client's conflicting feelings without making judgments, saying, for example, "You don't like having your son threaten you but you don't want him to be arrested either." If practitioners attempt to interpret rather than merely paraphrase a client's statements, they should be cautioned to make these interpretations in a tentative, nonthreatening manner, and not in a way that is beyond the elder's grasp (Golan, 1978). For example: "I'm wondering if you thought that if you were nice to him that he would stop bothering you."

If the client is not ready to pursue an intervention, the practitioner might say, "When you are ready to pursue . . . , I'll be ready to help you. Just let me know." This helps develop a feeling of acceptance, and allows the client to maintain control of his or her treatment.

## NEUTRALIZATION THEORY

Assisting the client with attaining a realistic understanding of what has happened or is happening is one of the first steps in treatment, but it is one of the greatest challenges for practitioners. A client's continuous denial of the mistreatment can be discouraging. In this section, neutralization theory will be summarized; then, its application to elder mistreatment will be considered.

Sykes and Matza (1957) developed neutralization theory to explain delinquency, not as a counterculture or as a subculture with values and norms that are inversely different from the dominant or conventional culture, but as part of a larger conventional social system—with the delinquent being affected by the norms and values of that system. Delinquents are partially committed to the dominant order, as is exhibited by their guilt or shame when apprehended. A premise is that historically, children or adolescents have been dependent on the adults in their social systems, and that delinquents can never be totally indifferent to the condemnation of their deviant acts by these adults. The delinquent recognizes the moral validity of the dominant culture, and commits criminal offenses only episodically.

Laws that reflect society's norms are not binding under all conditions. They are violated because they are not imperatives but serve as guides for action. Criminal laws are flexible in that intentionality, "blameworthiness," and defenses to crimes are taken into consideration. In most societies, if delinquents can prove lack of criminal intent, they can be free of moral culpability. Sykes and Matza (1957) theorize that delinquency is based on the extension of the defenses to crimes in the form of justifications and rationalizations for deviance, which are not seen as valid by society at large but are seen as valid by the delinquent.

The justifications and rationalizations preceding or following a deviant act neutralize the delinquent's internalized norms and mitigate the disapproval of those in the delinquent's social system. Social controls are thus rendered inoperative and the individual is free to engage in delinquent activities without serious damage to the self-image. The seven techniques of neutralization—five developed by Sykes and Matza, two by Minor (1980, 1981)—are: (1) denial of responsibility, (2) denial of injury, (3) denial of the victim, (4) condemnation of the condemners, (5) appeal to higher loyalties, (6) the defense of necessity, and (7) the metaphor of the ledger.

Wood (1974) argues that neutralization theory can be extended from delinquency to many types of adult crime. Just as it explains how delinquents episodically repudiate the standards and expectations to which they usually conform, neutralization theory can be used to explain why some people who are usually not abusive episodically abuse elders. The neutralization techniques cannot be viewed as direct causes of elder mistreatment; instead, they are interpreted separately as methods that weaken or neutralize the effect of bonds to the conventional order. If others excuse an initial act of mistreatment as necessary or due to extenuating circumstances, the abuser may use this feedback to justify the mistreatment and to feel that it is permissible to continue to commit similar acts. As shown in Figure 8-1, neutralization techniques are used before and after acts of elder mistreatment are committed; they provide an interaction effect and weaken the relationship between norms and elder mistreatment.

The following section presents examples of each of the neutralization techniques in the context of elder mistreatment. Some of these techniques can be utilized to explain some behaviors of the victim, the abuser, and the practitioner.

## Neutralization Techniques

1. *Denial of responsibility.* To begin, denial of responsibility occurs when an incident of delinquency is explained as an "accident" or as caused by forces beyond the delinquent's control, such as having unloving parents, bad companions, or poverty. Delinquents who deny responsibility refer to themselves as helpless individuals. Blame is attached to external social forces, and intraindividual interpretations for the act are avoided.

Denial of responsibility may be used by the elder abuser to claim that the abusive act was due to an accident or to claim that stress, the burdens of caregiving, lack of respite care, and lack of financial assistance contributed to the abusive acts. The abuser may also say that an acute illness or alcohol and drugs "made" him or her abuse the victim. Such abusers do

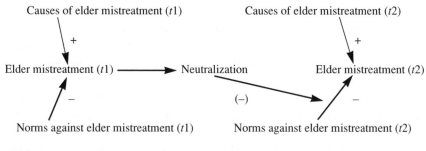

$t1$=Time 1
$t2$=Time 2

Figure 8-1　The use of neutralization techniques as a means of weakening the norms against elder mistreatment.

*Source:* Reprinted from Tomita, S.K. (1990). The denial of elder mistreatment by victims and abusers: The application of neutralization theory. *Violence and Victims,* 5(3), 171–184, p. 176.

not consider themselves "blameworthy." Rather, blame is placed on social circumstances or on society's failure to provide assistance. The victim may support the abuser's viewpoint and blame himself or herself for the mistreatment, saying, "Oh, I'm such a burden and that's why my son gets so angry; he's a nice man when he's not so stressed."

2. *Denial of the injury.* "Denial of the injury" refers to a situation in which the delinquent interprets the act as not being wrong because no one has been hurt by it (e.g., a car is stolen for a few hours' joyride). Vandalism and automobile theft may be defined as mischievous activities, and persons whose property has been destroyed can presumably afford to have the property destroyed. Delinquents may perceive support for this neutralization technique when adults in their social system refer to certain activities as merely "pranks."

In elder mistreatment situations, the victim and the abuser may use denial of injury to claim that the mistreatment did not cause significant harm. The victim may deny that the shove against the wall was injurious because he or she did not require medical attention. An abuser may justify financial exploitation by saying or thinking that an elder's wealth will be inherited anyway or that a parent can afford to sign away property and other assets. Taunting or emotionally abusing an elder may be seen as harmless teasing, whereas the elder interprets it as frightening—and such emotionally abusive acts may in fact cause severe problems such as clinical depression, feelings of helplessness, or suicidal ideation. Also, a victim who is mistreated repeatedly may deny the injuries, not realizing that such treatment is abnormal, perhaps owing to a lack of counteracting feedback from others.

3. *Denial of the victim.* The third technique, denial of the victim, means that the delinquent claims that the injurious act was not wrong, owing to the circumstances. The delinquent may interpret the victim as the wrongdoer or as someone deserving of the acts perpetrated. In addition, the victim may also be absent, unknown or an abstraction, as in cases where crimes are committed against property. The delinquent is unaware or has a diminished awareness of the victim's existence.

Denial of the victim may be used by the elder abuser to claim that the inflicted injury or the exploitation was an act of retaliation or punishment for unacceptable behavior. The victim is blamed as a "wrongdoer," deserving of exploitation or punishment. An elderly, confused victim may be perceived by the abuser as sometimes purposefully making caregiving a difficult job or as "faking" disability (e.g., "He just wants attention"), when in reality the elder is unable to do dressing or grooming tasks. Sykes and Matza note that the targets of delinquent acts are said to be people who have gotten "out of place"; similarly, the elder may be perceived as "out of hand" or "out of place" and deserving of being corrected or "put in place." Also, the abuser's diminished awareness of the victim, perhaps owing to a lack of frequent contacts or a lack of any history of closeness, can contribute to elder mistreatment. It could be that a strained relationship exists between a parent who may be considered the "wrong survivor" and an adult child who has never gotten along with that parent (Schmidt, 1980).

4. *Condemnation of the condemners.* The fourth technique of neutralization, condemnation of the condemners, is being used when delinquents accuse anyone who disapproves of their acts of being a hypocrite or a deviant in disguise, or of having a personal grudge against them. By blaming or attacking their critics, delinquents are able to deflect the focus away from their own wrongdoings. In elder mistreatment, this technique may be applied to explain the relationship between the abuser and the practitioners of agencies such as adult protective services (APS) who conduct investigations and provide interventions for both victims and alleged perpetrators. The abuser may accuse the investigator of being "snoopy" or intrusive, and may claim to be misunderstood by those outside the residence or to be "picked on," hoping to deflect attention from the deviant

acts. The abuser may hope that the investigator will never ask about the unusual bruises or injuries on the elder, or about the whereabouts of the victim's checkbook and other documents, which may indicate recent transactions benefiting the abuser.

5. *Appeal to higher loyalties.* Internal and social controls may be weakened by what is called an appeal to higher loyalties. In this process, the delinquent may choose friendship over legal constraints and commit a delinquent act to win approval from peers. In elder mistreatment situations, the abuser may tell the victim, "If you love me, you won't turn me in," and the victim may deny abuse to the investigator out of love or "higher" loyalty to the abuser. This technique may be utilized also by a male abuser who feels that he needs to hurt someone in order to be considered "a man" by others. Some abusers may continue to exploit or threaten to harm an elder because of pressure from others who say, "Why do you let your father get away with that?" (e.g., incontinence, slow movements) or "Why don't you be more firm, and stop taking that kind of behavior from him?"

6. *Defense of necessity.* Minor suggests that two more neutralization techniques be added to the list originated by Sykes and Matza. The sixth technique is the defense of necessity, which refers justifying an act as necessary and so preventing the perpetrator from feeling guilty. This defense may be used by a victim to excuse mistreatment as well as by an abuser to prevent guilty feelings—for instance, by perceiving a shove or a push as necessary in order to prevent a bigger problem or to protect the elder from self-inflicted harm. For example, an abuser may shove an elder at a store checkout stand to make him or her move faster in order not to inconvenience the clerk or others who are in line. To take another example, an abuser may rationalize beforehand that withdrawing $10,000 from an elder's account is necessary to prevent the elder from squandering the money, or to keep the elder from being exploited by others.

7. *The metaphor of the ledger.* Minor's other technique is the metaphor of the ledger, in which people who commit illegal acts may feel that they have been "good" and have a sufficient "supply" of good behaviors to their credit that it is permissible to indulge in an illegal act. A person who is usually good can do "evil" once in a while. This technique may be used by the elder and by the abuser to justify abusive acts, indicating that until the abusive act, the abuser had been a good provider and a good caregiver, and that because of such good behavior, he or she had a right to "slip" and to commit an improper act once in a while. The abuser may explain himself or herself as being a caregiver who has not had a vacation in 3 years, and who

has lapsed into this criminal behavior "just this one time, and I'll never do it again."

Minor points out that a limitation of neutralization theory is that it seems applicable only to offenders who still maintain a strong bond to the majority system's norms or to the conventional order—and that it is not applicable to hardened criminals. He proposes that neutralization be considered a facilitating element in the early stages of delinquency or predelinquency during which young people neutralize controls or rationalize their behavior in order to bring values and behavior into agreement. With a feedback process from the social system that sometimes lends support to neutralization techniques (e.g., a judge warns a delinquent to stay out of trouble and dismisses the charges), delinquents continue to commit violations until they no longer need to neutralize. Over time, a delinquent moves from an early phase of utilizing neutralization techniques to a later phase of committing violations without guilt or shame and without a need for neutralization techniques. Minor calls this the "hardening process."

In addition to explaining how neutralization can be a preincident or an ex post facto method of justifying behavior, Matza (1964) describes what initially motivates someone to commit delinquent acts and attempts to answer the question, "What causes the delinquent to be episodically released from the moral bind of a conventional order?" It is not due to compulsion or a commitment to an unconventional subculture but occurs when the delinquent is free to "drift" into delinquency during an episodic release from moral restraint. Will may or may not be exercised; it is an option that can be activated by two main factors, preparation and desperation. Preparation to willfully commit a delinquent act is described as the process of developing the realization that committing an act without being apprehended is feasible. During delinquents' "moral holiday," feedback from committing delinquent acts makes them realize that they can get away with such acts. If the chance of apprehension and captivity is found to be slight, the delinquent can discount the consequences of apprehension and feel comfortable about recommitting these acts.

Desperation is defined as a "mood of fatalism," a period in which delinquents see themselves as "effect," as being "pushed around." It develops when people lack mastery over their environment; for example, when a male feels a "loss of manhood" and commits an infraction in order to feel that he can be a "cause" and "make something happen." Matza describes desperation as providing the will to commit an infraction in order to experience a "jolt of humanism."

The concepts of preparation and desperation can be applied to elder mistreatment. Thus an abuser within the privacy of the residence may shove or threaten to kill an elder if the monthly Social Security check is not given up, and finds that these acts are easy to commit with no dire consequences. With no witnesses or external constraints, the risk of apprehension is small or nonexistent, and similar offenses are recommitted. Minor's suggested hardening process may ensue, and neutralization techniques may become unnecessary. Matza's "mood of fatalism" as an explanation for what propels someone to commit an infraction may also further explain Pillemer's postulate that an abuser may be abusive toward an elder out of feelings of powerlessness (1986).

It is important to note that practitioners working on cases of elder mistreatment are not themselves immune from utilizing neutralization techniques. Matza (1964) makes an interesting claim that judges, social workers, and psychiatrists mitigate illegal acts and support the delinquent's attribution of fault to the parent, community, society, and victim. Like Matza, the psychoanalyst T. Dorpat (1985) mentions that hospital personnel and physicians can support a patient's denial if they are in denial themselves. He feels that the patient's denial is affected by others' attitudes and communications. While Matza does not discuss the unconscious interactions of individuals, the similarities between Dorpat and Matza cannot be ignored: both warn practitioners against supporting directly, subtly, or indirectly, by attitudes or by actions, the condoning of inappropriate behavior. The authors present denial in two different contexts: Dorpat, the psychoanalyst, treats denial in the context of personal characteristics while Matza, the sociologist, interprets denial in relationship to norms within the social system.

## Implications of Neutralization Theory for Treatment

The main techniques for treatment involve diminishing the use of neutralization techniques and strengthening the norms against elder mistreatment. Finding constructive responses to denial has always posed a challenge to practitioners in the field of domestic violence. Roberts (1984) and Roy (1982) both mention denial as one of the frequent manifestations of resistance to treatment in battered women cases. Also, in an attempt to research elder mistreatment among APS workers' caseloads, one study found that abusers' denial prevented cases from being analyzed at all (Korbin, Anetzberger, & Eckert, 1989; Korbin et al., 1987). It has been difficult to formulate specific intervention techniques that deal with denial of the victim and the abuser, perhaps because denial has been treated in too general a manner: Denial that is defined psychiatrically as an unconscious, preverbal, and prereflective defense mechanism is lumped together with another form of denial, the type described by Sykes and Matza as an expressed justification or rationalization that stretches extenuating circumstances beyond a point originally conceived by the law. Perhaps by failing to define denial as having many forms, treatment methods have been too general to respond successfully to different client populations, for example, reatable abusers who deny in order to justify their acts, as opposed to untreatable hardened psychopaths who vehemently deny any wrongdoing despite the availability of convincing evidence.

In many clinical settings, despairing comments have been made about the impossibility of treating clients in denial. One benefit of applying Sykes and Matza's neutralization theory, and Minor's additions, to the study of elder mistreatment is that it forces practitioners to take another look at what is meant by the term *denial* and to consider developing interventions for each of the neutralization techniques. Some of these abusers may be in the early phases of the "hardening process," and if confronted early, may cease their abusive behavior. The use of neutralization theory may also allow the practitioner to inject energy into a stalemated situation in which both victim and abuser are using denial.

A small segment of the literature has presented specific counseling techniques with elder mistreatment victims (Breckman & Adelman, 1988; Ramsey-Klawsnik, 1993, 1995; Villamore & Bergman, 1981; Quinn & Tomita, 1986; Tomita, 1990), and a still smaller segment specifies techniques for intervention with the abuser. The first edition of this book tentatively provided techniques for intervention with the victim and the abuser, which were derived chiefly from learning theory, casework theory, psychotherapy, and spousal abuse. Some of the techniques that are presented here advance some of the original formulations within the context of neutralization theory, and augment rather than replace other therapeutic approaches.

## INTERVENTIONS WITH THE VICTIM

### Options

The intervention options available for the mistreatment client are diverse. The practitioner can provide reality testing, assist with restructuring the elder's environment, utilize educational and prevention models to develop the client's foresight, provide concrete assistance and services, and intervene indirectly. These options are detailed in this section.

The practitioner's main goal immediately after the mistreatment incident is to return the client to a state of equilibrium. Aguilera's paradigm for this process is based on three main balancing factors: (1) helping the client obtain a realistic perception of the event; (2) ensuring that the client has adequate situational support, and (3) determining that the client has adequate coping mechanisms. These steps are illustrated in Figure 8-2 (Aguilera, 1990). In the case of Hattie, an elderly woman who was abused by her husband, the absence of one or more of these balancing factors may block the resolution of elder mistreatment and may increase the client's disequilibrium.

### Expression and Management of Feelings

For cases in which the victim's denial of the severity of the mistreatment is due to loyalty to the abuser, it may be more productive for the practitioner to work on the expression and the management of the victim's feelings and on the discharge of tension than to dismiss the victim as "hopeless." The practitioner may say, "Mr. Jones, I believe you when you say you love your son. Even when he hurts you, you do not want him to be arrested." Sometimes, if the practitioner—without asking the victim to betray the abuser—repeats this statement perhaps 50 times during repeated visits, the client will eventually say, "Well, maybe love isn't worth this misery. Maybe I should do something else" (Elliot, 1983).

### Reality Testing

As representative of the community and of society in general, the practitioner's contacts with the victim are important opportunities, especially when the practitioner is the only person with whom the victim comes into contact. Providing information and advice can combat self-blame, excessive fantasies, and "magical" thinking—the idea that the mistreatment will

**CASE STUDY: HATTIE**

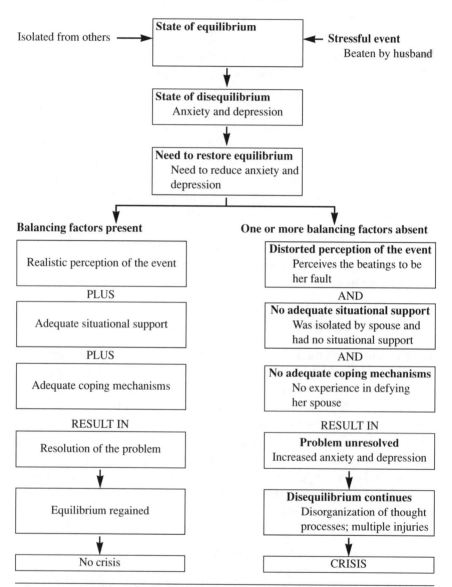

Figure 8-2    Paradigm: The effect of balancing factors in a stressful event.

*Source:* Adapted, with permission from the author and publisher, from Aguilera, D.C. (1990). *Crisis intervention: Theory and methodology.* St. Louis, MO: The C.V. Mosby Company.

end by itself. It can also curb other maladaptive coping patterns such as somatization and withdrawal from reality (Golan, 1978). Elders may attempt to dismiss a practitioner's offers of help, claiming that they are capable of handling their own affairs. But they may in fact be "pseudo-independent" and require assistance. For example, if the client, Mr. A., claims that he can do his own monthly budget, the practitioner, Ms. B., can ask him to sit down and do a budget with her. Or if Mr. A. says he is capable of doing his own grocery shopping, Ms. B. can ask him what he has been eating and ask him to show her what foods he has available in his refrigerator and cupboards. Mr. A should be allowed to arrive at his own conclusion that perhaps a little bit of help may be useful.

Some victims may maladaptively generalize their feelings after being victimized, and as a result may require reality testing. For instance:

> An elder whose trusted friend had expropriated $8,000 from his savings account began to verbalize a general mistrust of everyone. He began to jeopardize his social supports as he kept meaningful people at a distance, saying that people were interested only in his money and that no one should be trusted anymore. In her multiple contacts with him, the practitioner repeatedly reminded him, "That's how your friend was; not everyone is like him." She also helped him restore his faith in others by accompanying him to the bank and introducing him to the bank manager, who agreed to monitor the transactions of the elder's account.

In many instances, rather than rely on the client's self-determination, it is appropriate to advocate a particular course of action or to give an opinion about a maladaptive resolution to the elder's problem (Golan, 1978; Rapoport, 1970). A client who believes that a relative's abusive or neglectful behavior will cease through faith and hope will need to be reminded that wishing away a problem will not work and that perhaps other options should be considered.

The practitioner as an outsider can also reinterpret as inappropriate or illegal those acts to which the victim has become accustomed. For example, when the client says, "If I weren't such a burden, he wouldn't be so angry;" or, "Everyone would be better off if I were dead," the practitioner may react with, "Spilling a glass of water or wetting your bed does not justify a slap. No matter what you did, it is wrong to be hurt like that. No one deserves to be abused." In some instances, after making statements such as these to the client repeatedly—that the mistreatment was not his or her fault, and that to be mistreated is wrong—the client may surprise the practitioner by saying, "You know, you may have a point there; it isn't my fault. He has no right to blame me for things I can't help." In these instances, the intent is to interpret for the client what the community considers to be right or wrong, to interpret elder mistreatment as unacceptable behavior, and to prevent self-blame.

## Development of Foresight

Another method of providing the victim with a "dose of reality" is through the development of foresight, a form of intellectualization and a method to prepare the elder for the possibility of future incidents of mistreatment. To counteract the victim's denial of injury, the practitioner can ask the victim to seriously consider what he or she will do during the next abusive incident. Through behavior rehearsal, the practitioner can help the client consider an escape route, rehearse dialing emergency telephone numbers, develop steps to obtain his or her wallet and car keys, or develop self-protection techniques. By helping victims believe that they can escape under certain conditions, learned helplessness can be overcome. Walker states, "Learned helplessness does not mean that the woman is helpless, but rather, that she tends to only use behavior that has a high degree of predictability because she has lost the ability to predict the successful outcome for other low-level probability behaviors" (Walker, 1991, p. 24–25). In one case, the staff of an inpatient geriatrics unit rehearsed telephone dialing techniques and verbal rebuttals with a victim in anticipation of more abusive encounters with her grandchildren once the victim returned to her apartment.

Using anticipatory guidance, the client and practitioner can imagine scenarios that can result in further mistreatment by focusing on the previous incident. The elder is asked to recall the conflict situation or problems that led to the call for help, focusing on precipitating stressors. Then the practitioner and the elder can discuss new behaviors and plans which can be activated if a similar incident occurs. In one protective services agency, a potential client is asked to develop a future plan of escape from the batterer as a condition for receiving agency services. This requirement shows the client that the practitioner takes the abuse seriously and so must they. It also helps the clients to think beyond their current helpless feelings and to think about what solutions are possible. This anticipatory process can serve to restore an elder's emotional equilibrium.

## Tapping the Elder's Inner Strength

Podnieks found that although victims are often viewed as powerless and helpless, in many cases a significant personality characteristic—*hardiness*—was evident among victims in a prevalence study of elder mistreatment in Canada (1992a; 1992b). Many of these victims had learned coping and survival skills and self-reliance as a result of harsh experiences, including surviving the Depression years. Those skills helped them to withstand elder mistreatment incidents as well. This capacity may be emphasized and used to combat current and anticipated incidents, after reviewing with elders the ways they coped with previous disappointments, threats, and hardships. With such a review, a victim's self-confidence may improve.

## Educational Therapy

Teaching the client about new methods for dealing with mistreatment is extremely effective in combating minimization and denial. Practitioners can model appropriate behavior which an elder may adopt. They can also provide extensive information regarding their clients' social and legal rights, and they can intercede with medical and legal authorities to explain complex procedures. Modeling and teaching are effective during the "teachable moment" when a client is vulnerable and open to new information (Rapoport, 1970).

Clients can benefit from empowerment training that will help them acquire or strengthen a positive, powerful self-image. Clients' training may include taking assertiveness training classes to learn to say "no" to repeated requests for money and other unreasonable demands, and to stand their ground in times of adversity. For example:

> In one state with a large rural population, it was common for alcoholic sons to threaten their mothers with physical violence if they did not hand over their Social Security checks. The mothers, accustomed to sharing whatever they had, readily handed the checks over and then had no funds to purchase food for themselves. Community workers taught the mothers assertiveness, and thereafter they felt less intimidated by their sons. They were then able to refuse to give the adult sons the checks which they themselves needed for the basic necessities of life.

Training may include taking self-defense classes to overcome fear. Participants are taught to fend off an attacker and recognize situations in which they are vulnerable (Kenoyer & Batemen, 1982). These classes are offered in many senior centers and government-subsidized apartment houses for the elderly. Also offered in these settings are classes sponsored by local law enforcement agencies on how to secure one's residence. Clients can also be taught not to take the same route from their residence to the grocery store or bank while they are carrying cash and other valuables. Perpetrators may observe their patterns and then assault them. A handbag should be worn inside a woman's coat. In the home, cash and other valuables should be kept out of sight of visitors and family members. When possible, elderly clients should be educated about direct bank deposits of their Social Security or pension checks.

Clients may also be instructed on techniques of self-care to reduce their dependency on their abusers. For example, the practitioner may introduce aids that make the client less dependent, such as a reacher or dressing stick, a commode chair, simplified clothing, and special eating utensils. Catalogues that offer these items may be shown to an elder, who can peruse them to obtain ideas. Devices such as medication boxes enable an elder to take medications correctly and may also lessen the burden on the abuser.

Most important, the practitioner should also educate elders that battering is usually recurrent and escalates, and that action may be necessary to protect themselves. While a client may resist any interventions, the practitioner can still take an educational approach and inform the client about what is known so far of the cycle of violence: that battering can escalate in severity and frequency if no changes are made, and that it is understandable why victims may choose not to leave abusive relationships, especially in the calm, loving respite phase when a batterer is remorseful, attentive, and loving, and swears never to be abusive again (Walker, 1979). A client may experience an abuser's recurrent episodes of violent behavior followed by the respite phase for a long time before realizing that he or she is supporting a chronic condition by remaining in it. Educating clients and then being available when they make the final decision to seek active intervention may be all that a practitioner can do initially.

## Environmental Therapy

In short-term treatment, one of the practitioner's roles is to determine the client's capacity to understand and utilize community resources. Offering and delivering concrete services are proofs of the practitioner's sincerity about assisting the client. Practitioners may counteract past disappointments and help build a trusting relationship by delivering services when they say they will. If possible, the practitioner should act first on problems that are perceived by the elder and the suspected abuser. The general rule of thumb is to provide services while maintaining the client in the least restrictive environment. The Continuum of Care Scale (Figure 8-3) lists environmental options by degrees of restriction, beginning with the least restrictive environment at the bottom.

Services such as meals on wheels, chore services, and home nursing care allow clients to remain in their own familiar surroundings. For example, rather than relocating failing clients who are unable to prepare meals or pay their own bills, the practitioner can refer them to a home-delivered meal program and to a local service agency that dispatches volunteers to assist with paying bills on a monthly basis. Promises of services should not be made without knowledge of the client's income and assets, since qualifying for these services is based on income. The pertinent data obtained earlier in the assessment phase will now be useful. Only after all possible in-home services fail to maintain the client's freedom and safety at their own home should the client be approached about exploring other types of residential setting. The practitioner should keep in mind that there may be positive outcomes when clients are moved to more protective settings. The client may blossom from increased stimulation, regular meals, structured activities, and being surrounded by others.

Even the most impaired elders can be maintained at home if they are medically stable; if competent, caring attendants can be found; if there are funds to pay them; and if someone is available to supervise them. However, these conditions cannot always be met, and it may be necessary to impinge further on an elder's personal freedom for reasons of safety. It may be necessary to consider placement in a group setting if the elder is ambulatory, is fairly healthy, and can perform activities of daily living; or in a nursing home if the elder needs skilled nursing or medical care, is incontinent of bowel and bladder, or is not ambulatory (Quinn, 1990a).

Unfortunately, in some cases a client may require a move from a familiar environment. The main reason for such a move is the client's need for 24-hour care that cannot be provided in the home. Another reason is that the client's emotional and physical safety is seriously jeopardized by remaining in the home. Chapter 9, on legal interventions, will discuss measures to keep the abuser away from the home, but sometimes even legal interventions will not rectify the situation and the client must relocate. Relocation, especially to a more confining environment that results in the loss

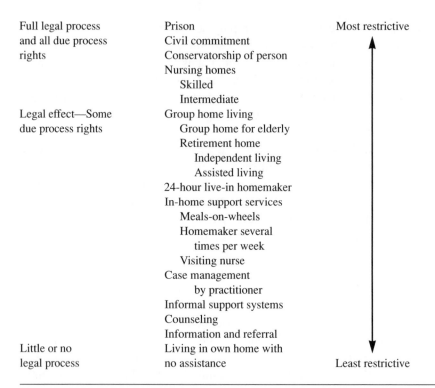

| Full legal process | Prison | Most restrictive |
| and all due process | Civil commitment | |
| rights | Conservatorship of person | |
| | Nursing homes | |
| |   Skilled | |
| |   Intermediate | |
| Legal effect—Some | Group home living | |
| due process rights |   Group home for elderly | |
| |   Retirement home | |
| |     Independent living | |
| |     Assisted living | |
| | 24-hour live-in homemaker | |
| | In-home support services | |
| |   Meals-on-wheels | |
| |   Homemaker several | |
| |     times per week | |
| |   Visiting nurse | |
| | Case management | |
| |   by practitioner | |
| | Informal support systems | |
| | Counseling | |
| | Information and referral | |
| Little or no | Living in own home with | |
| legal process |   no assistance | Least restrictive |

Figure 8-3    Continuum of care.

*Source:* Modified from Consortium for Elder Abuse Prevention, *Protocols,* UCSF/Mount Zion Center on Aging, San Francisco, 1983.

of privacy and familiar things, should be a plan of last resort. Some housing alternatives, depending on the client's functional abilities, are share-a-home, adult family home, boarding home, retirement home, assisted living, and nursing home. Elderly clients may be afraid to admit to being a victim of mistreatment because they envision being sent to a nursing home against their will. Their abusers may have intimidated them by saying things like, "If you tell them I hit you and took your money, they'll send you to a nursing home where you'll rot and die." Therefore, all the housing alternatives on the Continuum of Care Scale must be explored. If a nursing home is deemed the most appropriate choice, the nursing home staff should be made aware of the client's victimization, because it is not uncommon for an abuser to go to a nursing home to remove a client because he or she needs the client's monthly pension check. If not watched, such abusers may threaten their victims with harm, force them to sign over checks and property, and even hasten their death by suffocating them or turning off their oxygen supply.

The decision flow chart (Figure 8-4) adapted from O'Malley et al. (1983) may help determine what type of services can be offered.

## Preventive Counseling

Clients may feel that they are a burden to their caregivers or abusers; they may minimize their own needs; they may feel that they are not deserving of any improvement in their situation. The practitioner can encourage such clients to make reasonable requests before a buildup of emotions results in a confrontation (Schmidt, 1980). For example, a client may want someone to drive him or her to a local restaurant where friends meet regularly for coffee but, fighting dependency, may not have the nerve to speak up. Describing the agony of being dependent and waiting for others to help, Lustbader writes, "The more dependent we are on the mercy of others, the more waiting we have to endure. Dependency and waiting eventually become synonymous. . . . We begin to wonder, 'Is my life really worth all of this stress?' " (1991, pp. 6–9). In such instances, the practitioner's interventions are crucial. The practitioner can help the client rehearse requests and figure out how to broach the topic. The practitioner can also be present when clients make a first attempt at asserting their needs.

## Activity with Collaterals

Outside the family system, interpersonal and institutional resources can assist the client in developing a pattern of seeking and using help. Natural and created groups can provide comfort, support, and satisfaction from these relationships. Some elders benefit from a change of residence, or their environment can be made safer when friends, neighbors, and practitioners from different agencies and within the same agency develop a joint plan of action that is carried out by all.

Clients tend to feel more secure when they know their community will provide aid if necessary. Increased monitoring from outside of the home can come from daily telephone reassurance checks such as "dial-a-care," from a law enforcement agency, or from filling out a postal alert card, whereby the mail carrier will contact a local agency if the client fails to pick up mail for a specified number of days. "Neighbor helping neighbor"

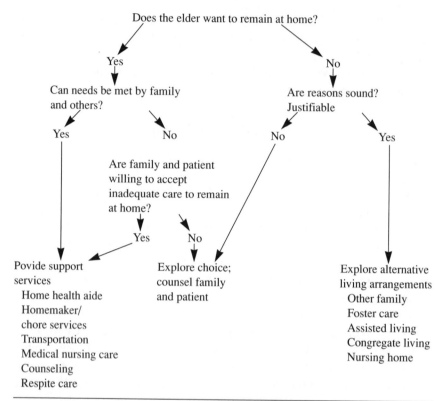

Figure 8-4    Decision flow chart for abuse or neglect of elderly person dependent on others for care.

*Source:* Modified, with permission from the authors and the publisher, from O'Malley, T., et al. (1983). Identifying and preventing family mediated abuse and neglect of elderly persons. *Annals of Internal Medicine, 98*(6), 998–1005. Copyright 1983, American College of Physicians.

programs and "gatekeeper" programs are a cost-effective way of assisting the elderly client. In some cities, utility meter readers, home fuel deliverers, and other groups have been trained to look for signs of foul play or neglect and to report their findings to a designated agency.

With the elder's permission, the practitioner can also call or visit people who come into contact with the elder and ask them what they think they can do to help. Some neighbors may choose not to get involved at all. Others may offer to "drop by," to do such things as wash and set the elder's hair, and to call the practitioner when there is a cause for concern. One home health aide reported that for families in which conflict was known to exist, she would stop by to bring fruit from her trees or other free items, to let the clients know that they had an ally, to provide support to the families, and at the same time to let them know that someone was watching their actions. Her attitude of helping everyone instead of taking an adversarial position served to dissipate some of the tension.

If the client belongs to a social group, its members may take turns transporting him or her to group activities. Many times neighbors who live alone exchange house keys and check on each other's well-being. Professionals in the community may help as well; as when an outpatient clinic social worker collaborates with an elder's protective services worker to arrange medical intervention when it is needed. Furthermore, the practitioner may help the client enroll in an adult day health center that provides a hot-meal program and transportation services to and from the center. In one case, the staff of one such center monitored for additional signs and symptoms of elder mistreatment, and talked to the client about his fears and concerns. Since this center was one of the few agencies that served elders beyond the assessment phase, it was in the best position to monitor the client's situation; the staff worked closely with the referring practitioner and the staff of the geriatrics clinic where the client received his medical care. The driver of the van played a crucial role as the conduit of information on the abusive son's comings and goings, and on the activities within the client's home.

Satisfactory resolution of financial exploitation incidents have necessitated collaborative activities by practitioners and financial institution personnel. In general, financial institutions are aware of attempts to exploit the vulnerable elderly and will try to monitor their regular customers' banking activities. In some cities, training has been conducted in some banks to make tellers aware of all possible fraudulent schemes. Some practitioners covering a certain geographic area have dropped in at local financial institutions and introduced themselves to the bank managers. Having cultivated a relationship, when a specific problem arises with a client, both sides have responded quickly.

Bank personnel welcome calls from workers who suspect that an elder's account is being exploited. The bank staff will look at signatures closely and may choose to withhold funds. They may put an alert on the account, or, as noted in Chapter 7, an administrative hold, which restricts withdrawals from the account. The alert may appear on the computer screen at the time a transaction is attempted, or the alert may be circulated by written communication between branches. Unfortunately, only the elder's "home" bank has the immediate alert; it is not possible to do a statewide alert all at once. If a client's funds are being withdrawn by a joint tenant of the account, the client or the client's substitute must close the account as soon as possible to avoid further depletion of funds. Once a signature is on the account, it is not removable. A new account will be opened in the client's name so that the client will have access to his or her funds. If someone attempts to withdraw funds by forging a client's signature or changing the amount on a check, the client is notified by the bank as soon as possible. The client then fills out a fraud form, "Affidavit of Forgery," if the amount involved is $350 or more. It is up to the client to fill out the form. If the client chooses not to fill it out, the bank will not pursue the matter further.

## Indirect Interventions with Victims

Indirect short-term interventions sometimes consist of documentation, reporting, and referral to another professional or agency for follow up. Documentation and treatment of elder mistreatment are done indirectly and directly and may take place in the home, an emergency room, or an outpatient clinic, or on a hospital inpatient floor. The in-home physical or occupational therapist, upon noticing suspicious signs of mistreatment, may refer the client to an agency nurse or social worker to study the problem, and they may work together to document symptoms of mistreatment and develop an interdisciplinary treatment plan. On the inpatient service, indirect interventions are also used where the mistreatment is documented and the assessment protocol is administered, but often no further action can be taken, primarily because the victim resists any changes in the situation. A client's denial of injury or being a victim can be frustrating to the staff. However, a small amount of comfort can be obtained from the realization that the mistreatment is clearly documented in the chart and that other staff members who treat the client on the next admission or the next visit to the emergency room will be alerted to the problem and will offer services again.

In order to be effective, the practitioner should become familiar with state laws about reporting elder mistreatment. In most states, practitioners—including nurses, psychologists, social workers, pharmacists, and physicians—are required to report possible cases of elder mistreatment. The agency mandated to accept all reports and to investigate them is usually the state's social and health services agency, staffed by protective service workers. Once a report is made, the protective services worker will conduct an investigation and offer appropriate services to the client, the suspected abuser, or both. If the referring practitioner chooses to remain involved with the client and to work with the protective services worker, that should be indicated at the time the report is provided by other agency practitioners. In many instances, protective services workers have collaborated with the referring practitioner because, realistically, the protective services worker will most likely be involved only until the allegations of elder mistreatment are substantiated or unsubstantiated, and then refer the case back to the referring practitioner for follow-up services.

## INTERVENTIONS WITH THE ABUSER

Pillemer's new information on dependency of the abuser (1986) as described in Chapter 2, reminds many practitioners and researchers to focus not only on the victim but on the abuser as well. Further, Pillemer and Finkelhor (1988) state that abuse appears to reflect the abuser's problems and general coping style more than the characteristics of the elderly victim. More recently, a comparative analysis of older women mistreated by their spouses and women mistreated by their adult children found two different profiles that require different approaches to treatment. While those mistreated by their spouses could benefit from legal and social interventions that are standard in the battered women's movement, those who were mistreated by their children could use assistance in obtaining counseling and rehabilitation services for their troubled and dependent children (Wolf & Pillemer, 1995). This study affirms the need to take a family approach rather than an individual, "client-only" approach whenever possible.

## Therapeutic Plan

### *Management of Practitioner's Feelings*

The practitioner's first difficulty is in the management of his or her own feelings toward the abuser. Feelings of anger, outrage, and disgust are aroused easily when the practitioner hears about abusive incidents and wants to make the abusers "pay" for their actions. Experts in child abuse remind all involved that "a hurt parent is a hurt child"; and an analogy can be drawn here: "A hurt abusive spouse or grown child is a hurt elder." Thus treatment must be offered to the abuser as well as the victim (Steele & Pollock, 1968). An abusive caregiver—such as an equally old spouse—who is overwhelmed with the tasks involved in taking care of an elder may enter the counseling relationship expecting to be attacked and may as a result be defensive. Such abusers may be yearning for recognition that they tried their best under the circumstances. It is advisable to ask abusers questions carefully and share similar situations in order to universalize their situation. Abusers' ability to identify with a practitioner is a good sign that they feel understood (Steele & Pollock, 1968).

In some cases, Walker contends, we must make "the shift from a unidimensional view of batterers . . . to an understanding that batterers and battering relationships are multidimensional. . . . Differences among types of batterers suggest the need for a 'triage' approach to the types of intervention and treatment available" (1995, p. 266). Time spent with abusers must not be used to focus on the client but should also focus on the abusers and their issues. It is wise to cultivate a relationship with an abuser and to develop a genuine liking for him or her. By paying attention to positive traits of the abuser—not just shortcomings—the practitioner can achieve the main goal: to stop the mistreatment. Simple things can help create a relationship between an abuser and a practitioner, such as admiring a picture on the abuser's wall. Talking about such items will help to develop a relationship on a genuine basis, and the abuser will feel more accepted. Sometimes simply talking about the weather will put both practitioner and abuser at ease. In turn, the abuser will probably be more cooperative about a suggested treatment plan.

Social isolation and having no one to talk to may contribute to decreased self-esteem and increased frustration. The practitioner's task is to help the abuser develop skills to engage in social activities. The task begins with the practitioner providing regular contacts, visiting the abuser regularly as time allows or requesting that a volunteer visit regularly, for the purpose of support and having a friendly visitor to share the day. Periodic phone calls to inquire about the abuser's progress may help. Once abusers feel accepted and comfortable with the practitioner as a friendly visitor, they may feel comfortable enough to consider increasing their contacts to include others in the community.

### *Acknowledgment of the Relationship's History*

In certain cases, the practitioner can acknowledge to the abuser an awareness of the history of the relationship. For instance, the practitioner, Mr. C., may tell the abuser, Ms. D., that he is aware that her situation has been a difficult one for many years, that her elderly relative has a history of being difficult to please, or that the elder has at times been unduly nasty toward Ms. D. While such acknowledgment does not condone the abusive or neglectful behavior, it will help abusers feel that they are being treated fairly and that the practitioner is not "taking sides." Sometimes an abuser's past difficulties with an elderly client began when he or she was a child and the elder was the powerful authority in control. With the tables turned, with the elder declining in function and in need of support and assistance, the abuser may still be living in the past and may have unrealistic expectations. In such cases, the elders may be barely managing their own affairs but tell their abusers little of what they want in the way of help. The role of the practitioner is to emphasize that "now" is not "then," that the client has aged (Schmidt, 1980). This attempt to improve reality testing may have to be repeated in ensuing counseling sessions. A useful tool is to show the abuser and others results of a client's mental status and functional assessments that indicate a mental or physical impairment or both.

An abuser in a caregiving role who must tolerate an elderly client's abuse may have ambivalent feelings yet still perform the tasks out of love, duty, or a strong sense or responsibility. The practitioner can promote a more positive relationship by acknowledging abusers' ambivalence, accepting their negativity, and pointing out that in spite of their negative feelings and past hurts, they are doing their best. For example, the practitioner may say, "Sometimes your father treats you like a slave and doesn't express gratitude, but you still visit him every day and try to help out. I can see why you sometimes feel like abandoning him." The practitioner can also suggest that the tasks be distributed among other family members and agency personnel.

The practitioner may discover that an abuser has been victimized at some point in the past, for example, as a victim of child abuse, as a victim of economic recession (being laid off from a job), or as a victim of a mugging. Exploring how such abusers feel or felt as victims may help them to understand the elder's feelings and to develop empathy. The abuser and victim may share similar feelings such as fear, hopelessness, self-blame, and anger.

### *Provision of Reality Testing and Structure*

The main methods for treating an abuser who utilizes neutralization techniques are to increase the abuser's apprehension of being "caught," to provide documentation and evidence to counteract the denial of injury and
responsibility, and to attack the abuser's mood of fatalism or feelings of
desperation. Abusers must be aware that while they may not perceive themselves as abusive or neglectful, others do. In such situations, it may help to
say, "Are you aware that some of your actions can be defined by the law as
theft?" or, "You may not think that you are doing anything wrong, but others may feel that you are breaking the law."

Collateral contacts, especially with persons who have known both the
elderly client and the abuser, are valuable for obtaining information that
can be presented to the abuser. One person may continue to deny abusive
or neglectful behavior in spite of the information, but another may realize
that he or she has been "caught" and cannot get away with the abusive or
neglectful behavior any longer (Ganley, 1981).

If there is a possibility of mistreatment, it is best for the practitioner to
be frank and honest, raising this concern with the abuser, and in a manner
that says help is available to correct the situation. The abuser may
acknowledge the mistreatment, but may not take responsibility and instead
may blame the victim or external factors, saying, for instance, "I didn't
get much sleep the night before and didn't realize what I was doing the
next day"; "I was so drunk I didn't realize what I was doing"; "He called
me a nasty name, so I had to teach him a lesson." The practitioner can refuse to support the externalization of blame and the abuser's denial, pointing out that while alcohol and drugs may have disinhibitive and cognitive
effects on some people and contribute to inappropriate behavior, other
people are not abusive when under the influence of alcohol or drugs. Mistreatment may coexist with alcohol and drug use, but there is no cause-
and-effect relationship.

Emphasizing self-control is another way to assist abusers with changing
their behavior. It is possible to encourage them to spend their energies on
learning to control their own behavior rather than focusing on the victim's
behavior and trying to control the victim. The abuser's behavior is not
caused by the victim; rather, that behavior may be a result of learned and
observed experiences—and it is possible for the abuser to change. The
abuser must also be reminded that while external stressors such as unemployment and lack of sleep cannot always be controlled, the response to

these stressors can be controlled, and acceptable methods of expressing stress can be learned. Perhaps the abuser's "mood of fatalism" and feeling of being an "effect" can be replaced by a mood of optimism and a feeling of being a "cause." Abusers can stop blaming others for their own unhappiness and stop waiting for others to make them feel happy. They can learn that as they take responsibility for their behavior, they can take control of it. Their happiness or unhappiness will be a result of what they do or do not do for themselves (Ganley, 1981).

An attempt to stop the abusive behavior can be made by focusing on clear expectations for behaving, usually with a time frame attached to them. For example, the practitioner can provide structure to the relationship by presenting verbal or written instructions to the abuser in the following manner:

1. Effectively immediately, you will make a conscious effort to stop assaultive behavior.
2. By February 25, you will return the items that you removed from your mother's home. You understand that failure to do so will result in a formal report to the authorities.
3. By March 1, you will identify someone to call and to talk to when you are feeling frustrated.
4. By May 1, you will use alternative behaviors rather than striking out. Alternative behaviors are: (a) Count to 20 before responding to the other person. (b) Walk around the block once. (c) Write a sentence beginning, "I feel _____ (frustrated, angry, upset) because _____ or _____."

In one case, an abusive husband ceased hitting his wife immediately when he was given a set of instructions similar to these. The list conveyed to him that the abuse was unacceptable and, at the same time, that others believed he was capable of behavioral change.

### Problem Resolution

Anticipatory counseling may be utilized to prevent family confrontations. The practitioner can sit down with the abuser and discuss items to be negotiated (e.g., leaving the elderly client in the care of a companion so that the abuser can have a free day) long before the situation arises. Discussion of touchy issues when both the elder and abuser have the time and energy to discuss them will help to avoid verbal and emotional confrontations that may further alienate them from each other. Sometimes the abuser may assume that the elderly client is incapable of engaging in making decisions regarding his or her care, especially if the elder suffers from some degree of cognitive impairment. The practitioner can help to relieve the abuser's guilt and frustration by holding joint family conferences and acting on the assumption that the elderly client is cognizant of the counseling activities and capable of participating in problem solving—for instance, deciding how often the abuser should have "days off" and deciding at what point the client will require 24-hour care in a facility. While impaired clients may not comprehend everything that is discussed, they may have moments of lucidity and make a few contributions (Schmidt, 1980). Most likely, they will have more of a commitment to a solution if they have been included in the problem-solving process.

By understanding the various neutralization techniques, perhaps the practitioner will be less likely to distance himself or herself from the abuser when threats and accusations of being "snoopy" are made; it could be that the abuser is only manifesting condemnation of the condemners in order to dissuade the practitioner from continuing with the investigation.

## Educational Plan

An educational approach to problem resolution is usually the least threatening counseling technique. Whenever possible, the practitioner can inform abusers of assistance for which they may qualify. Programs available may include respite care, volunteer visitor programs, and cash grants for caring for the elder. Abusive caregivers may be reluctant to accept outside help, thinking that they must do everything by themselves. Several sessions may be required to convince abusers, especially spouses who feel it is their responsibility to do everything alone, to accept help.

Abusers may be very threatened by the prospect of being on their own should an elder choose to ask them to leave the residence. They may not receive free room and board any longer. A victim may choose to vacate a residence and leave the abuser with the responsibilities of paying the rent and supporting himself or herself. Such abusers may not have the capacity to fend for themselves and may contemplate suicide. Taking a non-threatening, educational approach, the practitioner can discuss this with the abuser and agree on a plan if a crisis like this occurs (Ganley, 1981).

A practitioner may have heard ill-informed caregivers make such state-ments as, "Oh, he can walk if he wants; he's just faking it to get attention. To teach him a lesson, I just ignore his cries for help." To diminish unreal-istic expectations regarding the elder, the practitioner can attempt to teach the abuser what can and cannot be expected from the elderly client. Abusers can also be told of groups they can join to learn about subjects such as the psychological aspects of aging, chronic illnesses, sensory deprivation, com-munication, and use of community resources. The abuser can also be helped with literature written in lay terms which describes ways of taking care of a dementia patient in the home, home safety lists, and the do's and don'ts of drug use (Lustbader & Hooyman, 1994).

As abusers begin to conduct themselves in an appropriate manner and to fulfill their roles as caregivers and family members, praise and support must be given whenever possible. The practitioner can give suggestions and guidelines on what are appropriate caregiving tasks, such as laying out clothes for an elder who is unable to get to the closet, shopping, or prepar-ing a main meal daily.

Spousal abuse among the elderly has received increased attention in recent years (Homer & Gilleard, 1990; Paveza et al., 1992; Pillemer & Finkelhor, 1988; Pillemer & Suitor, 1992; Wolf & Pillemer, 1995), forcing elder mistreatment practitioners to join with domestic violence practitio-ners in developing appropriate interventions. Figure 8-5 was developed for a recent conference that united these groups. Currently, the main ap-proaches for male batterers are: (1) cognitive therapy, in which the abuser develops a better understanding of sexism, power, and control in intimate relationships; (2) behavioral therapy, to learn anger management tech-niques; and (3) a family systems approach involving all members. No one of these is more successful than the others (Sonkin, 1988).

While it is still not known how prevalent spouse battering is among elder mistreatment cases, it can be assumed that elderly clients can be in increased danger if they choose to remain in an abusive setting in which the abuser does not make an effort to change. The abuser must be taught that according to what is known so far from the literature on battered women, in many cases physical abuse can escalate in severity and frequency. There are three phases of battering: (1) tension building, in which the victim attempts to cope with minor battering incidents; (2) explosion or acute battering, in which there is no predictability or control; and (3) a calm, loving respite, in which the abuser is remorseful and obtains absolution by being kind and generous (Walker,

Figure 8-5    Power and control wheel for older battered women.

*Source:* Adapted from *Power and control wheel,* originally developed by the Domestic Abuse Intervention Project, Duluth, MN; and further developed by the Planning Committee for the Older Battered Women's Conference, Consortium for Elder Abuse Prevention, UCSF/Mount Zion Center on Aging, San Francisco, CA, 1996.

1979, 1987). There is no guarantee that the abuse will stop after the third phase unless the abuser's behavior changes.

Sometimes the only emotion that abusers have felt it acceptable to express is anger. They react with anger no matter what happens and no matter how else they may be feeling. Where other people might react with embarrassment if an elderly client yelled at them in public, or might be worried if the elderly client was 2 hours late coming home from an outing with others, an abuser may express embarrassment and anxiety by yelling at the elder. The abuser may never have learned to express the whole range of emotions such as hurt, disappointment, joy, shame, and worry. The practitioner can be helpful by interpreting some of these angry outbursts (Ganley, 1981; Sonkin & Durphy, 1982), saying, for example, "If my father had been that late coming home, I would have been worried sick"; or, "I always get embarrassed if someone yells at me in public, especially when I'm trying to be helpful and I feel that I don't deserve such rudeness."

## Resource Linkage

Resource linkage may occur as part of the educational plan but also can be implemented as a separate component. Locating respite care or day care for the elder in order to give family members a rest, obtaining cash grants for the abuser whenever possible, and identifying appropriate community resources are ways to relieve the burdens of caregiving on family members.

## Working with the Abuser: Summary

To summarize, working with the abuser may in the long run be an effective use of the practitioner's time. In reality, the majority of elder mistreatment victims will most likely choose to continue maintaining contact or living with the abuser. Extremely pathological abusers who are unwilling or unable to change their behavior probably constitute a small percentage of all abusers. It is possible for the practitioner to work with the abuser if the focus of the counseling is on stopping the abusive behavior. The practitioner's main task is to hold the abuser accountable for his or her behavior. The practitioner can teach abusers that their behaviors are not caused by the client, and that inappropriate behaviors are learned, can be unlearned, and can be replaced by more acceptable behaviors. If the practitioner provides support and acceptance and at the same time defines clear behavioral expectations, the abuser may become more comfortable in fulfilling appropriate roles. The abuse or neglect may then cease.

# TERMINATION

In short-term treatment, termination is often discussed and initiated in the first interview. The client—either the elder or the abuser—may negotiate with the practitioner the numbers of contacts and formulate the criteria for ending treatment. Termination may occur when clients *begin* to find solutions to their problems (Rapoport, 1970). It may be difficult to "let go" and tempting to maintain contact for a period beyond the predetermined time. Prolonging the treatment period may be justified by saying that the client is still "shaky." The focus of short-term treatment is not to promote dependency but to maximize change in the client's functioning and growth potential. For all people, not only those who are identified as clients, there are periods of adaptive and maladaptive functioning. Clients may be ambivalent toward help or may not want immediate assistance. They may take a while to decide to focus on solutions. For example, a client may change his or her mind about pressing charges against an abuser who has just stolen several thousand dollars. If practitioners can anticipate that ambivalence will be a common occurrence, they may be more realistic about treatment outcomes and not blame themselves if a client rejects what seems to be a sensible treatment plan.

In some cases, practitioners should allow themselves time away from a client. They may feel as if they are banging their heads against the wall when certain clients tax their patience—clients who, for instance, repeatedly change their mind about receiving help or show no progress in mastering their environment after multiple home visits. The practitioner may want a breather and should feel free to say to the client, "It's time for me to take a break from this situation. I feel that for the moment I've done all I can to assist you. I'm going to attend to some other matters for a few weeks and return to see you next month. Let's make an appointment to meet in 1 month and I will call you in 2 weeks to say hello." While practitioners may be tempted to terminate certain relationships permanently, distancing themselves temporarily may refresh them and enable them to examine these difficult situations with greater objectivity; new solutions or ideas may emerge from this break.

It is not a failure if an elder or an abuser refuses help or seems to make no progress within several treatment sessions. With an "open door policy," the elder or the abuser may return for help. Rapoport (1970) states:

> We expect that a problem solved should stay solved for all times. Reapplication for service should be viewed positively. Experience has shown that clients who return after a brief period of help need even briefer help the second time. They may use a second period of help to consolidate previous gains. In other instances, the need for help the second time may be unrelated entirely to the first situation, and should be dealt with in accordance with current need. (p. 303)

# ONGOING CLINICAL INTERVENTION

While many cases will be resolved during an immediate crisis or with short-term treatment, other cases will have to be followed for 2 years or longer. It may be that agencies identifying themselves primarily as delivering protective services will engage in more crisis and short-term treatment, while collateral agencies with fewer time and budget constraints will be better able to offer long-term services.

The practitioner should discuss with the caregiver resources that are available when the caregiver feels abusive and needs support. Crisis clinics exist in almost every city and are available 24 hours a day. Some are connected with inpatient psychiatric units of general hospitals. The practitioner's agency may have a 24-hour hot line, or the practitioner may give the abuser phone numbers of people available for crises. During anticipatory planning, these numbers and the plan of action for crises should be rehearsed (Aguilera, 1990; Parad & Parad, 1990).

A model in one state consists of maintaining contact with the victim beyond the initial phase. That model includes conducting 3-month follow-up contacts during the first year. If the client is not safe or stable within the first year, a referral is made for case management for long-term follow-up (Hwalek, Hill, & Stahl, 1989).

Some elder battered women need support as they sort through their feelings. Because of ambivalence, the victim may try to separate from the abuser several times before making a permanent break. The program manager of the Older Abused Women's Program at the Milwaukee Women's Center notes that in reality, it takes an average of seven or eight attempts to leave an abusive relationship. One of the first women she worked with took 2 years to leave. A professional working with the same woman earlier had labeled her a "help-rejecting complainer" (*Nexus*, 1995c).

In severe physical abuse cases where one party—the parent, the child, or the spouse—wants to be reunited with the other after a period of separation, there may be a gradual way of doing that. First, one party might send letters or tapes, either audio or video, to safely explore the other person's wishes. The next step may then consist of a gradual reintroduction of the victim or the abuser by short face-to-face visits, first with someone present. These should take place in a neutral setting, and such visits should be increased before the two are ever alone together again. Of course, at each of these steps the victim's desires must be monitored, and verbal and nonverbal cues must be interpreted. Supervised, gradual reunification may take months, and third-party monitoring would put the abuser on alert that some control is being imposed.

The following sections discuss specific forms of ongoing interventions.

## Ongoing Group Therapy

### *Group Settings*

Issues of domestic violence, including elder mistreatment, can arise in any group setting. They may emerge in direct statements, but more probably the references will be indirect, in such statements as, "I was harder on my daughter than I needed to be," or, "My son doesn't treat me right." Although these seem like minor clues, it is important to realize that abusers and victims tend to deny and minimize abuse incidents (Sonkin et al., 1985). Therefore, these statements are clues to be explored either within the group context or individually.

The issue of mistreatment may emerge if the group facilitator brings it up first, perhaps as part of mentioning several things that can be difficult in life. It could also emerge when current events are being discussed; there are frequently news stories about domestic violence in the newspapers and on television. Leaders may decide to provide education on the subject by way of helping elders spot, prevent, and combat mistreatment. In those instances, permission can be given for elders to speak to the leader privately or within the group. Conversely, there may be times when a leader will take the initiative and speak to an elder outside of the group, especially if the elder seems particularly upset about issues related to domestic violence, has talked openly about abuse, or has actually come to group meetings with bruises that are inadequately explained (see Chapter 6 for assessment techniques). When approaching an elder about possible personal mistreatment, practitioners should be prepared for initial denial, even if it is obvious that mistreatment is taking place. However, if a door is left open in the form of an accepting statement, the elder may return for help. Such a statement could be, "Well I'm glad to hear that everything is all right in your life. But I want you to know that often older people are abused, just as children and wives are sometimes abused. And it doesn't mean that you have a bad family or that you have to leave your family or that anyone has to go to jail. So if that ever happens to you, I want you to know that you can come to me and I'll help you."

Recently, specialty services in the form of elder victims' groups have been developed. Only 10 years ago, it was believed that no elder would want to join a group to discuss mistreatment, because of extreme humiliation and guilt. For many years, the elder victims' group at New York's Victim Services, staffed by volunteers, was apparently the only group in the nation. However, perhaps with increased publicity about mistreated elders and efforts by domestic violence groups to include the elderly as part of their target population, additional groups have since flourished. In New York, the Victim Services group was replicated by the Mount Sinai Medical Center Elder Abuse Project. Group members reported receiving more support from the group than from previous individual counseling (Wolf & Pillemer, 1994). In San Francisco, Family Service Agency has 6-week support group sessions for financially abused seniors. Speakers educate seniors on how to protect themselves against future abuse.

Groups for elderly men may be as essential as those for women. Walker and Griffin (1984), writing about group therapy for depressed elders, promote giving priority to men as members because in general they lack the support women have, are less communicative and more isolated, but have needs that are just as great.

With regard to offenders, in San Francisco an outpatient group treatment program for elder mistreatment offenders was attempted through Men Overcoming Violence Effectively (MOVE), in conjunction with the UCSF/Mount Zion Center on Aging. Insufficient membership has delayed its implementation. Available to men and women who have been physically, emotionally, verbally, or financially abusive to parents or elders in their care, the group is tentatively designed to meet weekly for 6 months. The treatment focuses on identifying abusive and controlling behavior, learning alternatives to violent behavior, understanding issues of power and control as they relate to the elderly, and learning communication skills.

### Groups for Older Battered Women

AOA-SPONSORED GROUPS.    Support groups have also been formed as part of an effort by the Administration on Aging (AOA) to increase services to elderly battered women. The five agencies selected by the AOA are the Vermont Network Against Domestic Violence and Sexual Assault, the Wisconsin Coalition Against Domestic Violence, the San Francisco Consortium for Elder Abuse Prevention (UCSF/Mount Zion Center on Aging), the Massachusetts Health Research Institute, and the Women's Center of

Bloomsburg, Pennsylvania (*Nexus*, 1995c). Groups for elderly battered women also exist in Seattle, Washington, and Milwaukee, Wisconsin.

THE MILWAUKEE WOMEN'S CENTER GROUPS.   In 1991, the Milwaukee Women's Center (MWC) initiated a program designed to serve elderly battered women. Conceived by a task force after a year of planning, it has served 120 elderly victims of physical and emotional abuse. The program includes a support group, case management, shelter, and counseling from volunteers. The age range of the elderly women is 53 to 91 years, with two-thirds being abused by their spouses and one-third by their children.

Contrary to the notion that women are attracted to abusive men and will repeatedly seek out similar types, in half of the cases of spousal abuse, the women were being abused by their second or third partners, and their first partners had usually not been abusive. Also important, the profile of the Center's victims further discounts the assumption that elder victims are frail and dependent on their abusers. On the contrary, few of the women had significant impairments, and still fewer were dependent on others for their care. It could be, however, that only healthy elders who are able to transport themselves to the sessions are being treated, and that frail elders are going without intervention.

Generally speaking, groups provide a chance for resocialization and for learning problem-solving techniques (*Nexus*, 1995c). At MWC, the focus of the group sessions may be on a particular theme, problem, or question. Some sessions have an educational component, covering the dynamics of power and control, the phases of battering, and the need to make safety and escape plans. Each member usually has a turn to speak and to obtain the support of the rest of the group. With such support, the victims may cope better and move from self-blame and ambivalence to accepting permanent solutions. As a note of caution, group developers must decide whether the location and times of the group meetings should be kept confidential. One group leader reported that some of the husbands have followed the participants to the group and have exhibited threatening behaviors.

## Ongoing Environmental Therapy: Developing Programs and Networks

### *Networking with Protective Services Agencies*

While APS agencies are usually designated to accept reports of elder mistreatment and to investigate them, they are often faced with financial constraints and understaffing. On the basis of figures from the census of 1990, annual APS funding averages $3.80 per elder 65 years old and older, but 25% of the states spend less than $1 per elder for protective services; some of the states spend nothing or as little as 22 cents per elder (Simon, 1992). Given these limitations, it is impossible for communities to expect APS to do everything on behalf of the elder. The protection of endangered elderly people is the responsibility of the entire community, not just one agency. In reality, most cases involve anywhere from two to 10 different agencies to achieve resolution.

Regardless of profession, practitioners working with the elderly subscribe to what is now known as the *APS Credo*. At the 1982 conference at the University of Southern Maine, "Improving Protective Services for Older Adults," which was attended by social work and legal professionals, a theory of adult protection was formulated with the hope of stimulating discussion and creating greater clarity with regard to the functioning of protective services. These four principles serve to guide everyone, not only the protective services practitioner (University of Southern Maine, 1982).

### *APS Credo*

1. *When interests compete, the practitioner is charged with serving the adult client.* The worker is not charged with serving the community's concern about the client's safety, the landlord's concern about crime or morality, or the concern of the client's family about their own health or finances. The client has a right to be annoying, eccentric, and even foolish. For example, clients may eat out of garbage cans; wear three shirts at once; be observed talking to themselves; own 12 cats; have candy and soda pop for breakfast, lunch, and dinner—and not be in need of any protective services.

A stressed caregiver or apartment manager have made a referral out of concern for the client. As much as the referrer may want to be helpful, it is the client's circumstances and wishes for help that are the primary determinants of intervention. The practitioner cannot always intervene just because the community says, "Do something." The practitioner's role is to be an advocate for the client, and to maintain and uphold the client's rights. Clients also have the right to divest themselves of their wealth, to give away their savings while they are alive. Wills may be contested by relatives after a client's death, but a relative may not dictate how the clients are to spend their money while they are still alive.

2. *When interests compete, an adult client is in charge of decision making until he or she delegates responsibility voluntarily to another or the*

*court grants responsibility to another.* Clients retain all constitutional rights unless they are declared incapacitated or incapable of giving consent or of handling their own affairs by a court of law. Services may not be imposed on those who are competent and who refuse to accept them. Deprivation of personal liberty must be carried out in accordance with due process law. Clients have a right to marry whomever they choose unless they have been declared by a court of law to be incapable of contracting a valid marriage. An agency may receive a complaint that an 80-year-old man is about to marry a 21-year-old woman who will probably inherit his $100,000 savings after his death. The woman is perceived by the referring caller to be exploitive, marrying the older person for his money. In such a case, if the 80-year-old man is capable of deciding what he wants for himself, the practitioner may not do anything.

On the other hand, depriving people of their rights can sometimes be protective. Owing to the immoral and unethical nature of some situations, the practitioner may be required to intervene, especially if funds are diverted and the client is subjected to undue influence. At times, a protective legal device may be necessary.

3. *When interests compete, freedom is more important than safety.* Clients have a right to be left alone; no matter how unsanitary and primitive their residences may be, and they have a right to refuse treatment. Recently, there have been several widely publicized cases involving elderly people who have refused medical treatment and for whom guardianship proceedings were initiated. Professionals were divided as to whether the clients were incapable of giving consent for medical care. These cases serve as a reminder that practitioners do not necessarily agree on what is best for clients, and that a client has the right to refuse treatment even if to do so would result in imminent death. It is sometimes very difficult for a practitioner to support a client's decision, especially when the client chooses not to alleviate a painful medical condition and subsequently dies. Every attempt should be made to gain the cooperation of the client before any action is taken. Involuntary intervention will not be initiated unless clients are incapable of caring for themselves or are in an emergency situation which is threatening to them or others. Only with proper evaluations and in the absence of all other reasonable alternatives will the practitioner obtain legal authority to remove the client's rights.

4. *In the ideal case, protection of adults seeks to achieve, simultaneously and in order of importance, freedom, safety, least disruption of lifestyle, and least restrictive care.* Services should be provided for the shortest

period of time and to the simplest extent necessary. The practitioner should involve those familiar to the client—including relatives, friends, and agencies—to the extent that they are willing and able to provide help. If no one else is available to assist or be an advocate for the client, the practitioner is obligated to assist the client. The intervention that is chosen will be balanced against the possible impact that it will have on the client's self-esteem, will to live, and feeling of control over his or her own life.

## Cooperation, Collaboration, and Networking

COLLABORATIVE APPROACHES.  Among clinicians, there is general agreement that a collaborative and multidisciplinary approach is essential in order to treat victims and their families successfully. Such an approach is especially effective with those cases that bounce from one agency to another and those that pose tremendous challenges. Working together assists with building creative solutions and comprehensive care plans, increasing individual expertise, and fighting fatigue. A great deal of discomfort arises in attempting to take legal action, especially against an extremely hostile perpetrator. Having backup and consultations available from colleagues allows the practitioner to go forward with the plans. Also, when multiple agencies take a concerted approach against a perpetrator, it is difficult for one agency or practitioner to be singled out or "dumped on."

Collaboration is crucial because although social service agencies provide treatment once mistreatment is uncovered, they are not necessarily the victim's first contact of choice. In a study conducted in 1991 with 21 older battered women in Milwaukee, it was found that the three agencies contacted most frequently were the police, doctors and nurses, and religious leaders. Often police received the first contact (Brandl, 1991).

Clinically, the nation is more informed and united in its efforts to prevent and intervene in cases of elder mistreatment, mainly owing to the efforts of the consortium of the National Center on Elder Abuse, and the National Committee for the Prevention of Elder Abuse (NCPEA).

NCPEA's *Journal of Elder Abuse and Neglect,* now in its eighth year, is a conduit for new information, research data, and ideas. NCPEA has also created a system by which local coalitions, councils, and groups of concerned citizens can become NCPEA affiliates. Its quarterly publication, *Nexus,* provides the most up-to-date information on national activities related to elder mistreatment. In 1992, professionals in Billings, Montana, developed the first local affiliate of the NCPEA. Additional affiliates have been or are being developed in Los Angeles, Santa Monica, and San Francisco, California; Cincinnati, Ohio; and Decatur, Georgia.

Many cities have long-standing groups with members representing the agencies in the area. In California, Sepulveda has the Elders at Risk Network, and Santa Clara has the Elder Abuse Task Force and the Multidisciplinary Elder Abuse Consultation Team (MEACT), which includes a physician specializing in geriatrics who provides valuable medical consultation to professionals in the area. The Multidisciplinary Team of the San Francisco's Consortium for Elder Abuse Prevention invites professionals to present cases for consultation. In Los Angeles, in response to numerous reported cases of financial abuse, the Fiduciary Abuse Specialist Team (FAST) was created to provide support to APS and Ombudsman staff. The FAST team is composed of consultants, including stockbrokers, bankers, realtors, insurance agents, law enforcement officers, attorneys, and a retired probate commissioner. With this collection of expertise and prompt response, millions of dollars have been recovered or protected in the city.

The Elder Abuse/Neglect Network in Seattle, Washington, now 12 years old, typifies networking bodies. It holds monthly meetings, and its members represent the Area Agency on Aging case management agency, APS, legal services, a police department victim and witness advocacy program, a home health agency that provides specialized mental health services to the elderly, a senior rights and assistance agency that relies heavily on volunteers, a mental health managed care agency, an older adults' program of a community mental health center, an adult day health center, a battered women's program, a nonprofit guardianship-payeeship agency, and the social work department of the University of Washington Medical Center. In addition to case presentations, the Seattle team evaluates problems on a system level and makes recommendations for improvement to government and other designated agencies.

In Massachusetts, a successful venture was developed between APS and the District Attorney's Office. It can be replicated elsewhere (Reulbach & Tewksbury, 1994).

THE MASSACHUSETTS MODEL.    In Massachusetts, an elder mistreatment reporting law was passed in 1983 that required APS workers to report serious cases to the District Attorney (DA). However, there were no clear guidelines on the types of cases to be reported, or what "serious" meant. In addition, APS was not allowed to share its files with the DA staff; this prevented the latter from taking any meaningful action on serious cases referred to them.

In 1988, the law was amended to allow APS to provide the DA's office with copies of materials from its files. In spite of this major change, in another area of the criminal justice system law enforcement personnel were not reporting to APS cases of elder mistreatment known to them, and in turn the APS workers knew little about law enforcement. Key staff members in the Office of Elder Affairs and the District Attorney's office in Middlesex County decided to develop interagency protocols. One of the first steps was to agree on terms such as "serious." A retrospective case review of their efforts revealed that both the DA and the APS agencies failed to follow up on the cases, the charges, or the victim's service plan.

A process was initiated to coordinate the investigations with law enforcement personnel and others, develop interagency service plans to support the victims throughout the criminal justice process, and develop role descriptions. As can be imagined, the planning process included many disagreements and strong differences of opinion, including which types of cases should be referred, which cases should be prosecuted, when case reviews should be completed, and what responses were appropriate under certain circumstances. With some general agreement achieved, specific guidelines were developed, answering questions such as, How soon? Who does what? What kind of information? A draft of the guidelines was circulated, amended after feedback was obtained, and tested. As they looked at the guidelines, some of the APS workers realized that they had been unaware that they were required to report serious cases. Important outcomes of this process included establishing the role of "second-line staff," or the supervisors, who were involved in important decision making activities; and a call-in system, designating one DA staff member and an alternate to answer questions from APS workers.

In subsequent cross-training sessions, two important questions were addressed: What happens if we disagree? Why should we report to you if no action will be taken? Protocols outlining steps to take for mediation and resolution among the agency workers were discussed. Reulbach and Tewksbury strongly recommend avoiding working on guidelines when feelings are running high right after a crisis within the shared caseload. The guidelines helped the APS workers learn that tardiness in reporting could result in the loss of physical, documentary, or testimonial evidence crucial in the criminal prosecution of a case. They also learned that not all cases referred to the DA's office were prosecutable, and that not all prosecuted cases

would necessarily involve incarceration. In turn, law enforcement personnel learned that if they failed to make a referral to APS, the victims lost out
on services for which they qualified, and that perhaps more appropriate
interventions outside the law enforcement system could not be pursued.
With streamlined access, the APS workers made more judicious use of the
system, and with consistency in feedback from the designated DA staff,
agreement was obtained on what were "serious" cases. This new system
identified gaps and led to new legislation addressing criminal neglect and
financial exploitation. The staff fought stereotypes and myths about each
other and increased their trust in each other's judgment. Also, having established personal relationships, they were able to introduce their colleagues
from other agencies to mistrustful victims, and quicker action was taken
on elder death cases. To take one example, a weekend call to the attorney
on duty facilitated an autopsy on a suspected victim before a cremation
ordered by the decedent's family for the following Monday. A cremation
would have destroyed any evidence of possible abuse.

In other areas of Massachusetts, a proactive approach to crimes against
the elderly was taken by creating multidisciplinary alliances and cross-training programs that were similar to those developed in Middlesex County. A
statewide Family and Community Crimes Bureau was also created, intend-
ing to highlight the victimization of the elderly, who were not as visible as
children or younger female victims. Adult protective services staff played a
primary role in the interventions, since most of the cases turned out to be
noncriminal in nature (Harshbarger, 1993).

In support of collaborative approaches such as those in Massachusetts,
Heisler (1991) lists the benefits of practitioners' being involved in the criminal justice system:

1. Stop the violence or other criminal behavior
2. Protect the victim
3. Protect the public
4. Hold the offender accountable for the conduct
5. Rehabilitate the offender
6. Communicate the societal intent to treat the conduct as a crime, not
   a private matter
7. Provide restitution to the victim (p. 9)

COLLABORATION WITH NURSING HOMES.    In another networking arena,
in San Luis Obispo County, California, one unique outcome of collabora-

tive efforts was the provision of free shelter for mistreated elders and dependent adults. The following report appeared in the January 1995 issue of *Nexus*:

### Nursing Homes Provide Free Shelter

Nursing home and residential care facilities in San Luis Obispo County, California, have agreed to provide up to seventy-two (72) hours of free shelter care to abused elders and dependent adults. The facilities accept referrals from police, fire departments, adult protective service workers, paramedics, and others. Preadmission paperwork is waived to permit emergency admissions. Operators of the facilities credit the program with "creating good relationships with referral sources as well as a more positive image of nursing homes." (Nexus, 1995a, p. 2)

### Ongoing Prevention and Awareness

PUBLIC AWARENESS.   Brochures and posters have been used extensively to make the public aware of elder mistreatment. Minnesota's Adult Protection Coalition has a poster with a cane on it, with the statement, "This isn't the only support system available to seniors." At the bottom of the poster is a blocked-out space for local agencies to list their names and phone numbers. The Coalition's brochure lists 33 supporting organizations, facts about elder mistreatment, and the activities of the Coalition.

Some groups have targeted special populations with special brochures. The "We Are Family" outreach project of the Consortium for Elder Abuse Prevention in San Francisco—with sponsorship from the Koret Foundation, San Francisco Commission on Aging, St. James Baptist Church, WAC-Lee Woodard Counseling, and Officers for Justice, San Francisco—published a brochure for African American elders to make them aware of what financial abuse is, what to do about it, and where they may call for additional information. The tie-in with African American cultural values and their churches as sources of strength and support is evident in the narrative. On the cover of the brochure, entitled "Money Sense for Seniors," are a photograph of an elderly African American couple, and a scripture from John 8:32, "You will know the truth, and the truth will make you free" (Njeri & Nerenberg, 1993).

In Washington, D.C., the National Hispanic Council on Aging (NHCA), in collaboration with the D.C. Area Agency on Aging (AAA) and Ayuda, Inc., the only community-based Latino agency providing legal and social services to undocumented Latinas and their children, have created a project to help midlife and older Latinas. The program includes a training program for professionals and elderly peer counselors, and a public awareness program for the community on the issue of domestic violence and elder abuse (*Nexus*, 1995b).

Kentucky's Adult Protective Services, whose motto is, "Abuse . . . It hurts at any age . . . Report it," created posters for Kentucky bank employees as a way of dealing with their many cases of financial exploitation. The poster states, "You can help protect your elderly customers from financial exploitation." It then lists suspicious behaviors and where to call for help.

Awareness of elder mistreatment was spread through note cards created and sold by the Elder Rights Coalition in Kansas. A pastel sketch of the artist at age 76 and her husband among flowers, titled "Self-Portrait with Glen," is on the cover, and the back of the folded card reads, "Prevent abuse through awareness. For information about elder abuse prevention contact the Elder Rights Coalition." It also lists the Coalition's address and phone number.

The Elder Abuse Task Force (EATF) of Santa Clara County, California has published an 8½- by 11-inch booklet titled "Elder Abuse—Guidelines for Professional Assessment and Reporting." Other communities may want to use it as a model for their own booklets because it is easily readable, with definitions and criteria for involvement clearly laid out. The booklet is divided into Identification, Assessment, Reporting, Prevention, and Resources. Indicators for each type of mistreatment and step-by-step instructions for filing a report are easy for practitioners to follow.

TRAINING AND EDUCATIONAL MATERIALS.    Local and national groups have made available training materials specifically for elder mistreatment education of professionals. Examples include one from Victim Services, Inc., in New York City (212-577-7700), which has a "train the trainers" manual with a video. It contains a core curriculum with supplemental curricula designed to address the specific concerns of law enforcement, court, and health care personnel. In addition, the manual contains sensitizing experimental exercises, such as the Labeling Game, which sensitizes the trainee to feelings that elders may have when they are talked down to, ignored, infantalized, or spoken to as if they were hard of hearing just because they are elderly. The San Francisco Consortium for Elder Abuse Prevention (415-750-4188), through the UCSF/Mount Zion Center on Aging, has issued *Building Partnerships,* which provides materials on the development of coalitions, interagency agreements, and teams related to elder mistreatment. Its *Elder Abuse Briefs* has information on four topics: *General Introduction to Elder Abuse and Neglect, Community Outreach in Elder Abuse Prevention, Guardianship,* and *Professional Training in Elder Abuse.* Many more creative and highly developed programs have been developed by practitioners in the various states, but it is not possible to list them all. The National Center on Elder Abuse (NCEA) has information on various programs, and practitioners may telephone the Center to obtain information about specific programs that they may be interested in starting in their own areas.

The National Center on Elder Abuse (NCEA) (202-682-0100)—established in 1993 to develop and provide information, data, and expertise to agencies, professionals and the public—is a consortium of the American Public Welfare Association (APWA), the National Association of State Units on Aging (NASUA), the University of Delaware Clearinghouse on Abuse and Neglect of the Elderly (CANE), and the National Committee for the Prevention of Elder Abuse (NCPEA, the Institute on Aging, Medical Center of Central Massachusetts). A variety of services are available: reports and monographs, training workshops, technical assistance and consultation, training guides and manuals, a computer bulletin board, teleconferences, and statistics and educational materials. In collaboration with the Texas Department of Protective and Regulatory Services, APWA, the lead agency for NCEA, cosponsors the annual Elder Abuse Prevention Conference in San Antonio, Texas. This annual event, begun in 1983, is extremely popular, drawing several hundred professionals from across the United States and from other countries.

Finally, practitioners who have access to computer information systems may want to check them for recent developments. The New York City Elder Abuse Coalition and Fordham University have just begun a Home Page on Elder Abuse and Neglect.

# IN CONCLUSION: COMMON OVERSIGHTS

Even experienced practitioners occasionally misjudge a situation. They should not castigate themselves for these lapses. The following situations illustrate typical errors and omissions and may help others to be alert to similar situations in their practice.

*Example 1:* An elderly man was seen in the emergency room after he collapsed in his home and was treated by an emergency response team. Because he was unconscious, the circumstances of the injuries were not explored. Three days later, an investigation found that the patient's adult daughter had attacked him from behind and had gouged his chest while standing behind him. In retrospect, it was clear that the patient's presenting condition should have been photographed and documented in the emergency room.

*Example 2:* A practitioner was called by the management of a facility to investigate a case of possible neglect. One of their patients, an elderly woman, was being cared for by private duty nurses who refused to let the staff of the facility examine her. When the staff forced the issue and were finally able to examine the patient, they found that she was covered with 13 pressure sores. Some of the sores were extremely wide and deep, exposing bone. Others were covered with black material. The staff took photographs of the pressure sores and showed them to the investigator. The practitioner did not go and look at the pressure sores herself—an error of omission, as she later realized. If she had been called to testify on the situation, she would not have qualified as an eyewitness to the client's condition. She also felt that had she personally assessed the client, she would have gained more energy to work on the case and advocate the elderly woman's interests more rigorously.

*Example 3:* A practitioner mistakenly interviewed the caregiver before the client. The client, a woman, became suspicious of the practitioner's motivations, feeling that since the practitioner had interviewed the caregiver first, he would side with the caregiver and not believe her explanation of the home situation. When the client was interviewed after the caregiver, she asked the practitioner why he had interviewed the caregiver first. The patient had been trying to alert the staff that she was being abused by the caregiver.

*Example 4:* One practitioner made the mistake of not watching a caregiver actually leave the premises as asked. The practitioner had asked the caregiver to wait her turn to be interviewed and meanwhile to walk around the block. He assumed that she had gone out of the house; however, as he began interviewing the client, the caregiver returned and was able to eavesdrop on the entire interview.

*Example 5:* A practitioner interviewed a caregiver first and accepted the caregiver's explanations of the condition of the elder, without verifying the information from third-party contacts. She closed the case and provided no assistance to the elder, who was, after all, her client.

*Example 6:* A practitioner looked for a family member in a tavern in order to interview him. The practitioner rationalized that in order to keep other family members from overhearing the interview with this particular individual, he would interview him in the tavern he frequented. When he was able to catch up with the family member, that person felt insulted that the practitioner had sought him in a tavern. He said that the practitioner must consider him a heavy drinker who had nothing better to do than to sit in a tavern all day long. As a result, he refused to cooperate with the practitioner, calling him a "meddlesome social worker." Looking back, the practitioner felt that he should have accorded the family member the courtesy of being sent an official letter requesting an appointment. If he had not responded to the letter, the practitioner would have been more justified in looking for him in his usual hangout.

*Example 7:* A practitioner allowed a family member to set up an interview with an elderly client without her knowledge. As a result, the client expressed surprise that the interview had been scheduled and refused to cooperate with the practitioner.

*Example 8:* A practitioner was hasty in removing a client from her home and assumed that he would be able to obtain short-term housing for her, either in the community or at a hospital. He was unsuccessful in placing his client immediately and realized that he should not have removed the client from her home without adequately planning and obtaining confirmation that housing was available.

*Example 9:* The practitioner failed to interview the alleged abuser, because of time constraints and because the proof seemed fairly substantial that he had perpetrated an act of enormous financial abuse upon the client. One year later he called the practitioner and threatened a lawsuit saying, "There must be some way I can get at you; you never talked to me and I never had a chance to tell my side of the story; I want to sue you. How can I go about it?" The practitioner realized that he should have interviewed the abuser and that if he had, he most likely would not have been subjected to the threats.

Practitioners should not permit themselves to become immobilized by errors of omission or commission. Acting in good faith, using commonly known techniques, and following agency policy will usually suffice. When errors are made, it is best to note them, to realize what corrective measures are necessary, and to rectify the situation to the extent possible.

# SUMMARY

Several interventions may be chosen from a diverse list of options in order to individualize a client's treatment. While it is not always possible to expect that a client or an abuser will exhibit permanent behavior changes within a short period of time, some positive outcomes can be expected. Short-term treatment may last from 3 to 6 months. With both individual counseling and therapy groups, elders and abusers may progress from denying the abuse or neglect and refusing to help, to feeling ambivalent toward each other and toward the practitioner, to finally accepting help in the form of a concrete service or, by receiving counseling, to explore alternative methods for handling abusive situations. Some clients and abusers never directly admit that mistreatment has taken place. Mainly through educational counseling and reality orientation, abused elders can develop foresight and learn what they can do to protect themselves and to develop a sense of autonomy. With regard to abusers, the practitioner can make them more accountable for their behaviors. In a few sessions, a practitioner can provide support, reality testing, and structure as well as teach abusers more appropriate ways of expressing themselves. With the guidance of national organizations and trailblazing models, collaborative intervention methods can also be developed by the practitioner. Concerned practitioners have opportunities to participate on many levels: individual, group, policy development and implementation, and collaboration. All levels are needed to combat the many forms of elder mistreatment.

# CHAPTER 9

# Intervention Phase

## III. Legal Intervention

The practitioner involved in elder abuse and neglect cases will undoubtedly be involved with the legal system. This chapter discusses legal options to be utilized by the practitioner. The advantages and disadvantages of these legal interventions are outlined. (Actual legal tools are given in Appendixes F and G.) In addition, suggestions are given on how practitioners can be involved with the criminal justice system, document findings, conduct themselves in a courtroom, give court testimony, and prepare for legal involvement.

### ACTING IN THE LEGAL MODE

Traditionally, service practitioners have had little to do with legal issues insofar as the client is concerned. In fact, they may have some fear of being involved in legal issues, as if such issues were beyond their ability to learn or to comprehend, or as if something terrible could happen to them. Furthermore, the prospect of being sued is always held over the practitioner's head: practitioners are often told that they must limit their activities because "you might be sued." However, while it is true that a suit can always be brought—since anyone can try to sue anyone for anything—the likelihood that a practitioner will be sued for work in the course of prescribed duties is extremely remote. This is not to say, of course, that practitioners should act without discretion. Practitioners should be aware that they are potentially liable for acts of omission as well as commission. They may expose themselves to liability if they fail to report acts of mistreatment, fail to report crimes, fail to treat a client according to agency guidelines, or fail to utilize the least restrictive alternative when treating a client. With regard to acts of commission, practitioners are liable if they breach confidentiality or fail to respect a client's right to due process. The latter may occur when practitioners subject clients to relocation or medical treatment against their will. In an emergency situation, the practitioner should consider calling either a law enforcement officer or a member of the fire department to transport a client instead of transporting the client in the practitioner's car. This would protect the practitioner from liability if an accident occurs in his or her vehicle or if a client dies en route to a treatment facility.

If practitioners feel comfortable with attorneys and legal issues, their clients will feel more at ease. Elder mistreatment clients need legal protection, and the practitioner needs to know what is available. The practitioner needs to be working in a legal mode at all times, because with elder mistreatment clients, there is always a possibility that a practitioner's report will be needed by a judge to validate the need for a conservatorship or guardianship, to keep an abusive relative from being appointed the conservator or guardian, or to provide the basis for a protective order. Practitioners cannot simply do the work and forget about going to court—not if they want to protect their clients and be involved in the "real" world. In fact, practitioners should assume that they will be going to court with each elder mistreatment case, and it is likely that abusers will have their own attorneys, who may try to disprove what a practitioner has to say. There are ways of protecting, of documenting, of giving testimony, and of proceeding in a calm and rational manner. There are certain things that judges and attorneys look for. Practitioners may be surprised to learn that they are viewed as experts, as people who will have solid, workable recommendations and who are knowledgeable about community resources, assessment, and clients' functioning—but practitioners do indeed have this expertise. It may even be possible to develop a team approach to an elder mistreatment situation when working with an attorney and a judge. One judge has suggested that practitioners attend court hearings and learn to understand court proceedings in their community; this would enable a practitioner to observe the manner in which the various parties conduct themselves and to become familiar with legal terminology. Another judge has agreed to preside over mock court hearings to help practitioners rehearse testimony and to help them be as comfortable as possible in the actual proceedings.

The practitioner can assist the client in obtaining legal counsel and may look to several subgroups in the legal profession for assistance. A private attorney who specializes in probate law may be most helpful when a guardianship or conservatorship is needed and in cases of complex financial exploitation. Government-funded legal services agencies, especially those with senior citizen units, may be helpful in actually representing an elderly client and suggesting legal options in cases involving fraud, financial exploitation, abuse, and other acts of domestic violence. Public defenders may sometimes become involved with victims of elder abuse and neglect. Some courts will pay a private attorney to represent clients who are unable to afford their own legal counsel.

## THE AMERICAN LEGAL SYSTEM

Most practitioners working with older adults have had limited experience with the American legal system. As a result, the legal system is underutilized in the prevention and resolution of elder mistreatment (Heisler & Quinn, 1995).

The legal system has two primary components: the civil justice system and the criminal justice system. The larger part is the civil justice system, which deals with matters such as divorce and child custody, personal injury and contract disputes, and guardianships and conservatorships. In civil law, the losing party generally pays money to the side that has won; in other words, money is the issue. In the criminal justice system, however, if someone is charged with a crime and found guilty, that person loses personal freedom, frequently must serve time in custody and may also lose some civil rights, such as the right to vote. The sentence in a criminal matter may result in probation, which is conditioned on the defendant's compliance with various requirements, such as participation in and completion of a rehabilitation program for substance abuse, anger management, or both; and perhaps psychiatric treatment.

Some states are passing laws that make it practical for elders who suffer from physical abuse, neglect, or financial exploitation from con artists, relatives, or staff in facilities to file civil suits and collect damages from people who hurt them. These laws have some unique features. First, the damage must be proved by clear and convincing evidence, as must the fact that the wrongdoer was guilty of recklessness in the commission of certain forms of abuse. Some of the laws are building in provisions that the abusers, when they lose, pay all the attorneys' fees. The other aspect being built in is that the damages may be awarded even if the victim dies; an executor or an administrator of a will can keep processing the lawsuit. This is particularly useful because abusers and their attorneys may try to prolong a lawsuit, hoping that the victim will die and that the lawsuit will then also die (Hankin, 1996).

The civil and the criminal system have similar goals, but they operate by different rules. One of the major rules the practitioner needs to be aware of is the concept of burden of proof. In both civil and criminal courts, the party making an accusation must provide evidence that proves, in the mind of the judge or jury, that he or she is correct to some degree of certainty. In the civil courts, the attorney needs to prove a case by one of two standards of proof. The first standard of proof is called *preponderance of the evidence;* this is the lowest level of proof—or slightly over 50 percent of certainty. The next level of proof in the civil system, a higher level of proof than preponderance of evidence, is *clear and convincing evidence.* This means that the accuser has the burden of providing evidence that an accusation is true to the point that a jury or a judge is *convinced.* For instance, the standard of proof for guardianship or conservatorship is clear and convincing evidence. In the criminal justice system, because a potential consequence to the defendant is a loss of personal freedom and civil rights, the law imposes the highest burden of proof on the state or government which brings the action against the individual: guilt *beyond a reasonable doubt.*

The legal system is adversarial in nature; in the clash between the parties and the search for the truth, the legal system mandates roles for the participants (Heisler & Quinn, 1995). On the civil side, the person who files a lawsuit is called the *plaintiff,* and that person must meet one of the two legal burdens previously described in order to win a case. Because a lawsuit generally concerns interaction of two or more parties, the parties themselves retain control of how the case flows. For instance, the plaintiff and the defendant can settle the case, come to agreements, and otherwise direct what takes place. Where guardianships are concerned, it is a little different. The person filing the case is typically called the *petitioner,* because traditionally, guardianship hearings have not been adversarial. Rather, there has been an assumption that the petitioner is acting on the behalf of someone—such as an older person—who needs help. However, this traditional view is giving way to many reforms as it is realized that sometimes persons seeking guardianships over others are acting in their *own* best interests rather than to assist, say, an elder in need. The result is that guardianship proceedings are becoming more complex and at times adversarial in nature. Legal rights of proposed wards are protected to a greater degree than previously.

The adversarial nature of the legal system is markedly different in criminal proceedings. There are two parties: the prosecution side, which represents the state or the government or "the people"; and the defense side, which represents the accused, called the *defendant.* The prosecution has no specific client. Rather, it represents society at large and is the chief law enforcement officer in the jurisdiction. The crime victim is a witness, although elder mistreatment victims, like other victims, are not always required to testify. Decisions concerning charging and final disposition of a criminal case are made by the prosecutor acting as a representative of the state and exercising legal discretion to decide how to act. The criminal defendant is represented by an attorney totally committed to representing the best interests of his or her client. Defense attorneys are required by strict rules of conduct to keep all communications from a client to themselves.

## LEGAL DEVICES

### The Concept of Least Restrictive Alternatives

The concept of the *least restrictive alternative,* a legal doctrine first articulated in the field of mental health, has gained wide acceptance among courts and service professionals. It creates an ethical duty for practitioners to fashion individualized solutions that are least intrusive upon their clients' personal freedom. The concept applies to the personal and environmental care of the elderly and the handling of material resources. It recognizes that elders may have capacities in some areas and lack capacity in other areas. Ideally, the more restrictive the option, the greater the due process protections and the greater the opportunities for an individual to object or to state preferences. The doctrine is primarily civil in nature, although it can be applicable in criminal matters when placement of persons who have been determined to be criminally insane is at issue (Heisler & Quinn, 1995; Quinn, 1990b).

In using the concept of the least restrictive alternative, practitioners should always keep in mind the following question: *The least restrictive alternative—for whom?* (J. Ferdon, personal communication, March 3, 1992). Least restrictive alternatives such as powers of attorney and trust have been used to take advantage of elders financially, and to subject them to other kinds of mistreatment. It is very difficult to use the concept of the least restrictive alternative, because the practitioner is walking a narrow line between abandoning the client and saying that the client just wants to be free, and, on the other hand, providing protections for the client that are suitable and appropriate.

Another issue the practitioner must give thought to is the realization that protection of the client is paramount, because anyone who is in a position of trust with a client is also in a position to abuse that client. People who look very trustworthy and reliable may nevertheless be in a position to abuse. Sometimes as people take care of an impaired elder, and the years go by and the impaired elder loses personality because of dementia, caregivers or those in charge of financial affairs come to think of the elder's assets as their own and start manipulating the assets to benefit themselves. A given legal device may be a means of preventing further abuse by placing more responsible and capable individuals in charge of the situation and moving the abusers out (Heisler & Quinn, 1995).

## A Continuum of Legal Alternatives

With regard to handling someone's financial affairs, there are several legal alternatives available. These alternatives form a continuum. At one end is the very simple situation in which someone handles his or her own money; at the other end, someone is totally in charge of someone else's affairs and is legally responsible for the other person (see Figure 9-1).

Legally speaking, the continuum of legal alternatives begins with a client who is unable to write checks because of some physical impairment, but is able to sign checks if someone else fills them out. In some cases, such clients can take care of their own financial affairs if someone helps them every month by going over the bills. However, these clients are at risk of exploitation if they are unaware of the amount of a check or cannot understand why a check is being written. The following sections describe the other points along the continuum.

### *Direct Deposit*

On the scale of options, direct deposit of the client's checks is the second least restrictive legal device. A client who receives Social Security benefits, supplemental Security Income (SSI), civil service benefits, pension checks, or Veterans Administration (VA) payments may have checks mailed directly to a bank, credit union, or savings and loan account. The advantages of direct

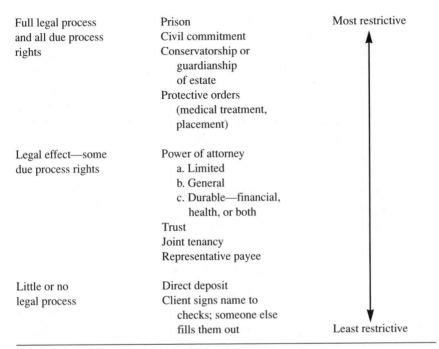

| | | |
|---|---|---|
| Full legal process and all due process rights | Prison<br>Civil commitment<br>Conservatorship or<br>   guardianship<br>   of estate<br>Protective orders<br>   (medical treatment,<br>   placement) | Most restrictive |
| Legal effect—some due process rights | Power of attorney<br>  a. Limited<br>  b. General<br>  c. Durable—financial,<br>     health, or both<br>Trust<br>Joint tenancy<br>Representative payee | |
| Little or no legal process | Direct deposit<br>Client signs name to<br>  checks; someone else<br>  fills them out | Least restrictive |

Figure 9-1    Continuum of legal alternatives.

*Source:* Modified from Consortium for Elder Abuse Prevention, *Protocols,* UCSF/Mount Zion Center on Aging, San Francisco, 1983.

deposit are that the check cannot be stolen, misplaced, or destroyed. In order to arrange for a direct deposit, the client may go to the bank to obtain the necessary forms to request it. The client may ask that the practitioner accompany him or her. Once the forms are filled out, the bank will send the completed form to the source of the client's monthly check, and in approximately 60 days the client's check will be deposited directly. A disadvantage of direct deposit is that the check may not arrive on the same day each month. The client may not know that a check is late being deposited and may write checks when there are insufficient funds to cover them.

### *Joint Tenancy*

Joint tenancy means that two people share equal title to an asset, a bank account, or a piece of property. When an asset is in joint tenancy it is not part of a will; on the death of one individual it immediately becomes part of the survivor's property whether or not is was the survivor's property originally. Joint tenancy can be used with bank accounts and real property. Most married couples hold all their assets in joint tenancy. An abuser who is intent on defrauding an elderly client may ask the client to add his or her name to the deed on real property, saying, "I will help you stay out of a nursing home if you will put my name on your property or deed." A perpetrator may mislead an elder by simply putting a document under the victim's nose, demanding that it be signed but not saying what it is for. Banks allow anyone to add a name to an elderly client's account, especially if the bank knows that the client has no transportation or is not ambulatory. More than one bank account has been cleaned out in this manner. However, banks are now becoming more concerned about exploitation of the elderly.

### Representative Payee

If clients are unable to manage their benefits properly, owing to a mental or physical disability or a problem with drugs or alcohol, they may require a representative payee. This is a person designated by the Social Security Administration or another federal agency to receive the client's check for the purposes of paying the client's bills. A relative, a friend, or an agency may ask to become the representative payee. If a suitable person cannot be found within the client's social circle, the Social Security Administration or another agency may help. Anyone may make a referral to the Social Security Administration to recommend that a client be assigned to a representative payee. In order to obtain a representative payee for a client, the practitioner may call the local Social Security Administration office, and information may be taken by phone. A field representative will then do an investigation and may request that the prospective payee go to the local office of the Social Security Administration to fill out forms. Sometimes the procedure can be done by mail. In any case, another form is sent to the client's medical practitioner, which asks for the practitioner's opinion regarding the client's ability or inability to handle finances. The form is then returned to the Social Security Administration. This process takes approximately 90 days. Caution should be taken in selecting the payee, for some payees have been known to abscond with the money.

The representative payee must make an accounting to the Social Security Administration upon request, usually annually. In practice, accounting is difficult to enforce and payees may abuse their privileges by simply keeping the money. A concerned person or the client may request removal of a payee either because the client feels that the payee is no longer needed or because the payee fails to fulfill the duties involved. Sometimes a form filled out by the client's physician will suffice as evidence that a client has improved mentally or physically and no longer requires a payee.

### Power of Attorney

A common legal device is a power of attorney. A power of attorney is a written agreement authorizing one or more persons to act for or represent the individual signing the document. The person granting the power of attorney must be competent at the time of signing the document; otherwise, the power of attorney is invalid. The power of attorney represents a voluntary action on the part of the person requesting it. It means giving up some control, sometimes upon recognizing that physical functioning is becoming impaired. The power of attorney can be granted on a permanent basis or on a temporary basis, and the person who serves can be a financial advisor, a relative, or a friend. The individual signing the power of attorney is called the *principal,* and the person to whom authority is given is called the *attorney-in-fact* or *agent.* In spite of the name, no lawyer is involved unless a lawyer prepares the document or serves as the attorney-in-fact. This power of attorney is revocable at any time by the principal. If practitioners find that a power of attorney is being abused, it is their responsibility to let the elder—the principal—know that the power of attorney is revocable and to assist the client in the process of revoking the instrument.

Powers of attorney may be limited and specific, or general. In addition, most states permit a power of attorney to be durable and to continue after the principal becomes incapable or incompetent. The *limited* or *specific power of attorney* is just what the term implies: for a specific act. For example, a limited power of attorney may be granted to cash a check or to draw on a bank account or to sell real property. This will allow a person who needs assistance in paying bills by writing and signing checks to grant another person access to the bank account without giving away as many rights as a joint tenancy would. Some financial institutions have their own power of attorney documents. An attorney-in-fact may use the funds only for the benefit of the principal. Creditors of the attorney-in-fact (unlike the creditors of a joint tenant) may not have access to the account. A *general power of attorney* usually gives the attorney-in-fact the right to handle all financial affairs. This type is often used when a person needing help has physical limitations. If the power to engage in real estate transactions is one of the powers given, then the power of attorney must be recorded with the county recorder. When a power of attorney does not have a durable clause, both limited and general powers of attorney become invalid when the principal becomes incompetent or incapable. In practice, however, many families continue to use the power of attorney long after the principal begins manifesting incompetent behavior.

*Durable powers of attorney* take two forms: one for health care and one for financial matters (see Appendix F). Generally, durable powers of attorney for the principal's health care and finances are two separate documents, and the attorney-in-fact handling the financial matters need not be the same person handling health matters. A durable power of attorney means that the principal, while presumably competent, designates an attorney-in-fact to make medical decisions or manage property, or both, in case of future incompetence. Either power of attorney may take effect at the time it is signed or may have a "springing" clause and take effect only when the principal is declared incompetent as specified by the principal. For example, principals sometimes designate that a durable power of attorney will take effect when two physicians agree that they can no longer handle their own affairs. Support for this type of power of attorney is increasing across the country among both attorneys and state legislators. The underlying assumption of a durable power of attorney is that self-determination ahead of time is preferable to a guardianship or a conservatorship which may be imposed involuntarily at a later time, is public, may be expensive and complicated, and might be imposed for only one act of mismanagement on the part of an elderly client.

While a power of attorney may be entirely appropriate in many cases, it has some implicit limitations. Chief among them is that there is no supervision of the attorney-in-fact. Most states provide that the court can make an investigation if there are charges of impropriety, but the community at large may not know that, and an overburdened court may not have designated a staff to make the necessary investigations. Another problem is that no attorney-in-fact is bonded. If there is dishonesty or wasting of funds, there is no means of recovering lost assets. Nevertheless, a power of attorney can be a useful tool, especially when people long known and trusted are available to serve and there are others who are in contact with the elderly client on a regular basis and could spot abuse. It is likely that more powers of attorney will be used in the near future, especially the durable power of attorney for health care.

In general, the more specific the terms of a power of attorney, the less likely it will be abused. The practitioner may suggest that the client limit the conditions of the power of attorney and that the conditions for revocation and continuation be spelled out. Power of attorney forms are available in most stationery stores. However, extreme caution must be taken in filling out a general power of attorney form, to avoid giving the attorney-in-fact more privileges than are desired by the principal.

Powers of attorney do not need to be recorded with the county recorder's office, but it is a good idea to record them. Any power of attorney may be revoked immediately if the principal so desires. A revocation has been done even if the capacity of the principal is in question, and even after the principal has been found incapable. This may be done when a client does not recall granting the power of attorney in the first place, and there appears to be abuse. If a client is unconscious or incapacitated and is unable to revoke the power of attorney, and the power of attorney is being abused, an interested person or practitioner may have to find a way to revoke it. This can be done by having a guardian or conservator appointed. When revocation of a power of attorney is being initiated, the principal or a substitute should call the attorney-in-fact immediately and state that a revocation is forthcoming. This telephone call should be documented in writing. The phone call gives the attorney-in-fact due notice to immediately cease using the power of attorney and is followed by a letter sent by certified mail. If the attorney-in-fact uses the power of attorney after the oral notification (the phone call), the courts may hold him or her liable. A revocation may be written simply as in the following example:

> Jane Doe
> Cherry Lane
> Des Moines, CA 02222
> June 8, 19—

Mr. Richard Roe
P.O. Box 12345
222 Box Street
Los Angeles, CA 91111

Dear Mr. Roe:

I, Jane Doe, rescind the general power of attorney that was granted to Richard Roe on December 24, 19—.

I request that all copies of records of my accounts, bank books, and check-books, and my identification cards be turned over to me by July 9, 19—.

Thank you for your prompt attention to my request.

Sincerely,
Jane Doe

A durable power of attorney for health care can be revoked orally at any time as long as the principal has capacity. The burden is on the principal or the substitute to notify all parties who may be relying on the power of attorney about the revocation as soon as possible before further actions take place. Courts take a durable power of attorney for health care very seriously and may well leave the power for decision-making about health care to the attorney-in-fact even after a conservator or guardian has been appointed. The court may choose to revoke that power only upon a specific showing that it would be better for a guardian or conservator of the person to have that power. This means that a durable power of attorney for health care can persist and continue even though a guardianship has been established unless specific court action has been taken to revoke the durable power of attorney for health care (Quinn, 1996).

Any type of power of attorney can be abused:

A durable power of attorney for health care was abused by a son who was the attorney-in-fact. The son, under his mother's durable power of attorney for health care, had his mother kept alive with a nasogastric tube even though she had expressly stated she did not want that intervention. In fact, the treating physician learned that the mother had actually written a book on the subject. When the treating physician found this out, he contacted the court, and a neutral conservator was appointed to take care of the mother's medical problems. The son had been keeping his mother alive so that he could collect payments on an unsecured loan that he made with his mother's money and to collect his mother's Social Security checks. The feeding tube was ordered removed by the guardian who had authorized it, and the woman was fed by hand.

This case makes it clear that clinical and legal practitioners must be thoughtful and cautious when recommending legal alternatives. To repeat: It is always wise to ask, "Least restrictive—for whom?"

### *Protective Orders*

A protec*tive* order must not be confused with a protec*tion* order, the latter being a tool under the laws of domestic violence. (The protection order will be covered in the section on criminal remedies later in this chapter.) Protective orders fall between conservatorships and powers of attorney in terms of restriction. As with a conservatorship, the courts become involved; but unlike a conservatorship, in which the powers of the conservator are broad, a protective order is specific—for one particular situation. For instance, a protective order may enable a client to be medically treated or moved from a dangerous residence. Judges must be presented with convincing evidence before they will sign such an order. Some states have time-limited guardianships that operate on the same principle as protective orders.

Often the protective legal orders that affect clients are done "for their own good." Often the order is an involuntary measure; the client does not want it. Most states provide no formal avenue for clients to voice their own opinions or objections about the order, and there is wide disagreement as to who should be subjected to these protective procedures. Often the lawyer and the practitioner involved with a shared client may seem to be at odds. The social worker may say that a client needs help, and the lawyer may say that the client's most important right is the right to be left alone, the right to personal freedom. Disagreements are real and valid for both disciplines. The truth may be in the middle and could be discovered if each knew more about the other's discipline—so that the practitioner would not think that all lawyers are heartless and want to prevent frail elderly people from getting help, and the attorney would not think that every practitioner wants all clients to be under guardianships over their objections and without any civil rights protections.

### *Trusts*

Trusts are often used for purposes of financial management and to avoid probate. A trust requires a trustee, generally someone other than the person creating the trust. The trustee can be any person qualified to serve or any entity qualified to serve, such as the trust department of a bank. With this type of arrangement, financial management is ensured, but the client's personal and medical needs will not be supervised. A trust officer will not go to the client's home on a regular basis to supervise the care he or she is receiving.

## Conservatorships and Guardianships

*Conservatorships* are called *guardianships* in many states. Some states have both conservatorships and guardianships; the first is for the purposes of handling a client's estate and the second is for the purposes of handling a client's personal affairs. In other states, there are conservatorships only, which pertain to the handling of both personal and financial matters. In still other states, only guardianships exist, and they also pertain to the handling of both financial and personal affairs. The two terms will be used interchangeably throughout this chapter.

Conservatorships or guardianships have not always enjoyed a good press or good public relations. In truth, they have been the alternative of choice in too many situations where a less restrictive legal option might have been appropriate if only there had been someone available to serve and if the client had been capable of giving consent. There are several reasons why conservatorships have been used as the "solution" to the unmet needs of a dependent adult. One common reason for resorting to conservatorships is lack of awareness of other legal options available for handling finances and personal affairs. A second reason may be convenience: that is, time may be pressing and a nursing home wants a "responsible party" to sign a client in and to make sure that the bills get paid. In one city, some nursing home operators tried for a time to insist that everyone who was admitted to their facilities should be under guardianship. A third reason for turning to a conservatorship may be necessity. Very sick, confused patients in an acute care ward of a hospital who are unable to handle their affairs may require a conservatorship. There is no way of knowing whether their physical health and mental status will return to baseline functioning. After a conservatorship is established, a patient may improve considerably and may no longer require a conservatorship, at which point the conservatorship may be terminated. Fourth, urgent matters may also create the need for a guardianship. Perhaps finances are being dissipated by a person who is in the manic phase of a manic-depressive illness, and there is concern about protecting bank accounts so that money will not be lost entirely. Fifth, most people know that a guardianship is under court supervision and guardians are bonded; this can be very reassuring. With regard to this fifth reason, however, it should be noted that the quality and quantity of court supervision may vary from state to state.

Just as practitioners are learning to discard the idea of nursing home placement as the only way to take care of physically and mentally frail elderly people, so the practitioner must learn to think of using legal devices other than guardianship. Why have conservatorships been viewed so negatively by some professionals involved with the elderly? There are many good reasons, and some states have moved to revise their laws to incorporate the objections of civil libertarians, whose main focus is the preservation of due process protections. One main objection is that in many states, certain medical or psychiatric diagnoses alone can make adults eligible for a conservatorship, no matter how well they are functioning and taking care of their personal and financial needs. Thus, a person who is labeled "schizophrenic" could be subject to a conservatorship. Similarly, "old age" is still accepted in many states as a sole reason for needing a conservatorship. Some people have called that ageist. The criterion for a conservatorship should be functional ability: that is, the ability to manage financial resources and to provide for personal needs, such as food, clothing, shelter, and medical care. A second objection has to do with the global concept of "incompetence." In most states, incompetence means that a conservatee or ward can do nothing for him- or herself. The conservator or guardian is in total control. It has been argued that conservatorships should be tailored to assist the individual only in areas where there are difficulties. There should be flexibility, and conservatees should be allowed control over those areas where they are capable of making decisions. A third objection is that court proceedings for appointing a conservator are sometimes too informal, that they are done without due process protections for the proposed conservatee or ward, or that not all the requirements for notice to a proposed conservatee or ward are strictly followed. For instance, proposed conservatees may never be informed of an impending conservatorship or may be discouraged from attending the proceedings even though they are capable of doing so. Thus, unless they have hired attorneys to represent them—which is highly unlikely—there may be no opportunity for the proposed conservatees to put forth their position. Another objection is the expense involved in setting up the conservatorship. There are fees and costs which can range from $1,000 to $5,000, depending on the problems involved in the case.

Courts are prejudiced in favor of granting guardianships, not denying them. Families and relatives, the usual heirs to an elder's estate, are viewed more favorably by the law as proposed guardians than are friends and strangers, even though there may be obvious conflicts of interest. For example, a guardian may not want to spend money for a ward's care and support, in order to preserve the estate and later inherit as much as possible.

On the other hand, there may be no one else available to serve as the guardian, and it may be the wish of the proposed ward that this particular individual serve. When a spouse or relative is unable to serve, the court can appoint others as guardians. Some states have public guardians or nonprofit corporations that meet certain criteria for serving as guardians. Professional people and agencies are increasingly serving as guardians and now are able to earn a living as professional guardians. The court sometimes holds a professional guardian to a higher standard than a family member, who may not have the opportunity to know resources and agencies.

REFORMS OF CONSERVATORSHIP AND GUARDIANSHIP LAWS.  In 1987, in an attempt to address many of these objections, the Associated Press undertook a nationwide study of over 2,000 conservatorships and guardianships. As a result, the Subcommittee on Housing and Consumer Interests of the Select Committee on Aging in the House of Representatives held extensive hearings (1989). Numerous model revisions were proposed for conservatorship and guardianship law. Some of these proposed revisions included more emphasis on due process protections for the proposed ward or conservatee, more reliance on medical and social information that would be made available to the court, greater accountability of a conservatorship or a guardianship once it was established, and provisions ensuring that a guardianship or conservatorship would be imposed only to the extent that individuals were incapable of taking care of their own affairs.

For example, in California, the concept of conservatorship was created to eliminate what was felt to be the stigma of guardianships in which a person was legally labeled "incompetent" or "insane." Now an individual under a conservatorship is simply called the "conservatee." A guardianship now applies only to children. There are no findings of incompetence, and the law looks strictly to functional abilities, not diagnoses, to determine the need for a conservatorship. The term *old age* does not appear in the text of the law. A conservatee retains certain rights unless the court makes specific determinations. These are the right to vote, the right to handle any earnings, the right to have an allowance, the right to marry, and the right to make medical decisions. Although the law may not be as flexible as some would like, there is an obvious attempt on the part of the legislature to allow judges to tailor the conservatorship to the conservatee.

One outgrowth of the Associated Press articles in 1987 has been the recommendation that courts educate people who are becoming conservators and guardians. There has been a proliferation of films and videotapes which are shown to prospective guardians at the time of their appointment. In addition to the videos, many jurisdictions have undertaken to write handbooks for conservators that include detailed clinical information. These handbooks are available at the time the conservator is appointed.

Another result of this Associated Press study and the hearings held in Congress (Subcommittee on Health and Long-Term Care, 1987) was that most states undertook to revise their conservatorship or guardianship laws to answer the objections that had been raised. Many states incorporated within their laws the role of what could be called the court visitor or court investigator—or someone who is independent and goes out, actually sees the impaired person, and reports back to the court.

In California, each of the 58 counties has at least one court investigator, and the larger counties have more than one. The investigator is responsible to the judge he or she serves and must make reports on proposed conservatees and supervise existing conservatorships on a regular basis. The investigator generally sees a proposed conservatee prior to the appointment of a conservator, 1 year thereafter, and then every 2 years. The investigator also responds to complaints from conservatees or others, including practitioners in the community. The investigator follows up on problem situations such as elder mistreatment, makes recommendations to the judge, and informs conservatees and proposed conservatees of their legal rights. For instance, those who are subjected to a conservatorship have the right to attend the hearing, protest the establishment of a conservatorship, ask for a conservator other than the person proposed, and have legal representation. If a court investigator thinks an attorney is needed to protect the rights of the proposed conservatee, the investigator can make that recommendation to the judge, who then will appoint an attorney. On review of the conservatorship, the investigator determines whether the conservatorship is still needed, and if not, assists the conservatee in obtaining a termination of the conservatorship. Before the existence of investigators, conservatees usually were unaware that termination was a possibility. The court investigator represents the judicial system's best attempt to humanize situations that are difficult for all concerned.

Some states are not charging the estate of the elder (if there is any) for the preappointment investigation or for any subsequent review investigations during the time the guardianship or conservatorship is in existence. In one jurisdiction, the charge is $425 per investigation, no matter how complex the investigation is.

Because of financial limitations, some states have chosen to work with the American Association of Retired Persons and to train and supervise sophisticated volunteers to do this monitoring of guardianships. Some states have even had the volunteers train to go out and see people who are the subject of a proposed conservatorship or guardianship in order to report back to the court as to the necessity of the conservatorship or guardianship.

UTILIZING GUARDIANSHIPS OR CONSERVATORSHIPS.   Conservatorships or guardianships are not always imposed involuntarily. In fact, most are uncontested. Individuals can nominate anyone they choose to serve as a guardian prior to the need for a guardianship. They may state, in writing, that should they become incapable of handling their own affairs, they would like a specific individual appointed as guardian. Thus, some self-determination is possible. Some states have conservatorships which pertain to involuntary mental health commitment and are distinctly different from traditional probate conservatorships.

When should a practitioner consider a conservatorship for a client? First, the practitioner must make sure that the code requirements are met by the client. Generally speaking, now that other legal devices are available, a conservatorship should be used only when another device will not do the job adequately: when more protection is needed, or when an elder has become too impaired to sign a power of attorney, or when third parties such as banks, brokerage houses, and title companies will not recognize a power of attorney but will honor a conservatorship. A conservatorship may be a way of permanently blocking an abuser from access to an elder's financial assets. It can also be valuable when there are a number of adult children and only one or two want to be involved with the parent. The fact that the court records are public and can be examined by the other children at any time may serve to avert family feuds. Conservatorships are also advised where there are substantial assets, so that the person managing those assets is bonded. Many older persons want conservatorships because they know there is court review. Prospective conservators may welcome a conservatorship for the same reason. A conservatorship is appropriate for people who need help and object to help but clearly lack the capacity to carry on for themselves. In fact, although civil libertarians see conservatorships as always imposed on unwilling subjects, most older people do not object to a conservatorship. Many welcome it and feel relieved that they do not have to be responsible for their affairs or that, at last, help is available. Some elderly people know that they are losing the capacity to handle their affairs.

Many state laws incorporate the concept of *undue influence* in their restrictions on guardianship or conservatorship. Undue influence occurs when one person uses his or her role and power to exploit the trust, dependency, and fear of another (Nerenberg, 1996). The abuser uses power deceptively to gain control of the decision-making of the other person. Healthy elders who are recently widowed or who have lost any intimate significant other may be the most vulnerable to undue influence.

The process of unduly influencing a frail elder may consist of several steps. First, the elder—whom we will Mrs. E.—may be deliberately isolated by those hired to take care of her. The isolation may start with telling Mrs. E. there have been no phone calls for her. The abuser, whom we can call Mr. F., censors the mail and turns people away at the door, and convinces Mrs. E. that he is the only one who cares about her. Mr. F. may start to infantilize Mrs. E., or increase her medication, or overdose her with tranquilizers or sleeping pills, or give her a little shove so that she feels unsteady or even falls. In these ways, an abuser fosters dependency until a fragile elder feels totally dependent. The next step in the process is to start handling small amounts of money, and then gradually take over the finances completely. Another approach is to create a "siege mentality" by leading an elder to think that enemies are lurking everywhere. In such cases, the abuser may poison the elder against the practitioner and service providers.

Several characteristics of undue influence or overpersuasion have been described by Nievod and Singer to assist courts in determining if undue influence was used to induce people to sign contracts or enter into agreements (Nerenberg, 1996):

- Discussion of the transaction at an unusual or inappropriate time
- Consummation of the transaction in an unusual place
- Demand that the business be finished at once
- Extreme emphasis on the consequences of delay
- Use of multiple persuaders by the dominant side against a vulnerable, single person
- Absence of third-party advisers

An abuser who wields undue influence may be one of several types. Some abusers, who may be labeled "psychopaths" or "sociopaths," take the elder's money and have no conscience about it. Others may have defects of character or may simply be greedy. Some are just easily tempted. Some rationalize the abuse. In the previous example, for instance, Mr. F. might rationalize his abuse by saying that Mrs. E. was abusive to him and therefore deserves to have money taken from her. Or Mr. F. may feel that Mrs. E. was crotchety and did not say thank you enough, and so he has developed a sense of entitlement and feels justified in taking her money. There are also abusers who feel that the world owes them a living. If an elder has money, they see no reason why it should not be theirs.

In spite of the revisions in conservatorship and guardianship laws across the country, these laws remain overly broad in their definitions. In fact, if they had been taken very seriously, most of the population over the age of 75 would have been affected. Therefore, practical considerations need to be taken into account when trying to decide whether or not to pursue a conservatorship or a guardianship. Some practical considerations have been developed by Quinn (1989; 1996):

1. There is a sudden and catastrophic physical impairment due to a stroke or an accident.
2. There are transactions that require a surrogate decision-maker, such as divorce, selling a house or other property, establishing a trust, splitting assets when one spouse is in a convalescent hospital, or settling a personal injury lawsuit or another type of lawsuit.
3. The elder does not grasp the severity of the situation and refuses desperately needed assistance.
4. A family is quarreling over custody or assets of the elder. It is interesting to note that sibling rivalry can persist even among people who are in their seventies and eighties.
5. One adult child wants to claim an inheritance prematurely or influence the elder to make out a new will.
6. Guardianship is a condition for probation or for receiving funds from a trust or the Social Security Administration, or in the settlement of a lawsuit.
7. There has been a gradual decline in the elder's functioning, resulting in incapacity. There is now a crisis precipitated by a physician or banker, who becomes uncomfortable about medical consent or the handling of financial assets. There may also be concern about placement, and the physician says that a guardianship is needed to be the elder's advocate. Perhaps someone tells the family that a gen-

eral power of attorney they have been using for years is no longer valid because the elder lost capacity some years previously.

8. There is an adequate support system but the elder does not trust the support system.
9. The estate is too complex, and everyone is more comfortable with having it under court supervision.
10. There is abuse of a less restrictive legal option.

Depending on their capabilities and on state law, people under guardianships may lose civil rights such as (1) the right to manage property, or personal and financial affairs; (2) the right to contract; (3) the right to vote; (4) the right to drive; (5) the right to choose a residence; and (6) the right to refuse or consent to medical treatment. Removal of such rights is a very serious act, and the practitioner should recommend to the court the removal of as few rights as possible.

For expediency, some states have forms available for medical practitioners to fill out which indicate the client's functional ability. Other states ask that physicians comment only on whether or not the client is physically able to be present in court, since the criterion for conservatorship is the client's functional ability and not a medical diagnosis. For states in which medical letters are currently required, it is important that the medical practitioner write a letter which includes a functional assessment of the client.

In some states a special guardianship or a limited guardianship is available for a specific situation. For example, if a proposed ward is in need of emergency surgery and is not able to consent to surgery and no next of kin can be found, a limited guardianship may be initiated by an agency or a hospital attorney. A limited guardianship automatically terminates after the specified intervention is completed or on a predetermined date.

The shortcomings of a conservatorship must be mentioned. For states in which the ward or conservatee is still labeled "incompetent," the psychological ramifications of being stigmatized by such a label may be considerable. The public and open nature of the proceedings can also be a disadvantage. The proposed ward may feel humiliated and on the "hot seat." Conservatorships in states with no court investigators as described in this section generally are not fully monitored by the court system. Although termination of a conservatorship is possible, it is very difficult to effect, especially when the ward or conservatee is unaware of being abused or neglected (Judicial Council of California, 1992). If a conservator is found to be abusing his or her privileges, anyone may ask to modify or terminate the conservatorship. Terminating a conservatorship requires returning to court for a hearing, and this process must be coordinated. It is difficult for conservatees to effect a termination by themselves. It can be costly to hire an attorney to terminate the conservatorship except in states where there are public defender agencies willing to do the task.

After guardianships or conservatorships, the remaining items on the continuum of legal alternatives are civil commitment and prison. These are the most restrictive devices and they carry the most due process rights protections. These options are shown on the scale so that the practitioner can see the progression of deprivation of rights and have some idea of the meaning of due process protections.

## CRIMINAL REMEDIES

### Working with the Police

A case involving the criminal justice systems begins with a call to a law enforcement agency to request assistance. The standard emergency telephone number can be used to make a report. The practitioner can begin by identifying himself or herself and giving the purpose of the call. It is preferable to speak to supervisors who are sergeants; they will probably have more experience in matters related to elder mistreatment. A uniformed officer will usually be dispatched to take a report from a victim. When possible, however, the practitioner should request that the client be interviewed by an officer in street clothes instead of a uniform: A uniform can intimidate victims and prevent them from disclosing important information. After making the phone call, the practitioner should remain with the client at the scene of the incident to provide information to the officer and to be a source of support.

A practitioner who has difficulty gaining access to a client and fears for the client's safety can call the standard phone number and ask an officer to "check on the well-being" of the client. A law enforcement officer will visit the client's residence but may not use force to enter on the first visit unless the client is considered to be in immediate danger. It may take additional reports of concern for the officer to make a forced entry.

The practitioner may ask that the responding officer bring a camera if the elder has sustained physical injuries or if the residence is in a state of extreme neglect. The practitioner should ask officers to make a report on each incident to which they respond so that a paper trail is established and there will be documentation which may be used at a later date. A practitioner may say to an officer, "I am establishing a chain of evidence, and I need you to make a report." The practitioner should always obtain the police report number for future reference.

In some states, a law enforcement officer may not arrest anyone on the scene unless there is repeated or ongoing violence. In states where domestic violence laws stipulate automatic arrest of perpetrators, officers have no choice but to arrest them. Some states have penal code sections that hold caregivers responsible for abuse they have willfully inflicted (see Appendix G). In cases where explicit threats are made involving weapons, an officer may confiscate the weapon for "safekeeping."

After evidence is gathered, the report by the law enforcement officer is turned over to the prosecutor's office. The prosecutor, a lawyer for the government in a criminal case, determines whether or not there is sufficient evidence to press charges for which a case is brought to court. It is up to the prosecutor to decide whether or not to file charges against a wrongdoer. Very few cases of elder mistreatment reach the criminal justice system, partly because of elderly victims are often reluctant or unable to ask that charges be pressed, especially if the charges are against a relative or someone else they have known for a long period. Prosecutors are reluctant to bring cases of elder mistreatment to trial when the elderly victim is unable to be a credible witness, especially when the victim is incapable of recalling details of the crime, because of anxiety or an intermittent memory loss.

A person who is abusive may be charged with criminal trespass, false imprisonment, malicious mischief, reckless endangerment, or one of several types of assault. For theft and fraud, an abuser may be charged with one of several degrees of theft or burglary, extortion, forgery, or possession of stolen property. It is very difficult to make a charge of neglect; however, a person held against his or her will may have the perpetrator charged with false imprisonment. The wrongdoer may also be charged with malicious mischief or reckless endangerment (Evergreen Legal Services, 1983).

Theft charges are very difficult to prove unless a paper trail is developed to prove that the crime did take place. Proof of intent to deprive the client of funds or property is very difficult, especially if the victim is unable to counter claims by the wrongdoer that the property was a gift or had been promised.

Successful intervention by the criminal justice system must credit and validate the victim's traumatic experience without making the victim responsible for the ultimate action taken against the offender (Heisler, 1991). There are several procedures and resources available within the criminal justice system to assist the victim. They include:

1. Placing ultimate responsibility for arrest, charging, and disposition of a criminal case with the police, prosecution, court, probation, and corrections departments
2. Offering victims support services and state mandated indemnification programs through local victim witness or advocacy units
3. Implementing special procedures in cases with elderly victims
4. Prosecuting elder mistreatment cases in a vertical manner, that is by having the same attorney handle the case throughout the entire criminal justice process
5. Providing an array of sentencing alternatives for the court, ranging from diversion programs to imprisonment
6. Using protective orders to ensure the victim's safety and nonharassment by the alleged offender. (Heisler, 1991, pp. 6–7)

## Role of the Practitioner

The practitioner can play an important role in helping the elderly victim deal with the criminal justice system. In some instances it may be helpful to tell the victim that as a result of criminal prosecution, the abusive family member will get court-ordered counseling or treatment in a substance abuse problem. When pressed charges result in a conviction, the wrongdoer may also be mandated to make restitution to the victim for medical care and loss or destruction of property. The wrongdoer may also be ordered to have no more contact with the victim, thus providing a safer situation for the elder. Wrongdoers may be deterred from committing further abusive acts if they know that they may be arrested and charged.

When prosecutors press charges, it can be difficult for the victim. The benefits to the victim and to society at large must be weighed against the strain of pressing charges. It is not the responsibility of the victim to decide whether criminal charges will be brought against an alleged abuser. In fact, that decision is made by prosecutors. When the criminal justice system takes responsibility for prosecuting a case away from the victim, society makes it clear that the conduct is a public concern, not a mere private family affair. Further, when the prosecutor rather than the victim is responsible for deciding the charges, the offender learns that threatening, coercing, or manipulating the victim will be ineffective in avoiding criminal responsibility (Heisler, 1991). Nevertheless, a victim may feel that it is wrong to imprison a member of the immediate family, no matter who does it (Brownell, 1996). Having to recount the fraud or abusive incident may be too traumatic for the victim, who may refuse to participate in the criminal proceedings. The practitioner should accompany the victim when he or she is interviewed by the prosecutor, who must decide whether adequate evidence is available and whether the victim will be a cooperative witness. Some communities have victim and witness advocacy groups that can provide supportive counseling to victims during the criminal court proceedings. Practitioners can work with victim-witness counselors to help victims devise ways to protect themselves as well as decompress after the trial.

Prosecutors specializing in domestic violence cases advise practitioners to counsel a client carefully before deciding to proceed with the prosecution process, which can be lengthy. Only the prosecutor can dismiss charges prior to the trial (Heisler, 1991). While one victim may refuse to be involved in criminal proceedings, another victim may want justice to prevail, and it is important for the practitioner to support a victim who wants to pursue every avenue of prosecution. The victim must withstand multiple delays in the criminal proceedings, be willing to be interviewed by both the prosecutor and the attorney for the defense, be consistent in telling the story, and not be afraid of being tormented by the abuser, who sometimes may be out of jail on bail.

Over the last 10 years, prosecutors have become more and more involved in elder mistreatment and in fact are creatively developing prosecutorial strategies to actually bring charges against and successfully prosecute people who abuse older people. Medical and service professionals must work closely with prosecutors and others in the criminal justice system so that abusers will be charged. Impeccable documentation and medical assessments are necessary in order for prosecutors to do their job.

## Protection Orders

A protection order directly addresses an abusive situation. Most states make protection orders available through domestic violence laws. Originally designed to address the problem of spouse abuse, these laws can also be applied to the older adult who is being abused. They make it possible for a judge to order an abuser to move and stay out of the house and order the abuser not to contact the abused in any way. A judge can also order the offender to pay the fees for the victim's attorney, and to obtain counseling. These orders are enforced by the police if the abuser violates them. A violation is deemed a crime, and the abuser can be arrested. An abuser can also be ordered to make restitution to the abused, to "make whole" or return the victim to the status enjoyed prior to the abuse.

A protection order is not to be confused with a protective order, which was discussed earlier. It is also different from a restraining order and a no-contact order. In some states a restraining order can be obtained only when the victim is involved in another legal action such as a divorce, guardianship, or child custody proceeding. One benefit of a protection order is that it can be granted whether or not another legal action is pending. A no-contact order can be issued to an alleged offender to keep him or her from making contact with the alleged victim pending the outcome of the trial.

A protection order can be issued in situations of domestic violence, which include not only actual physical harm or injury but also threats or actions that cause a victim to fear immediate physical harm. The victim can obtain immediate help by filing a request with the court for a protection order. In many cases a temporary protection order is issued immediately, pending an investigation and a hearing, which usually occurs within 14 days. A practitioner should advise victims that once they file a protection order, they should not invite the abuser into their homes. This has been known to happen; the abused victim files a request for a protection order, is granted the protection order, and then has a change of heart. Such a scenario makes it difficult for the police officer and the prosecutor to do their share of law enforcement.

## Other Criminal Justice Remedies

Many practitioners may not realize that the criminal justice system has a variety of remedies that can be imposed on abusers who have been convicted of an elder abuse crime. Heisler (1991) lists some of them:

1. Period of confinement in a county jail
2. Work furlough program
3. Home detention
4. Counseling for control of family violence, anger, or substance abuse; psychiatric or psychological treatment in residential or outpatient centers
5. Performance of community service

6. Payment of restitution
7. Regular chemical testing for substance abuse
8. Prohibitions against possession of weapons
9. Waiver of Fourth Amendment protections against warrantless searches and seizures without probable cause
10. Order to seek and maintain employment
11. Regular reporting to a probation officer .
12. Obeying all the laws of the community
13. Payment of probation costs incurred in supervising the offender's probation
14. Payment of a fine
15. Estate or victim indemnification program

The court may also order the defendant to stay away from and have no contact with the victim, or order that all visits must be supervised by a third party or occur in a particular location for the duration of the probation. The court may order periodic reports concerning the defendant's progress on probation and compliance with the terms and conditions of the probation. Violation of these terms and conditions may result in revocation of probation and the defendant's commitment to the state penitentiary.

## DOCUMENTING FOR COURT

A booklet by Collins and LaFrance (1982) on protective services and the law outlines what documentation is necessary for successful court intervention: case notes, statutory chart recording, compilation of exhibits, and casework recording. Additionally, many courts give credence to documented quotations gathered during the practitioner's assessment.

From the beginning of his or her involvement, the practitioner should record all dates, contacts, home visits, and telephone calls. Firsthand knowledge of a client's behavior is weighted more than behavior that is reported by others. Hearsay evidence sometimes is admissible in the court. Statutory chart recording consists of recording observations factually and applying them to statute and policy definitions of situations such as emergency, abuse, incomptence, and imminent danger. The booklet recommends that the practitioner develop a chart listing the definitions in one column and, in an adjoining column, the practitioner's gathered facts and dates related to the specific situation. In addition, witnesses, their addresses, and their phone numbers should be listed. Such a chart can be read easily by the court and provides clear data to help the court make necessary decisions.

Documentation counters denial. It is important to realize that there is a great deal of denial regarding elder mistreatment—even health professionals may deny that it happens. Frequently, the practitioner must testify about matters which occurred a year or more earlier. All forms of documentation, including notations of observations, statements, and especially photographs, are helpful for convincing judges and juries. In one incredible case:

> An 85-year-old woman was bitten over 20 times by her daughter, who was thought to have been drunk at the time. The judge had difficulty believing that the daughter—a very respectable-looking professional, well-educated woman—could have done such a thing. Photographs had been taken in the emergency room and were critical in convincing the judge that the mother had actually been bitten by her daughter. Also, skin grafts had been needed, and the plastic surgeon was able to point to before-and-after photographs in her testimony.

Judges and juries frequently are sympathetic to elder abusers, particularly when the defense is that the perpetrator became stressed in the care of the elder or where there are allegations that the elder was demanding. Savvy prosecutors counteract that defense by obtaining information as to the functioning of the elder the day before the assault and the day after (C. Heisler & T. Jackson, personal communication, January 28, 1994). In the case of the mother who was bitten, the defense tried to portray the daughter as a stressed caregiver. However, evidence was introduced to show that the mother was capable of self-care and that she had been out watering the lawn the day before the assault and talking to her neighbors. The day after the attack, she could not walk or verbalize. Defense attorneys may also try to portray their clients as incapable of performing the acts in question by insisting that the client loves the elder. Practitioners should realize that they may counter this argument by saying, "Yes, I'm sure that your client does love the victim. It is possible to love people and also abuse them at the same time."

## PROVIDING COURT TESTIMONY

As more cases of elder mistreatment are being brought before courts, the need for testimony has begun to grow. Practitioners who are involved in diagnosing and treating elder mistreatment cases are increasingly likely to find themselves involved in court proceedings. They need to be aware of types of proceedings where testimony may be required as well as some key legal concepts. They also need to know the role of the professional as well as the types of witnesses and the rights and duties of witnesses (Heisler, 1994).

## Background: Types of Legal Proceedings

Requests to give testimony frequently come in the form of telephone calls from attorneys who feel that the practitioner possesses information which may benefit their clients. Or practitioners may receive a subpoena ordering them to appear at a deposition or a specific courtroom in order to give testimony. Usually, the contact with the practitioner will come well after legal proceedings are under way. Practitioners may be asked to give testimony in civil court cases, in criminal court cases, and in depositions which take place prior to court trials.

### *Depositions*

Depositions are commonly taken in civil matters. The purpose of a deposition is to obtain the sworn testimony of a witness prior to trial. The attorney wants to know what the practitioner knows, how the practitioner will testify, how credible the practitioner is, and how useful the information is. Information given in depositions can determine if a case should be settled without a trial as well as the amount of money that should be offered or accepted in civil cases.

Depositions are often taken in an attorney's office, and attorneys from both sides will question the practitioner or witness. Those who are present will include the attorneys for the parties involved, a court reporter who records all testimony given, and the witness. The parties involved in the case have the right to be present also. Usually depositions are conducted in informal surroundings, often attorneys' conference rooms. During deposition testimony—unlike a court trial—practitioners or witnesses may confer with the attorney who subpoenaed them. In addition to getting the factual information the practitioner has to give, both attorneys will use the time to "size up" the practitioner in terms of dress, ability to speak well, truthfulness, sincerity, and honesty. Typically, a serious, calm, thoughtful style, along with a neat, professional, conservative appearance, will serve the witness well.

Testimony given in deposition must be consistent with that given later at trial. If the two are different, the witness's credibility will be questioned (Antoine, 1987). When acting as witnesses, practitioners should always ask to review a copy of their deposition testimony for accuracy and make corrections promptly if any errors are discovered. State law may provide that depositions are to be reviewed and corrected within a certain number of days.

Frequently, the information obtained in deposition will lead to the settlement of a civil case without a court trial. Settlements can take place up to the very moment the trial begins, and even during the trial; judges frequently encourage parties to settle in order to avoid the time, strain, and costs involved in court trials.

## Court Proceedings

When there is a trial, it could be a civil proceeding or it could be a criminal proceeding. In civil court trials, the practitioner will commonly be involved in guardianships, will contests, civil commitment proceedings, or other types of lawsuits. It is less common for a practitioner to be involved in criminal cases where a perpetrator has been charged with a crime against an elder. Civil courts deal with an alleged wrong done by someone to another party. The person who is alleged to have done the wrong is called the *defendant* and the person who is alleged to have been wronged is the *plaintiff.* Typically in a civil trial, money is the issue: the plaintiff seeks to get money from the defendant for the wrong. If the defendant loses, he or she must compensate the plaintiff with monetary damages.

Criminal cases are a bit different; as noted earlier, they are brought by a district attorney or prosecutor on behalf of the people. The outcome of a criminal case may well be the loss of personal freedom. Those who are convicted may have to serve time in prison. In criminal elder mistreatment cases, judges have wide discretion in sentencing; their orders may include counseling, drug and alcohol rehabilitation, job skills training, no contact with the elder, and continuing employment so that the abuser can make financial restitution to the elder, thus rendering the elder "whole" (Heisler & Tewksbury, 1991).

Criminal proceedings have several steps (Heisler, 1991). The first contact is most likely the police, who would do the initial investigation and refer the matter for prosecution after an arrest has been made. Prosecutors have wide discretion to decide which cases they will take, depending on the evidence that is available, the seriousness of the offense, the offender's criminal history, and the desires of the victim. If the prosecutor takes the case, there may be time constraints between the arrest and the time the prosecutor "charges" the case. At that time, the practitioner may be contacted to provide witnesses, written statements, or a taped interview. Prosecutors know that practitioners may have information that is crucial to the case and critical to successful prosecution. As was mentioned earlier, documentation is of utmost importance. Victims may not always have to testify, especially if they are not reliable owing to dementia. Once the first two steps of prosecution have been completed—the arrest and the charging of the case by the prosecution—the next step is court proceedings.

In the first court appearance, frequently called the arraignment, defendants are advised of the charges against them and given an opportunity to retain an attorney. Bail may be set, and the defendant will make a plea. Most often, the plea will be not guilty. When defendants are released on bail or on their own recognizance, a prosecutor may request a stay away or no contact order, directing a defendant to leave a victim alone.

After arraignment, the next step may be that a grand jury will further evaluate the evidence to determine if there is sufficient evidence for an indictment, that is, if there is sufficient evidence to warrant a trial. Alternatively, a preliminary hearing may be held in front of a judge to determine if there is sufficient evidence to have a trial. Practitioners may be called to testify in front of a grand jury or at the preliminary hearing. If the grand jury or judge decides there is sufficient evidence for a trial, a date is set. Most cases result in a plea of guilty prior to trial. If this does not happen, the case will most likely be tried in front of a jury.

The actual court trial starts with the selection of a jury, after which the prosecutor makes an opening statement outlining the evidence that will be introduced. The defense may or may not make an opening statement. Then the prosecutor presents his or her case by calling witnesses and questioning them. Defense counsel will cross-examine the witnesses. Physical evidence and exhibits may be introduced. When the prosecution has finished presenting its case and called all its witnesses, the defense may choose to present a case or may choose not to present evidence or witnesses. The defense may at that time make a motion to have the case dismissed entirely for failure of proof. If that is denied by the judge, the defense may then decide to present a case, at which time witnesses are called and questioned, and this time they are cross-examined by the prosecution. Next, the prosecution may counter or attempt to invalidate the defense's case. Eventually, both the defense and the prosecution rest.

This process is then followed by a summation of the case by the prosecution and then by the defense. The judge then instructs the jury, which then deliberates the facts. If the jury finds there is guilt beyond a "reasonable doubt and to a moral certainty," the defendant is found guilty. The sentencing phase then follows.

A defendant who is found not guilty is released. If the defendant is found guilty, a probation report will be made between the court trial and the sentencing phase. The victim will be contacted to see what he or she wants and what restitution will be sufficient. Other involved parties, including other practitioners, may be consulted. Both the defense and the prosecution may have input in the probation report. Once the sentencing phase begins, the defense may ask for a new trial. If the judge grants the request, a new trial is held; if not, the judge sentences the defendant. As mentioned earlier, judges have many options when sentencing. An appeal to a higher court may follow the sentencing (Heisler, 1991).

## Testifying in Court

Being called upon to give testimony in a deposition or a court trial, whether as a percipient witness or an expert witness, can sometimes be terrifying. Practitioners are rarely trained to give testimony and may not be certain as to what is expected. They may feel intimidated by the process or may fail to understand the limits of the role and may then overreach. Some practitioners may "clam up" and feel they have nothing to say; some may feel they have a great deal to say, but what they say does not always have a bearing on the case. On the other hand, testifying is an educational experience which can be exhilirating and can have the effect of bringing a fresh focus to the practitioner's work.

### *Types of Witnesses*

In either civil or criminal courts, a practitioner may be called as a *percipient* or *lay* witness or as an *expert* witness. A percipient or lay witness is someone with firsthand knowledge who was an observer or a participant in a factual situation and who must now describe the event. A percipient witness is generally not permitted to give interpretations, impressions, or other opinions (Havemeyer, 1980). Only expert witnesses can do that.

Practitioners may also be called upon to testify as expert witnesses, but less commonly. When a judge questions a practitioner, it is up to the judge to decide if the practitioner can testify as an expert. The judge will base that decision upon the education, skills, and experience of the practitioner. Only judges can admit a practitioner to expert witness status. An expert witness is a allowed to give an opinion on a "subject that is sufficiently beyond common experience," in order to assist the court (Antoine, 1987). Expert witnesses give opinions to the court and may not have been professionally involved in the case in which they are asked to give testimony. In fact, an expert might be called only during the sentencing phase of the trial in order to give information with regard to recommendations to the judge or jury.

There are some principles for giving testimony. They should be reviewed repeatedly prior to having to give testimony or whenever encountering the legal system.

Many practitioners request that they be given a subpoena by the attorney who wants their testimony. As a result, the other side is given notice that the practitioner is being asked for information. This will help preserve the practitioner's neutrality and reinforce the importance of the information to be given. In testifying, the role of the practitioner is to give information to the judge, and the jury if there is one. Practitioners' main allegiance is to the information they have to give, not to the attorney who is requesting their involvement (Slade, personal communication, January 31, 1994). In this situation, unlike clinical situations, the practitioner's allegiance is not to the elder (Brodsky, 1989). Taking sides or skewing information to favor one side reduces the effectiveness and credibility of the information the practitioner has to give the court. Once a practitioner has lost credibility in the courts, it is not possible to get it back.

### Common Subjects of Testimony

Regardless of which court a percipient or expert witness appears in, the subjects the witness will be asked to testify about will pertain to an individual case. Common subjects are bruises, falls, head injuries, failure to thrive syndrome, and the physiology of Alzheimer's disease or other brain changes, failing memory, or incontinence (Brodsky, 1989). Other subjects include competency, dynamics between the abuser and the victim, substance abuse, undue influence, and details of financial transactions or the signing of legal documents. It is important to remember that most testimony will be *percipient,* and practitioners will be allowed to testify only to factual matters, that which they have personally seen or heard (Havemeyer, 1980).

Physicians will typically be asked to testify about diagnosis, treatment, and prognosis of a particular medical condition. The physician who has documented changes, including mental status, will be in a stronger position on the witness stand than the physician who has not documented.

## *Preparation for Testifying*

Preparing for the testimony is critical and will provide the practitioner with solid support when actually testifying. Preparation should include reviewing all relevant documents, learning what evidence will be introduced, identifying key issues in the litigation, and determining the practitioner's role in the lawsuit. The relationship between practitioner and attorney is very important. Each will need to learn from the other. Practitioners should know what level of proof will be applied to their testimony. Practitioners who are called upon to give testimony should insist that the attorney calling them be candid and fully brief them on the issues and the players as well as on anticipated questions, critical issues in the case, anticipated cross-examination issues, and what exhibits will be introduced that the practitioner may be asked to comment upon. Attorneys may be unfamiliar with the practitioner's discipline or with issues that concern the practitioner. Practitioners should go over their information and be aware of "holes" or potential weaknesses. It is likely that there will be another attorney representing the other side who will cross-examine the witnesses. If a practitioner has not testified frequently before, it can be helpful to talk with others who have given testimony. Even if they did not feel they had a "good" experience, the practitioner can learn from that information.

The cross-examination is the most difficult part of giving testimony. The legal system is adversarial, and the opposing attorney's job is to try to shake the practitioner's testimony. The practitioner may be accused of making up the story, or of having a personal interest in bringing the case to court, or of acting on emotions and not on facts. A practitioner may not be used to being attacked for "doing good" but should not take these accusations personally, because it is the defense attorney's job to defend the accused, even an abuser (Havemeyer, 1980).

Witnesses are not expected to remember every fact. Practitioners may bring actual documents to court and use them when testifying. They may also wish to bring a portfolio that has been prepared for the lawsuit. If the case is complex, the practitioner may want to write notes on a small piece of paper or a card as an aid to memory, keeping in mind that either attorney has the right to see the card. Knowing the data "backward and forward" will enable the practitioner to feel more comfortable and to speak more easily.

### *Guidelines for Testifying*

In general, there are several "rules" for giving testimony. They are summarized here:

1. The role of a witness is to give information to the trier of fact. The trier may be a judge or jury. Therefore, it is helpful if you keep in mind that your job is to inform the judge or jury. It is helpful to face the judge or jury when talking about the information you have to give rather than to face the attorney asking the questions.
2. Testify only as to what you actually know. Do not speculate, guess, or overreach beyond what you know with certainty. Do not "fake it" or "wing it." The judge and jury can tell.
3. Do not be afraid to say you do not know.
4. Realize that the attorney for the other side may try to exploit your discomfort by frequently objecting or interrupting or by using a tone of voice meant to "throw you off."
5. Answer questions simply, clearly, and as briefly as possible. It is the attorney's role to ask the questions and to get the information from the witness.
6. Do not name-call, editorialize, or give asides.
7. Self-presentation affects credibility. Witnesses whose grooming and dress are conservative in style and color and on the more formal side will be more believable to a judge or jury. Look and sound like the professional you are.
8. Practitioners who testify as expert witnesses on a certain subject must keep current with the field and must keep records of where they have testified and the names of those cases, as well as of articles and lectures they have produced on the subject at hand.
9. If an attorney refers to an article you are not familiar with, indicate that you do not know it. In some jurisdictions, you may be able to request a recess to review the article.

10. Consider using the "admit-deny" response when confronted with a question that is only partially accurate, even if the attorney tries to get you to say yes or no (Brodsky, 1989). In this kind of reply, the witness admits the part of the question that is true and vigorously denies the part that is inaccurate. For instance, an attorney may say, "My client, who is accused of beating his mother, loves her. How can anyone who loves his mother beat her? He is innocent. Don't you believe he loves his mother?" You may respond, "I believe that he loves his mother. However, it is possible to love someone and also physically abuse that person."

11. Take questions seriously but not personally. It is important to remain nondefensive. Common questions from attorneys who are cross-examining will call into question your credentials and training. Expert witnesses will be asked if they are being paid to give their testimony, the implication being that they are hired guns who will say whatever is requested. The expert witness can reply that he or she is being paid, as are the attorneys and other professionals in the case. Another question from the attorney may be whether you are only giving your opinion, in which case you can reply that it is much more than an opinion, since it is based on education, training, and experience (Slade, 1994).

12. Do not get into arguments, but do not be afraid to disagree with the attorney either.

13. Realize that if one attorney calls you as a witness, the attorney for the other side will also have the right to question you.

14. Ask to refer to your notes if that would be helpful.

15. Do not interrupt the judge or an attorney, however much you might like to.

16. Maintain good posture and speak clearly. Appear confident even though you may be nervous.

17. Be prepared to give intervention options if asked by the judge or any of the other parties. The practitioner may have information that no one else in the case has.

18. Ask to have a question repeated if the question was unclear.

19. Understand and be able to spell any technical terms you may use. Avoid technical terms as much as possible.

20. If a question is interrupted by an objection from an attorney, wait to answer the question until instructed to do so by the judge.

# MAKING AN IMPACT ON THE LEGAL SYSTEM

As practitioners become more aware of laws that affect older people, they will want to become more familiar with those laws. They will also want to have more access to the courts in order to gain the best results for their clients.

Practitioners must realize that a court is an independent body, not in existence to support only their stance. They may feel angry at the court if their "side" does not prevail, but the court must consider all facts and all evidence before making a final decision. Given this lengthy system of checks and balances, it is incumbent upon the practitioner to be as prepared as possible.

Practitioners may find themselves feeling intimidated by judges, court personnel, court processes, and even the appearance or the courtroom itself. There are reasons why a court is more formal than other settings, such as a social worker's or doctor's office. The decisions made in court have a public impact on someone's life, and they are serious decisions. The intent of the formality is to help people realize that everyone there has the task of seeking justice for an individual person. All participants must take what they are doing in the courtroom with the utmost seriousness.

Practitioners can write to a judge or an attorney if they feel they have information that will be helpful in a particular case or if they want to establish an ongoing relationship. A practitioner can do this by writing a letter introducing himself or herself. The letter should be brief, respectful, and professionally typed or keyboarded. Practitioners may well have special information about a case that no one else has. For example, they can be reasonably certain that neither the attorney nor the judge has ever been in the home of the abuser or the victim. They may be the only ones who can give the facts of a situation and prevent an abusive caregiver from becoming a guardian or conservator. They may have important information about the mental status of a client. However, the legal standard for incompetency or incapacity to determine guardianships may be different from the practitioner's standards. Each profession seems to have its own standards for this subject, and a judge's standard must be the same as those legislated by the state. If practitioners understand the standards under which attorneys and judges must function, they will be less frustrated.

Instead of waiting for a court hearing to take place, practitioners may want to request a meeting with a judge to discuss shared concerns. For example, a practitioner may approach a judge by saying, "I often have information on cases that come before you. I would like to discuss with you how I might best make this information available to you on a regular basis so that you will have all of the facts in front of you at the time of the hearings you conduct." Not all judges will respond, but some will, and the practitioner must remember that judges cannot be stereotyped. They may be liberal, progressive, naive, isolationist, sophisticated, unexpectedly compassionate, or unfamiliar with assistance. A judge may come from a different economic class than the client and may never have been exposed to the kinds of problems faced by the protective services practitioner. Some judges may be thinking in terms of their own life experiences; therefore, it is crucial for the practitioner to provide information that will make a difference in the outcome of a proceeding.

At times a practitioner may ask for a meeting in a judge's chambers. Time in chambers is an informal problem-solving practice that enables all parties to get away temporarily from the legal procedure, which is a sparring, adversarial process, and to get to the point. It also saves certain people from being exposed publicly regarding embarrassing information, such as sexual information or information pertaining to substance abuse. Judges may be able to assist people in airing out situations or do some quasi-mediation between family members when there are issues about which they are unable to agree, such as medical treatment of an elder, or whether or not an elder should be treated with extraordinary medical measures. At the hearing, the practitioner may request the client's attorney to ask the court if it would entertain a chamber session. This can be done at the beginning of the court process. What goes on in chambers is not recorded. It is a discussion process. Decisions made in open court go on record.

When practitioners go to court, it is advisable for them to remain during the entire course of a hearing to make sure that everything they want to have expressed or presented in court is accomplished. At times attorneys, who have many different pieces of information to present, may lose a piece or two and may benefit from prompting by the practitioner.

When having contact with the legal system, practitioners should not present themselves as impassioned over any particular cause or issue, because that turns people off. If practitioners show a lot of emotion, their credibility will be questioned. If they have strong feelings about a case, they are advised to discuss and ventilate these feelings with a coworker or supervisor, but not in court. When a practitioner is speaking to legal professionals, it is best to understate a case and use facts to convince, not feelings. When first making contact with a court, practitioners must realize that they will have to prove themselves to the court over a period of time, sometimes for months or 1 to 2 years. They should not "buddy up" to court personnel, who serve the general public and must not give the appearance of being biased toward certain practitioners. Court workers are very aware that some people will try to curry favor with them, and they will be on guard. The practitioner needs to be sincere and consistent in working with court personnel. They will help when possible.

Another way for practitioners to make an impact on the legal system is to learn about the laws that affect their clients. The practitioner can begin by going to the law library and asking for information on state laws regarding guardianship, conservatorship, and power of attorney. Groups may be formed to study and understand the laws. A practitioner who has located a sympathetic attorney may invite the attorney to attend the study group. The attorney chosen should be one who is both knowledgeable about the laws in question and sympathetic to the practitioner's position, or at least willing to learn about it. An attorney who specializes in issues regarding the elderly is most knowledgeable in this instance. The practitioner should look to the attorney not as the sole authority on legal matters but rather as someone who can give information, and perhaps one side of the issue, as the practitioner travels on the road to becoming an expert on protective services laws. The practitioner may also want to find out who is available for public speaking and guest lectures, and who will come to the practitioner's agency to teach the staff about geriatric law. There is probably at least one legislator in the practitioner's state who is sympathetic to older people and their problems. The practitioner can attempt to find out who the sympathetic legislators are and make acquaintance with them and their staffs. Practitioners can learn about impending legislation and give input so that the laws are realistic and can support their practice. Some practitioners are now being asked for input on proposed legislation and are able to effect appropriate changes in protective services laws.

Practitioners may want to find out when hearings are held on conservatorships or guardianships in their county. Since most of these hearings are public, anyone has a right to attend them. Practitioners may call the superior court and attend these hearings to acquaint themselves with the judicial mind. If anyone should ask them why they are present, they should speak honestly. Practitioners may say that they often have a client who comes under guardianships and that they want to educate themselves so that they can be more knowledgeable about the field. Courts tend to respect the learner, the practitioner who methodically and rationally tries to learn more about the functioning of the court with an altruistic goal in mind. Court personnel on the whole like to think that they are helping people; they are aware that going to court can be a momentous experience for most people, and they will make it easier if they can. Some judges are very supportive of the practitioner's desire to learn more about the court system. These judges have offered to perform mock court, to give practitioners a tour of the court system, and to run them through a typical hearing. Agencies may want to consider these judges' offers and make court tours and rehearsals a standard part of their staff training program.

The practitioner has a right to approach judges and legislators. They are public officials, appointed or elected. They must be responsive to their constituencies. Most are aware that there are increasing numbers of older people who vote and that their livelihood depends in part on these voters. Additionally, older people have a good press now, and there is a national consciousness of many of the problems that are part of old age. There is also a climate for practitioners to become involved. They have a better chance of finding a sympathetic ear now than 10 years ago. The field of geriatric law is moving rapidly, and the practitioner is in a very good position to influence it.

## SUMMARY

Practitioners who make it a point to understand all legal options available to their clients will be able to serve those clients in an expeditious and efficient manner. The practitioner should expect to be involved in court proceedings and should therefore become familiar with the state civil and criminal justice systems and their personnel. Practitioners can work on issues involving elder mistreatment in several ways: as clinicians helping clients understand legal mandatory reporting laws, for example, and as an advocate of practitioner-attorney teamwork whenever possible.

# CHAPTER 10

# Epilogue

Much of what is now known about elder mistreatment has been presented in the preceding chapters. In this epilogue, issues that merit further study and attention in order to advance the field of elder mistreatment are discussed, and in some areas specific recommendations are made.

## RESEARCH

With the recent information regarding double direction violence among caregivers and impaired elders (Homer & Gilleard, 1990; Paveza et al., 1992; Pillemer & Suitor, 1992), the concepts of elder dependency and stressed caregiver are being revisited and regaining prominence as variables of interest. Additional data from research that focuses on the context of, and the relationship between, a caregiver and an impaired elder may reveal that victims fall into several categories: well elders whose children and others exploit them financially, elder spouses who have a long history of physical abuse, frail elders who are neglected by caregivers in need of assistance and training, and impaired elders who are provocative and disruptive within a caregiving context. Abusers and neglecters may also fall into specific categories which could guide practitioners in selecting interventions that are most appropriate for their circumstances.

More research is needed among ethnic groups. Perhaps elder mistreatment exists in any ethnic group, but it is unknown what culturally normative behaviors are considered to be mistreatment and what norms protect against or promote those forms of mistreatment. Some elders in certain ethnic groups dread psychological abuse (name-calling, saying unkind things about the elder within earshot, mocking) and psychological neglect (ignoring, isolating, excluding from activities) more than physical abuse and neglect. Perhaps the fear of being isolated from their families and not being involved in family activities compels some elders to put up with mistreatment. A research question to pursue could be, "How much mistreatment would you be willing to put up with in order not to be excluded from your family?" (Anetzberger et al., 1996).

For those cultures that emphasize nonverbal interaction, telephone interviews may not be an appropriate method of measuring family dynamics. In-person interviews by culturally proficient interviewers may result in a different profile of elder mistreatment victims in this country (Tomita, 1995).

## TRAINING ISSUES

All professional schools should incorporate issues of elder mistreatment into their curricula. This includes curricula for all health care professionals as well as legal professionals and those who are being trained in gerontology. Certain professions may see one kind of abuse more often than others. Recently, some schools of pharmacy have begun teaching detection techniques, since pharmacists are in a very good position to inquire about the care of an elder and to detect mistreatment—especially in the form of under- and overmedication, and an abuser's use of an elder's medication.

Annual conferences such as those sponsored by the Gerontological Society of America (GSA) and the American Society on Aging (ASA) now have distinct adult protection and elder mistreatment tracks, which encourage the submission of recent research and treatment papers for discussion and which advance the field. Professional conferences, including the annual APS conference in San Antonio cosponsored by the Texas Department of Protective and Regulatory Services and the American Public Welfare Association, routinely offer sessions on issues of elder mistreatment, usually facilitated by practitioners who have caseloads that involve elder mistreatment. Their clinical methods are fresh, and they are able to speak directly from experience. Some seasoned practitioners voluntarily train other professionals in their communities by serving as consultants and information sources, knowing this will help to develop cohesiveness among the various agencies and lend credibility to the issue of elder mistreatment.

# RESOURCES

There has historically been a lack of temporary shelters for victims of elder mistreatment, but this is changing. Some existing facilities, such as convalescent hospitals and retirement homes, are offering this resource. Undoubtedly victims of elder mistreatment require different levels of care, and it may be that retirement homes could take in an elder who is continent, alert, and oriented. An elder who is incontinent and impaired, and wanders, would be better cared for in facilities such as the three nursing homes in San Luis Obispo County, California, which have agreed to provide up to 3 days of emergency shelter free of charge to elderly victims of abuse, neglect, and abandonment.

A 24-hour hot line, which people who are concerned about elder mistreatment or are victims themselves can call to report the mistreatment, is available in some states. Ideally, before 24-hour hot lines are installed, support services should be available on a 24-hour basis to back them up. Then callers need not be told to wait until the next morning, when a staff comes on duty to take care of their problems.

Another issue having to do with resources is that adult protective services agencies are typically understaffed. These are the official agencies to which most mandatory reporting of elder mistreatment must be directed, but they are increasingly unable to meet the needs of all frail elders in the community. The size of caseloads continues to increase dramatically, but the amount of money allotted for staffing, training, and education continues to diminish.

# THE LEGAL SYSTEM

Some observers have suggested that special laws be passed with regard to the mistreatment of elders; and others feel that current laws are sufficient. Many laws are on the books with regard to assault and battery, financial exploitation, and harassment of individuals in general. These laws should be enforced when they apply to elders as well as to other age groups. There should be a continued expansion of the court investigation system in all states. Courts should have direct, impartial knowledge of the situations in which frail elders find themselves when they are the subject of a conservatorship or any other proceeding.

In some states, bank personnel have been given immunity from civil suits if they report financial abuse to the police or the court. These employees as well as judges and attorneys are in the best position to observe financial abuse. Laws need to be passed in all states to address this issue.

In some jurisdictions, prosecutors take elder mistreatment cases just as seriously as they do any other case, and they press charges just as they do with other cases. They also have set up special procedures for dealing with these cases. In addition, some police jurisdictions have a special category for indicating when a case involves elder mistreatment. This facilitates data collection and prompt referrals to special units within the department and to other agencies.

## REPORTING LAWS

Currently, mandatory reporting laws are uneven across the states as regards definitions and penalties for not reporting. Furthermore, these laws tend to concentrate only on physical abuse and neglect and financial abuse. This ignores psychological abuse and neglect, which have been reported in preliminary studies (Anetzberger et al., 1996; Tomita, 1995) and which may be tantamount to psychological torture as defined by Amnesty International. The National Committee for the Prevention of Elder Abuse promotes bringing uniformity to the various reporting laws and definitions, since inconsistencies have prevented agencies from obtaining and comparing incidence data. At present a number of professions are mandated to report, but bank personnel, judges, and attorneys—those who are most familiar with financial abuse—are not mandated to report and probably should be.

## PRACTICE ISSUES

Practitioners are likely to find themselves working with the entire family system in elder mistreatment cases, especially when family "we-ness" takes precedent over individual needs. Some agencies and practitioners feel they can be only pro-victim and may want to leave the treatment of batterers to other, specialized agencies and practitioners. However, because most victims will probably choose to continue living with their abusers, especially if the abusers are family members, the practitioner will most probably treat the family as a system, using family and joint counseling techniques.

Given the strong desire of elder victims to continue their relationships with the abusers, techniques used by child abuse practitioners to reunite victims and their parents are now being studied to evaluate their applicability to elder mistreatment situations. The level of reunification will most likely vary, depending on the victim's wishes, the nature of the mistreatment, and the reliability of the abuser. Any blanket application of a reunification policy in any agency should be approached with extreme caution, especially if long-term monitoring efforts cannot be guaranteed.

Specific counseling techniques to be used beyond the initial assessment and intervention phase are underdeveloped. Practitioners are encouraged to study available theories, such as exchange and social control, and apply them to their practice. Experimenting with new techniques is encouraged, with initial thoughts and problems presented at conferences for feedback and improvement of those techniques.

Some elders do not realize that they are victims, because many associate the term *elder mistreatment* only with overt forms of physical abuse and neglect and with cases that have been sensationalized in the print and television media. Data have not been collected on what many elders dread most—psychological abuse and neglect—and thus practitioners in any setting need to be reminded to ask elders about these more subtle, yet equally lethal, forms of mistreatment.

A specialty practice may develop for those who are working with elder mistreatment. One school of social work developed a master's level training unit in adult protective services and placed students and a full-time instructor in the APS office. The APS agency was pleased to have two students join them upon graduation (Wolf & Pillemer, 1994). Such an APS curriculum might be considered too narrow to some students. One suggestion is to incorporate the program with curricula involving gerontology and clinical work with the elderly, especially since anyone working with elderly will come across instances of elder mistreatment. These curricula in different professional schools should give students training in legal issues, medical conditions that traditionally affect the elderly, domestic violence investigation and intervention techniques, and the legislative process for problem-solving on a state level.

Elder mistreatment clinicians are developing closer working relationships with domestic violence clinicians. In April 1996, a conference entitled "Older Battered Women" was held in San Francisco, bringing researchers and clinicians from both fields together to integrate knowledge, perspectives, and methods of treatment in order to improve services for older battered women. Sharing common dilemmas and problems, the two groups may band together to lobby for effective legislation and budgets to meet the needs of domestic-violence victims. In some parts of the country, attempts are being made to form "family violence coalitions" composed of agencies that treat the various types of domestic violence: child abuse and neglect, sexual assault, spouse abuse, and elder mistreatment. These groups call attention to the learned nature of family violence, the common history of maltreatment of family members who are relatively more vulnerable, and the strong likelihood that the number of reported victims of domestic violence will increase. Relatedly, guided by spousal abuse programs and experts, therapy groups are being formed to treat both elder victims and their abusers. This trend should continue, and the information should be shared with others.

Another practice issue concerns recommendations to judges and to officials who deal with judges, such as probation officers. The judges who often determine the treatment of the batterer and grant protection orders for the victim are usually generalists, and they are seldom well trained in domestic-violence issues. They often welcome specific recommendations from a practitioner, especially if those recommendations are backed up by a clear-cut rationale showing how the practitioner arrived at a conclusion. Judges also tend to be impressed by the person who actually appears in front of them. Therefore, practitioners concerned about the treatment of a batterer or victim should go to court to give their reports. This kind of follow-through by the practitioner will ensure better treatment for the batterer and the victim.

The contents of this book only begin to teach the practitioner how to assess and treat elder mistreatment. A great deal of work remains to be done in the areas of research, training, development of legal responses, resource development, and clinical practice.

# Harborview Medical Center Elder Abuse Diagnostic and Intervention Protocol*

The following is a written protocol for identification and assessment.

### *"Tools" Needed*

1. Sketch sheet or trauma graph.
2. Tape measure.
3. Camera, film, flash attachment.
4. Paper and pen.
5. Consent and release of information forms.

### *General Interview Techniques*

1. Privacy.
2. Pacing.
3. Planning.
4. Pitch.
5. Punctuality. (Oregon Office of Elder Affairs, 1981)

*Modified from the version originally created by Tomita, Clark, Williams, and Rabbitt (1981), and Tomita (1982).

# ASSESSMENT

## History

### *Methodology/Technique*

1. Examine client alone without caregiver.
2. Explain to caregiver he/she will be interviewed separately after client is interviewed; this is part of routine exam.
3. Do not rush during interview. Provide support to client and caregiver. Work questions into conversation in relaxed manner.
4. Do not be judgmental or allow personal feelings to interfere with providing optimal care. Do not *prematurely* diagnose client's case as elder abuse or neglect; do not tell caregiver what treatment plans are until all facts are gathered.
5. Pay special attention to trauma, burns, nutrition, recent change in condition, and financial status.
6. Do collateral contacts as soon as possible with others—e.g., visiting nurse, neighbors, friends—to obtain additional information.

## Presentation

### *Signs and Symptoms Suspicious for Abuse/Neglect*

1. Client brought in to hospital emergency room by someone other than caregiver.
2. Prolonged interval between trauma/illness and presentation for medical care (e.g., care of gross decubiti).
3. Suspicious history: Client is new to system, with history of "shopping" or "doctor hopping." Description of how injury occurred is inconsistent with the physical findings, either better or worse; client has injuries not mentioned in history; client has history of previous similar episodes; there are too many "explained" injuries or inconsistent explanations over time.
4. Medication bottles or the client's pharmacy profile indicates that medications are not being taken or given as prescribed.

## *Functional Assessment Evaluation*

1. Administer Mental Status exam, such as Folstein and Folstein's Mini-Mental Status Exam or Goldfarb's Dementia Scale, to determine current mental status. (Goldfarb Dementia Scale: 1 point each if patient knows age, day, month, year, day of birth, year of birth, street, address, city, president of United States, previous president of United States. Poor = 0-2; fair = 3-7; good = 8-10).
2. Collect pertinent data: e.g., length of time at residence, medical insurer, source(s) of income.
3. Assess activities of daily living: self-care; ambulation; ability to prepare meals, pay bills, shop; mode of transportation; etc.
4. Ask client to describe a typical day to determine degree of independence or dependence on others, and most frequent and significant contacts (who is seen and how often).
5. Ask client about role expectations for self and caregiver.
6. Have client report any recent crisis in family life.
7. Ask if there is alcohol use, drug use, mental illness, or behavior dyscontrol among household or family members.
8. Ask directly if patient has experienced:
   a. Being shoved, shaken, or hit (record, verbatim, when and where on body; examine body).
   b. Being left alone, tied to chair or bed, or left locked in a room (record, verbatim, when and duration).
   c. Having money or property taken or signed over to someone else. Determine current assets, financial status (specify).
   d. Withholding of food, medication, or medical care; being oversedated with medication or alcohol.
   e. Being threatened by or experiencing fear of caregiver (99% of all patients answer yes or no; 50% of those who answer yes identify the abuser).
9. Assess if patient senses being ignored or is made to feel like a burden or in the way.
10. Assess how client responds in situations listed above.
11. Ask client how he/she copes with stress and upsetting incidents; how much abuse he/she is willing to put up with.
12. Assess degree of patient's dependence on caregiver alone for financial, physical, and/or emotional support.

### *Physical Exam*

1. In medical setting, a standard comprehensive examination should be completed on an undressed, gowned patient (no exceptions). In home, attempt review of body while protecting client's modesty.
2. If injury is due to an accident, document circumstances (e.g., client was pushed, client has balance problem, patient was drowsy from medications and fell).
3. Examine closely for effects of undermedication or overmedication; assess nutrition, hygiene, and personal care for evidence of abuse/ neglect (e.g., dehydration or malnourishment without illness-related cause).
4. Assess for:
   a. Burns, unusual location or type.
   b. Physical or thermal injury on head, scalp, or face.
   c. Bruises and hematomas:
      (1) Bilaterally on soft parts of body, not over bony prominences (knee and elbows).
      (2) Clustered, as from repeated striking.
      (3) Shape similar to an object or thumb/fingerprints
      (4) Presence of old and new bruises at the same time as from repeated injury, injuries in different stages of resolution (see table below).
      (5) Presence of bruises after changing health care provider or after prolonged absence from health care agency.
   d. Changes from previous level in mental status and neurological exam
   e. Fractures, falls, or evidence or physical restraint. Contractures may indicate confinement for long periods.

**Dating of Bruises**

| | |
|---|---|
| 0–2 days | Swollen, tender |
| 0–5 days | Red-blue |
| 5–7 days | Green |
| 7–10 days | Yellow |
| 10–14 days | Brown |
| 2–4 weeks | Clear |

    f. Ambulation status: Poor ambulation may be suggestive of sexual assault or other "hidden" injuries.

5. Observe and document:
    a. No new lesions during patient's hospitalization.
    b. Family/caregiver(s) do not visit or show concern.
    c. Client's affect and nonverbal behavior: abnormal/suspicious behavior of client—extremely fearful or agitated; overly quiet and passive; expresses fear of caregiver.
    d. Your intuition that all is not well between patient and caregiver.
    e. Client-caregiver interaction: If the caregiver yells at client and client yells back, determine whether they "need" to yell at each other and/or whether this is a long-term pattern with which both are comfortable. If the verbal threats and yelling are "new" behaviors and the content of the yelling indicates escalation toward more abusive acts or severe verbal abuse, the practitioner should be concerned.

6. In medical setting, diagnostic procedures as indicated by history of exam may include:
    a. Radiologic screen for fractures or evidence of physical restraint
    b. Metabolic screen for nutritional, electrolyte, or endocrine abnormality.
    c. Toxicologic screen or drug levels for over- or undermedication.
    d. Hematologic screen for coagulation defect when abnormal bleeding or bruising is documented.
    e. CAT for major change in neurological status or head trauma that could result in subdural hematoma.
    f. Gynecologic procedures to rule out STD by sexual assault.

## Interview with Possible Perpetrator

*"Thank you for waiting while I interviewed your mother. Now it's your turn. I need your help—I am doing an assessment* (a psychosocial assessment) *of* (for example) *your mother's current functioning and situation in order to determine what services are appropriate at this time. I would like to spend some time with you and have you tell me your perception of how things are here."*

1. *"Tell me what you want me to know about your mother."*
2. *"What is her medical condition? What medicine does she take?"*
3. *"What kind of care does she require?"*
4. *"How involved are you with your mother's everyday activities and care?"*

5. *"What do you expect her to do for herself?"*
6. *"What does she expect you to do for her?"*
   a. *"Do you do these things?"*
   b. *"Are you able to do them?"*
   c. *"Have you had any difficulties? What kinds of difficulties?"*
7. Please describe a typical day for yourself.
8. *"How do you cope with having to care for your mother all the time?"*
9. *"Do you have supports or respite care?"*
   a. *"Who and what?"*
   b. *"Are there other siblings who help?"*
10. *"What responsibilities do you have outside the home? Do you work? What are your hours? What do you do?"*
11. *"Would you mind telling me your income?"* (If this question seems touchy to caregiver, say, *"I just wondered if the pills she needs to take are affordable for your family."* At the same time, you are assessing the caregiver's degree of dependence on the elderly client's income/pensions/assets.)
12. *"Is your mother's Social Security check deposited directly in the bank?"*
13. *"Who owns this house? Do you pay rent? Whose name is on the deed?"*
14. *"If you help your mother pay her bills, how do you do it? Is your name on her account? Do you have power of attorney? Does it have a durable clause? When did you get it?"*

Save more delicate questions for last:

1. *"You know those bruises on your mother's arms (head, nose, etc.)? How do you suppose she got them?"* (Document response verbatim. If possible, follow up with request that caregiver demonstrate how injury may have happened.)
2. *"Your mother is suffering from malnourishment and/or dehydration"* or *"Your mother seems rather undernourished and thin. How do you think she got this way?"*
3. *"Is there a reason for waiting this long to seek medical care for your mother?"*
4. *"Caring for someone as impaired as your mother is a difficult task. Have you ever felt so frustrated with her that you either pushed her*

*a little harder than you expected? How about hitting or slapping her? What were the circumstances?"* (Record verbatim.)

5. *"Have you ever had to tie your mother to a bed or chair, or lock her in a room when you go out at night?"*

6. *"Have there been times when you've yelled at her or threatened her verbally?"*

### *Signs of High-Risk situation:*

1. Perpetrator has history of alcohol, drug abuse, or mental illness.
2. Perpetrator and victim are alienated, depressed, and socially isolated, and have poor self-image.
3. Perpetrator is young or immature, and behavior indicates own dependency needs have not been met.
4. Perpetrator is forced by circumstances to care for patient who is unwanted.
5. Perpetrator is unemployed, without sufficient funds, dependent on client for housing and money.
6. Perpetrator's and/or client's poor health or chronic illness may exacerbate poor relationship.
7. Perpetrator exhibits abnormal behavior, e.g., overtly hostile or frustrated; secretive; shows little concern; demonstrates poor self-control; "blames" client; exhibits exaggerated defensiveness and denial; lacks physical, facial, or eye contact with client; shows overconcern regarding correcting client's bad behavior; visits patient with alcohol on breath.

## Collateral Contacts

1. Have a philosophy of inclusiveness, not exclusiveness.
2. Make collateral contacts promptly, before caregiver attempts to collude with them.
3. Number of contacts may range from 2 to 15.

## Diagnosis

Integrate patient's history, physical exam, perpetrator's history, and information from collateral contacts.

1. No evidence of elder abuse/neglect
2. Suspicious for neglect
3. Suspicious for abuse
4. Positive for abuse/neglect, gross neglect

## Types of Clients

1. Capable, consenting
2. Capable, nonconsenting
3. Incapable
4. Emergency

# INTERVENTION OPTIONS

## Agency/Professional Intervention

### *Indirect Intervention*

1. Documentation—review of chart may later point to abuse.
2. Reporting—most states have Adult Protective Services Units. Forty-nine states have some form of reporting law; some are mandatory reporting laws and some are voluntary reporting laws.
3. Referral out—refer the case to another agency for follow-up.

### *Direct Intervention with Client*

1. Diagnostic plan:
   a. Home visit or in-clinic assessment by geriatric evaluation team.
   b. Short hospital stay or repeated contact for further assessment and case planning.
   c. Administer written protocol and refer case out for execution of treatment plan.
2. Therapeutic plan:
   a. *Repeated* home visits or follow-up appointments in office to gain trust; to combat denial; to bargain with and persuade elderly client; to help elder with decision making, ventilation, and problem solving (might take 2 years).
      (1) Acknowledgment of love and ambivalence.

      (2) Reality orientation.

      (3) Useful next step.

  b. Legal intervention: use least restrictive alternative possible—e.g., apply for guardianship or protective payee status; press charges and/or prosecute; provide medical documentation promptly for the legal process.

  c. Financial crisis intervention:

      (1) Call the bank to place an alert on the account.

      (2) Transport the client to the bank to discuss the incident with bank managers.

      (3) Bring bank personnel to the client's home.

      (4) Report the incident(s) to the Social Security Office.

      (5) Attempt to void the client's signature on forms signed without the client's knowledge; or recall forms signed under duress or when the client most likely was legally incompetent.

3. Education plan/empowerment training to acquire/strengthen positive, powerful self-image:

  a. Develop awareness of new resources.

  b. Assertiveness training.

  c. How to fend off an attacker.

  d. How to care better for self to reduce dependency on perpetrator.

  e. Advise elder not to have observable pattern of behavior (e.g., change your route regularly when you walk to and from store, bank, etc.).

4. Environmental change; use the least restrictive environmental alternative possible:

  a. Block watch.

  b. Move to safer place (e.g., elderly housing, another friend, relative, adult foster home, boarding home).

  c. Home improvements.

  d. Increased contacts outside of home (e.g., day care center).

5. Advocacy/resource linkage:

  a. Assist elder with obtaining meals-on-wheels, chorework service.

  b. Link elder to natural helpers and "gatekeepers."

  c. Telephone checks (e.g., Dial-A-Care).

### Direct Intervention with Perpetrator

1. Therapeutic plan:

  a. Repeated home or office visits for family counseling to clarify role

expectations, promote accountability, reduce conflict, and combat denial.
   (1) Criminalize the act.
   (2) Suggest alternative forms of expression.
   (3) Provide information.
2. Resource linkage:
   a. Strengthen resources and social supports available to caregivers (e.g., chorework, home health aide).

## Staff Training

1. Teach your colleagues how to detect abuse/neglect, what are intervention options, what is being done elsewhere.
2. Offer team approach to care of high-risk patients/clients; offer to do follow-up, share information.

## Community Intervention

1. Train support system to watch for symptoms of inability to care, of abuse, and of neglect; and to report to case manager when an elder has not been seen for a long time.
2. Maintain contact and provide support to the natural helpers.
3. Whenever possible, engage the natural helper's or elder's own social systems in carrying out the treatment plan.

## Follow-Up Process

1. In general, make appointments for home and clinic visits.
2. Consider dropping in on client for second visit to put all involved "on warning" but also to display earnestness.
3. Third appointment is generally a scheduled appointment.

## Limitations/When to Terminate

1. The client dies.
2. The client is competent and chooses not to accept the practitioner's help.
3. The client is no longer in danger.

# Resources

1. 587-5620   Adult Protective Services (Seattle)
2. 448-3110   Senior Information and Assistance (Seattle)
3. 624-7382   Columbia Legal Services (Seattle)

# Dementia Scale*

1. What is the name of this place?
2. Where is it located (address)?
3. What is today's date?
4. What is the month now?
5. What is the year?
6. How old are you?
7. When were you born (month)?
8. When were you born (year)?
9. Who is the president of the United States?
10. Who was the president before him?

Poor = 0–2
Fair = 3–7
Good = 8–10

*Reprinted, by permission of the author and the publisher, from R. L. Kahn et al., Brief objective measures for the determination of mental status in the aged. *American Journal of Psychiatry, 1960. 117*(4):326–328. Copyright © 1960, The American Psychiatric Association.

# Mini-Mental Status Exam*

### *Orientation*

Ask each of the following, and score 1 for each correct answer.
1. What is the day of the week __ , month __ , date __ , year __ , season __                                                ( )/5
2. Where are we: state __ , county __ , town __ , residence number __ , street name __ (or hospital and floor)        ( )/5

### *Registration*

- Name 3 unrelated objects slowly and clearly (e.g., horse, watch, phone).
- Ask the client to repeat them. Tell client to remember objects because he/she will be asked to name them in a few minutes. Score first try. Repeat objects till all are learned, up to 6 trials.                                  ( )/3

### *Attention and Calculation*

- Ask the client to perform serial 7 subtraction from 100 or serial 3 subtraction from 20. Stop after 5 numbers and score 1 for each number (93, 86, 79, 72, 65) or (17, 14, 11, 8, 5).                                                ( )/5

*Reprinted, by permission of the authors and the publisher, from M. F. Folstein, S. E. Folstein, & P. R. McHugh, Mini-Mental State. *Journal of Psychiatric Research,* 1975, *12*(3): 189–198. Copyright © 1975, Pergamon Press, Ltd.

### *Recall*

- Ask the client to recall the names of the 3 unrelated objects which you asked him/her to repeat above. Score 1 for each correct name ( )/3

### *Language*

1. Naming—point to 2 objects and ask the client to name them. Score 1 for each correct name (e.g., tie and pencil). ( )/2
2. Repetition—ask the client to repeat "No ifs, ands, or buts." Allow only 1 trial. Score 0 or 1 ( )/1
3. Three-stage command—ask the client to "Take a paper in your right hand, fold it in half and put it on the floor." Score 1 for each part correctly executed. ( )/3
4. Reading—print on a blank card "Close your eyes," ask the client to read the sentence and do what it says. Score 1 if eyes are closed. ( )/1
5. Writing—ask the client to write a sentence; do not dictate. It must contain a subject and verb, and make sense. Correct grammar and punctuation are not necessary. Score 0 or 1. ( )/1
6. Copying—ask the client to copy this figure exactly. All 10 angles and intersection must be present to score 1. ( )/1

Total ( )/30 possible points

(Refer to source for scoring guidelines.)

# ADL Evaluation Form*

*Instructions:* For each area of functioning listed below, check description that applies.

### *Bathing*

[  ] Independent—Receives no assistance (gets in and out of tub by self if tub is usual means of bathing).

[  ] Independent—Receives assistance in bathing only one part of body (such as back or leg).

[  ] Dependent  —Receives assistance in bathing more than one part of body (or not bathed).

### *Dressing*

[  ] Independent—Gets clothes and gets completely dressed without assistance.

[  ] Independent—Gets clothes and gets dressed without assistance except for tying shoes.

[  ] Dependent  —Receives assistance in getting clothes and getting dressed or stays partly or completely undressed.

*Reprinted, by permission of the authors and the publisher, from S. Katz et al., Studies of illness in the aged—The index of ADL: A standardized measure of biological and psychosocial function. *Journal of the American Medical Association, 185*(12):914–919. Copyright © 1963, American Medical Association.

### Toileting

[   ] Independent—Goes to toilet, cleans self, and arranges clothes without assistance (may use object for support such as cane, walker, or wheelchair and may manage night bedpan or commode, emptying same in morning).

[   ] Dependent  —Receives assistance in going to toilet or in cleansing self or in arranging clothes after elimination or in use of night bedpan or commode.

[   ] Dependent  —Does not go to room termed "toilet" for the elimination process.

### Transfer

[   ] Independent—Moves in and out of bed as well as in and out of chair without assistance (may be using object for support such as cane or walker).

[   ] Dependent  —Moves in or out of bed or chair with assistance.

[   ] Dependent  —Doesn't get out of bed.

### Continence

[   ] Independent—Controls urination and bowel movement completely by self.

[   ] Independent—Has occasional "accidents."

[   ] Dependent  —Supervision helps keep urine or bowel control; catheter is used or is incontinent.

### Feeding

[   ] Independent—Feeds self without assistance.

[   ] Dependent  —Feeds self except for getting assistance in (e.g.) cutting meat or buttering bread.

[   ] Dependent  —Receives assistance in feeding or is fed partly or completely by using tubes or intravenous fluids.

# Symptoms of Depression*

1. Dysphoria—dissatisfaction, restlessness, malaise.
2. Sleep disturbance.
3. Poor concentration; slowed thoughts.
4. Change in appetite or weight.
5. Loss of interest in usual activities.
6. Psychomotor agitation or retardation.
7. Suicide ideation, recurrent thoughts of death.
8. Sense of worthlessness, self-reproach, excessive guilt.
9. Loss of energy.
10. Symptoms are present at least for 2 weeks with no other major psychiatric or organic disorder present and are not due to bereavement.

*D. W. Goodwin and S. B. Guze. *Psychiatric Diagnosis* (3rd ed.), New York and Oxford: Oxford Press, Inc., 1984.

# Powers of Attorney*

## DURABLE POWER OF ATTORNEY

THIS DURABLE POWER OF ATTORNEY SHALL NOT BE AF-
FECTED BY SUBSEQUENT INCAPACITY OF THE PRINCIPAL.
This is an important legal document. It creates a durable power of attorney.
Before executing this document, you should know these important facts:

1. This document may provide the person you designate as your attorney-in-fact with broad powers to dispose of, sell, convey, and encum-
   ber your real and personal property.
2. These powers will exist for an indefinite period of time unless you
   limit their duration in this document. These powers continue to exist
   notwithstanding your subsequent disability or incapacity.
3. You have the right to revoke or terminate this durable power of attorney at any time.

### Article I. Declarations

1.1 Effective date of this Power: _____

1.2 Name and address of the Principal: _____
_____

The first person pronoun, "I," and its variations, "ME," "MINE," and
"MYSELF," refer to the Principal.

---

*Used by permission of Support Services for Elders, Inc., San Francisco, undated.

1.3  Name and Address of the Attorney in Fact: Support Services for elders, Inc., 50 Oak Street, San Francisco, CA 94102.

The second person pronoun, "YOU," and its variations, "YOUR," and "YOURSELF," refer to the ATTORNEY-IN-FACT.

When you, as my Attorney-in-Fact, sign on my behalf under the powers I give you in this document, you shall use the following form as authorized in California Civil Code Section 1095:

"_____,  by SUPPORT SERVICES
         My name           FOR ELDERS, INC., his/her
                                  Attorney-in-Fact.

1.4  My cancelation of any part of this document: IF, BEFORE I SIGN THIS DOCUMENT, I cross out or write through any part of this document, and I put my initials opposite the canceled part, then I eliminate that part from the powers I give you in this document.

## Article II. Powers Given to the Attorney-in-Fact

2.1  I, as Principal, appoint you as my Attorney-in-Fact, with full power of substitution, revocation, and delegation. I give you the powers in this document to use for my benefit and on my behalf. You shall use these powers in a fiduciary capacity.

2.2  As to any assets (a) standing in my name, or (b) held for my benefit, or (c) acquired for my benefit, and subject to Paragraph 1.4, I give you these powers:

1. As to any commercial, checking, savings, savings and loan, money market, Treasury bills, mutual fund accounts, safe deposit boxes, in my name or opened for my benefit—to open, withdraw, deposit into, close, and to negotiate, endorse, or transfer any instrument affecting those accounts.

2. As to any promissory note receivable, secured or unsecured, or any accounts receivable—to collect on, compromise, endorse, borrow against, hypothecate, release and reconvey that note and any related deed of trust.

3. As to any shares of stock, bonds, or any documents or instruments defined as securities under California law—to open accounts with stockbrokers (on cash or on margin), buy, sell, endorse, transfer, hypothecate, and borrow against.

4. As to any real property—to collect rents, disburse funds, keep in

repair, hire professional property managers, lease to tenants, negotiate and renegotiate leases, borrow against, renew any loan, sign any documents required for any transaction in this Paragraph 4, and to sell , subject to confirmation of court, any of the real property.

5. To hire and pay from my funds for counsel and services of professional advisors, including SSE, Inc., according to the then current fee schedule, without limitations—physicians, dentists, accountants, attorneys, and investment counselors.

6. As to my income taxes and other taxes—to sign my name, hire preparers and advisors, and pay for their services from my funds, and to do whatever is necessary to protect my assets from assessments as though I did those acts myself.

7. To apply for government and insurance benefits, to prosecute and to defend legal actions, to arrange for transportation and travel, and to partition community property to create separate property for me.

8. To sign and deliver a valid disclaimer under the Internal Revenue Code and the California Probate Code, when, in your judgment, my own and my heirs' best interests would be served; to that end, to hire and to pay for legal and financial counsel to make that decision as to whether to file that disclaimer.

9. To manage tangible personal property, including but not limited to, moving, storing, selling, donating, or otherwise disposing of said property.

## Article III. Miscellaneous

3.1 *Severability.* If any provision of this document is not valid, all other provisions shall remain valid.

3.2 *Your freedom from liability when you show good faith.* You are not liable to me or any of my successors when, in good faith, you act or do not act under this document; but this freedom from liability is not effective in the event of your willful misconduct or gross negligence.

3.3 Where required, the singular includes the plural and plural includes the singular.

3.4 *California governing law.* California law governs this durable power of attorney in all respects.

3.5 *Reliance on photocopies.* Any person dealing with my Attorney shall have the right to rely on a photocopy of this Durable Power of Attorney declared by my attorney as being genuine, as if it were the signed, original Durable Power of Attorney.

3.6 *Signing*. I, the Principal, sign this Durable Power of Attorney on date
set opposite my signature.

SIGNATURE _____ Date _____

..........................................................................................................

State of California              )
                                ) ss:

City and County of San Francisco  )

On this __ day of __ in the year __ , before me, the undersigned, a Notary
Public, State of California, duly commissioned and sworn, personally
appeared _____ , known to me (or proved to me on the basis of satisfactory evidence) to be the person whose name is subscribed to the within
instrument and acknowledged to me that s/he executed the same.

In witness whereof I have hereunto set my hand and affixed my official seal
in the County of San Francisco the day and year in this certificate first
above written.

_____

Notary Public, State of California

My commission expires _____

..........................................................................................................

Any of the following are authorized to act for SUPPORT SERVICES FOR
ELDERS, INC. on behalf of _____

_____

_____ (seal)

_____

_____

(Signed) _____

# DURABLE POWER OF ATTORNEY (SPRINGING)*

THIS DURABLE POWER OF ATTORNEY SHALL BECOME EFFEC-
TIVE UPON THE INCAPACITY OF THE PRINCIPAL.

This is an important document. It creates a durable power of attorney.
Before executing this document, you should know these important facts:

1. This document may provide the person you designate as your attorney-in-fact with broad powers to dispose of, sell, convey, and encum-
   ber your real and personal property.
2. These powers will exist for an indefinite period of time unless you
   limit their duration in this document. These powers continue to exist
   notwithstanding your subsequent disability or incapacity.
3. You have the right to revoke or terminate this durable power of attorney at any time.

## Article I. Declarations

1.1 Effective date of this Power: _____

1.2 Name and Address of the Principal: _____

_____

The first person pronoun, "I," and its variations, "ME," "MINE," and
"MYSELF," refer to the Principal.

1.3 Name and Address of the Attorney in Fact: SUPPORT SERVICES
FOR ELDERS, INC., 50 Oak Street, San Francisco, CA 94102.

The second person pronoun, "YOU," and its variations, "YOUR," and
"YOURSELF," refer to the ATTORNEY-IN-FACT.

When you, as my Attorney-in-Fact, sign on my behalf under the powers I give you in this document, you shall use the following form as
authorized in California Civil Code Section 1095:

"_____," by SUPPORT SERVICES
    My name        FOR ELDERS, INC., his/her
                        Attorney in Fact.

1.4 My cancelation of any part of this document: IF, BEFORE I SIGN
THIS DOCUMENT, I cross out or write through any part of this doc-

---

*Used by permission of Support Services for Elders, Inc., San Francisco, undated.

ument, and I put my initials opposite the canceled part, then I eliminate that part from the powers I give you in this document.

## Article II. Powers Given to the Attorney-in-Fact

2.1 I, as Principal, appoint you as my Attorney-in-Fact, with full power of substitution, revocation, and delegation. I give you the powers in this document to use for my benefit and on my behalf. You shall use these powers in a fiduciary capacity.

2.2 As to any assets (a) standing in my name, or (b) held for my benefit, or (c) acquired for my benefit, and subject to Paragraph 1.4, I give you these powers:

1. As to any commercial, checking, savings, savings and loan, money market, Treasury bills, mutual fund accounts, safe deposit boxes, in my name or opened for my benefit—to open, withdraw, deposit into, close, and to negotiate, endorse, or transfer any instrument affecting those accounts.

2. As to any promissory note receivable, secured or unsecured, or any accounts receivable—to collect on, compromise, endorse, borrow against, hypothecate, release, and reconvey that note and any related deed of trust.

3. As to any shares of stock, bonds, or any documents or instruments defined as securities under California law—to open accounts with stockbrokers (on cash or on margin), buy, sell, endorse, transfer, hypothecate, and borrow against.

4. As to any real property—to collect rents, disburse funds, keep in repair, hire professional property managers, lease to tenants, negotiate and renegotiate leases, borrow against, renew any loan, sign any documents required for any transaction in this Paragraph 4, and to sell, subject to confirmation of court, any of the real property.

5. To hire and pay from my funds for counsel and services of professional advisors, including SSE, Inc., according to the then current fee schedule, without limitations—physicians, dentists, accountants, attorneys, and investment counselors.

6. As to my income taxes and other taxes—to sign my name, hire preparers and advisors, and pay for their services from my funds, and to do whatever is necessary to protect my assets from assessments as though I did those acts myself.

7. To apply for government and insurance benefits, to prosecute and to

defend legal actions, to arrange for transportation and travel, and to partition community property to create separate property for me.

8. To sign and deliver a valid disclaimer under the Internal Revenue Code and the California Probate Code, when, in your judgment, my own and my heirs' best interests would be served; to that end, to hire and to pay for legal and financial counsel to make that decision as to whether to file that disclaimer.

9. To manage tangible personal property, including but not limited to, moving, storing, selling, donating, or otherwise disposing of said property.

## Aricle III. Miscellaneous

3.1 *Severability.* If any provision of this document is not valid, all other provisions shall remain valid.

3.2 *Your freedom from liability when you show good faith.* You are not liable to me or any of my successors when, in good faith, you act or do not act under this document; but this freedom from liability is not effective in the event of your willful misconduct or gross negligence.

3.3 Where required, the singular includes the plural and plural includes the singular.

3.4 *California governing law.* California law governs this durable power of attorney in all respects.

3.5 *Reliance on photocopies.* Any person dealing with my Attorney shall have the right to rely on a photocopy of this Durable Power of Attorney declared by my attorney as being genuine, as if it were the signed, original Durable Power of Attorney.

3.6 *Signing.* I, the Principal, sign this Durable Power of Attorney on date set opposite my signature.

SIGNATURE _____ Date _____

····································································································

|                                      | )       |
| State of California                  | ) ss:   |
| City and County of San Francisco     | )       |

On this __ day of __ in the year __ , before me, the undersigned, a Notary Public, State of California, duly commissioned and sworn, personally appeared _____ , known to me (or proved to me on the basis of satisfactory evidence) to be the person whose name is subscribed to the within instrument and acknowledged to me that s/he executed the same.

IN WITNESS WHEREOF I have hereunto set my hand and affixed my official seal in the County of San Francisco the day and year in this certificate first above written.

_____

Notary Public, State of California

My commission expires _____

..............................................................................................................

Any of the following are authorized to act for SUPPORT SERVICES FOR ELDERS, INC. on behalf of _____

_____

_____ (seal)

_____

_____

_____(Signed) _____

# CALIFORNIA MEDICAL ASSOCIATION: DURABLE POWER OF ATTORNEY FOR HEALTH CARE DECISIONS*

## 1. CREATION OF DURABLE POWER OF ATTORNEY FOR HEALTH CARE

By this document I intend to create a durable power of attorney by appointing the person designated below to make health care decisions for me as allowed by Sections 4600 to 4753, inclusive, of the California Probate Code. This power of attorney shall not be affected by my subsequent incapacity. I hereby revoke any prior durable power of attorney for health care. I am a California resident who is at least 18 years old, of sound mind, and acting of my own free will.

## 2. APPOINTMENT OF HEALTH CARE AGENT

*(Fill in below the name, address and telephone number of the person you wish to make health care decisions for you if you become incapacitated. You should make sure that this person agrees to accept this responsibility. The following may not serve as your agent: (1) your treating health care provider; (2) an operator of a community care facility or residential care facility for the elderly; or (3) an employee of your treating health care provider, a community care facility, or a residential care facility for the elderly, unless that employee is related to you by blood, marriage or adoption. If you are a conservatee under the Lanterman-Petris-Short Act (the law governing involuntary commitment to a mental health facility) and you wish to appoint your conservator as your agent, you must consult a lawyer, who must sign and attach a special declaration for this document to be valid.)*

I, _____, hereby appoint:
                    *(insert your name)*

Name _____

Address _____

Work Telephone (_____) _____ Home Telephone (_____) _____

as my agent (attorney-in-fact) to make health care decisions for me as authorized in this document. I understand that this power of attorney will be effective for an indefinite period of time unless I revoke it or limit its duration below.

(Optional) This power of attorney shall expire on the following date: _____.

*California Probate Code Sections 4600–4753.

## 3. AUTHORITY OF AGENT

If I become incapable of giving informed consent to health care decisions, I grant my agent full power and authority to make those decisions for me, subject to any statements of desires or limitations set forth below. Unless I have limited my agent's authority in this document, that authority shall include the right to consent, refuse consent, or withdraw consent to any medical care, treatment, service, or procedure; to receive and to consent to the release of medical information; to authorize an autopsy to determine the cause of my death; to make a gift of all or part of my body; and to direct the disposition of my remains, subject to any instructions I have given in a written contract for funeral services, my will or by some other method. I understand that, by law, my agent may not consent to any of the following: commitment to a mental health treatment facility, convulsive treatment, psychosurgery, sterilization or abortion.

## 4. MEDICAL TREATMENT DESIRES AND LIMITATIONS (OPTIONAL)

*(Your agent must make health care decisions that are consistent with your known desires. You may, but are not required to, state your desires about the kinds of medical care you do or do not want to receive, including your desires concerning life support if you are seriously ill. If you do not want your agent to have the authority to make certain decisions, you must write a statement to that effect in the space provided below; otherwise, your agent will have the broad powers to make health care decisions for you that are outlined in paragraph 3 above. In either case, it is important that you discuss your health care desires with the person you appoint as your agent and with your doctor(s).*

*(Following is a general statement about withholding and removal of life-sustaining treatment. If the statement accurately reflects your desires, you may initial it. If you wish to add to it or to write your own statement instead, you may do so in the space provided.)*

I do **not** want efforts made to prolong my life and I do **not** want life-sustaining treatment to be provided or continued: (1) if I am in an irreversible coma or persistent vegetative state; or (2) if I am terminally ill and the use of life-sustaining procedures would serve only to artificially delay the moment of my death; or (3) under any other circumstances where the burdens of the treatment outweigh the expected benefits. In making decisions about life-sustaining treatment under provision (3) above, I want my agent to consider the relief of suffering and the quality of my life, as well as the extent of the possible prolongation of my life.

*If this statement reflects your desires, initial here:* _____

Other or additional statements of medical treatment desires and limitations: _____

_____

_____

_____

*(You may attach additional pages if you need more space to complete your statements. Each additional page must be dated and signed at the same time you date and sign this document.)*

## 5. APPOINTMENT OF ALTERNATE AGENTS (OPTIONAL)

*(You may appoint alternate agents to make health care decisions for you in case the person you appointed in Paragraph 2 is unable or unwilling to do so.)*

If the person named as my agent in Paragraph 2 is not available or willing to make health care decisions for me as authorized in this document, I appoint the following persons to do so, listed in the order they should be asked:

*First Alternate Agent:* Name _____

Address _____

Work Telephone ( _____ ) _____   Home Telephone ( _____ ) _____

*Second Alternate Agent:* Name _____

Address _____

Work Telephone ( _____ ) _____   Home Telephone ( _____ ) _____

## 6. USE OF COPIES

I hereby authorize that photocopies of this document can be relied upon by my agent and others as though they were originals.

## DATE AND SIGNATURE OF PRINCIPAL
(You must date and sign this power of attorney)

I sign my name to this Durable Power of Attorney for Health Care at _____, _____

(City)        (State)

on _____ · _____

(Date)        (Signature of Principal)

## STATEMENT OF WITNESSES

*(This power of attorney will not be valid for making health care decisions unless it is either (1) signed by two qualified adult witnesses who are present when you sign or acknowledge your signature or (2) acknowledged before a notary public in California. If you elect to use witnesses rather than a notary public, the law provides that none of the following may be used as witnesses: (1) the persons you have appointed as your agent and alternate agents; (2) your health care provider or an employee of your health care provider; or (3) an operator or employee of an operator of a community care facility or residential care facility for the elderly. Additionally, at least one of the witnesses cannot be related to you by blood, marriage or adoption, or be named in your will. IF YOU ARE A PATIENT IN A SKILLED NURSING FACILITY, YOU MUST HAVE A PATIENT ADVOCATE OR OMBUDSMAN SIGN BOTH THE STATEMENT OF WITNESSES BELOW AND THE DECLARATION ON THE FOLLOWING PAGE.)*

I declare under penalty of perjury under the laws of California that the person who signed or acknowledged this document is personally known to me to be the principal, or that the identity of the principal was proved to me by convincing evidence;* that the principal signed or acknowledged this durable power of attorney in my presence, that the principal appears to be of sound mind and under no duress, fraud, or undue influence; that I am not the person appointed as attorney in fact by this document; and that I am not the principal's health care provider, an employee of the principal's health care provider, the operator of a community care facility or a residential care facility for the elderly, nor an employee of an operator of a community care facility or residential care facility for the elderly.

*First Witness:* Signature _____

Print name _____

Date _____

Residence Address _____

*Second Witness:* Signature _____

Print name _____

Date _____

Residence Address _____

### (AT LEAST ONE OF THE ABOVE WITNESSES MUST ALSO SIGN THE FOLLOWING DECLARATION)

I further declare under penalty of perjury under the laws of California that I am not related to the principal by blood, marriage, or adoption, and, to the best of my knowledge I am not entitled to any part of the estate of the principal upon the death of the principal under a will now existing or by operation of law.

Signature: _____

---

*The law allows one or more of the following forms of identification as convincing evidence of identity: a California driver's license or identification card or U.S. passport that is current or has been issued within five years, or any of the following if the document is current or has been issued within five years, contains a photograph and description of the person named on it, is signed by the person, and bears a serial or other identifying number: a foreign passport that has been stamped by the U.S. Immigration and Naturalization Service; a driver's license issued by another state or by an authorized Canadian or Mexican agency; or an identification card issued by another state or by any branch of the U.S. armed forces. If the principal is a patient in a skilled nursing facility, a patient advocate or ombudsman may rely on the representations of family members or the administrator or staff of the facility as convincing evidence of identity if the patient advocate or ombudsman believes that the representations provide a reasonable basis for determining the identity of the principal.

## SPECIAL REQUIREMENT: STATEMENT OF PATIENT ADVOCATE OR OMBUDSMAN

*(If you are a patient in a skilled nursing facility, a patient advocate or ombudsman must sign the Statement of Witnesses above __and__ must also sign the following declaration.)*

I further declare under penalty of perjury under the laws of California that I am a patient advocate or ombudsman as designated by the State Department of Aging and am serving as a witness as required by subdivision (e) of Probate Code Section 4701.

Signature: _____     Address: _____

Print Name: _____                  _____

Date: _____                  _____

## CERTIFICATE OF ACKNOWLEDGMENT OF NOTARY PUBLIC

*(Acknowledgment before a notary public is __not__ required if you have elected to have two qualified witnesses sign above. If you are a patient in a skilled nursing facility, you __must__ have a patient advocate or ombudsman sign the Statement of Witnesses on page 3 __and__ the Statement of Patient Advocate or Ombudsman above)*

State of California               )

                         )ss.

County of _____)

On this _____ day of _____, in the year _____,

before me, _____,
                                       *(here insert name and title of the officer)*

personally appeared _____
                                       *(here insert name of principal)*

personally known to me (or proved to me on the basis of satisfactory evidence) to be the person(s) whose name(s) is/are subscribed to this instrument and acknowledged to me that he/she/they executed the same in his/her/their authorized capacity(ies), and that by his/her/their signature(s) on the instrument the person(s), or the entity upon behalf of which the person(s) acted, executed the instrument.

WITNESS my hand and official seal.

_____
     *(Signature of Notary Public)*

                                               **NOTARY SEAL**

## COPIES

YOUR AGENT MAY NEED THIS DOCUMENT IMMEDIATELY IN CASE OF AN EMERGENCY. YOU SHOULD KEEP THE COMPLETED ORIGINAL AND GIVE PHOTOCOPIES OF THE COMPLETED ORIGINAL TO (1) YOUR AGENT AND ALTERNATE AGENTS, (2) YOUR PERSONAL PHYSICIAN, AND (3) MEMBERS OF YOUR FAMILY AND ANY OTHER PERSONS WHO MIGHT BE CALLED IN THE EVENT OF A MEDICAL EMERGENCY. THE LAW PERMITS THAT PHOTOCOPIES OF THE COMPLETED DOCUMENT CAN BE RELIED UPON AS THOUGH THEY WERE ORIGINALS.

# California Penal Code §368 Person Causing Pain to or Suffering of Dependent Adult; Theft or Embezzlement by Caretaker*

(a) Any person who, under circumstances or conditions likely to produce great bodily harm or death, willfully causes or permits any elder or dependent adult, with knowledge that he or she is an elder or a dependent adult, to suffer, or inflicts thereon unjustifiable physical pain or mental suffering, or having the care or custody of any elder or dependent adult, willfully causes or permits the person or health of the elder or dependent adult to be injured, or willfully causes or permits the elder or dependent adult to be placed in a situation such that his or her person or health is endangered, is punishable by imprisonment in the county jail not exceeding one year, or in the state prison for two, three, or four years.

(b) Any person who, under circumstances or conditions other than those likely to produce great bodily harm or death, willfully causes or permits any elder or dependent adult with knowledge that he or she is an elder or a dependent adult, to suffer, or inflicts thereon unjustifiable physical pain or mental suffering, or having the care or custody of any elder or dependent adult, willfully causes or permits the person or health of the elder or depen-

*Standard California Codes. (1995). New York and Oakland, CA: Matthew Bender.

dent adult to be injured or willfully causes or permits the elder or dependent adult to be placed in a situation such that his or her person or health may be endangered, is guilty of a misdemeanor.

(c) Any caretaker of an elder or a dependent adult who violates any provision of law proscribing theft or embezzlement, with respect to the property of that elder or dependent adult, is punishable by imprisonment in the county jail not exceeding one year, or in the state prison for two, three, or four years when the money, labor, or real or personal property taken is of a value exceeding four hundred dollars ($400), and by fine not exceeding one thousand dollars ($1,000) or by imprisonment in the county jail not exceeding one year, or both, when the money, labor, or real or personal property taken is of a value not exceeding four hundred dollars ($400).

(d) As used in this section, "elder" means any person who is 65 years of age or older.

(e) As used in this section, "dependent adult" means any person who is between the ages of 18 and 64, who has physical or mental limitations which restrict his or her ability to carry our normal activities or to protect his or her rights, including, but not limited to, persons who have physical or developmental disabilities or whose physical or mental abilities have diminished or whose physical or mental abilities have diminished because of age. "Dependent adult" includes any person between the ages of 18 and 64 who is admitted as an inpatient to a 24-hour health facility, as defined in Section 1250, 1250.2, and 1250.3 of the Health and Safety Code.

(1) As used in this section, "caretaker" means any person who has the care, custody, or control of or who stands in a position of trust with, an elder or a dependent adult. Leg. II, 1983 ch. 968, 1984 ch. 144 (amended and renumbered from 367a), 1986 ch. 769.

# References

Ackley, D. (1977). A brief overview of child abuse. *Social Casework,* 58(1), 21–24.

Adelson, L. (1974). *The pathology of homicide.* Springfield, IL: Thomas.

Aguilera, D. C. (1990). *Crisis intervention: Theory and methodology.* St. Louis, MO: Mosby.

Alliance/Elder Abuse Project (1983). *An analysis of state mandatory reporting laws on elder abuse.* Syracuse, NY: Author.

American Association of Retired Persons (1992). *Abused elders or older battered women?* Report on the AARP Forum, October 29–30, 1992. Washington, DC: Author.

American Association of Retired Persons (1994). *A profile of older Americans: 1994.* Washington, DC: Author.

American Medical Association (1992). *Diagnostic and treatment guidelines in elder abuse and neglect.* Chicago: Author.

American Public Welfare Association/National Association of State Units on Aging. (1986). *A comprehensive analysis of state policy and practice related to elder abuse.* Washington, D.C: Author.

Anastasio, C. J. (1981). *Elder abuse: Identification and acute care intervention.* Paper presented at the National Conference on Abuse of Older Persons, Boston.

Anderson, S. (1981). *Management of child abuse and neglect, overview and protocol.* Seattle, WA: Harborview Medical Center.

Andres, R., Bierman, E. L., & Hazzard, W. R. (1985). *Principles of geriatric medicine.* NY: McGraw-Hill.

Aneshensel, C., Pearlin, L., Mullan, J., Zarit, S, & Whitlatch, C. (1995). *Profiles in caregiving: The unexpected career.* San Diego, CA: Academic.

Anetzberger, G. J. (1987). *The etiology of elder abuse by adult offspring.* Springfield, IL: Thomas.

Anetzberger, G. J., Korbin, J. E., & Austin, C. (1994). Alcoholism and elder abuse. *Journal of Interpersonal Violence, 9*(2), 184–193.

Anetzberger, G. J., Korbin, J. E., & Tomita, S. K. (1996). Defining elder mistreatment in four ethnic groups across two generations. *Journal of Cross-Cultural Gerontology, 11*(2), 1996, 187–212.

Antone, M. (1987). Litigation and the nurse witness. *California nursing review,* Nov.–Dec., 32–8.

Aronson, M. K. (1984). Update of Alzheimer's: Introduction. *Generations, Quarterly Journal of the Western Gerontological Society, 9*(2), 5–6.

Attorney General's Task Force on Family Violence (1984). *Final Report,* Washington, DC.

Axinn, J. (1989). Women and aging: Issues of adequacy and equity. In J. Garner & S. Mercer (Eds.). *Women as they age: Challenge, opportunity, and triumph* (pp. 339–362). NY: Haworth.

Bergeron, L. R. (1989). Elder abuse and prevention: A holistic approach. In R. Filinson & S. R. Ingman (Eds.), *Elder Abuse: Practice and Policy* (pp. 218–228). NY: Human Sciences.

Bendik, M. (1992). Reaching the breaking point: Dangers of mistreatment in elder caregiving situations. *Journal of Elder Abuse and Neglect 4*(3), 39–59.

Blau, P. (1964). *Exchange and power in social life.* NY: Wiley.

Blazer, D. G. (1989). The epidemiology of psychiatric disorders in late life. In E. V. Busse and D. G. Blazer (Eds.), *Geriatric Psychiatry* (pp. 235–62). Washington, DC: American Psychiatric Press.

Block, M. R. (1983). Special problems and vulnerability of elderly women. In J. Kosberg (Ed.), *Abuse and maltreatment of the elderly: Causes and interventions.* Littleton, MA: John Wright-PSG.

Block, M. R., & Sinnott, J. D. (Eds.). (1979). *The battered elder syndrome: An exploratory study.* College Park, MD: University of Maryland Center on Aging.

Blom, M. F. (1985). Dramatic decrease in decubitus ulcers. *Geriatric Nursing, 6*(2), 84–87.

Blunt, A. (1993). Financial exploitation of the incapacitated: Investigation and remedies. *Journal of Elder Abuse and Neglect, 5*(1), 19–32.

Bookin, D., & Dunkle, R. E. (1989). Assessment problems in cases of elder abuse. In R. Filinson & S. R. Ingman (Eds.). *Elder Abuse: Practice and Policy* (pp. 65–85). NY: Human Sciences.

Brandl, B. (1991). *Older battered women in Milwaukee.* Milwaukee, WI: Community Care Organization of Milwaukee, Milwaukee Foundation and Milwaukee Coalition Against Domestic Violence.

Brantley, P. J., & Sutker, P. B. (1984). Antisocial behavior disorders. In H. E. Adams & P. B. Sutker (Eds.), *Comprehensive handbook of psychopathology.* New York: Plenum.

Braun, J., Wykle, M. H., & Cowling, W. (1988). Failure to thrive in older persons: A concept derived. *Gerontologist, 28*(6), 809–812.

Breckman, R., & Adelman, R. (1988). *Strategies for helping victims of elder mistreatment.* Beverly Hills, CA: Sage.

Bristowe, E. & Collins, J. B. (1989). Family mediated abuse of noninstitutionalized frail elderly men and women living in British Columbia. *Journal of Elder Abuse and Neglect, 1*(1), 45–64.

Brody, E. M. (1985). Parent care as a normative family stress. *Gerontologist, 25*(1), 19–29.

Brody, E. M., & Spark, G. (1966). Institutionalization of the aged: A family crisis. *Family Process, 5,* 76–90.

Brodsky, S. (1989). Testimony about elder abuse and guardianship. *Journal of Elder Abuse and Neglect, 1*(2), 9–15.

Brown, A. (1989). A survey on elder abuse at one Native American tribe. *Journal of Elder Abuse and Neglect, 1*(2), 17–37.

Brown, S. (Dec. 1978). *The second forty years.* Coalition for the Medical Rights of Women. Transcription of a speech to the 5th Annual Conference of the California Psychiatric Association, San Francisco.

Brownell, P. (1994). Elder abuse: policy & practice for social workers. In I. R. Guthell (Ed.) *Work With Older People: Challenges and Opportunities* (pp. 85–108). NY: Fordham University Press.

Brownell, P. (1996). Social work and criminal justice responses to elder abuse in New York City. In A. R. Roberts (Ed.), *Helping Battered Women: New Perspectives and Remedies* (pp. 44–66). NY: Oxford University Press.

Burnside, I. M. (1976). *Nursing and the aged.* New York: McGraw-Hill.

Burr, J. J. (1982). *Protective services for adults.* U. S. Department of Health and Human Services (Pub. No. [OHDS] 82-20505), Washington, DC.

Butler, R. N. (1975). *Why survive? Being old in America.* New York: Harper and Row.

Butler, R. N., & Lewis, M. I. (1973). *Aging and mental health: Positive psychosocial approaches.* St. Louis, MO: Mosby.

Butler, R. N., & Lewis, M. I. (1982). *Aging and mental health: Positive psychosocial and biomedical approaches, Third edition.* St. Louis, MO: Mosby.

Caffey, J. (1946). Multiple fractures in the long bones of children suffering from chronic subdural hematoma. *American Journal of Roentgenology, 56,* 163.

California Civil Code Sections 206 and 242 (1995). *Standard California codes.* New York and Oakland, CA: Bender.

California Penal Code Section 270c (1995). *Standard California codes.* New York and Oakland, CA: Bender.

Cantor, M. (1991). Family and community: Changing roles in an aging society. *Gerontologist, 31*(3), 337–346.

Carkhuff, R. R., & Anthony, W. A. (1979). *The skills of helping.* Amherst, MA: Human Resource Development.

Carson, D. (1995). American Indian elder abuse: Risk and protective factors among the oldest Americans. *Journal of Elder Abuse and Neglect, 7*(1), 17–39.

Cazenave, N. (1983). Elder abuse and black Americans: Incidence, correlates, treatment, and prevention. In J. Kosberg (Ed.), *Abuse and maltreatment of the elderly: Causes and interventions* (pp. 187–203). Boston: Wright.

Chester, B., Robin, R., Koss, M. P., Lopez, J., & Goldman, D. (1994). Grandmother dishonored: Violence against women by male partners in American Indian communities. *Violence and Victims, 9*(3), 249–258.

Clark, A. N. G., Mankikar, G. D., & Gray, I. (1975). Diogenes syndrome: A clinical study of gross neglect in old age. *Lancet, 1*(790), 366–368.

Collins, M., & La France, A. B. (1982, September). *Improving protective services of older Americans: Social worker role.* Portland, ME: Human Services Development Institute, Center for Research and Advanced Study, University of Southern Maine.

Conklin, E. (1993, May 21). Secret hell of a hoarder's home. *Seattle Post Intelligencer.*

Consortium for Elder Abuse Prevention. (1983). *Protocols.* San Francisco: Author.

Cook, K. (Ed.). (1987). *Social exchange theory.* Beverly Hills, CA: Sage.

Cook, K., & Emerson, R. (1978). Power, equity, commitment in exchange networks. *American Sociological Review, 43*(5), 721–739.

Cormier, W. H., & Cormier, S. L. (1985). *Interviewing strategies for helpers.* Monterey, CA: Brooks/Cole.

Crossman, L., London, C., & Barry, C. (1981). Older women caring for disabled spouses: A model for supportive services. *Gerontologist, 21*(5), 454–470.

Crystal, S. (1986). Social policy and elder abuse. In K. Pillemer & R. Wolf (Eds.), *Elder abuse: Conflict in the family* (pp. 331–340). Dover, MA: Auburn.

Culter, L. (1985). Counseling caregivers. *Generations: Quarterly Journal of the American Society on Aging, 10*(1), 53–57.

Daly, M., & Wilson, M. (1982). Homicide and kinship. *American Anthropologist, 84,* 372–378.

Deets, H. B. (1993). AARP study sheds new light on elder abuse. *AARP Bulletin, 34*(3), 3.

Dorpat, T. (1985). *Denial and defense in the therapeutic situation.* New York: Aronson.

Douglass, R. L., & Hickey, T. (1983). Domestic neglect and abuse of the elderly: Research findings and systems perspective for service delivery planning. In J. I. Kosberg (Ed.), *Abuse and maltreatment of the elderly: Causes and interventions.* Littleton, MA: John Wright-PSG.

Douglass, R. L., Hickey, T., & Noel, C. (1980). *A study of maltreatment of the elderly and other vulnerable adults.* Ann Arbor: Institute of Gerontology, University of Michigan.

Dowd, J. J. (1975). Aging as exchange: A preface to theory. *Journal of Gerontology. 30,* 585–594.

Dubin, T., Garcia, R., Lelong, J., & Mowesian, R. (1986). *Family neglect and self-neglect of the elderly: Normative characteristics and a design for intervention.* Austin, TX: Hogg Foundations for Mental Health, Family Eldercare, Inc.

Duke, J. (1991). A national study of self-neglecting adult protective services clients. In T. Tatara & M. Rittman (Eds.), & K. J. Kaufer Flores (Coordinator), *Findings of five elder abuse studies* (pp. 23–53). Washington, DC: National Aging Resource Center on Elder Abuse.

Ebersole, P., & Hess, P. (1981). *Toward healthy aging: Human needs and nursing response.* St. Louis, MO: Mosby.

Ebersole, P., & Hess, P. (1985). *Toward healthy aging: Human needs and nursing response* (2nd ed.). St. Louis, MO: Mosby.

Ebersole, P., & Hess, P. (1994). *Toward Healthy Aging: Human needs and nursing response* (4th ed.). St. Louis, MO: Mosby.

Elliot, C. (1983, December). Notes from talk given on domestic violence and rape in marriage to King's County Prosecutor's Office, Seattle, WA.

Emerson, R. (1972a). Exchange theory, Part I: A sociological basis for social exchange. In J. Berger, M. Zelditch, & B. Anderson (Eds.), *Sociological theories in progress, Vol. 2* (pp. 38–57). Boston: Houghton Mifflin.

Emerson, R. (1972b). Exchange theory, Part II: A sociological basis for social exchange. In. J. Berger, M. Zelditch, & B. Anderson (Eds.), *Sociological theories in progress, Vol. 2* (pp. 58–87). Boston: Houghton Mifflin.

Emerson, R. (1987). In K. Cook (Ed.), *Social exchange theory* (pp. 11–46). Beverly Hills, CA: Sage.

English, R. W. (1977). Combating stigma toward physically disabled persons. In R. P. Marinelli & A. E. Dell Orto (Eds.), *The psychological and social impact of physical disability.* New York: Springer.

English, R. W. (1980). *Elder Abuse.* Philadelphia: Franklin Research Center.

Evergreen Legal Services. *Advocate's guide to elder abuse, neglect, and exploitation* (1983). Seattle, WA: Author.

Fabian, D., & Rathbone-McCuan, E. (1992). Elder self-neglect: A blurred concept: In E. Rathbone-McCuan & D. Fabian (Eds.), *Self-neglecting elders: A clinical dilemma* (pp. 3–12). Westport, CT: Auburn.

Ferguson, D., & Beck, C. (1983). H.A.L.F.—A tool to assess elder abuse within the family. *Geriatric Nursing, 4,* 301–304.

Filinson, R. (1988). Introduction. In R. Filinson & S. Ingman (Eds.), *Elder Abuse: Practice and Policy* (pp. 166–178). NY: Human Sciences.

Fillenbaum, G., & Smyer, M. (1981). The development, validity, and reliability of the OARS multidimensional assessment questionnaire. *Journal of Gerontology 36,* 428–434.

Finklehor, D. (1983). Common features of family abuse. In D. Finkelhor, R. J. Gelles, G. Hotaling, & M. Straus (Eds.), *The dark side of families: Current family violence research.* Beverly Hills, CA: Sage.

Fitting, M. D., Rabins, P. V., & Lucas, M. J. (1984, November). *Caregivers for dementia patients: A comparison of men and women.* Paper presented at the 37th Annual Scientific Meeting of the Gerontological Society of America, San Antonio, TX.

Fitting, M., & Rabins, P. (1985). Men and women: Do they give care differently? *Generations: Quarterly Journal of the American Society on Aging, 10*(1), 23–26.

Fleming, C. F. (1992). American Indians and Alaska Natives: Changing societies past and present. In M. Orlando, R . Weston, & L. G. Epstein (Eds.), *Cultural competence for evaluators* (pp. 147–172). Rockville, MD: U.S. Dept. of Health and Human Services.

Folstein, M. F., Folstein, S. E., & McHugh, P. R. (1975). Mini-mental state. *Journal of Psychiatric Research, 12*(3), 189–198.

Foner, N. (1984). *Ages in conflict: A cross-cultural perspective on inequality between old and young.* NY: Columbia University Press.

Foster, J. R., & Foster, R. P. (1983). Group psychotherapy with the old and aged. In H. I. Kaplan (Ed.), *Comprehensive group psychotherapy.* Baltimore: Williams & Wilkins.

Fraser, J. G. (1900). *The golden bough: A study in magic and religion* (2nd ed.). NY: Macmillan.

Fulmer, T. T., & O'Malley, T. A. (1987). *Inadequate care of the elderly: A health care perspective on abuse and neglect.* NY: Springer.

Fulmer, T., Street, S., & Carr, K. (1984). Abuse of the elderly: Screening and detection. *Journal of Emergency Nursing, 10*(3), 131–140.

Gambrill, E. (1983). *Casework: A competency-based approach.* Englewood Cliffs, NJ: Prentice-Hall.

Ganley, A. L. (1981). *Court mandated counseling for men who batter: A 3-day workshop for mental health professionals.* Washington, DC: Center for Women Policy Studies.

Gaspar, P. M. (1988). Fluid intake: What determines how much patients drink? *Geriatric Nursing, 9*(4), 221–224.

Gelles, R., & Straus, M. (1988). *Intimate violence: The causes and consequences of abuse in the American family.* NY: Simon and Schuster.

George, L., & Gwyther, L. (1986). Caregiver well-being: A multidimensional examination of family caregivers of demented adults. *Gerontologist, 26,* 253–259.

Gesino, J. P., Smith, H. H., & Keckich, W. A. (1982, Fall). The battered woman grows old. *Clinical Gerontologist, 1*(1), 59–67.

Giordano, N. H., & Giordano, J. A. (1984). *Individual and family correlates of elder abuse.* Paper presented at the 37th Annual Scientific Meeting of the Gerontology Society of America, San Francisco.

Glascock, A., & Feinman, S. (1981). Social assessment of burden: Treatment of the aged in non-industrial societies. In C. Fry (Eds.), *Dimensions: Aging, culture, and health* (pp. 13–31). NY: Praeger.

Godkin, M., Wolf, R., & Pillemer, K. (1989). A case-comparison analysis of elder abuse and neglect. *International Journal of Aging and Human Development, 28*(3), 207–225.

Golan, N. (1978). *Treatment in crisis situations.* New York: Free Press.

Golan, N. (1979). Crisis theory. In F. J. Turner (Ed.), *Social work treatment: Interlocking theoretical approaches,* New York: Free Press.

Golan, N. (1987). Crisis intervention. In A. Minahan (Ed.), *Encyclopedia of social work* (18th ed., pp. 360–372). Washington, DC: National Association of Social Workers.

Goodwin, D. W., & Guze, S. B. (1984). *Psychiatric Diagnosis* (3rd ed.). New York and Oxford: Oxford University Press.

Gordon, R. (1992). Material abuse and powers of attorney in Canada: A preliminary examination. *Journal of Elder Abuse and Neglect, 4*(2), 173–193.

Gottlieb, N. (1989). Families, work, and the lives of older women. In J. Garner & S. Mercer (Eds.). *Women as they age: Challenge, opportunity and triumph* (pp. 217–244). NY: Haworth.

Grant, I. H., & Quinn, M. J. (in press). Guardianship and abuse of dependent adults. In G. H. Zinny & G. T. Grossberg (Eds.), *Guardianship of the elderly: Medical and judicial aspects.* NY: Springer.

Greenberg, D. (1987). Compulsive hoarding. *American Journal of Psychotherapy, XLI*(3), 409–416.

Greenberg, D., Witztum, E., & Levy, A. (1990). Hoarding as a psychiatric symptom. *Journal of Clinical Psychiatry, 51*(10), 417–421.

Griffin, L. W. (1994). Elder maltreatment among rural African Americans. *Journal of Elder Abuse and Neglect, 6*(1), 1–27.

Griffin, L. W., & Williams, O. (1992). Abuse among African American elderly. *Journal of Family Violence, 7*(1), 19–35.

Hankin, M. (1996). Making the perpetrators pay: Collecting damages for elder abuse, neglect, and exploitation. *Aging, 367,* 66–70.

Harshbarger, S. (1993). From protection to prevention: A proactive approach. *Journal of Elder Abuse and Neglect, 5*(1), 41–55.

Havemeyer, H. (1980). *Key points for adult services testimony.* Lakewood, CO: Jefferson County Department of Social Services.

Hayes, C. L. (1984). *Elder abuse and the utilization of support groups for the relatives of functionally disabled older adults.* Unpublished manuscript, Center on Aging, Catholic University of America.

Heisler, C. (1991). The role of the criminal justice system in elder abuse cases. *Journal of Elder Abuse and Neglect, 3*(1), 5–33.

Heisler, C. (1994). *Elder abuse.* Paper presented at Family Violence and the Courts:

A Coordinated Response, sponsored by the Judicial Council of California, Administrative Offices of the Courts, Los Angeles, CA.

Heisler, C., & Quinn, M. J. (1995). A legal perspective. *Journal of Elder Abuse and Neglect, 7*(2/3 ), 141–156.

Heisler, C., & Tewksbury, J. (1991). Fiduciary abuse of the elderly: A prosecutor's perspective. *Journal of Elder Abuse and Neglect, 3*(4), 23–30.

Henson, T. (1987). Medicolegal role in detection and prevention of human abuse. *Holistic Nurse Practitioner, 1,* 75–84.

Herr, J. J., & Weakland, J. H. (1979). *Counseling elders and their families.* New York: Springer.

Heston, L. L., & White, J. A. (1983). *Dementia: A practical guide to Alzheimer's disease and related illnesses.* New York and San Francisco: Freeman.

Hickey, T., & Douglass, R. L. (1981). Neglect and abuse of older family members: Professionals' perspectives and case experience. *Gerontologist, 21*(4), 171–176.

Holt, M. G. (1993). Elder sexual abuse in Britain: Preliminary findings. *Journal of Elder Abuse and Neglect, 5*(2), 64–71.

Homans, G. (1974). *Social behavior.* New York: Harcourt Brace Jovanovich.

Homer, A., & Gilleard, C. (1990). Abuse of elderly people by their carers. *British Medical Journal, 301,* 1359–1362.

Hotaling, G., & Sugarman, D. (1986). An analysis of risk markers in husband to wife violence: The current state of knowledge. *Violence and Victims, 1*(2), 101–124.

Hudson, M. (1989). Analysis of the concepts of elder mistreatment: Abuse and neglect. *Journal of Elder Abuse and Neglect, 1*(1), 5–25.

Hudson, M. (1994). Elder abuse: Its meaning to middle-aged and older adults. Part II: Pilot results. *Journal of Elder Abuse and Neglect, 6*(1), 55–81.

Hunter, R., & Kilstrom, N. (1979). Breaking the cycle in abusive families. *American Journal of Psychiatry, 136* (October 1979),1320–1322.

Hwalek, M., Hill, B., & Stahl, C. (1989). The Illinois plan for a statewide elder abuse program. In R. Filinson & S. Ingman (Eds.). *Elder abuse: Practice and policy.* NY: Human Sciences.

Hwalek, M., Sengstock, M. C., & Lawrence, R. (1984, November). *Assessing the probability of abuse of the elderly.* Presented at the Annual Meeting of the Gerontological Society of America.

Jensen, G. D., & Oakley, F. B. (1980). Aged appearance and behavior: An evolutionary and ethnological perspective. *Gerontologist, 20*(5), 595–597.

John, R. (1988). The Native American family. In C. Mindel, R. Habenstein, & R. Wright, Jr. (Eds.), *Ethnic families in America* (pp. 325–363). New York: Elsevier.

Johnson, C. L., & Catalano, D. J. (1983). A longitudinal study of family supports to impaired elderly. *Gerontologist, 23*(6), 612–618.

Johnson, D. (1981). Abuse of the elderly. *Nurse Practitioner, 6,* 29–34.

Johnson, R. A. (1983). Mobilizing the disabled. In J. Freeman (Ed.), *Social movements of the sixties and seventies.* New York, Longman.

Johnson, T. (1986). Critical issues in the definition of elder mistreatment. In K. Pillemer & R. Wolf (Eds.), *Elder abuse: Conflict in the family* (pp. 167–196). Dover, MA: Auburn.

Judicial Council of California (1992). *Handbook for conservators.* San Francisco: Author.

Kahn, R. L., Goldfarb, A., Pollack, M., & Peck, A. (1960). Brief objective measures for the determination of mental status in the aged. *American Journal of Psychiatry, 117*(4), 326–328.

Kane, R., Ouslander, J., & Abrass, I. (1994). *Essentials of clinical geriatrics* (3rd ed.). NY: McGraw-Hill.

Kaneko, Y., & Yamada, Y. (1990). Wives and mothers-in-law: Potential for family conflict in post-war Japan. *Journal of Elder Abuse and Neglect, 2*(1/2), 87–99.

Katz, S., Ford, A. B., Moskowitz, R. W., Jackson, B. A., & Jaffe, M. W. (1963). Studies of illness in the aged—The index of ADL: A standardized measure of biological and psychosocial function. *Journal of the American Medical Association, 185*(12), 914–919.

Kempe, C. H., & Kempe, R. S. (1978). *Child abuse.* Cambridge, MA: Harvard University Press.

Kennedy, T., Graham, W., Miller, S., & Davis, T. (1977). Management and prevention of pressure ulcers. *American Family Physician, 15*(16), 84–90.

Kenoyer, L., & Bateman, P. (1982). *Peace of mind: Senior citizen self-protection.* Seattle, WA: Alternatives to Fear.

Kirkpatrick, C. (1955). *The family as process and institution.* New York: Ronald.

Klingbeil, K. (1979). *Domestic abuse—battered woman syndrome: Medical and social work protocol.* Seattle, WA: Harborview Medical Center.

Klingbeil, K. S., & Boyd, V. D. (1984). Emergency room intervention: Detection, assessment, and treatment. In A. R. Roberts (Ed.), *Battered women and their families.* New York: Springer.

Korbin, J., Anetzberger, G., & Austin, C. (1995). The intergenerational cycle of violence in child and elder abuse. *Journal of Elder Abuse and Neglect, 7*(1), 1–15.

Korbin, J., Anetzberger, G., & Eckert, J. K. (1989). Elder abuse and child abuse: A consideration of similarities and differences in intergenerational family violence. *Journal of Elder Abuse and Neglect, 1*(4), 1–14.

Korbin, J., Anetzberger, G., Thomassen, R., & Austin, C. (1991). Abused elders who seek legal recourse against their adult offspring: Findings from an exploratory study. *Journal of Elder Abuse and Neglect, 3*(3), 1–18.

Korbin, J., Eckert, K., Anetzberger, G., Whittemore, E., Mitchell, L., & Vargo, E.

(1987). *Elder abuse and child abuse: Commonalties and differences.* Paper presented at the 3rd National Family Violence Research Conference, Durham, NH.

Krassen Maxwell, E., & Maxwell, R. J. (1992). Insults to the body civil: Mistreatment of elderly in two Plains Indian tribes. *Journal of Cross Cultural Gerontology, 7*(1), 3–23.

Lachs, M. S., Berkman, L., Fulmer, T., & Horwitz, R. I. (1994). A prospective community-based pilot study of risk factors for the investigation of elder mistreatment. *Journal of the American Geriatrics Society, 42,* 169–173.

Langsley, D. G., & Kaplan, D. M. (1968). *The treatment of families in crisis.* New York: Grune and Stratton.

Lau, E. A., & Kosberg, J. I. (Nov. 1978). *Abuse of the elderly by informal care providers: Practice and research issues.* Paper presented at the 31st Annual Meeting of the Gerontological Society of America, Dallas, TX.

Lau, E. A., & Kosberg, J. I. (1979, September–October). Abuse of the elderly by informal care providers. *Aging,* 299–300, 10–15.

Levinson, D. (1989). *Family violence in cross-cultural perspective.* Newbury Park, CA: Sage.

Longres, J. (1995). Self-neglect among the elderly. *Journal of Elder Abuse and Neglect 7*(1), 69–86.

Longres, J., Raymond, J., & Kimmel, K. (1991). *Black and white clients in an elder abuse system.* Unpublished manuscript.

Lowry, F. (1957). Caseworker in short contact services. *Social Work, 2*(1), 52–56.

Lustbader, W. (1991). *Counting on kindness: The dilemmas of dependency.* New York: Free Press.

Lustbader, W., & Hooyman, N. (1994). *Taking care of aging family members: A practical guide.* New York: Free Press.

MacAndrew, C., & Edgerton, R. B. (1969). *Drunken comportment: A social explanation.* Chicago: Aldine.

Macey, S. M., & Schneider, D. F. (1993). Deaths from excessive heat and excessive cold among the elderly. *Gerontologist, 33*(4), 497–500.

Manfreda, M. L., & Krampitz, S. D. (1977). *Psychiatric nursing* (10th ed.). Philadelphia: Davis.

Martin, D. (1976). *Battered wives.* New York: Pocket Books.

Matlaw, J. R., & Spence, D. M. (1994). The hospital elder assessment team: A protocol for suspected cases of elder abuse and neglect. *Journal of Elder Abuse and Neglect, 6*(2), 23–37.

Matza, D. (1964). *Delinquency and drift.* New York: Wiley.

May, P. A. (1987). Suicide and self-destruction among American Indian youths. *American Indian and Alaska Native Mental Health Research, 1,* 52–69.

Mayeux, R., & Schofield, P. (1994). Alzheimer's disease. In W. Hazzard, E. Bierman, J. Blass, W. Ettinger, Jr., & J. Halter (Eds.), *Principles of geriatric medicine and gerontology* (3rd ed., pp. 1035–1050). New York: McGraw-Hill.

McIntosh, J. L., and Hubbard, R. W. (1988). Indirect self-destructive behavior among the elderly: A review with case examples. *Journal of Gerontological Social Work 13*(1-a), 37–48.

Miller, R., & Dodder, R. (1988). The abused-abuser dyad: Elder abuse in the state of Florida. In R. Filinson & S. Ingman (Eds.), *Elder abuse: Practice and policy* (pp. 166–178). New York: Human Sciences.

Minor, W. (1980, May). The neutralization of criminal offense. *Criminology, 18*(1), 103–120.

Minor, W. (1981, July). Techniques of neutralization: A reconceptualization and empirical examination. *Journal of Research in Crime and Delinquency,* 295–318.

Moon, A., & Williams, O. (1993). Perceptions of elder abuse and help-seeking patterns among African-American, Caucasian American, and Korean-American elderly women. *Gerontologist 33*(3), 386–395.

Mitchell, W. (1973). Bargaining and public choice. In H. Leavitt & L. Pondy (Eds.), *Readings in managerial psychology* (2nd ed.). Chicago: University of Chicago Press.

Murdach, A. (1980). Bargaining and persuasion with nonvoluntary clients. *Social Work, 25*(6), 458–461.

National Center on Elder Abuse (NCEA). (1995). *Understanding the nature and extent of elder abuse in domestic settings. An NCEA Summary Sheet.* Washington, DC: Author.

Nerenberg, L. (1995). LAPD's fiduciary SWAT team. Nexus: *A Publication for NCPEA Affiliates, 1*(2), 4–5. San Francisco: National Committee for the Prevention of Elder Abuse Affiliate Program, UCSF/Mount Zion Center on Aging.

Nerenberg, L. (1996). Hornswoggled? An interview with Margaret Singer on undue influence. *Nexus: A Publication for NCPEA Affiliates, 2*(1), 4–6 San Francisco: National Committee for the Prevention of Elder Abuse Affiliate Program, UCSF/Mount Zion Center on Aging.

*Nexus* (1995a). Nursing homes provide free shelter. *Nexus: A Publication for NCPEA Affiliates, 1*(1), 2. San Francisco: National Committee for the Prevention of Elder Abuse Affiliate Program, UCSF/Mount Zion Center on Aging.

*Nexus* (1995b). Protecting elderly Latinas against domestic violence. *Nexus: A Publication for NCPEA Affiliates, 1*(2), 2. San Francisco: National Committee for the Prevention of Elder Abuse Affiliate Program, UCSF/Mount Zion Center on Aging.

*Nexus* (1995c). Services for older battered women offer hope and healing. *Nexus: A Publication for NCPEA Affiliates, 1*(3), 1; 4–7. San Francisco: National Committee for the Prevention of Elder Abuse Affiliate Program, UCSF/Mount Zion Center on Aging.

Njeri, M., & Nerenberg, L. (1993). WE ARE FAMILY: Outreach to African-American Seniors. *Journal of Elder Abuse and Neglect, 5*(4), 5–19.

Nuessel, F. H. (1982). The language of ageism. *Gerontologist, 22*(3), 273–275.

Nuttbrock, L., & Kosberg, J. I. (1980). Images of the physician and help-seeking behavior of the elderly: A multivariate assessment. *Journal of Gerontology, 35,* 241–248.

O'Malley, H. C., Segars, H., Perez, R., Mitchell, V., & Knuepel, G. M. (1979). *Elder abuse in Massachusetts: A survey of professionals and paraprofessionals.* Boston: Legal Research and Services for the Elderly.

O'Malley, T. A., Everett, E. D., O'Malley, H. C., & Campion, E. W. (1983). Identifying and preventing family mediated abuse and neglect of elderly persons. *Annals of Internal Medicine, 90*(6), 998–1005.

Ory, M. G. (1985). The burden of care. *Generations: Quarterly Journal of the American Society on Aging, 10*(1), 14–17.

Ostrovski (Quinn), M. J. (1977). Life review and depression in late life. Unpublished master's thesis.

Ostrovski (Quinn), M. J. (1979). Transition to adulthood. In I. M. Burnside, P. Ebersole, & H. E. Monea (Eds.), *Psychosocial caring throughout the life span.* New York: McGraw-Hill.

Ostrovski-Quinn, M. J. (1985). The frail vulnerable old. In P. Ebersole & P. Hess (Eds.), *Toward healthy aging: Human needs and nursing response* (2nd ed.). St. Louis, MO: Mosby.

Parad, H. J. (1971). Crisis intervention. In *Encyclopedia of social work* (Vol. 1). Washington, DC: National Association of Social Workers.

Parad, H. J., & Parad, L. G. (Eds.) (1990). *Crisis intervention, Book 2: The practitioner's sourcebook for brief therapy.* Milwaukee, WI: Family Service America.

Parad, H. J., Selby, L., & Quinlan, J. (1976). Crisis intervention with families and groups. In R. W. Roberts & H. Northern (Eds.), *Theories of social work with groups.* New York: Columbia University Press.

Paveza, G. J., Cohen, D., Eisdorfer, C., Freels, S., Semla, T., Ashford, J. W., Gorelick, P., Hirschman, R., Luchman, R., Luchins, D., & Levy, P. (1992). Severe family violence and Alzheimer's disease: Prevalence and risk factors. *Gerontologist, 32*(4), 493–497.

Payne, B., & Cikovic, R. (1996). An empirical examination of the characteristics, consequences, and causes of elder abuse in nursing homes. *Journal of Elder Abuse and Neglect, 7*(4), 61–74.

Pedrin, V., & Brown, S. (1980). Sexism and ageism: Obstacles to health care for women. *Generations: Quarterly Journal of the Western Gerontological Society, 4*(4), 20–21.

Phillips, L. R. (1983). Abuse and neglect of the frail elderly at home: An exploration of theoretical relationships. *Journal of Advanced Nursing, 3,* 379–392.

Phillips, L. R. (1986). Theoretical explanations of elder abuse: Competing hypotheses and unresolved issues. In K. Pillemer & R. Wolf (Eds.), *Elder abuse: Conflict in the family* (pp. 197–217). Dover, MA: Auburn.

Pillemer, K. (1985a). *Domestic violence against the elderly: A case-control study.* Unpublished doctoral dissertation. Department of Sociology, Brandeis University.

Pillemer, K. (1985b). The dangers of dependency: New findings on domestic violence against the elderly. *Social Problems, 33*(2): 146–157.

Pillemer, K. (1986). Risk factors in elder abuse: Results from a case control study. In K. Pillemer & R. Wolf (Eds.), *Elder abuse: Conflict in the family* (pp. 239–263). Dover, MA: Auburn.

Pillemer, K., & Finkelhor, D. (1985, October). *Domestic violence against the elderly: A discussion paper.* A paper prepared for the Surgeon General's Workshop on Violence and Public Health, Leesburg, VA.

Pillemer, K., & Finkelhor, D. (1988). The prevalence of elder abuse: A random sample survey. *Gerontologist, 28*(1), 51–57.

Pillemer, K., & Moore, D. (1989). Abuse of patients in nursing homes: Findings from a survey of staff. *Gerontologist, 29,* 314–320.

Pillemer, K., & Moore, D. (1990). Highlights from a study of abuse of patients in nursing homes. *Journal of Elder Abuse and Neglect, 2*(1/2), 5–29.

Pillemer, K., & Suitor, J. (1992). Violence and violent feelings: What causes them among caregivers? *Journal of Gerontology, 47,* S 165–S 172.

Pizzey, E. (1974). *Scream quietly or the neighbors will hear.* Baltimore: Penguin.

Podnieks, E. (1992a). National survey on abuse of the elderly in Canada. *Journal of Elder Abuse and Neglect 4*(1/2), 5–58.

Podnieks, E. (1992b). Emerging themes from a follow-up study of Canadian victims of elder abuse. *Journal of Elder Abuse and Neglect 4*(1/2), 59–111.

Podnieks, E., Pillemer, K., Nicholson, J., Shillington, T, & Frizzel, A. (1990). *National survey on abuse of the elderly in Canada.* Toronto: Ryerson Polytechnical Institute.

Quinn, M. J. (1985). Elder abuse and neglect raise new dilemmas. *Generations: Quarterly Journal of the American Society on Aging, 10*(2), 22–25.

Quinn, M. J. (1989). Probate conservatorships and guardianships: Assessment and curative aspects. *Journal of Elder Abuse and Neglect, 1*(1), 91–101.

Quinn, M. J. (1990a). Elder abuse and neglect: Treatment issues. In S. M. Stith, M. B. Williams, & K. Rosen (Eds.). *Violence hits home* (pp. 277–292). New York: Springer.

Quinn, M. J. (1990b). Elder abuse and neglect: Intervention strategies. In. S. M. Stith, M. B. Williams, & K. Rosen (Eds.). *Violence hits home* (pp. 293–302). New York: Springer.

Quinn, M. J. (1996). Commentary—Everyday competencies and guardianship: Refinements and realities. In M. Smyer, K. W. Schaie, & M. B. Kapp, *Older adult's decision-making and the law* (pp. 128–141). New York: Springer.

Quinn, M. J., & Tomita, S. (1986). *Elder abuse and neglect: Causes, diagnosis, and intervention strategies* (1st ed). New York: Springer.

Radbill, S. (1968). A history of child abuse and infanticide. In R. E. Helfer & C. H. Kempe (Eds.), *The battered child*. Chicago: University of Chicago Press.

Ramsey-Klawsnik, H. (1991). Elder sexual abuse: Preliminary findings. *Journal of Elder Abuse and Neglect, 3*(3), 73–90.

Ramsey-Klawsnik, H. (1993). Interviewing elders for suspected sexual abuse: Guidelines and techniques. *Journal of Elder Abuse and Neglect, 5*(1), 5–18.

Ramsey-Klawsnik, H. (1995). Investigating suspected elder maltreatment. *Journal of Elder Abuse and Neglect, 7*(1), 41–67.

Rapoport, L. (1962). The state of crisis: Some theoretical considerations. *Social Service Review, 36*(2), 211–217.

Rapoport, L. (1970). Crisis intervention as a mode of brief treatment. In R. W. Roberts & R. H. Nee (Eds.), *Theories of social casework*. Chicago: University of Chicago Press.

Rathbone-McCuan, E. (1978, November). *Inter-generational family violence and neglect: The aged as victims of reactivated and reverse neglect*. Presented at International Conference of Gerontology, Japan.

Rathbone-McCuan, E. (1980). Elderly victims of family violence and neglect. *Social Casework, 61*(5), 296–304.

Rathbone-McCuan, E. (1982). Older women: Endangered but surviving species. *Generations: Quarterly Journal of the Western Gerontological Society, 6*(3), 11–12, 59.

Rathbone-McCuan, E., & Bricker-Jenkins, M. (1988). *Self-neglect and adult protective services*. TN: Tennessee Department of Human Services.

Rathbone-McCuan, E., & Voyles, B. (1982). Case detection of abused elderly parents. *American Journal of Psychiatry, 139,* 189–192.

Rathbone-McCuan, E., Travis, A., & Voyles, B. (1983). Family intervention: Applying the task centered approach. In J. Kosberg (Ed.), *Abuse and maltreatment of the elderly: Causes and intervention*. Littleton, MA: John Wright-PSG.

Reedy, D. F. (1988). How can you prevent dehydration? *Geriatric Nursing, 9*(4), 225–226.

Reinharz, S. (1986). Loving and hating one's elders: Twin themes in legend and literature. In R. Wolf & K. Pillemer (Eds.), *Elder abuse: Conflict in the family* (pp. 25–48). Dover, MA: Auburn.

Reulbach, D., & Tewksbury, J. (1994). Collaboration between APS and law enforcement: The Massachusetts Model. *Journal of Elder Abuse and Neglect, 6*(2), 9–21.

Roberts, A. R. (1984). Intervention with the abusive partner: In A. R. Roberts (Ed.), *Battered women and their families: Intervention strategies and treatment programs*. New York: Springer.

Roberts, A. R. (1996). Epidemiology and definitions of acute crisis in American society. In A. Roberts (Ed.), *Crisis management and brief treatment*. Chicago: Nelson-Hall.

Rosenbaum, A., & Maiuro, R. (1990). Perpetrators of spouse abuse. In R. T. Ammerman & M. Herson (Eds.). *Treatment of family violence: A sourcebook* (pp. 280–309). New York: Wiley.

Roy, M. (Ed.) (1982). *The abusive partner: Analysis of domestic battering.* New York: Van Nostrand Reinhold.

Salamone, A., & Berman, J. (1995). *The use of domestic violence shelters by elder abuse Victims.* Paper presented at the 48th Annual Scientific Meeting of the Gerontological Society of America, Los Angeles.

Salend, E., Kane, R. A., Satz, M., & Pynoos, J. (1984). Elder abuse reporting: Limitations of statutes. *Gerontologist, 24*(1), 61–69.

Schier, R. W. (1982). *Clinical internal medicine in the aged.* Philadelphia: Saunders.

Schmidt, M. G. (1980). Failing parents, aging children. *Journal of Gerontological Social Work, 2*(3), 259–268.

Seaver, C. (1995, October). Comments made in an interview, Moving towards a peaceful life: Carole Seaver talks about the Milwaukee Women's Center and its Older Battered Women's Program. *Nexus, 1*(3), 4–7.

Seligman, M. E. P. (1975). *Helplessness.* San Francisco: Freeman.

Sengstock, M. C., & Hwalek, M. (1983a, November). *A critical analysis of measures for the identification of physical abuse and neglect of the elderly.* Presented at the Annual Meeting of the Gerontological Society of America.

Sengstock, M. C, & Hwalek, M. (1983b, November). *Sources of information used in measures for the identification of elder abuse.* Presented at the Annual Meeting of the Gerontological Society of America.

Shanas, E. (1962). *The health of older people: A social survey.* Cambridge: Harvard University Press.

Sharon, N. (1991). Elder abuse and neglect substantiations: What they tell us about the problem. *Journal of Elder Abuse and Neglect 3*(3), 19–35.

Simon, B. K. (1970). Social casework theory: An overview. In R. W. Roberts, & R. H. Nee (Eds.), *Theories of social casework.* Chicago: University of Chicago Press.

Simon, M. L. (1992). *An exploratory study of adult protective services programs' repeat elder abuse clients.* Washington, DC: American Association of Retired Persons.

Slade, M. (1990). Forensic toxicology and domestic violence: A connection. Paper presented at the 42nd Annual Meeting of the American Academy of Forensic Sciences, Cincinnati, OH.

Slade, M., Daniel, L., & Heisler, C. (1991). Application of forensic toxicology to the problem of domestic violence. *Journal of Forensic Sciences,* JFSCA, *36*(36), May, 1991, 708–713.

Snyder, M. (1982). Self-fulfilling stereotypes. *Psychology Today, 16*(7), 60–68.

Sommers, T. (1984). Untitled article. *WGS Connection. Newsletter published by the Western Gerontological Society, 5*(1), 1.

Sommers, T. (1985). Caregiving: A woman's issue. *Generations: Quarterly Journal of the American Society on Aging, 10*(1), 9–13.

Sonkin, D. (1988). The male batterer: Clinical and research issues. Special Issue: Wife assaulters. *Violence and Victims, 3*(1), 65–79.

Sonkin, D. J., & Durphy, M. (1982). *Learning to live without violence.* San Francisco: Volcano.

Sonkin, D., Martin, D., & Walker, L. (1985). *The male batterer.* New York: Springer.

Star, B. (1978). Treating the battered woman. In J. Hanks (Ed.), *Towards human dignity: Social work in practice. 5th NASW Symposium.* Washington, DC: National Association of Social Workers.

Stearns, P. N. (1986). Old age family conflict: The perspective of the past. In R. Wolf & K. Pillemer (Eds.), *Elder abuse: Conflict in the family* (pp. 3–24). Dover, MA: Auburn.

Steele, B. F., & Pollock, C. B. (1968). A psychiatric study of parents who abuse infants and small children. In R. E. Helfer & C. H. Kempe (Eds.), *The battered child,* Chicago: University of Chicago Press.

Steinmetz, S. K. (1978). Battered parents. *Society, 15*(15), 54–55.

Steinmetz, S. K. (1980). *Elder abuse: The hidden problem.* Statement prepared for the briefing by the Select Committee on Aging. United States House of Representatives. 96th Congress, June 23, 1979. (pp. 7–10). Boston, MA, Washington, DC.

Steinmetz, S. K. (1981, January–February). Elder abuse. *Aging,* 315–316, 6–10.

Steinmetz, S. K. (1983). Dependency, stress and violence between middle-aged caregivers and their elderly parents. In J. I. Kosberg (Ed.), *Abuse and maltreatment of the elderly.* Boston: John Wright-PSG.

Steinmetz, S. K. (1988a). *Duty bound: Elder abuse and family care.* Newbury Park., CA: Sage.

Steinmetz, S. K. (1988b). Elder abuse by family caregivers: Processes and intervention strategies. Special Issue: Coping with victimization. *Contemporary Family Therapy: An International Journal, 10*(4), 256–271.

Stenback, A. (1975). Psychosomatic states. In J. G. Howells (Ed.), *Modern perceptions in the psychiatry of old age.* New York: Brunner-Mazel.

Steuer, J., & Austin, E. (1980). Family abuse of the elderly. *Journal of American Geriatric Society, 28,* 372–376.

Stone, G. (1979). Patient compliance and the role of the expert. *Journal of Social Issues, 35*(1), 34–59.

Straus, M. A. (1979a). *A sociological perspective on the causes of family violence.* Paper presented at American Association for the Advancement of Science, Houston, TX.

Straus, M. (1979b). Measuring intrafamily conflict and violence: The Conflict Tactics Scale. *Journal of Marriage and the Family, 41,* 75–88.

Straus, M. A., Gelles, R., & Steinmetz, S. K. (1980). *Behind closed doors: Violence in the American family.* Garden City, NY: Anchor/Doubleday.

Strickler, M., & Bonnefil, M. (1974). Crisis intervention and social casework: Similarities and differences in problem solving. *Clinical Social Work Journal, 2*(1), 36–44.

Subcommittee on Health and Long-Term Care. (1987). *Abuses in guardianship of the elderly and infirm: A national disgrace.* Select Committee on Aging, U.S. House of Representatives, 100th Congress, First Session (Committee Print, 1987). Washington, DC: Author.

Subcommittee on Housing and Consumer Interests. (1989). *Surrogate decision-making for adults: Model standards to insure quality guardianship and representative payee services.* Select Committee on Aging, U.S. House of Representatives, 100th Congress, Second Session, December, 1988. Committee Publication 100-705. Washington, DC: U.S. Government Printing Office.

Sykes, G., & Matza, D. (1957). Techniques of neutralization: A theory of delinquency. *American Sociological Review, 22,* 664–670.

Szaz, T. S., & Hollander, M. H. (1956). A contribution to the philosophy of medicine: The basic models of the doctor-patient relationship. *Archives of Internal Medicine, 97*(5), 585–592.

Tatara, T. (1993). Understanding the nature and scope of domestic elder abuse with the use of state aggregate data: Summaries of the key findings of a national survey of state APS and aging agencies. *Journal of Elder Abuse and Neglect, 5*(4), 35–57.

Tomita, S. K. (1982). Detection and treatment of elderly abuse and neglect: A protocol for health care professionals. *PT and OT in Geriatrics, 2*(2), 37–51.

Tomita, S. K. (1988). The state of exchange theory on the topic of elder mistreatment. Unpublished manuscript.

Tomita, S. K. (1990). The denial of elder mistreatment by victims and abusers: The application of neutralization theory. *Violence and Victims, 5*(3), 171–184.

Tomita, S. K. (1994). The consideration of cultural factors in the research of elder mistreatment with an in-depth look at the Japanese. *Journal of Cross-Cultural Gerontology 9,* 39–52.

Tomita, S. K. (1995). An exploration of elder mistreatment among Japanese Americans within a broad context of conflict: Conditions and consequences. Ph.D. dissertation, University of Washington.

Tomita, S. K., Clark, H., Williams, V., & Rabbitt, T. (1981). *Detection of elder abuse and neglect in a medical setting.* Paper presented at the National Conference on Abuse of Older Persons, San Francisco.

Uhlmann, R. F, Larson, E. B., Rees, T. S., Koepsell, T. D. (1989). Relationship of hearing impairment to dementia and cognitive dysfunction in older adults. *Journal of the American Medical Association, 261*(13), 1916–1919.

University of Southern Maine (1982). *Improving protective services for older Americans: A national guide series.* Portland, ME: Author.

Umana, R. F., Gross, S. J., & McConville, M. T. (1980). *Crisis in the family.* New York: Gardner.

U.S. Bureau of the Census. (1983). *Current Population Reports,* Series P–23, No. 128. *American in transition: An aging society.* Washington, DC: Government Printing Office.

U.S. Bureau of the Census. (1984). *Current Population Reports,* Series P23, No. 138. *Demographic and socioeconomic aspects of aging in the United States.* Washington, DC: Government Printing Office.

U.S. Bureau of the Census. (1992). *Current population reports, Special Studies,* Series P23–178. *Sixty-five plus in America.* Washington, DC: U.S. Government Printing Office.

U.S. Department of Health and Human Services. (1984). *Alzheimer's disease* [DHHS Publication No. (ADM) 84-1323]. Washington, DC: Government Printing Office.

U.S. House of Representatives Select Committee on Aging. (1981). *Elder abuse: An examination of a hidden problem.* 97th Congress (Comm. Pub. No. 97–277), Washington, DC: Government Printing Office.

U.S. House Select Committee on Aging. (1990). *Elder abuse: A decade of shame and inaction.* Publication No. 101–752. Washington, DC: U.S. Government Printing Office.

U.S. Senate Special Committee on Aging in conjunction with the American Association of Retired Persons. (1984). *Aging America: Trends and projections* (2nd ed.). Washington, DC.

Vickers, R. (1992). Psychiatric and biomedical considerations in self-neglect. In E. Rathbone-McCuan & D. R. Fabian (Eds.), *Self-neglecting elders: A clinical dilemma* (pp. 46–70). Westport, CT: Auburn.

Villamore, E., & Bergman, J. (Eds.) (1981). *Elder abuse and neglect: A guide for practitioners and policy makers.* Manual prepared for the Oregon Office of Elder Affairs by the National Paralegal Institute, San Francisco, and Legal Research and Services for the Elderly, Boston.

Vinton, L. (1992). Battered women's shelters and older women: The Florida experience. *Journal of Family Violence, 7*(1), 63–72.

Walker, L. (1979). *The battered woman.* New York: Harper and Row.

Walker, L. (1984). *The battered woman syndrome.* New York: Springer.

Walker, L. (1987). Identifying the wife at risk of bettering. *Medical Aspects of Human Sexuality, 21*(7), 107–114.

Walker, L. (1991). Post-traumatic stress disorder in women: Diagnosis and treatment of battered women syndrome. *Psychotherapy, 28*(1) Spring, 1991, 21:29.

Walker, L. (1995). Current perspectives on men who batter women—Implications for intervention and treatment to stop violence against women: Comment on Gottman et al. (1995). *Journal of Family Psychology 9*(3), 264–271.

Walker, M., & Griffin, M. (1984). Group therapy for depressed elders. *Geriatric Nursing, 5*(7), 309–311.

Wasserman, S. L. (1979). Ego psychology. In J. F. Turner (Ed.), *Social work treatment: Interlocking theoretical approaches*. New York: Free Press.

Weston, J. T. (1968). The pathology of child abuse. In R. E. Helfer & C. H. Kempe (Eds.), *The battered child*. Chicago: University of Chicago Press.

Williamson, J., Stokoe, I. H., Gray, S., Fisher, M., Smith, A., McGhee, A., & Stephenson, E. (1964). Old people at home: Their unreported needs. *Lancet, 1*(1743), 1117–1120.

Wisconsin Department of Health and Social Services. (1991). *1990 Wisconsin report on elder abuse*. WN: Department of Health and Social Services, Division of Community Services, Bureau on Aging.

Wolf, L. E. (1982). *Minnesota's American Indian Battered Women: The cycle of oppression: A cultural awareness training manual for non-Indian professionals*. St. Paul, MN: St. Paul Indian Center.

Wolf, R. S. (1986). Major findings from Three Model Projects on elderly abuse. In K. Pillemer & R. Wolf (Eds.), *Elder abuse and neglect: Conflict in the family* (pp. 218–238).

Wolf, R. S. (1990). Testimony on behalf of the Committee on Prevention of Elder Abuse before the U.S. Select Committee on Aging, Subcommittee on Human Services. *Journal of Elder Abuse and Neglect, 2*(1/2), 137–150.

Wolf, R. S., Godkin, M. A., & Pillemer, K. A. (1986). Maltreatment of the elderly: A comparative analysis. *Pride Institute Journal of Long Term Home Health Care, 5*(4), 10–17.

Wolf, R. S., & Pillemer, K. A. (1984). *Working with abused elders: Assessment, advocacy, and intervention*. Worcester, MA: University of Massachusetts Medical Center.

Wolf, R. S., & Pillemer, K. A. (1989). *Helping elderly victims: The reality of elderly abuse*. New York: Columbia University

Wolf, R. S., & Pillemer, K. A. (1994). What's new in elder abuse programming? Four bright ideas. *Gerontologist, 34*(1), 126–129.

Wolf, R. S., & Pillemer, K. A. (1995). *The older battered woman: Spouse abuse and parent abuse compared*. Paper presented at the 48th Annual Scientific Meeting of the Gerontological Society of America, Los Angeles.

Wolf, R. S., Strugnell, C., & Godkin, M. A. (1982). *Preliminary findings from Three Model Projects on elderly abuse*. Worcester, MA: University of Massachusetts Medical Center, Center on Aging.

Wood, A. (1974). *Deviant behavior and control strategies*. Lexington, MA: Heath.

Yen, P. K. (1989). The picture of malnutrition. *Geriatric Nursing, 10*(3), 159.

Zarit, S. W., Reever, K. E., & Bach-Peterson, J. (1980). Relatives of impaired elderly: Correlates of feelings of burden. *Gerontologist, 10*(6), 649–655.

Zarit, S. W. (1985). New directions. *Generations: Quarterly Journal of the American Society on Aging, 10*(1), 6–8.

# Index

# Springer Publishing Company

# Older Adults' Misuse of Medicines, Alcohol, and Other Drugs

**Anne M. Gurnack**, MSW, PhD

The chapters contained in this volume offer the latest thinking and research findings on alcohol and drug misuse in later life. Anne Gurnack has assembled an internationally known multidisciplinary team of experts to review this underserved population.

Part I reviews the epidemiology and assessment of problem drinking. It includes a useful review of medical manifestations of alcoholism; techniques on how to detect early versus late onset of alcoholism; and treatment alternatives for alcohol abusers.

Part II focuses on prescriptive and illicit drug abuse. The topics include misuse of prescription drugs; interactions between alcohol and drugs; and drug misuse in nursing homes.

*Contents:*

- Epidemiology of Problem Drinking Among Elderly People, *W.L. Adams. MD, MPH* and *N. Smith Cox. PhD*
- Alcohol Use Disorders in Older Adults: Screening and Diagnosis, *S.S. DeHart. MSN, PhD, RN* and *N.G. Hoffman, PhD*
- Medical Manifestations of Alcoholism in the Elderly, *J.W. Smith*
- Early Versus Late Onset of Alcoholism in the Elderly, *J.G. Liberto, MD* and *D.W. Oslin. MD*
- Treatment Alternatives for Older Alcohol Abusers, *L. Schonfeld, PhD* and *L. Dupree, PhD*
- Alcoholism and Dementia, *D.M. Smit, MD* and *R.M. Atkinson, MD*
- Misuse of Prescription Drugs, *R. Finlayson, MD*
- Interactions Between Alcohol and Other Drugs, *W.L. Adams, MD, MPH*
- Illicit Drug Use and Abuse Among Older People, *H. Rosenberg, PhD*
- Alcohol and Drug Misuse in the Nursing Home, *C. Joseph, MD*

*1996    0-8261-9500-8    hardcover*

536 Broadway, New York, NY 10012-3955 • (212) 431-4370 • Fax (212) 941-7842